DATE DUE

DEMCO 38-296

Infant Tongues

INFANT
TONGUES

THE VOICE
OF THE CHILD IN
LITERATURE

EDITED BY
Elizabeth Goodenough
Mark A. Heberle
and
Naomi Sokoloff

WITH A FOREWORD BY
Robert Coles

WAYNE STATE UNIVERSITY PRESS   DETROIT

Infant tongues

Copyright © 1994 by Wayne State University Press,
Detroit, Michigan 48201. All rights are reserved.
No part of this book may be reproduced without formal permission.
Manufactured in the United States of America.
99 98 97 96 95 94   5 4 3 2 1

Library of Congress Cataloging-in-Publication Data

Infant tongues : the voice of the child in literature / edited by
Elizabeth Goodenough, Mark A. Heberle, and Naomi Sokoloff ; with a
foreword by Robert Coles.
    p.   cm.
Includes bibliographical references and index.
ISBN 0-8143-2430-4   (alk. paper). —
ISBN 0-8143-2431-2   (pbk. : alk. paper)
    I. Children in literature.   2. Children's literature—History and
criticism.   3. Children as authors.   I. Goodenough, Elizabeth.
    II. Heberle, Mark A.   III. Sokoloff, Naomi B.
            PN56.5.C46I54   1994
        809'.93352054—dc20   94-25751

Designer: Joanne Elkin Kinney

The cover illustration, from John Trusler's *The Progress of Man and Society* (1791), is reproduced
from the Children's Book Collection, University Research Library, University of California,
Los Angeles. The editors would like to thank Mitzi Myers, Andrea Immel, Jeff Rankin, and
James Davis of UCLA for their assistance.

CONTENTS

Foreword

☯

Robert Coles

As I read this book's essays I couldn't help but go back to my medical school days and my hospital residency days, when I was learning to be a pediatrician, then a child psychiatrist—and when I had the great good fortune to know an ailing but quite alert, strong-minded, expressive physician and poet, William Carlos Williams. Once, as we sat in his Rutherford office, and recalled earlier medical trips to Paterson, where so many of his poor and vulnerable patients lived, he stopped to reflect on the children he had treated over the years and decades, and, too, on himself as not only their doctor but an observer of them, one who wanted to comprehend them, first, then take that more idiosyncratic and rare (and terribly challenging step) of conveying to others what had been learned.

At one point he said this: "I spent years trying to get children to talk to me, break out of a silence—a perfectly understandable silence. (Why *should* they talk to this stranger with a black bag, a bag of instruments, of tricks!) Sometimes I succeeded—hell, I should put it this way: *we* succeeded. Sometimes [that is], we had a good talk, and I knew a kid, or I thought I did, and maybe the kid got to know this doc sitting there in the apartment as less of a scary one than before— I'm being careful here, using my negatives to inch toward a possible positive! But the toughest assignment I ever gave myself was to come back here [to his office, where he pointed at his typewriter] and start pounding out those words—as if I had the right (and the ability) to speak for those kids, to be their voice. Was I—was I their voice, or were they instruments of my voice, or is this a foolish question that leads to futile efforts called answers? All I know is the thin ice: I was afraid I'd sink as I tried to imagine how a kid thought and how a kid would talk under the various circumstances of those stories I constructed—an 'errand into the wilderness,' as your friend put it [Perry Miller, who had been my college tutor]. True, I'd heard kids bellow and cry and whimper and I'd seen them cower

vii

or run or explode with angry combativeness—all fists or all 'fast feet' toward the door—but those were moments, often isolated moments, and when you write a story you're trying to go beyond all of that: give a real coherence to those noises, those outbursts, those times of truculence or terror, of anger or fear or flight. Maybe I succeeded, but I can't be sure—and the kids, who ought to be the judges of my achievement or my failure, they're not there, they're not here, to give us their conclusions! So, we have, instead, you and me talking—the adults called readers and writers and critics!"

Such a blunt and even acerbic appraisal. Such a brave and unpretentious and modest self-arraignment, stated in ordinary language, in a vernacular, actually, that Dr. Williams had learned in Paterson (rather than, say, Princeton) kept coming to my mind as I shared with these writers (what a reader does) the central struggle that informs their various essays: with what accuracy, with what subtlety and amplitude of sensibility do we "grown-up" writers render a child's thoughts, a child's speech, a child's effort to glimpse the world, take its measure, respond to it through words? Of course, an irony is always at work here. Literature is given us by those who have become comfortable with words, proficient at using them— the very definition of our adult humanity: we are the creature who possesses both consciousness and a language, and arguably, without them, we cease to be our distinctive selves, human beings. Children, then, can be defined not only as boys and girls who have yet to be full-grown physically, but as the ones among us who have yet to master a language, develop a full-fledged consciousness (the two are obviously very much connected). In a sense, then, "infant tongues" are no efforts of documentary expression, or autobiographical accounts of those yet to enter a particular world, but evidence of a leap of the imagination: adults flexing their verbal prowess, trying hard with thoughts and words to evoke, to render (to remember, surely) and thereby, proving themselves to be—grownups. "Infant tongues," then, give us adult sounds: one more measure of our human capability— and at that, as these essays amply demonstrate, no small measure, indeed. I rather think the Dr. Williams of "The Girl with the Pimply Face," or "The Use of Force," would perk up, take notice, immerse himself in what follows, find himself interested, informed, instructed.

ACKNOWLEDGMENTS

This collection of essays emerged out of a session at the 1987 convention of the Modern Language Association in San Francisco. Four of the contributors to this volume—Elizabeth Goodenough, Mark Heberle, Naomi Sokoloff, and Mary Galbraith—participated in a panel there on the topic "*Infans:* Representing the Language of the Child in Literature." Through the discussion we discovered a range of common interests. As plans for the volume progressed, we further discovered that our interests in the voices and language of children in literature defined a point of contact that binds together work done by scholars and writers in a variety of fields. We would like to thank the other participants in that MLA panel, Steve Curry and Mary Jane Hurst, as well as everyone who submitted manuscripts for the volume. Every contribution was valuable in helping us to define the scope of this collection.

The publication of this volume was supported by grants from Claremont McKenna College, the Research Relations Fund of the University of Hawaii, and the University of Washington Graduate School Fund. Our thanks go to those institutions for helping make this project possible. We would also like to thank Arthur Evans, director of Wayne State University Press, for guidance and ongoing support that brought this project to fruition. We wish to express our appreciation to Kathy Wildfong, our project editor, and to Suha Kudsieh, who helped with preparing the index.

Successful completion of this work wouldn't have been possible without the patience and personal support of a number of other individuals. We would like to express our appreciation to Doug Berry, Rachel Berry, and Michelle Berry, Cristina Bacchilega, Barry Menikoff, Mike Riley, Nick Warner, and Gil Leaf.

INTRODUCTION

ELIZABETH GOODENOUGH, MARK A. HEBERLE, AND NAOMI SOKOLOFF

> Children at this age [6] give us no such
> information of themselves: and at what time
> were we dipped in the Lethe, which has
> produced such utter oblivion of a state so
> godlike? There are many of us that still possess
> some remembrance, more or less distinct,
> respecting themselves at six years old; pity that
> the worthless straws only should float, while
> treasures, compared with which all the mines of
> Golconda and Mexico were but straws, should
> be absorbed by some unknown gulf into some
> unknown abyss.
> —S. T. Coleridge, "Defects of Wordsworth's
> Poetry," *Biographia Literaria*

Over the past two decades, literary studies have been revolutionized through
the recovery and interpretation of works, writers, and discourses previously
disregarded by scholars and critics. The perspectives of feminism, popular culture,
and ethnic studies, among others, have fruitfully unsettled the literary canon and
redefined literature itself by recognizing the importance of articulate voices, past
and present, that have gone previously unheard. The proliferation of new divisions
and special sessions in the Modern Language Association over the past decade
(including a 1993 panel on "Literature by Children") reflects this ferment, as
does the expansion of English department offerings to include courses devoted to
female and minority writers, popular music and culture, film, and folk tales.

Much recent critical practice is concerned with the question of otherness,
analzying or questioning how the apparent coherence of literary works, as well as
the institution of literature itself, has depended upon defining and then marginalizing, erasing, or ignoring alternative subjects. The recognition, recovery, and validation of otherness in literary criticism has been decried by traditionalists inside

I

and outside the academy, for it inevitably threatens the ideal of hierarchial difference that may seem necessary to serious thought. At its best, however, this apparently subversive criticism is part of a postcolonialist, postfeminist, postmodern discontent with old borders that is reshaping thinking itself.[1] To be aware of how our own identity is fashioned by the construction of the Other is initially deconstructive but ultimately liberating, since it strengthens self-awareness without requiring the misrepresentation of other selves.

Until very recently, however, this ongoing critical revolution has given little attention to how literature written for adults represents children, whose interests in general are too often marginalized within the deracinated and improvident urgencies of postmodern society.[2] The border between the child and the adult is necessarily controlled by the latter, but not necessarily in the interest of that other self whom the adult has effaced or transcended. Within the institution of criticism itself, the child in adult literature tends to be benignly neglected as well, like some domesticated Other. On the other hand, literature written *for* children has received critical attention for years in specialized scholarly journals, and elective courses in children's literature are beginning to be offered in many English departments. Such official respectability, however, has come at the cost of bracketing it as a peripheral species of literature, its significance weakened by its childish subjects and audience.

Only recently have studies of children in literature begun to recognize the complex interaction between adult and child which produces such works; nor has much criticism focussed upon the representation of children's language, a crucial issue in defining the conventional boundary between childhood and adult consciousness. Works like Mary Jane Hurst's study of child language in American literature (1990), Peter Hunt's union of *Criticism, Theory, and Children's Literature* (1991), and James Kincaid's *Child-Loving: The Erotic Child in Victorian Culture* (1992) raise such issues prominently, however. The purpose of *Infant Tongues* is to illustrate the promise of these areas of inquiry and to encourage further investigation into the ways in which child consciousness requires adult construction and mediation in order to be voiced in written representations.

Although the child presents a relatively neglected yet distinctively challenging and fertile subject for writers and readers alike, significant studies of literary children in adult texts have heretofore been largely descriptive, like Peter Coveney's classic survey of child characters in post-1800 English literature, or broadly thematic, like Robert Pattison's study of child figures in English literature in relation to the fall of man and original sin.[3] Most previous studies assume a relatively unproblematic view of the relationship between author, character, and work, in which the child, like any other literary character, is given full fictional presence in a narrative or dramatic imitation of life. Such criticism understandably passes over a radical problem addressed by many of the articles in this collection: the uniquely difficult accessibility of children's consciousness to the adult imagination, let alone its articulation, and the attendant complexities entailed in speaking for children,

2

or in their names. Even the best of recent studies tend to ignore the vast corpus of texts written for children by adult authors, who are doubly affected by this issue, both in representing child character and in imagining the consciousness of a presumed reader who is a child. Nor do they consider texts by child authors that have been published—that is, filtered through the expectations of an adult editor.

The problematic of child language and consciousness is radically signified by *enfant*, the French term for child, and its Latin cognate *infans*, "unspeaking." The English derivative, "infant," defines one who cannot speak and whose progressive attempts at articulation must be translated by adults into a world of discourse not yet fully inhabited by the child. Coleridge's lament in *Biographia Literaria* (quoted above) identifies the problem faced by writers who find in the child a figure pregnant with significance. His remark implies that the experience of childhood is unutterable and thus lost to the adult: the child goes through it, but lacks the language to convey its reality to others, while the adult writer commands the full resources of language but is largely cut off from children's consciousness. Thus, the experience of being a child may be irrecoverable in a way that being a woman, an African-American, or a gay is not; furthermore, what children actually say may not be considered interesting discourse to adult writers and readers, who after all define what is literary for both mature and juvenile audiences. As Richard Coe, in his study of childhood autobiography points out, attempts to imitate the verbal and cognitive worlds of children, which concern themselves with what may often seem trivial to adults, must convince the reader of its significance (xii). In the end, how to present a child's voice that is genuinely mimetic or rhetorically significant is a problem faced by every writer who creates child characters and invents a language for them.

The relative inarticulateness of children makes any representation of their consciousness necessarily a tentative and fundamentally artificial construction of adult writers and audiences, of which literary fictions may be among the most disinterested and, hence, most valuable. Ultimately, however, the history of literature for or about children—like the history of childhood in general—has been one of manipulation, power, and desire. Child-centered writing is never free from adult concerns, whether to indoctrinate young minds or to wrest young minds free of conventional assumptions. The problem is not limited to children in adult literature; these fundamental issues have been raised by such critics of children's literature as Jacqueline Rose, Juliet Dusinberre, and Jack Zipes. Rose has suggested that children's literature itself is an "impossibility," predicated on the Romantic myth of a universal childhood. Such fictions (composed and produced exclusively by adults) mollify and address our own discontents, she argues, imagining "a primitive or lost state to which the child has special access. The child restores these worlds to us, and gives them back to us with a facility or directness which ensures that our relationship to them is, finally, safe" (9). Although her analysis of children's literature threatens to devalue it, as Perry Nodelman has noted,

Rose's emphasis upon the latent adult desires that generate such texts (an important topic in James Kincaid's *Child Loving*) returns us to the problem that underlies any attempt at the representation of children.

Moreover, the intersection of children's experiences and adult interests determines the content and form of child-authored texts. If literature written for children has a dual audience in which the child's participation may be less important than the adult's, the few published works written by children effectively have dual authors. It is not the child writer but the adult editor or publisher, using criteria of which the child is unaware, who determines the final content of work written by children. This inescapable limitation of child authorship is cleverly represented in Stephen Millhauser's two novels, *Edwin Mullhouse* and *Portrait of a Romantic*, which purport to present directly the childhood experiences of fictional authors.[4]

Other relatively suppressed or unacknowledged voices—those of women, minorities, non-Western authors, noncanonical or non-"literary" writers—can at least offer their own words, even if they go unheard. Certainly such authors have experienced a range of difficulties in finding their own modes of expression and making themselves heard as they struggle with or against the vocabulary and conventions of the dominant literary discourse. Children, however, are often more radically alienated from their own words in literary texts. Yet, as Coleridge's comment suggests, it is the very wordlessness of children that makes them so significant. To recognize the child's exclusion from adult language and discourse does not mean that children's voices are condemned to being disabled in literary representations. On the contrary, many texts written from a child's viewpoint are brilliantly creative, subversive, or compensatory precisely because children speak from a realm as yet unappropriated, or only partially appropriated, by social or cultural intentionality.[5] Indeed, full acquisition of language marks the dissolution of childhood, as the child's consciousness is progressively defined within a system of signs communicated by parents and siblings in the first instance, but ultimately imposed by social convention. Voices from that earlier realm of human self-awareness can put into relief the shortcomings or blindspots of adult discourse as the child, in naivete or incomprehension, interprets the world and words in a new way.

This novelty of vision is constantly changing, too, as experience brings the young person to challenge limits and to redefine "self" and "other" in his or her relation to adults. The created or edited voice of the child is often exceptionally resonant to adults because of its familiarity as well as its startling novelty or subversiveness. The child's state is one that we have all shared, male or female, whatever our age, or ethnic and social identity.

The development of verbal consciousness in the child is crucial to two fundamental concerns of recent literary theory: how subjects are constituted or constitute themselves and how meaning itself is established. Because children occupy a borderland beyond which social and cognitive reality, adult identity, and literature itself have defined themselves, many of the different strands of contemporary literary criticism (e.g., semiotics, reader response, psychoanalytic, dialogic, feminist) converge in studying children's language.

The preverbal creature, the infant, is truly on the margin of discourse, but voiceless only for a short time. Then the child begins to acquire language, which is constantly changing and becoming more complex, along with his or her existence as a subject. At every point, however, the child is less than fully informed by the verbal code of adults as well as underrepresented in fiction by and for adults. But those authors who are seriously involved with giving a voice to the child are crossing back over the border and, in doing so, are not only simply representing children but implicitly uncovering for themselves and for their readers the distinctive psychological, social, and discursive practices that constitute adult identity and that normally go unremarked and unexamined. Therefore, while Coleridge's labeling of the child's state as "godlike" may seem outmoded, his acknowledgment of the child as a site of fundamental significance is well justified. Ultimately, as the work of the contributors to *Infant Tongues* demonstrates, the representation of child consciousness and children's language in literary texts raises issues important to anyone interested in linguistics, psychology, social history, ideology, and the human sciences in general, as well as in literary criticism, theory, and production.

The editors of this volume believe that the complexity of such issues has not been sufficiently recognized; indeed, for most earlier writers, Coleridge's fascination with childhood would have been a puzzling fixation, for children were almost never significant subjects in their own right. According to Robert Pattison, Aristotelian anthropology defined them as undeveloped human beings, while Augustinian theology saw the child as a synechdoche for fallen human nature in general (x). The first viewpoint encouraged the literary characterization of children as virtually a separate species, inferior to adults; the latter used them as symbols or reflectors of adult actions. Children seldom speak in pre-Romantic literature, and they almost never develop as human beings. Dante's work is typical: the *infanti* are left in Limbo, and no children are consigned to Hell, Purgatory, or Paradise because the *Divine Comedy* only has places for fully developed human souls.

In fact, recognition of childhood in the West as a discrete and theoretically privileged period of life seems to begin only after the Renaissance, and is of course symptomatic of Romanticism. The Romantic revaluation of childhood is epitomized in Wordsworth's paradox (in "My Heart Leaps Up") that "The Child is father to the Man." This dramatic assertion of the priority and significance of the child also reflects the problem of representation noted by Coleridge: the metaphor of development integrates child with adult as unified personality, yet the separate identities of father and offspring that sustain the metaphor make the child and adult distinct figures. The Romantic concern with the child was an integral part of its more general concern with human consciousness. Romantic literature is a precursor of the scientific study of the mind, and psychology, founded as a science by Gustave Fechner in the 1860s (Hall 11) may be regarded as the offspring of "modern" (Romantic) literature itself. For Freud, who claimed that poets and philosophers had discovered the unconscious and that he had merely discovered the means by which it could be studied, the child is almost literally the father of the man, but he is shorn of his Romantic glory and mystification. Post-Freudian theorists of the mind have followed his lead by finding in literature and myth a key to understanding the unconscious and the traces of childhood itself. For Jung, the figure of the child that emerges out of the collective unconscious is a symbol of psychic wholeness. For Lacan, the child's entrance into discursive language, and the symbolic order generally, displaces the imaginary wholeness experienced before the mirror stage of infantile development.

This relationship, between the use of language and the development of the child, has been studied more empirically by investigators in several fields, beginning with Darwin, who in 1840 began to keep a minutely detailed record of the activities of William Erasmus, his infant son.[6] Contemporary attempts to understand the development of either childhood or language necessarily involve studying both: developmental psychologists, following Piaget, try to trace and define the stages of verbal behavior in order to define how children grow; psycholinguists, in the wake of Chomsky, have found in children's acquisition of language the key to explaining this uniquely human characteristic. And in the field of developmental linguistics, pioneered in America by Roger Brown only three decades ago, the growth of children and the development of language are inextricable from each other. Much current research, influenced by the work of the Soviet psycholinguist L. S. Vygotsky, complicates the relatively straightforward paradigms of Piaget, finding the language of the child both more individualistic, subjective, and imaginative *and* more influenced by the rhetorical and social context of children's communication than earlier psychologists had determined.[7] Such developments are analogous to the rebirth of biographical, historical, and social criticism within literary studies, all of which situate works within complex purposes and contexts rather than seeing them as stable and self-unified.

Conclusions about children and language since the Romantic discovery of childhood are themselves inescapably culture-bound, of course, and Western conceptions of the child in general may not be fully relevant when applied to Asian or Islamic societies, for example.[8] The history of childhood in the West, inaugurated as a species of cultural history by Philippe Ariès's classic study, *Centuries of Childhood* (1965), helps us realize to what extent childhood is a historically situated invention of the adult mind and a social construction of Western educational and ideological systems—as well as an existential fact. Ariès's work traces European attitudes toward the child from centuries of relative lack of interest to near obsession from the eighteenth century onward. Later social historians like Lloyd De-Mause and Lawrence Stone have extended Ariès's work, though his astringent conclusions about pre-Enlightenment parents' indifference to their children have been sharply questioned by Linda Pollock; nonetheless, his outline of the development of childhood as a concept remains sound, particularly the role of public and private education in characterizing children as a distinctive social group and extending the years of enforced segregation that help define them. As historians, like literary critics, explore previously ignored or slighted subjects, it seems certain that the child will assume increasing significance; for example, Mark Golden and Thomas Wiedemann, writing on ancient Greek and Roman children, have extended the account of Western children beyond the medieval prelude to *Centuries of Childhood.*

As the subtitle of Ariès's own book suggests, his interest in children was largely the starting point for a more comprehensive subject, the history of the family, which in turn has been extended into the massive five-volume *Histoire de la vie privée* (1985–87), the first four volumes of which have been translated into English. Therefore, while children are at last regarded as important figures, they are inevitably studied as a part of more general social and cultural histories. In this case, the professional rediscovery of children reinscribes them into history as ancillary to more important or more comprehensive concerns.

Thus, the problem of representation attending literary re-creations of children reflects a situation inescapable in all organized attempts at understanding the child. Adult purposes and conceptions of significance and coherence always threaten to define children in our terms rather than in their own. In selecting the essays that make up this volume, the editors have been particularly concerned with this fundamental issue. The studies that follow show how adults have spoken the child's voice—that is, how the literary enterprise, as an adult domain, has allowed the voice of children to be sounded. The variety of critical approaches and disciplines drawn upon by our contributors illustrates both the complex issues raised by writers' attempts to represent childhood from the Renaissance to the present as well as the resources of contemporary critical practice and theory.

The first three essays in *Infant Tongues*, which deal with representations of children in the early modern period, recover children's voices that have been generally ignored by social historians and literary critics alike. Gillian Avery, examining Puritan accounts of exemplary children, traces a long tradition of pedagogical texts that report children's speech as filtered through adult editors and compilers. She shows that such speech was given representation from the early Tudor period onward but that the voices that sound familiar are, ironically, those of truancy and mischief, which come through to us relatively unaffected by the paradigm of proper child discourse. Mark Heberle examines the roles and the language of children in Shakespeare's plays, arguing for a revaluation of both that would call attention to the importance of preserving the integrity of childhood for Shakespeare's contemporary audiences. Focussing primarily upon *King John*, he questions whether the apparent marginalizing of children in these plays is a product of Shakespeare's imagination or our own. Dealing with texts even more canonical than Shakespeare's plays, Ruth B. Bottigheimer examines German children's Bibles between the seventeenth and eighteenth centuries, deducing a shifting consensus about the consciousness of child readers among the adult editors of such works.

Two essays on early nineteenth-century texts for and by children recover distinctly noncanonical texts neglected and distorted in the wake of the Romantic apotheosis of the child. Mitzi Myers shows how Maria Edgeworth's dialogic stories for children, free of the perils of both Romantic transcendentalism and Victorian sentimentality, manage to span the boundaries between child and adult, female and male, individual and community, entertainment and pedagogy. And Alexandra Johnson recovers an early nineteenth-century child's journal by Marjory Fleming from the encrustations of her Victorian publishers, who gave a second life to "Pet Marjory," shaping the literary expression of a child's voice in accordance with their own agenda.

The Romantic revaluation of childhood, signalized initially by Rousseau and Wordsworth, made the rendering of child consciousness itself an important subject for European and English writers throughout the nineteenth century. Examining the work of Pushkin, Tolstoy, and Belyi, Andrew Wachtel shows how Russian writers, late but enthusiastic heirs of the cult of the child, adapted the use of multiple perspectives from history writing to their representations of childhood, producing multiply-voiced works that attempt to combine past and present, child and adult. Similar attempts to mediate between adult and child awareness may be found in the works of Dickens. Focussing intensively upon the first chapter of *Great Expectations*, Mary Galbraith provides a linguistic analysis that unravels the presence of three voices—adult novelist, adult narrator, and child narrator—while focussing on the problem of formulating an antecedent state of identity in a literary work. And in a Freudian study of Rimbaud's poetic language, Michael Lastinger uncovers traces of childhood sexual abuse that may explain this prodigy's precipitous entrance into adult language, yet so scrambled the borderline between child and adult in the writer that he remained radically voiceless as well as homeless throughout his short life.

As heirs of the Romantics, the great modernists continued to find the consciousness of children a fertile subject for their own imaginations, though their perspectives were deeply affected by the replacement of Romantic with psychoanalytical myths of childhood. In a study of D. H. Lawrence's child characters that draws upon the author's own speculations about psychological development, Carol Sklenicka and Mark Spilka examine the evolution of Lawrence's rhetoric of childhood. For Lawrence, children are highly individualized and, at their best, retain a passionate relationship with external and internal forces that Lawrence found lacking in most adults and in the overly refined consciousness of his modernist contemporaries. That the development of language can impoverish as well as empower the consciousness of the child is also an important theme in Virginia Woolf, as Elizabeth Goodenough demonstrates. She shows how Woolf's aesthetic iconoclasm in her attraction to the inchoate as a literary strategy includes a romantic identification of childhood experience with the creative imagination. In another study of a major modernist, Brian McHale uses psycholinguistic data to canvass the speech of the twelve child characters in Dos Passos's *U.S.A.*; his analysis shows how literary representation mediates between characteristics of actual child speech and linguistic stereotypes, and he argues that the contexts of literary discourse render any direct mimesis of children's speech an impossibility.

Each of our final three critical essays deals with a body of texts and addresses the multiple purposes served by child-centered works. Suzanne Rahn shows how black children have spoken a very different language in children's books of 1930, 1960, and 1990, reflecting the attempts by their authors—reinforced by the illustrations—to create an image for young (mainly white) readers of what black children are like and how one should relate to them. Naomi Sokoloff examines the voices of children in literary texts of the Holocaust, including representations of children in adult, child-authored, and juvenile fiction. She concludes with a reading of David Grossman's "Momik" (the first section of his novel *See Under: Love*), a work that cuts across the other categories of child-centered literature and suggests that to understand how the voice of the child expresses itself requires an awareness of the interconnection between all three modes. Maria Tatar examines fairy tales, a category of texts with multiple incarnations. Basing her position upon recent studies of child-generated tales, she argues that careful attention to the voices of children as interpreters of these tales is important if they are to serve their purpose for parents and their children.

Perhaps even more than readers and critics, it is the authors of child-voiced stories who most fully experience the mutuality of child and adult consciousness that informs such texts. The essays by Mark Harris, David Shields, and Darrell Lum (appended to his story, "Giving Tanks") discuss their own stories in relation to the experiences of childhood out of which they have arisen. Each writer also examines the voice of the child in himself that is recovered so forcefully in his written work. Finally, in his Afterword, Laurie Ricou uses all of the essays to reflect upon children's places in literature and literature's place in the lives of children.

As this description of the collection demonstrates, our principle of selection deliberately blurs boundaries between genres. Included here are analyses of child characters in adult fiction, juvenile fiction and children's literature, and writing by children. These texts are bound together by a shared theoretical issue, however: in all, the child's voice has been mediated, modified, or appropriated by an adult voice. Exploring the interaction of adult and child consciousness is perhaps the most important emphasis of *Infant Tongues* relative to the study of child-centered discourse, but it is only one of the ways in which this collection hopes to encourage recognition of such discourse as an important site for other border crossings. While criticism of children's literature still struggles for respectability in academic and scholarly circles, it is crucial to recognize the importance of such study and its kinship with recent concerns of literary theory, including questions of otherness, subject positions, and the constitution of meaning.

Our juxtaposition of genres itself demonstrates the interaction of canonical and noncanonical literatures in revealing children's voices. Adult fiction has certainly learned from juvenile fiction and absorbed its conventions in a variety of ways, as the example of David Grossman indicates—*See Under: Love* portrays a little boy's mind as it develops through his appropriation and reinterpretation of Arthur Conan Doyle, fairy tales, boy's adventure stories, Jewish legends, and biblical stories. In *Alice to the Lighthouse,* Juliet Dusinberre has shown how children's literature heavily influenced the avant-garde adult literature of the early twentieth century (27–28). Lewis Carroll's classic itself is a prime instance of a children's book that will be always be postmodern as well.

Conversely, the models of adult literature have on many occasions affected children's literature. Suzanne Rahn's essay suggests that many writers of juvenile fiction take their cue from ethnic sensitivity and consciousness in adult writing. Indeed, some theorists of children's literature have argued that juvenile texts are by nature derivative, subordinate to, and more conservative than adult writing. Yet Peter Hunt argues that children's books "are probably the most interesting and experimental of texts, in that they use mixed-media techniques which combine word, image, shape, and sound" (17). The conflicting evidence on this issue invites further debate on the interactions of adult and children's texts within the literary system as a whole.

Moreover, studying noncanonical texts of various sorts—including works written for, by, and about children—reveals much about the values, interests, and limitations of the dominant literary culture. Marjorie Fleming's diary throws into relief the Victorian values that dictated the rewriting and editing of little girls' thoughts; Maria Edgeworth's pedagogical stories were innovative not only in voicing the everyday language of children but also in providing an arena wherein women's voices could begin to empower themselves. An awareness of the subliteratures that have developed alongside the normative canon may encourage scholars to re-examine and redefine the emphases of literary history more comprehensively.

These specifically literary questions ultimately raise matters of importance to an understanding of broader cultural issues involving childhood. Beyond critical concerns, literature can help us understand children in ways that may vitalize and complement the disciplines of linguistics, psychology, sociology, and history by recreating the feel of experience from within. Earlier literature for children tended to present values or ideals that adults wanted them to internalize. But in America, Israel, and elsewhere, children's literature has increasingly come to adopt child narrators, perspectives, and diction in attempts to express for children what they feel but cannot articulate for themselves, a project Maria Tatar would extend to the interpretation of such literature as well. Writers are usually ahead of their time, as Freud recognized, released through the play and imaginative perceptiveness that accompany artistic re-creation from the conventional insouciance, adjustment, and repression that govern our daily lives. If there is to be a social and political recuperation of the child at the center rather than on the margin of contemporary societies, it is probably already germinating within the works of contemporary poets, dramatists, and fiction writers.

Although this volume does not directly address the proliferation of children's voices in extra-discursive media such as television, movies, and children's theatre and folklore, the editors hope others will do so and thereby extend discussion of issues raised in *Infant Tongues*. The always complex and sometimes problematic purposes of childhood representation certainly merit scrutiny in connection with television and movies. Indeed, media-generated characterizations of children are particularly subject to commercial and stereotyping pressures, as the remarkable furor over the Barney-the-Dinosaur phenomenon, or the packaging of child actor Macaulay Culkin attests. The interviews on NBC's *Today* show and other programs which promoted the publication of *The Diary of LaToya Hunter* (1992), a twelve-year-old offered a five thousand dollar advance for the daily record of her first year in a Bronx junior high school, indicate the increasing value that publishers and the mass media find in actual children who can put their experience before the public eye. At the same time, different art forms and media raise quite distinct questions about representation, voice, and adult mediation of children's views. While these are increasingly compelling and challenging questions, as technology changes the images and stories our culture creates about ourselves, these questions are beyond the scope of this volume, which focuses on written texts. In any case, as the essays in *Infant Tongues* demonstrate, written representations of childhood foreground the adult-child relation and remind us that neither can be defined without the other. These articles explicitly or implicitly emphasize how all that we can know of children's identities is produced by the work of adult writers or editors.

Moreover, when we consider why writers create child characters for their readers, we can appreciate how important children are in constituting our own identities. For authors, of course, the return to childhood through writing enables a revisiting of the time when they first began to establish meaning through words. Putting children into texts is thus a way of getting to the truth of oneself as well, and the author's self-recapitulation may be shared by the reader, who was also a child, if never an author. In addition, the recent explosion of literary memoirs (e.g., those by Mary McCarthy, Arthur Miller, John Updike, William Styron, and Denis Donoghue) and the development of a new literary genre, the autobiographi-cal "childhood" (Coe 8–9), indicate a widespread contemporary trend to use literature as a medium of self-understanding.[9] The recovery of childhood and its continued presence within the adult protagonist is also the subject of autobio-graphical novels recently published by the German writer Marie Luise Kaschnitz and Canada's Margaret Atwood. At the very least, all such literary autobiography provides evidence of childhood remembered; beyond that, it may constitute the reassumption or acceptance of a previously lost or neglected self necessary to complete one's adult identity.

As psychologists and social scientists themselves turn to literary methods and to narrative, lyric, and drama as ways of knowing, literature will remain a crucial province of expression for, or sensitivity to, the perspective of the child. Currently high on the agenda of various schools of thought in the field of psychology is the attempt to establish a conversation with one's early self. Building on Jung's perception, in "The Psychology of the Child Archetype," of the inner child as a symbol of the unified self, "the part of the human personality which wants to develop and become whole," recent therapies tap the child within the adult as a source of creative energy. Writers such as Bruno Bettelheim, Alice Miller, Robert Coles, Scott Peck, Jeremiah Abrams, and John Bradshaw have turned to literature— myth, poetry, song, novels, and stories—to elaborate their theories of personality, finding the inner child motif "as ancient as religion and as current as Hollywood comedy" (Abrams 6).

The variety of attempts to comprehend the child over the last two centuries indicates how seductive and elusive the nature of childhood continues to be. Its very unknowability stimulates the imagination of adult observers: perhaps we believe that in pursuing this liminal figure we may know children as we do not understand ourselves. As our sense of endangered nature on this shrinking planet becomes acute, children become the last frontier, embodiments of existences without bounds, of freedom, of possibility, purity, primitivism: they provide a perspective on the exotic, the unknown, or on what Gaston Bachelard calls "antecedence of being" (108). As E. M. Forster noted, at their best literary representations of the child illuminate "a single point, a point which, when rightly focused, may perhaps make all the surrounding landscape intelligible" (cited in Coveney 270). The editors hope that the essays presented in *Infant Tongues* will help to enlighten readers by encouraging them to listen to the voices of children in literature and in life.

NOTES

1. Michel Foucault's investigations of outcast and marginalized groups within Western culture and society (e.g., criminals and the insane) helped initiate critical and theoretical study of the construction of otherness in a variety of contexts. Important examples include Edward Said's *Orientalism* (New York: Random House, 1978), which discusses Western misappropriation of Islamic culture. Recent prominent studies include Henry Louis Gates's *"Race," Writing, and Difference* (Chicago: University of Chicago Press, 1986), a collection of essays dealing with African and African-American subjects, and Trin Minh Ha's *Woman Race Other: Writing Postcoloniality and Feminism* (Bloomington and Indianapolis: Indiana University Press, 1989), an Asian feminist critique of Western feminism that discusses films and folk tales as well as literary texts.

2. Recent studies by Laurie Ricou, *Everyday Magic: Child Languages in Canadian Literature* (Vancouver: University of British Columbia Press, 1987), Mary Jane Hurst, *The*

Voice of the Child in American Literature: Linguistic Approaches to Fictional Child Language (Lexington: University Press of Kentucky, 1990), and Andrew Wachtel, *The Battle for Childhood: Creation of a Russian Myth* (Stanford: Stanford University Press, 1990) suggest growing interest, however, in this important subject.

3. But see also the studies by Reinhard Kuhn and Richard N. Coe. Both works are surveys in effect if not in form, but they also discuss problems of representing children in literature.

4. In *Edwin Mullhouse*, the child writer is twice-removed from the adult author, whose persona is a child biographer; in *Portrait of a Romantic*, a parody of Goethe's *Werther* (among other sources), the autobiographer, Arthur Grumm, who is recalling his childhood and adolescence with minute detail, is yet another fictional stand-in for Millhauser.

5. These ideas are more fully discussed in Naomi B. Sokoloff, *Imagining the Child in Modern Jewish Fiction* (Baltimore: Johns Hopkins University Press, 1992).

6. Darwin's conclusions, based on his daily record of the baby's activities, were published in *Mind* (1877): 286–94.

7. Piaget's extensive work began with *Language and Thought of the Child* (1926). Chomsky's attack upon behavioristic theories of language acquisition began with a review of B. F. Skinner's *Verbal Behavior* in *Language* 35 (1959): 26–58; his own philosophy of language is presented in *Language and Mind* (New York: Harcourt, 1968). Roger Brown's seminal work is *A First Language: The Early Stages* (Cambridge, MA: Harvard University Press, 1973). The major issues and current research in this area are presented in *Child Language: A Reader*, ed. Margery B. Franklin and Sybil S. Barten (London: Oxford University Press, 1987), which includes a discussion of Vygotsky.

8. Not much cross-cultural work on children's language has been attempted, though a revealing comparison of children's differing development is presented in Joseph Jay Tobin and David Y. H. Yu, *Preschool in Three Cultures: Japan, China, and the United States* (New Haven: Yale University Press, 1989). Ethnocentric distortions of childhood are present within American culture as well—see Craig Howes, "Hawaii through Western Eyes: Orientalism and Historical Fiction for Children," *The Lion and the Unicorn: A Critical Journal of Children's Literature* 11 (1987): 68–88.

9. Numerous literary childhoods have appeared over the past few years, among them Annie Dillard's in *An American Childhood* (New York: Harper and Row, 1987), John Updike's in *Self-Consciousness: Memoirs* (New York: Knopf, 1989), and Robert MacNeil's in *Wordstruck* (Harmondsworth: Penguin, 1989).

Works Cited in Text

Abrams, Jeremiah, ed. *Reclaiming the Inner Child*. Los Angeles: Jeremy P. Tarcher, 1990.

Ariès, Philippe. *Centuries of Childhood: A Social History of Family Life* Trans. Robert Baldick. New York: Knopf, 1965.

Ariès, Philippe, and Georges Duby, eds. *A History of Private Life.* 4 vols. Cambridge, MA: Belknap/Harvard University Press, 1987.

Atwood, Margaret. *Cat's Eye.* New York: Doubleday, 1989.

Bachelard, Gaston. *The Poetics of Reverie.* Boston: Beacon, 1971.

Coe, Richard N. *When the Grass Was Taller: Autobiography and the Experience of Childhood.* New Haven: Yale University Press, 1984.

Coleridge, S. T. *Biographia Literaria or Biographical Sketches of My Literary Life and Opinions.* Ed. James Engell and W. Jackson Bate. *The Collected Works of Samuel Taylor Coleridge,* volume 2. Bollingen Series 75. Princeton University Pres, 1983.

Coveney, Peter. *The Image of Childhood: The Individual and Society: A Study of the Theme in English Literature.* Harmondsworth: Penguin, 1957.

DeMause, Lloyd. *The History of Childhood.* New York: Psychohistory Press, 1974.

Donoghue, Denis. *Warrenpoint.* New York: Knopf, 1990.

Dusinberre, Juliet. *Alice to the Lighthouse: Children's Books and Radical Experiments in Art.* London: Macmillan, 1987.

Golden, Mark. *Children and Childhood in Classical Athens.* Baltimore: Johns Hopkins University Press, 1990.

Hall, Calvin S. *A Primer of Freudian Psychology.* New York: New American Library, 1954.

Hunt, Peter. *Criticism, Theory, and Children's Literature.* Oxford: Basil Blackwell, 1991.

Hunter, LaToya. *The Diary of LaToya Hunter.* New York: Crown, 1992.

Jung, C. G. "The Psychology of the Child Archetype." In his *The Archetypes and the Collective Unconscious.* Trans. R. F. C. Hull. *The Collected Works of C. G. Jung,* volume 9. Bollingen Series 20. New York: Pantheon, 1959.

Kaschnitz, Marie Luise. *The House of Childhood (Das Haus der Kindheit).* Trans. Anni Whissen. Lincoln: University of Nebraska Press, 1990.

Kincaid, James R. *Child-Loving: The Erotic Child in Victorian Culture.* New York: Routledge, 1992.

Kuhn, Reinhard. *Corruption in Paradise: The Child in Western Literature.* London: University Press of New England for Brown University Press, 1982.

McCarthy, Mary. *How I Grew.* New York: Harcourt, 1988.

Miller, Arthur. *Timebends.* New York: Harper Collins, 1988.

Millhauser, Stephen. *Edwin Mullhouse: The Life and Death of an American Writer, 1943–1954, by Jeffrey Cartwright.* New York: Knopf, 1972.

———. *Portrait of a Romantic.* New York: Knopf, 1977.

Nodelman, Perry. "The Case of Children's Fiction: Or the Impossibility of Jacqueline Rose." *Children's Literature Association Quarterly* 10.3 (Fall 1985): 98–100.

Pattison, Robert. *The Child Figure in English Literature.* Athens, GA: University of Georgia Press, 1978.

Pollock, Linda. *Forgotten Children.* New York: Oxford University Press, 1983.

Rose, Jacqueline. *The Case of Peter Pan or The Impossibility of Children's Fiction.* London: Macmillan, 1984.

Said, Edward W. *Orientalism.* New York: Random, 1978.

Stone, Lawrence. *The Family, Sex, and Marriage in England, 1500–1800.* New York: Harper and Row, 1977.

Styron, William. *Darkness Visible: A Memoir of Madness.* New York: Random, 1990.

Wiedemann, Thomas. *Adults and Children in the Roman Empire.* New Haven: Yale University Press, 1990.

Wordsworth, William. *Selected Prose and Prefaces.* Ed. Jack Stillinger. Boston: Houghton Mifflin, 1962.

Zipes, Jack. *Fairytales and the Art of Subversion: The Classical Genre and the Process of Civilization.* New York: Wildman, 1983.

The Voice of the Child,
Both Godly and Unregenerate,
in Early Modern England

GILLIAN AVERY

"Children, like women, are what anthropologists like to call a muted group," wrote Sir Keith Thomas in an admirable essay on children in the early modern period (roughly 1500–1800) (47). His argument was, however, that in spite of the once fashionable theories of such historians as Philippe Ariès, there was plenty of material to show that childhood as a distinctive phase of life was recognized long before the eighteenth century. Deftly manipulating a wide range of documentary evidence, he proceeded to construct a picture of a juvenile subculture, often rambunctious and anarchic, and usually encompassing "a casual attitude to private property, an addiction to mischief, and a predilection for what most adults regarded as noise and dirt" (57). He showed Tudor and Stuart children as ubiquitous, behaving in a way inconsistent with the values of adult society. Even choirboys shamelessly and aggressively begged for money; some were accused of "pissing upon stones in the Churche . . . to slide upon, as upon ysse" (57). The more undisciplined ran riot on feast days, stole fruit, horrified passersby with their foul language. On a milder note, there are allusions to children playing with drums, hobby horses, dolls, marbles, kites, tops. And there are references to a mass of different games and sports.

Keith Thomas was drawing upon sermons, letters, treatises and diaries, all, naturally, written from an adult point of view. But what children thought and how they expressed themselves is more elusive, especially what one might term children caught unawares—playing, skirmishing, talking among themselves. Iona Opie, the folklorist of childhood, prefaced her *The People in the Playground* with the explanation she used to give the schoolchildren from whom she was gathering her material: "I tried to explain to the people in the playground why I turned up every week and wrote down whatever was happening. . . . 'I think it will be interesting in 100 years' time,' I said. 'I wish somebody had done the same 100 years ago, then we would know what it was like'" (viii).

Probably she said "100 years" because she felt that to a seven- or eight-year-old a longer period was unimaginable. But as she knew well, by the Victorian period children and their sayings, games, rhymes were recognized to be of great interest, though no one as yet was bringing the same scholarly and scientific interest to the subject as she and Peter Opie were to devote to it, beginning with the *Oxford Dictionary of Nursery Rhymes* in 1951. Nobody before 1744, for instance, had apparently thought it worthwhile to write down and publish the traditional rhymes sung to children, and that children chanted to each other. In that year, Mary Cooper, a London music publisher, printed two little volumes, the first of which has disappeared and whose contents can only be guessed at, and *Tommy Thumb's Pretty Song Book voll.* [sic] *II*, of which a single copy exists in the British Library. In this there are songs that still form part of the Mother Goose canon. Most often, as the Opies have demonstrated, these were not written specifically for children, but were fragments of songs and ballads, perhaps sung in taprooms, on the stage, in barracks, on street corners. But Mary Cooper also included some examples of crude abuse where we do detect the voices of children (the children who talked to Iona Opie in their Hampshire playground in the 1970s had the same scatological tastes):

Piss a Bed,
Piss a Bed,
Barley Butt,
Your Bum is so heavy,
You can't get up.

and

Lyer Lyer Lickspit,
Turn the Candlestick,
What's good for Lyers,
Brimstone and Fire.

and

Spit Cat, Spit,
Your tongue shall be slit,
And all the Dogs in our Town
Shall have a Bit.

(In the twentieth century children are more likely to call out "Tell Tale tit.") There is no way of knowing how old these rhymes were when Mary Cooper

17

published them, but one would surmise at least that she herself had known them as a child.

The 1740s saw the beginnings of a recreational literature for children. Sarah Fielding's *The Governess* (1749), the first juvenile novel, included dialogue. But it was far from being the first time that children had been presented with conversation in their books. The best-known instance (discussed later in this article) is James Janeway's *A Token for Children*, published in the early 1670s, a time when Puritan educators were searching for new ways to bring their message home to the young.

But for centuries before this there had been schoolmasters who had tried to make learning (and this in effect meant the learning of Latin) "full of pleasant allurement," as John Brinsley put it in the "epistle dedicatory" of *Corderius Dialogues Translated* in 1614. They would probably not have been treated with such trusting informality as Iona Opie was, but they have always been in a position to see what went on among the young, and many of them did indeed draw upon their observations. It is in their compilations of Latin conversation for schoolboys that we first hear children talking among themselves. Latin being the lingua franca of all European educated classes, for centuries boys learnt to speak it, and indeed were not expected to use the vernacular while they were on the school premises. So pedagogues tried to supply them with a vocabulary for work and for play, and it was traditional to put this into dialogue form. "Because Children learne first to talke familiarly with their fellowes or others, Dialogs are most easie for their capacitie," wrote one schoolmaster (William Kempe) in 1588 (*The Education of Children*). John Brinsley, a Puritan schoolmaster, who edited Cordier's *Colloquies* in 1614, put an English translation in the margin because, as he says in the "epistle to the reader," "whilst wee seeke to get Grammar and Latine, wee lose purity and propriety in our owne tongue." (This was indeed one of the disadvantages of a Latin-centered education, and Brinsley was to draw attention to it in other educational works.)

Many other compilers also included vernacular translations, one of the earliest being Aelfric, abbot of Eynsham (fl. 1006), who composed a book of dialogues, presumably for children in monastic schools. His *Colloquy* has an Anglo-Saxon translation of the Latin sentences, and begins with one of the boys begging to be taught Latin, even if it means being flogged. This request does not carry conviction; it seems to be pious pedagogical hope. For centuries boys were certainly flogged into their Latin, but the comment of an unknown fifteenth-century writer must be far nearer what they themselves felt about this. The manuscript (Balliol MS 354, ij CXXX) is in the library of Balliol College in Oxford. Since boys then went up to the university at the age of fifteen, it is reasonable to speculate that the poem was written by someone who had not left childhood very far behind. The writer laments that though he does want to acquire learning, it is a painful process.

I wold ffayn be a clarke
but yet hit is a strange werke;
The byrchyn twiggis be so sharpe,
hit makith me haue a faynt harte.
    what avaylith it me thowgh I say nay?

He says he would rather go twenty miles twice than go to school on Mondays. And when he does get there, late, he is tempted to give the master an insolent excuse, that he has been milking ducks. Naturally he gets a beating.

My master lokith as he were madde:
"Wher hast thou be, thow sory ladde?"
"Milked dukkis, my moder badde":
hit was no mervayle thow I were sadde.
    what vaylith it me thowgh I say nay?

My master pepered my ars with well good spede
hit was worse than ffynkll [fennel] sede;
He wold not leve till it did blede.
Myche sorow haue he for his dede!

And savagely he wishes that his master was a hare, and he himself the jolly hunter. He would blow his horn lustily and rally the hounds, "for if he were dede I wold not care." It seems to be one of the very few instances of youthful comment that has come down to us unrevised by adults.

Many of the collections of aphorisms and sentences schoolmasters put together for their pupils were intended to teach morality and good manners as well as Latin. They also contain much adult matter. For instance William Horman, an early headmaster of Eton, presumably wrote his *Vulgaria* in 1519 with his Eton scholars in mind. He covered many topics, and in the section De Coniugialibus included such conversational gambits as: "I begot the first night that I laye with my wife" (*f*o 146), and "I muste bye cradell clothes." (*f*o 146). But in "De Scholasticis" there are several very convincing schoolboy observations:

He is a mychar. [to mitch, to play truant] (*f*o 89)
Me thynke I begynne to take fauour and increase
in grammer. (*f*o 85)
My boke hathe be sought and better soughte: but he
can nat be founde no where. (*f*o 85)
He begynneth to tell shrewed talys vpo me to the maister.
He was foule entreated and sore beate. (*f*o 85)
He made a sore complaynt, and shewed openly his naked
body al to bete. (*f*o 85)

19

Gyve me my boke or els I shall make the. (fo 85)
I put to the this ryddyl. (fo 86)
We haue played a comedi of greke. (fo 87)
Lend me thy Terence for this seuynnyght [week]. (fo 87)
I have left my boke in the tennys playe. (fo 86)

The most engaging schoolbook of the period is *Linguae Latinae Exercitatio* by the Spanish humanist Juan Luis Vives (1492–1540), published the year before he died. Vives believed that the colloquial Latin spoken in his time was a debased form, and wished schoolboys to be grounded in purer, classical Latin, as Cicero had written it. But though this desire to return to a discarded usage might be considered misjudged, the dialogues he composed are delightful, and show an informality unique in schoolbooks at that time and for centuries to come. It is known to have been used in a few English schools in the sixteenth and seventeenth centuries, and in 1908 was translated and presented to the general reader as a portrait of Tudor schoolboy life. In fact, it does not show English life at all, but a Mediterranean culture where the relationship between children and parents is far less formal than we find in any Tudor book of manners. When the boy comes down to breakfast he calls merry greetings to his father, his mother whom he addresses with an affectionate diminutive ("mea matercula"), and his little brothers ("mei germanuli"). His mother makes fond enquiries after his health: "May Christ preserve you, my light. What are you doing, my darling? How are you? How did you rest last night?" (6) She is desperately worried when she hears that he has had a headache, and only relieved when he tells her it lasted less than "an eighth of an hour." We see him playing with Ruscio, his dog, then being persuaded by his father that it is time for his education to begin so that he can be a man rather than a mere animal like Ruscio. He spends a first day at school and when he comes home proudly with his writing tablet, his little sister shrieks to their mother that Tulliolus has been drawing pictures of ants and gnats. "Be quiet, you silly thing, they are letters," says Tulliolus indignantly (21). Vives shows the children playing games—dice, draughts, cards, throwing nuts (games of chance that certainly would not have been countenanced by Tudor moralists). There is much about school life, including school meals, and an exchange between a boy and a fruit vendor which carries great conviction. The vendor has told him indignantly that she is not going to give her fruit away.

BOY: That dirt which you have on your hands and neck was not given to you, was it?

WOMAN: Unless you take yourself off, you impudent boy, your cheeks will see some of this dirt on them.

BOY: How will my cheeks feel, when you have it on your hands?

WOMAN: Give those cherries back, you young rogue.

BOY: I am merely sampling, for I wish to buy them.

WOMAN: Then buy.

BOY: Provided they have pleased me (17).

Its 1908 translator quoted a tribute to Vives's text by a sixteenth-century German scholar who had edited the book in 1582. "As a boy I so loved Vives that not even now do I feel my old love for him has faded" (li). Not many schoolbooks can have inspired this sort of sentiment.

After 1666 there appears to have been no further school edition of Vives in England. It sprang out of a Catholic culture, and that would have made it suspect. More popular was the *Colloquiorum scholasticorum libri quatuor* by the French pedagogue and grammarian Mathurin Cordier (1479–1564). The fact that he had been converted to Protestantism, indeed, was a friend of Calvin, must have made him attractive to English schoolmasters. The *Colloquies*, first published in Geneva in 1563, are long and diffuse in their original form, and were usually presented as *Colloquia Selecta*. Many of them were exchanges between schoolboys and their masters, but Cordier, far more than Vives, is concerned with the nitty-gritty of classroom matters such as Latin grammar and the preparing of pens. In his edition of 1614, John Brinsley used idiomatic speech with a literal translation in the margin. In the first dialogue a boy rebukes a new pupil who suggests play: "O thou foolish boy, what sayest thou? Thou hast scarcely entered the schoole, and doest thou already speake of play?" (1). However, by the eighth dialogue the scholar is emboldened to ask the master: "I and my schoolefellows haue beene set hard to our books, almost al these three dayes: is it not lawfull to refresh our minde with play a little?" (14). This the master allows, provided the boy asks for it correctly in Latin. (And he does so, admitting that a companion has taught him the formula.) There is less detail about the play than the expansive Vives gave, though there is talk of hand ball, and playing "in the gallerie" when it rains, for "pinnes or walnuts." In Book II, dialogue 31, Dominic expresses outrage that Barrase has eaten his nuts. "O wretch hast thou eaten them? Wherefore didst thou not keepe them rather to play?" (159). And we get an interesting glimpse of how the boys who are getting this sort of superior education are mocked by "dissolute knaves" who "laugh at us with full cheekes, because wee speake Latin in the streetes" (170).

In 1617 John Brinsley, who had the care of the school of Ashby de la Zouch in Leicestershire, translated the anonymous *Pueriles Confabulatiunculae* to which he gave the subtitle *Children's Dialogues*. The Latin origin has not been traced, but Charles Hoole, another schoolmaster, said in his edition of 1659 (which he translated as *Children's Talk*) that it was "writ heretofore (as is probable) in Dutch and Latine by Evaldus Gallus." It is less arid than Cordier, and it is certainly possible that children could have enjoyed it. As in Vives, a boy's day is described through dialogues. His mother tries to wake him, and he says: "Mother, depart, I will rise by and by" (fo 4). He gets into trouble with his schoolmaster; there is much lament about misappropriated pens, missing knives, and an interesting exchange between the master and a boy whose hair is uncombed. The boy says his parents are too poor to buy a comb, and that no one will lend him one: "We have most of us scabbed heads; I thinke men do shun that" (*f* o 14). The reader is provided with the Latin for different excuses for leaving the room.

I pray you Master give me leave,
That I may purge my belly
That I may go to the privie
That I may go to make water
That I may lighten my bladder
That I may fetch our kine (*f* o 3)

One whole dialogue is devoted to the heinous crime of speaking English instead of Latin, which the accused Quintin hotly denies. And there is particularly convincing playground horseplay.

HENRY: Sit where dogs sit.
GERARD: And where do dogs sit?
HENRY: Upon their buttocks.
GERARD: I do in like manner.
HENRY: But doest thou know how thou sittest?
GERARD: Like a man.
HENRY: And knowest thou where?
GERARD: In thy lap.
HENRY: But now thou liest on me with thy face upward.
GERARD: Thou shalt never doe this to me scot-free.
HENRY: I weigh not thy threats of a locke of woole. (*f* o 7)

Brinsley did not translate the whole of the book, remarking that it was not fit, and that he preferred Cordier. The unfitness might have been the references to Catholic practices, or he may have found some of the dialogue too coarse.

He hath all to be pist my shooes
He hath bemarred my paper
He will not let me mind my booke
He jeeres mee
He farts at us

Charles Hoole in his later edition however restored all this, together with the prayers and the riddles that concluded the book in its original state.

The sceptic will find exchanges like the above more convincing than the utterances of exemplary children which began to be used in the mid-seventeenth century as a way of persuading young readers into "early piety"—the state so much desired by Puritan parents and preachers. These were always said to be the voices of real children; fiction was abhorrent to Puritans, and anything less than the truth was a lie, and therefore damnably wicked. But the trouble is that children are natural mimics. One can suspect that much of what was said was a formula, and that many of the later accounts of the lives and deaths of godly children stemmed from James Janeway's *Token*. Its full title is *A Token for Children, being an Exact Account of the Conversion, Holy and Exemplary Lives, and Joyful Deaths of several Young Children*. The first part was probably published in 1672, the second in 1673. Janeway, a dissenting preacher who had a chapel at Rotherhithe in London, died of consumption in 1674, and could not possibly have foreseen the far-reaching influence of his work.

Individually, the contents were not innovative; other Puritan divines such as Isaac Ambrose and Samuel Clarke, both a generation older, had recorded the sayings and doings of such children and there is a strong family likeness in them all. The great impact came from the fact that it was the first compilation entirely devoted to stories of children. Janeway was adamant that it was a faithful and true record, though in fact none of the children seems to have been known to him; some of them died when he himself was a child, and two of them—Susanna and Jacob Bicks—had lived in Holland. He relied on the reports of others: "He had a friend that oft watched him, and listened at his Chamber-door, from whom I received this Narrative," he says on one occasion (23). On another: "This Narrative I had from a judicious holy man un-related to him, who was an eye and ear-witness to all these things" (72). And in the preface to the second part he was indignant about people who had disbelieved one of his accounts. He had had it, he said, from "Mrs. Jeofries in Long-Lane in Mary Magdalen Bermondsey Parish, in the county of Surry . . . and as a reverend Divine said, Such a Mother in Israel, her single Testimony about London, is as of much authority almost as any one single Minister's."

The narratives therefore are at best hearsay rather than accurate reporting. Janeway himself claimed no sort of originality for his work, and indeed drew on some of his predecessors. The work that may have inspired *A Token* was Thomas White's *A Little Book for Little Children* (1671?) which was warmly recommended by Janeway himself. It is addressed to the very young "who canst not read yet" and the tender, homelike details (through interspersed with horrific accounts of infant martyrs) still have power to move the reader. There is the mother who takes her small son on to her lap and asks him why he cries. On his deathbed he names his sins: he whetted his knife upon the Lord's Day; he did not reprove one he heard swear; he once omitted prayer to go to play; he omitted prayer because he thought God was angry; when his mother called him he answered Yes, and not Forsooth (60). Many young Puritans were to feel guilt over similar sins of omission or commission, but the simplicity of this account is what makes it linger in the memory. In White's third story there is a little child "which would go to Prayer alone, before it could speak plain." When he is five, he is whipping a top, but

23

flings away his whip and says: "O Mother, I must go to God, will you go with me?" (71). A month later he sickens and dies, repeating these words.

The words of some of Janeway's children are similarly touching. "Away then all that is in the world," says Jacob Bicks, "dying of a very sore sickness upon the sixth of August, 1664" (II, 61). "Away with all my pleasant things in the world; away with my Dagger for where I go there is nothing to do with Daggers and Swords; men shall not fight there but praise God" (II 63). But more often the children's ejaculations of joyful expectation have a recognizable sameness, as do their responses to those who are catechizing them. It was part of the Puritan tradition to demand an abnormal religious response from children.

"It is evident that children were not only expected to have the same religious experience as the adult—they really had that experience. The result of this forcing process was that children frequently manifested religious precocity, and they assumed positions of prominence and spoke with a certain censoriousness which were most unnatural" (Fleming 178). Thus we find that all thirteen of Janeway's children, ranging in age from five to just over twelve, not only show the same desired characteristics but also speak with a similar voice. It is recorded of all of them that from an early age they took a delight in secret prayer and serious discourse. They are no respecters of persons. Anne Lane corrected her parents "if she saw anything in them that she judged would not be for the honour of Religion" (II, 17), and grieved if she saw others talk too long to her father of common things. John Harvy, who died when he was eleven, reproved his mother thus: "Once he had a new suit brought from the Tailors, which when he looked on, he found some ribbons at the knees, at which he was grieved: asking his Mother, whether those things would keep him warm. No, Child said his Mother; why then said he, do you suffer them to be put here, you are mistaken, if you think such things please me" (II, 75). In similar style another Puritan minister, Henry Jessey, recorded in 1672 the instance of a five-year-old who had turned her back on vanity.

> She had a new plain Tammy Coat, and when she was made ready, was to be carried with other children into Morefields. But having looked upon her Coat, how fine she was, she presently went to her Chair, sate down, her tears running down her eyes, she wept seriously by her self. Her mother seeing it, said to her, How now? Are you not well? What is the matter that you weep? The Child answered, Yes, I am well, but I would I had not been made ready, for I am afraid my fine Cloaths will cast me down to Hell. (Jessey 7)

Finally, dying, the children responded eloquently to the catechizing of their elders, and were able to quote the Scriptures with remarkable aptness and to the inspiration of those who gathered marvelling in the bedchamber. In this again their upbringing had been a preparation. Mary Livermore, born in Boston in 1820 but brought up in "the Calvinistic faith in its entirety and severity as it was taught and believed a hundred years before" gave some account of her religious education. (She might have said "two hundred years before," for Cotton Mather's children were brought up in the same way.) Before she was ten years old, she said, she had the whole Calvinist theological system at her tongue's end, and could restate it and dovetail it together like a theological expert. Every child in the family from the age of seven was expected to read the Bible through once a year, in addition to the twice daily readings by the father, so that it became "ingrained in my memory, a part of my very self." It will come as no surprise, therefore, that the Janeway children, brought up in similar style, should speak with so uniform a voice, articulate the same truths, quote similar texts.

John Evelyn's little son was five when he died, though "he did excel many that I have known of fifteene," his father said sorrowfully. In an introduction dedicated to his own brothers, the boy's uncles, to *The Golden Book of St John Chrysostom, Concerning the Education of Children* (1659), Evelyn set down a record of the child's life and attainments.

> But that I may conclude and show how truely jealous this child was, least he should offend God in the least scruple, that very morning, not many howers before he fell into that sleepe which was his last, being in the midst of his *Paroxysme*, he called to me, and asked of me whether he should not offend, if in the extremity of his pain, he mentioned so often the name of God, calling for ease; and whether God would accept his prayers if he did not hold his hands out of bed in the posture of praying? Which when I had pacified him about, he prayed till his prayers were turned into eternal praises. Thus ended your Nephew, being but five years, five monethes, and three dayes old.

Nothing in the more expansive Janeway is more poignant or more convincing than this.

Interestingly, a book of moral and religious maxims, *The Last Advice of Mr. Ben Alexander* (1659), used the dialogue method of Vives and Cordier to introduce children to religion.

SARAH: I pray thee, Brother, let us sit under yonder green tree.
BEN: I will, Sister, for it is pleasant weather. But why wilt thou go to day?
SARAH: Because I am now at leisure, and would speak to thee in private.
BEN: Let us go.
SARAH: Pray tell me one thing, Brother?
BEN: Doubt not, Sister, I will if I can.
SARAH: I have seen my Father of-times on his knees in the hall, and sometimes in the parlour, what doth he mean by that?

And the brother is drawn on to expound Christian doctrine to his sister and teaches her how to pray. It is stilted and unremarkable in itself, but worth noting as a very early example (the earliest that I have found) of conversation composed for children in the vernacular.

But if we want to hear more convincing children we can find them in another book of precepts written some forty years later—Robert Russel's *A Little Book for Children* (London, c. 1696). Russel had described how a good child conducted himself—all familiar from Janeway; he prays by himself, he loves his book, he discourses with like-minded children "about God and Christ, and the matters of another World," he reads his Bible. This is no doubt an ideal, but in the subsequent account of how children ought *not* to behave we hear what seem to be authentic, recognizable voices.

All the time his Father is a Reading, or at Prayers, he sits laughing, and playing with his Brothers and Sisters, not minding anything that is said. Then another time, his Father and Mother being in the Shop at work, and leaving him and his Brothers and Sisters within, charging every one of them to read their Books, and his Brothers and Sisters being almost as bad as he, instead of reading their Books they play and rude with each other: and, oh! there is such a frolic and flutter amongst them as if none was to be heard but themselves. Then they play so long, until at last they fall out and quarrel with one another, and call one another all to nought; one is called Dog, another is called Bitch, and another is called Rogue, and another is called Bastard; then it may be they go to fighting, and fling one another down in the House. Then John goes with a Story to his Mother that Mary hit him in the face. Then Mary and Betty go with a Story to their Mother that the Boys do nothing but tear them about, and will not let them alone. Then Tom goes with a story to his mother, saying, Mother, William flung me aground and hurt my Arm. Then William goeth with a story to his Mother, saying, Mother, Tom hit me with his Batt. Then Tom crys out, But you Lye, I did not touch you, you flung me aground first. But you lye: and you lye: And you lye: and you lye.

Books of moral precepts indeed can surprise us with their grasp of real life. Who would have expected the hymn writer, Dr. Isaac Watts (1674–1748), a scholarly bachelor who led a sheltered life as domestic chaplain in a wealthy house, could successfully capture the tones of the eternal rebellious teenager, long before any work of fiction attempted to do so? Having in the second part of *The Improvement of the Mind* (1741) set out what he considered suitable pastimes for the young, he imagined their complaints. "But the Children of our Age will pertly reply, 'What, we must live like No-body! Must we turn old Puritans again? Must we look like fools in Company, where there is scarce any Discourse but of Plays, Operas and Masquerades, of Cards, Dice, and Midnight-Assemblies? And pray what Sin is there in any of them?' " (181). Fashions in juvenile godliness change over the centuries; the voice of mutinous youth hardly varies.

WORKS CITED

Alexander, Benjamin. *The Last Advice of Mr. Ben. Alexander . . . to his Children*. London: For N. Ekins, 1659.

"The Birched School-boy." Balliol MS 354 ij CXXX. Printed in Early English Text Society vol. 32, 403. London: N. Trübner, 1867.

Brinsley, John, trans. *Pueriles Confabulatiunculae or Children's Dialogues.* London: Printed by H. L. for Thomas Man, 1617.

[Cordier, Mathurin]. *Corderius Dialogues Translated Grammatically.* Trans. John Brinsley. London: Humfrey Lownes, 1614.

Evelyn, John. *The Golden Book of St. John Chrysostom, concerning the education of children.* London: printed by D. M. for G. Bedel and T. Collins, 1659.

Fleming, Sandford. *Children and Puritanism.* New Haven: Yale University Press, 1933.

Hoole, Charles, trans. *Pueriles Confabulatiunculae.* London: For the Company of Stationers, 1659.

[Horman, William]. *Vulgaria.* London: Richard Pynson, 1519.

Janeway, James. *A Token for Children.* [1672?; Pt II, 1673]. Facsimile of 1676 ed., New York: Garland Publishing, 1977.

Jessey, Henry. *A Looking-glass for Children.* London: Robert Boulter, 1673.

[Kempe, William]. *The Education of Children.* London: T. Orwin for J. Potter and T. Gubbin, 1588.

Livermore, Mary. *The Story of My Life.* Hartford, CT: A.D. Worthington, 1897.

Opie, Iona. *The People in the Playground.* Oxford: Oxford University Press, 1993.

Russel, Robert. *A Little Book for Children.* London: J. Blare [1696?].

Thomas, Sir Keith. "Children in Early Modern England." In *Children and Their Books,* ed. Gillian Avery and Julia Briggs. Oxford: Oxford University Press, 1989.

Tommy Thumb's Pretty Song Book voll. II. London: Mary Cooper, 1744.

Vives, Juan Luis. *Tudor School-Boy Life: the dialogues of Juan Luis Vives.* Trans. Foster Watson. London: J.M. Dent, 1908.

Watts, Isaac. *The Improvement of the Mind, to which is added A Discourse on the Education of Children and Youth.* London: printed for J. Buckland, T. Longman, T. Field and C. Dilly, 1784.

White, Thomas. *A Little Book for Little Children.* 12th ed. London: Tho. Parkhurst, 1702.

"Innocent Prate":
King John and Shakespeare's Children

MARK A. HEBERLE

The moral climax of Shakespeare's *King John* is a scene (act 4, scene 1) of displaced infanticide: Hubert, the king's loyal servant, has been ordered to blind Arthur, a young boy whom John has just captured in battle, after pledging to end the boy's life two scenes earlier. The child is not only Duke of Brittany (a title created for him by John himself) and the king's nephew but, as son of John's deceased older brother Geoffrey Plantagenet, a legitimate claimant for John's own crown; indeed, the battle just completed has been waged unsuccessfully by Arthur's French supporters in order to put him on the English throne. Unaware that the irons being heated in the room are intended for his own eyes, the boy laments his imprisonment to Hubert near the beginning of the scene:

> Mercy on me!
> Methinks nobody should be sad but I:
> Yet I remember, when I was in France,
> Young gentlemen would be as sad as night,
> Only for wantonness. By my Christendom,
> So I were out of prison, and kept sheep,
> I should be merry as the day is long;
> And so I would be here, but that I doubt
> My uncle practices more harm to me.
> He is afraid of me, and I of him:
> Is it my fault that I was Geoffrey's son?
> No, indeed is't not; and I would to heaven
> I were your son, so you would love me, Hubert. (4.1.12b–24)[1]

Hubert responds in an aside to the audience:

> If I talk to him, with his innocent prate

28

He will awake my mercy, which lies dead:
Therefore I will be sudden and dispatch.

In the event, however, the child's words prove irresistible, as Hubert and the audience in whom he confides ultimately wish: as the scene goes on and the boy becomes aware of the horror about to be perpetrated, his pleas to the man whom he would have his father overcome Hubert's loyalty to the king. By the end of the scene, the heated irons have cooled and Hubert has pledged to protect the "little prince" (9b) "for the wealth of all the world" (130).

In the BBC/Time-Life Royal Shakespeare Company video, a definitive late twentieth-century performance of this rarely performed play, the final nine lines of Arthur's speech are cut, along with thirty more lines of the more than eighty that the boy speaks in the rest of the scene. Cutting is of course necessary in even the best of productions, but the silencing of the boy in this scene, the longest continuous dialogue involving a child in Shakespeare, seems to suggest that his words are relatively unimportant. It implies that the child's role is less essential to this scene than Hubert's and, in doing so, it resembles the contemporary critical depreciation of children's voices and roles in the most canonical of English writers. This essay attempts to explain what may account for such a judgment, to question it, and to suggest that the silencing of children's voices in the largest sense is an important theme for Shakespeare and would have been for his audience.

Over the last decade, feminist, cultural, and New Historicist criticism has enriched and altered the study of characterization in Shakespeare. The old paradigm of isolated, internalized development is being replaced by work that sees character development as relational, and the relationship of children to parents is perhaps the most important of these post-individualist emphases. Typically, such work has focussed upon adult children such as Rosalind and Orlando, or Prince Hal, or Lear's daughters, and the like. While such studies address anew the importance of child-parent relationships in the plays and in English Renaissance society generally, they make almost no mention of children characters who are pre-adolescent and whose roles would have been played by child actors on the Elizabethan and Jacobean stage.[2] Indeed, the few critics who have called attention to these figures have dismissed them as insignificant, uninteresting, and unrealistic, speaking a language that seems preternaturally sophisticated (Pendleton 40, Clemen 100–1, Spilka 162) and that Leah Marcus finds typical of sixteenth-century literary children in general (24–25).

This depreciation of child characters and their language reflects a broader view concerning pre-Enlightenment attitudes toward children that is most significantly represented in Philippe Ariès's *Centuries of Childhood: A Social History of Family Life*. For Ariès and the social historians influenced by him, the idea of childhood, "that particular nature which distinguishes the child from the adult, even the young adult" (128), was nonexistent in medieval Europe and became paradigmatic only in the eighteenth century. For literary critics, influenced by Peter Coveney's groundbreaking study, the appearance of significant children in English works begins even later, with Romantic literature and the beginning of the nineteenth century.

Over the last decade, however, the Ariès thesis has been powerfully questioned by other social historians who have examined previously neglected primary sources such as diaries and autobiographies.[3] Moreover, several important recent studies of literary children in sixteenth- and seventeenth-century texts demonstrate that the child emerges as an important and complex subject in English literature during this period, its innocence and need of guidance both defining its own nature and also symbolically reflecting contemporary social and cultural tensions.[4] A re-examination of Shakespeare's child characters seems appropriate in light of such new conceptions of Renaissance children, literary and otherwise. My primary focus for such re-examination is *King John*, one of the most neglected works in the canon and the one in which children are most important. In this play, Shakespeare has altered his sources drastically so that the work's dramatic structure and political theme depend crucially upon two child characters, the royal princes Arthur and Henry. In addition, Arthur speaks more lines than any child character in Shakespeare, so an analysis of what he does and does not say illustrates *how* Shakespeare makes dramatic use of the words of children rather than simply dismissing such language as unmimetic. Looking at the child figures in *King John* also furnishes an opportunity to redefine generally the significance of Shakespeare's literary children within their sixteenth-century literary, social, and political context as well as our own failure to take them seriously.

The critical dismissal of Shakespeare's children derives from a sense that their roles are trivial, their characters one-dimensional, and their speeches either uninteresting or too adult-like. There are altogether thirty-nine child characters in the canon, and several of these roles are indeed insignificant, presenting little that is distinctly childlike, the boy actor merely functioning as a servant, messenger, or performer (e.g., Benedick's boy in *Much Ado About Nothing*, Mariana's page in *Measure for Measure*, and Lucius in *Julius Caesar*).[5] Similarly insignificant roles for adult messengers, servants, and subalterns may be found in the plays as well, however, and the appearance of *any* children on the stage is unusual in drama and reminds us that actual children were not only part of Shakespeare's own acting company, but enormously popular on stage throughout this period. Peter Thomson notes that there has been little recognition of or even awareness of this phenomenon among social historians or drama critics: "Something about Elizabethan acting ought to be made clearer by the popularity of the boy players, yet that something remains elusive" (112).[6] One thing suggested by such popularity is a striking new interest in childhood and children within Elizabethan society, an interest capitalized upon by Shakespeare as well as other dramatists.

While the number of Shakespeare's child characters may not seem large in itself, it is extraordinary in comparison to the work of post-Renaissance dramatists writing for an adult audience. The pre-adolescent child nearly disappears in later theater, and for good reason: of all literary genres, drama is most dependent upon voluble and articulate speech. Characters, like children, whose speech is limited in articulation are seldom represented in plays for adults. Depreciation of Shakespeare's articulate child characters ignores the peculiar difficulty faced by dramatists in giving significant voice to the child and threatens to throw the baby out with the bath water. Given significant speech by child characters in these plays, perhaps we should ask how it functions and how is it perceived by other characters in the plays rather than whether it is convincingly childlike to us.

Beyond its naively mimetic assumptions, such criticism seems anachronistic in another way. Ariès's own argument for the evolution of our present conception of childhood defines the Renaissance as a transitional period in which children were gradually regarded as different from adults on the basis of their innocence and ignorance, in need of coddling and loving attention on the one hand and carefully supervised education on the other (128–33). Shakespeare himself uses the schoolboy as the archetypal child in Jacques's speech on the Seven Ages of Man in *As You Like It* (2.7.144–46). The few adult remarks on children's speech in these plays typically note its innocence or its precociousness (e.g., *Richard III*, 2.2.17–19; 3.1.132–35). Given the strong Humanist emphasis upon developing and refining the child's potential through education, eloquent boys and girls may not have struck sixteenth-century parents and theatergoers as premature adults, but as perfected children. Indeed, upper-class sixteenth-century children in England "were expected to greet their parents with formalized demonstrations of respect," notes Marcus (29), and since nearly all of Shakespeare's child characters are noble or gentle and speak only to adults, their language may have seemed more ideal *and* natural to his audience than it does to us.

The significance of child characters in Shakespeare does not primarily depend upon how closely they adhere to our conception of realistic, individualized children's behavior and speech, in any case. Their importance drives from an Elizabethan audience's sense of the special nature of children: their innocence—which demands protection by and isolation from the harsher aspects of adult society—and their ignorance—which requires education to enable a child's successful integration into that society. Children are significant agents of the breakdown and/or reintegration of adult society in a number of plays, depending upon how they are received by adults. In the four late romances and the romance-like *Comedy of Errors*, familial and/or social catastrophe is marked by the apparent destruction or loss of infants or children by their parents, while recovery accompanies the children's reappearance years later as adults.[7] Thus, in *The Winter's Tale*, the death of the boy Mamillius fully reveals the moral corruption of his father Leontes and virtually freezes the king and his wronged wife in place, while the return of Leontes's daughter Perdita ("Lost") brings regeneration to Sicily and rebirth for her mother. These plays posit a direct relationship between social health and the welfare of children and may reflect that increasing attention to children's distinctive needs by English Renaissance parents that recent social historians have begun to document. Since the lost children of these plays are recovered as adults, however, there is no representation of children's speech and consciousness, with one exception. The boy Mamillius is represented as an innocent whose words and responses are used by his morally diseased father to further energize Leontes's pathological suspicions of his wife's adultery. Seeing the boy in front of him, the king briefly questions even this child's legitimacy and uses Mamillius's ignorance of his mother's imagined infidelity to help confirm his own certainty that she has been unfaithful.[8]

Leontes's orders to imprison his wife and destroy her infant daughter, whom he rejects as a "bastard," are the response of a patriarchal arrogance turned murderous. Ironically, in separating Mamillius from Hermione in order to keep the boy uncontaminated by his mother's imagined stain, the King of Sicilia destroys the young child's will to live and is left without an heir. Mamillius's fate is representative of a number of child figures, found most characteristically in the history plays. With one exception (Clarence's daughter in *Richard III*), all of these children are boys. With three exceptions, including Prince Henry in *King John*, all of the significant child characters in the history plays are killed or murdered in the course of political and military conflict, or imprisoned, or forced to participate in murderous violence by adult parental figures.[9] The terrible fate of children in these plays, particularly in the first tetralogy, constitutes an implicit indictment of the aggressive pursuit of power for its own sake that characterized the ambitions of Renaissance sovereigns, who tended to identify the welfare of the commonwealth with their own glory. As dramatized in Shakespeare's histories and some of the tragedies (e.g., *Macbeth* and *Coriolanus*), this will to power, implicitly or explicitly patriarchal, is variously and ironically undercut by its effects upon children. First, the need to advance one's own power in order to insure the patrimony of the Crown results in the destruction of everyone else's sons and, ultimately, in the first tetralogy, in the annihilation of the entire male Plantagenet clan. Second, the violence that disfigures or destroys each boy in these plays derives from the very political and military virtues that he is expected to emulate as a youth, the exercise of force to defend or advance himself. Finally, while a rightly ordered public world would protect and develop the potential inherent in childhood, increasingly recognized as a moral and personal imperative by Shakespeare's audiences, the disfiguring of children by the political *ethos* of these plays calls into question the values of that world.

King John is probably the most striking indictment of politics as usual in the canon, and the role of child characters in this play both reflects and advances beyond the representation of children in the first tetralogy that had preceded it (the three parts of *Henry VI* and *Richard III*). Frequently produced during the eighteenth and nineteenth century (Beaurline 1), yet labeled the most cynical of Shakespeare's plays by R. S. White (51), seldom read or taught, and infrequently addressed even by professional Shakespeareans, the play is an anomaly among Shakespeare's works. *King John* was written between the composition of the first tetralogy and the second (*Richard II*, the two parts of *Henry IV*, and *Henry V*), and it is Shakespeare's only history play written during the Elizabethan period that is not part of a larger four-part structure. Lying outside the providential or political purposiveness that links those two epic dramatizations of pre-Tudor English history, it has room in which to be subversive. A contemporary play, *The Troublesome Raign of John, King of England* (1591), has been generally regarded as Shakespeare's direct source but also as an inferior, propagandistic adaptation of Shakespeare's play, so that the date of *King John* has been variously proposed as 1588–90 or 1595–96.[10] Its titular subject, who had defied Roman authority in 1207 but been forced to reconsecrate his crown to the Pope in 1213, had become a Protestant hero after the break from Rome. A vigorously martial ruler, his reign was ultimately unsuccessful: embroiled in inconclusive civil conflicts with his nobles that resulted in the Magna Carta (1215), his regime lost most of England's continental possessions before the king's premature death in 1216, attributed by some sources to his having been poisoned by a treacherous monk. A more mixed combination of virtues and weakness, accomplishments and failures, could scarcely be found in Holinshed and the other chronicle sources. Furthermore, the extreme remoteness in time of John's reign from Renaissance England seems to have provided Shakespeare with an opportunity to question Renaissance political morality in the guise of memorializing a Protestant hero.

Whether Holinshed or the Holinshed-derived *Troublesome Raign* is Shakespeare's primary source, the play is remarkably centered around John's conflict with a child, Prince Arthur, who, as noted above, was the son of the king's older brother Geoffrey. In *King John*, history is drastically rearranged to make Arthur's conflict with his uncle define the shape of John's rule. John's conflict with Arthur generates the king's invasion of France and the dynastic marriage between his niece and the French king's son Lewis that temporarily stymies Arthur's claim by granting the boy the duchy of Brittany, events of 1200 that take up the first two acts of the play. But Arthur's dismissed dynastic claims also reinforce the papal legate's excommunication of John in act 3, an event that occurred historically four years *after* Arthur's death in 1203. The further outbreak of war between France and England that follows in act 3 and results in Arthur's capture by John is thus waged under a Papal interest in the boy's rights that is unhistorical. And John's order for Arthur's death, quickly regretted by the king, results in a revolt of some of John's nobles and a complementary French invasion of England that did not occur until the 1214–1216 period and had nothing at all to do with avenging or rectifying Arthur's demise at John's hands. As Saccio has noted: "The claims and the ultimate fate of Arthur . . . become the mainspring of the plot, the hinge upon which the whole of John's reign is made to turn" (202).

Shakespeare had earlier made the death of royal children the turning point of action, in the first tetralogy: young Rutland's murder by Clifford at the beginning of *3 Henry VI* sets in motion the calculus of vengeful slaughter that is Shakespeare's dramatization of the Wars of the Roses in that play; and Richard III's first order upon assuming the throne, the murder of the Yorkist princes in the Tower, triggers his inevitable downfall. Although the king is not directly responsible for Arthur's death in *King John* (the child is killed as a result of a fall, trying to escape from his prison just after Hubert has spared him), Shakespeare telescopes and rearranges events unhistorically in this play even more drastically than he had done in the earlier history plays. His replotting of history makes John's treatment of Arthur the fundamental action of his whole reign.

The play's moral catastrophe is centered upon Arthur's claim to the throne: John opposes it by warfare in the first two acts; frustrates it through a dynastic marriage with the French in act 3; tries to eliminate it by destroying Arthur in captivity after war breaks out again; and is ultimately consumed by it even after the child's death. Unlike both Holinshed and *The Troublesome Raign*, Shakespeare presents this claim as legitimate, for John's mother admits the legal illegitimacy of her son's rule in the first scene of the play (43). This striking innovation from all previous accounts of John's rule, which never questioned his legitimacy, makes Arthur's cause just, and the child himself a figure of powerless virtue, manipulated for their own purposes by all the adult characters in the play. Even the Bastard, John's most loyal and most morally prescient supporter, memorializes the fallen child as a personification of values that are compromised everywhere else in the play:

> From forth this morsel of dead royalty,
> The life, the right and truth of all this realm
> Is fled to heaven, and England now is left
> To tug and scamble and to part by th' teeth,
> The unowed interest of proud swelling state. (4.3.143–47)

Finally, in addition to centering his action upon Arthur's claims and valorizing them, Shakespeare is responsible for making Arthur a child. Historically, the prince was sixteen when he died in 1203, and Holinshed notes that he helped lead the army that captured John's mother in Anjou in 1202, an exploit dramatized in scene 3 of *The Troublesome Raign*. In *King John*, by contrast, the boy actor playing Arthur was so small that he could be carried off the stage by Hubert alone after his death scene (Holmes 140–41). Thus, Shakespeare has deliberately recast the martial youth as a child, powerless in himself but a vehicle of power for his ambitious mother, King Philip of France and his son Lewis, and the Papal legate Pandulph, all of whom support his claim to England for their own interests.

Prior to Arthur's terrible encounter with Hubert, the disfigurement of the child's innocence is dramatized by the suppression of his voice. Arthur's first words in the play are addressed to the Duke of Austria, purportedly the slayer of Richard Coeur de Lion (the boy's uncle) and one of the commanders under King Philip of France, who is supporting Arthur's cause:

God shall forgive you Cordelion's death
The rather that you give his offspring life,
Shadowing their right under your wings of war.
I give you welcome with a powerless hand,
But with a heart full of unstained love:
Welcome before the gates of Angier, Duke. (2.1.12–17)

This speech, acknowledging his own weakness, is the only moment in the play in which the boy makes any reference to the political struggle between adults that ultimately consumes him. Elsewhere, his responses are what we might expect of a child, a political innocent scarcely interested in the murderous game of claim and counter-claim played out by the adults who purport to be acting in his behalf. When his mother Constance and his grandmother Elinor vie for his allegiance later in the scene, the boy exclaims in frustration: "Good my mother, peace! / I would that I were low laid in my grave. / I am not worth this coil that's made for me" (163–65). After the dynastic marriage between John's niece and Philip's son that eliminates Arthur's claim to the throne while creating him Duke of Brittany, he responds to his mother's apoplectic grief and anger with a simple plea ("I do beseech you, madam, be content," 2.2.42) that indicates how his subjection to adult political conflict has disturbed him. His mother's initial response to the outbreak of peace between John and Philip betrays whose interests are really being served by her insistence on the boy's right to John's throne: "Lewis marry Blanch! O boy, then where art thou? / France friend with England, what becomes of me?" (34–35). The boy's implicit indifference to and distaste for pursuing his dynastic claim (which would have been unthinkable in the historical Arthur) is answered by a nearly hysterical reiteration of that claim by his mother, who claims to be protecting his rights rather than her own desire for power.

In the scene that follows, alliances shift again: John's excommunication by Pandulph, the papal legate, forces Philip to break the recent armistice and resume war against England in the name of the Church and Arthur's rights. During this long and complicated exchange of threats and insults, the boy remains silent, his interests supposedly being advanced by the political power-broking and casuistry of the self-interested adults all about him. Because Arthur speaks no words in this scene, he has been literally written out of it in some modern editions (e.g., Matchett, Braunmuller), even though there is no stage direction for his exit in the First Folio source text of the play.[11] Removing Arthur from the scene in such editions ironically replicates the dismissal of the child that the adult contestants' political quarrels betoken. The physical presence of Arthur and the boy actor representing him during this fusillade of speeches would strikingly remind an audience of the marginality of his true interests as a child. Kings, mothers, and papal legates claim to speak "for" or "against" him, but he is given no words of his own. Ultimately, Arthur's innocence is used *against* him: once John has captured his little rival, Pandulph and Lewis plot an invasion of England in the boy's name, certain that John will execute his captive and that the revulsion sure to follow among the English will enable Lewis himself, now the sole claimant, to depose John.[12]

In the interim, however, John's murderousness outruns Pandulph's scenario, for the king orders Hubert to have Arthur done away with even before Lewis's Church-sanctified invasion. John's ultimately self-destructive attempt to remove the threat of Arthur suggests uncertainty about his own patrilineal claim to the throne, and his murderous orders suggest how morally illegitimate he has become as a result. The king insists on a public re-coronation of himself once he is convinced that Hubert has carried out his instructions, even though his nobles rightly point out that such ceremony betokens deep insecurity and demand Arthur's release from imprisonment. The king's frantic scrambling to win them back after they are convinced of his murder of the child indicates no remorse over Arthur's fate that is not politically motivated. And his subsequent, feckless relinquishing of command to the Bastard ("Have thou the ordering of this present time"; 5.1.77) suggests that the man who ordered Arthur's death is no longer fit to be king. In the end, the illness that afflicts him on his final battlefield, coming after all the catastrophes prompted by Arthur's death, is made to seem an internal punishment for his moral darkening: "This fever, that hath troubled me so long, / Lies heavy on me: O, my heart is sick!" (5.3.3–4)

John's criminality as an infanticide is presented ironically by Shakespeare. His desire to have Arthur killed has become an order to blind him by the time Hubert fails to carry it out; the child is *not* directly destroyed by John, but dies of a fall when he tries to escape his prison.[13] John is therefore not guilty of killing Arthur, but he is ultimately punished for simply having the intention to do so. The switch from execution to blinding suggests a politically calculated pulling back from murder that is morally even more repugnant—Arthur will live, but be incapable of replacing his uncle as king. Indeed, John's initial instructions to Hubert just after Arthur has been captured suggest the king's recognition of the moral squalor of his intentions:

KING JOHN: dost thou understand me?
              Thou art his keeper.
HUBERT: And I'll keep him so
              That he shall not offend your Majesty.
KING JOHN: Death.
HUBERT: My lord.
KING JOHN: A grave.
HUBERT: He shall not live.
KING JOHN: Enough.

This extraordinarily truncated exchange dramatizes the unspeakability of the crime about to be committed and leads to the encounter between child and executioner. Here the child, increasingly silenced as a political object in the rest of the play, speaks for himself and saves his life. As the dialogue between Hubert and Arthur proceeds from the boy's initial ignorance of Hubert's intentions to horror to final release, Shakespeare emphasizes the power of the boy's "innocent prate" through Hubert's reactions. "His words do take possession of my bosom," (32) he reflects to the audience as he shows the royal order to the prince. After Hubert has dismissed the other executioners and Arthur breaks his agreement to accept his mutilation without speaking, Hubert attempts to silence him so that the king's will may be done:

> HUBERT: Is this your promise? Go to, hold your tongue.
> ARTHUR: Hubert, the utterance of a brace of tongues
> Must needs want pleading for a pair of eyes;
> Let me not hold my tongue! let me not, Hubert!

From a contemporary perspective, the child's words in this scene may seem overly studied at points, overly simple-minded at others, and the Royal Shakespeare production on video has made cuts based on those criteria, one presumes. Dramatically, of course, *all* the words in this scene convert Hubert from political to parental imperatives and remind us that the child's voice must be silenced, in this play and beyond it, if adults are to ignore children's rights to live as children.

Two scenes later, as Arthur, disguised as a shipboy, prepares to leap to freedom, Shakespeare gives him the only monologue by a child in the canon:

> The wall is high, and yet will I leap down.
> Good ground, be pitiful and hurt me not!
> There's few or none do know me; if they did,
> This ship-boy's semblance hath disguised me quite.
> I am afraid, and yet I'll venture it.
> If I get down, and do not break my limbs,
> I'll find a thousand shifts to get away
> As good to die and go, as die and stay. (4.3.1–8)

Touchingly childish in its apostrophizing and simple exposition, the speech emphasizes the abuse of childhood that Shakespeare's plays powerfully dramatize for his own audience and ourselves. Defined by others only as claimant to the English crown, Arthur sees himself, rightly, as one whom few do know; in leaving the only person who has protected his childhood innocence, the boy vainly hopes to "get away" from a world in which his identity is politically defined and politically controlled. There is no implication that he intends to find his mother, who is part of the problem that he is running away from.

In fact, although Arthur would be unaware of this, her death was announced to John in the preceding scene, fulfilling the boy's prophecy after his capture that "this will make my mother die with grief!" (3.2.15). Constance's demise belies her name and seems oddly selfish, leaving her imprisoned son behind her, and we might wonder whether she died of grief simply for Arthur's sake or for the sake of the crown that had been lost by his capture.

Arthur's disguise is typical of romance protagonists like Julia in *Two Gentlemen of Verona* or Viola and Sebastian in *Twelfth Night*, but unlike theirs it will not bring escape or transformation. In fact, Arthur's bold attempt to alter his identity and take control of his life by risking it suggests a passage from childhood to youth that is invariably lethal for male children in the history plays. In the event, he dies upon the ground after his leap from the prison walls: "O me! my uncle's spirit is in these stones! / Heaven take my soul, and England keep my bones!" (4.3.9–10). Arthur's apostrophe appropriately identifies John as his murderer morally, and the uncle's spirit may be seen as a synechdoche for the world of political calculation and power-seeking that ultimately has used and discarded this child.

Arthur's fate resembles that of male children in the first tetralogy, but the destruction of children by adult political power is handled with greater irony and complexity in *King John*. As noted, the structure of the play centers about the treatment of Arthur from beginning to end (the inconclusive war that ends with John's death in act 5 is brought on by the death of the boy), unlike earlier plays in which the destruction of children was one crucial element in a succession of catastrophes (the *Henry VI* plays) and the maniacal rise and fall of a tyrant (*Richard III*). Moreover, Arthur's successful appeal to Hubert and the latter's protection of the prince provide a positive picture of the paradoxical strength of childish words and childhood innocence. Hubert, together with the Bastard, is the moral hero of this play, the only adult to protect an innocent child who happens to be Duke of Brittany.

Finally, while Arthur perishes, the play ends by valorizing another character who is both child and legitimate heir to John. Prince Henry, the king's son, appears only in the final act, surrounded by the English nobles who had revolted from John to the French as a result of the death of Arthur. Since Henry was only nine years old when his father died in 1216, Shakespeare's child character was probably played by the same small boy who had portrayed Arthur. In a graphic way, then, Henry is Arthur, that "right and truth of all this realm" mourned by the Bastard, reborn and come again, as if the disguised shipboy had both escaped and returned. (A comparable effect is produced in the BBC/Time-Life production: though different boy actors play Arthur and Henry, each is the same size and wears the same royal clothing.) Young Henry's speech tends to be formal and rhetorical, as in his opening words to the assembled lords concerning his father's fatal poisoning:

It is too late: the life of all his blood
Is touched corruptibly, and his pure brain
Which some suppose the soul's frail dwelling house,
Doth, by the idle comments that it makes,
Foretell the ending of mortality. (5.7.1–5)

He goes on to analyze the progress of the disease, using an elaborate and typical metaphor of assault upon a fortress, later reflecting upon John's feverish singing through the myth of the swan-song:

> 'Tis strange that death should sing!
> I am the cygnet to this pale faint swan,
> Who chants a doleful hymn to his own death,
> And from the organ-pipe of frailty sings
> His soul and body to their lasting rest. (5.7.20–24)

Such language may seem unchildish to us, but it simply illustrates that the allowable repertoire of children's stage language for an Elizabethan audience is different than our own. The stage presence of the boy actor himself would directly ensure a representation of boyhood, and the rhetorical control and elaboration engaged in by Henry here would be dramatically appropriate for a scene in which his father is dying and the son is about to be called upon to succeed him. Here, as elsewhere in Shakespeare, childishness is registered by the reactions of the other characters as well as Henry's own words and acts: he needs to be comforted by Salisbury concerning John's state; he cannot hold back his tears when his father's litter is brought in; and he breaks down at the end of the play, when all of John's adult attendants kneel in homage to him as King Henry III: "I have a kind soul that gives thanks, / And knows not how to do it but with tears" (108–9).

Henry's boyish eloquence throughout this scene, together with this final tableau of adult subjects pledging him their allegiance, presents the most positive valorization of the child in Shakespeare's histories and tragedies.[14] In the first tetralogy, only one child character escaped the murderous effects of political fratricide, the young Henry, Earl of Richmond, who is blessed by Henry VI (*3H6* 4.6) before he is rushed by his noble protectors overseas to avoid being murdered by Edward IV. Although Richmond, founder of the Tudor line, returns in *Richard III* to rid England of the "usurper," the child in *3H6* does not speak a single word and his quick disappearance emphasizes the lethal conflict between adult politics and the nurturing of children that is ever-present in Shakespeare. In *Henry VIII*, his last play, Shakespeare presents the only other child in a history play not disfigured or destroyed by history. At the very end of the play, the infant Elizabeth is brought out on stage and saluted with glorious prophecies of her reign (long since past at the time *Henry VIII* was produced).

In contrast to these silent icons of the Tudor era, who have no part to play in the action of their works, Prince Henry's assumption of the title of his father and the right of his cousin involves both words and actions and combines childhood and political power positively. As William Matchett has noted, the Bastard's decision to pledge his allegiance to another powerless child reverses John's initial frustration and ultimate destruction of Arthur's rights (xxiv). It also prompts the

English nobles who had earlier abandoned John to acknowledge his son as their ruler.

The problem of child kings had been dealt with throughout the first tetralogy and would even darken the final chorus of the triumphalist *Henry V*, which reminds the audience that what Henry had accomplished would be lost under the reign of his infant successor. Thus, the final scene of adult political leaders kneeling before a child might be uncertain or even ominous, particularly since Henry has appeared without previous reference in the play to his existence. Yet this scene ultimately corrects the grim scenario that precedes it. As the political abuse of one child had led to catastrophe for England, so the homage paid to another suggests a different outcome. While the disfiguring of childhood in *King John* is used to question the pursuit of political power, its preservation validates and symbolizes what is politically just. Led by the Bastard, John's nobles become Henry's, pledging their loyalty to a mourning child whom Shakespeare's audience knew as the longest-ruling monarch in English history (1216–1272):

> And happily may your sweet self put on
> The lineal state and glory of the land!
> To whom, with all submission, on my knee
> I do bequeath my faithful services
> And true subjection everlastingly. (101–5)

In this concluding mise-en-scène of four noblemen kneeling before a boy, Shakespeare graphically pays homage to both the potential and the integrity of childhood and suggests that protecting, nurturing, and assisting the child is fundamental to that just political order so rarely found in the history plays, or in the world outside the theater.

Notes

1. All Shakespeare quotations are taken from *The Complete Signet Classic Shakespeare*, with act, scene, and line number references included in the text.

2. See for example Erickson, *Patriarchal Structures* (which deals with *As You Like It*, *Henry V*, *Hamlet* and *King Lear*); Leverenz, "The Woman in Hamlet"; McFarland, "Image of the Family in King Lear"; Adelman, "Feeding, Dependency, and Aggression in Coriolanus." Marjorie Garber discusses the overall movement from childhood to adulthood in the second chapter of *Coming of Age in Shakespeare*, and C. L. Barber deals with parent-child relationships more generally in "The Family in Shakespeare's Development." Diane Dreher studies the relationship between fathers and daughters in *Domination and Defiance*. Both Garber (36) and Barber (199) are typical, however, in dismissing actual child characters in the plays as unimportant to Shakespeare and his audience, while Dreher does not discuss them at all.

3. See Wrightson 106–7; Ozment 2, 133, 137; Hanawalt 171. Linda Pollock concludes *Forgotten Children* by questioning the earlier viewpoint: "Contrary to the belief of such writers as Ariès, there was a concept of childhood in the 16th century. This may have become more elaborated through the centuries, but, none the less, the 16th century writers did appreciate that children were different from adults and were also aware of the ways in which children were different—the latter passed through certain recognisable developmental stages; they played; they required discipline, education, and protection" (267–68).

4. Marcus's study of seventeenth-century poets from Herbert to Marvell is acknowledged in Wooden's account of mid-century Marian sermons, homilies, and plays. Both writers show how childhood became the site of a reimagined return to an earlier, more harmonious, and happier state of English society, Anglican and Roman Catholic respectively. Estrin's close analysis of the foundling motif in Malory and English Renaissance literature suggests that such a theme imaginatively and happily resolved recalcitrant issues of contemporary child-raising (18–26).

5. My count is based upon specific references within the plays showing that a role was cast for a boy actor. For example, the Lancastrian Prince Edward in *3H6* is variously addressed by the York brothers as "youthful Edward," "so young a thorn," "brat," "wilful boy," and "untutored lad" during his final scene in the play (5.5.11, 13, 27, 31, 32).

6. Within Shakespeare's own company, there were probably twelve adult and four boy actors between 1594 and 1599 (Ringler 125–26). There were seven all-boy companies in London between 1558 and 1603—compared to six major mens' companies—and they had a repertory of eighty plays produced during those years (Murray xvi, Shapiro 261–67).

7. Besides the Antipholi and Dromii, Marina, Guiderius and Arviragus, Mamillius and Perdita, and Miranda, we might note several analogous figures, including Rosalind, Helena, Imogen, and Ferdinand, adult children whose unexpected recoveries by their parents provide happy endings and lead to their own marriages.

8. See 1.2.119–37, 160–63, 186–90, 207–8, 211; 2.3.13–17. In the final passage, Leontes attributes his son's fatal decline to shame over his mother's adultery, which Leontes alone has imagined. Mamillius's death is clearly a function of his innocence, which has been destroyed, along with his life, by his father's insane charges against Hermione.

9. There are nineteen child characters in these plays: two, Prince Edward (*3H6, R3*) and Falstaff's page (*2H4, H5*) appear in two plays; two, the traveler's boy in *1 Henry IV* and Gardiner's page in *Henry VIII*, are negligible as child figures. The other fifteen are all thematically and structurally significant, including such a figure as the page whom Richard III misuses to find him a murderer of the royal princes.

10. In the New Arden Edition (1954), Honigmann calls into question the priority of *The Troublesome Raign*, and Matchett (1966) also argues for *King John*'s being the source of the anonymous play. In the two most recent editions of Shakespeare's play, Braunmuller regards *The Troublesome Raign* as Shakespeare's source, while Beaurline be-

lieves *King John* is the earlier play. In his edition of *The Troublesome Raign*, Sider reviews the evidence on both sides of the issue through 1979 and finds it ultimately inconclusive.

11. The most recent editor, Beaurline, restores Arthur to this scene, however, and the silent child remains on stage in the BBC/Time-Life production.

12. This infanticide by proxy is absent from *The Troublesome Raign*, where Pandulph regards Arthur as "safe" with John and encourages Lewis to claim the English crown directly in his own right (Sider 75: v. 36–41).

13. Holinshed presents three different explanations of Arthur's death—he died of grief, he was murdered, he fell to his death trying to escape—of which Shakespeare chose the most ironic (cited in Matchett 177).

14. In *The Troublesome Raign*, Prince Henry, like Arthur, is presented as a youth rather than as a child. Among the orders that he issues is a request that Swinsted Abbey be eradicated, since his father has been poisoned by the monks within (xvi.159–62). Such shrill appeals to vengeance and transparent anti-Catholic propaganda are foreign to Shakespeare's more subtly hopeful conclusion.

Works Cited

Adelman, Janet. " 'Anger's My Meat': Feeding, Dependency, and Aggression in *Coriolanus*." In *Shakespeare: Pattern of Excelling Nature*, eds. David Bevington and Jay L. Halio, 108–24. Newark: University of Delaware Press, 1978. Rpt. in Schwartz and Kahn 129–49.

Ariès, Philippe. *Centuries of Childhood: A Social History of Family Life*. Trans. Robert Baldick. 1960. New York: Vintage, 1962.

Barber, C. L. "The Family in Shakespeare's Development: Tragedy and Sacredness." In Schwartz and Kahn, 188–202.

Beaurline, L. A., ed. *King John*. By William Shakespeare. Cambridge: Cambridge University Press, 1990.

Braunmuller, A. R., ed. *The Life and Death of King John*. Oxford: Clarendon Press, 1989.

Clemen, Wolfgang. *A Commentary on Shakespeare's "Richard III."* London: Methuen, 1968.

Coveney, Peter. *The Image of Childhood: The Individual and Society: A Study of the Theme in English Literature*. Harmondsworth: Penguin, 1957.

Dreher, Diane Elizabeth. *Domination and Defiance: Fathers and Daughters in Shakespeare*. Lexington: University Press of Kentucky, 1986.

Erickson, Peter. *Patriarchal Structures in Shakespeare's Drama*. Berkeley: University of California Press, 1985.

Estrin, Barbara. *The Raven and the Lark: Lost Children in Literature of the English Renaissance*. Lewisburg, PA: Bucknell University Press, 1985.

Garber, Marjorie. *Coming of Age in Shakespeare*. London: Methuen, 1981.

Hanawalt, Barbara A. *The Ties that Bound: Peasant Families in Medieval England*. New York: Oxford University Press, 1986.

Holmes, Martin. *Shakespeare and Burbage*. London and Chichester: Phillimore, 1978.

Honigmann, E. A. J., ed. *King John*. By William Shakespeare. London: Methuen: Cambridge, MA: Harvard University Press, 1954.

Leverenz, David. "The Woman in Hamlet: An Interpersonal View." *Signs: Journal of Women in Culture and Society*. 4.2 (1978): 291–308.

McFarland, Thomas. "The Image of the Family in King Lear." In *On "King Lear,"* ed. Lawrence Danson, 91–118. Princeton: Princeton University Press, 1981.

Marcus, Leah. *Childhood and Cultural Despair: A Theme and Variations in Seventeenth-Century Literature*. Pittsburgh: University of Pittsburgh Press, 1978.

Matchett, William H., ed. *The Life and Death of King John*. New York and Toronto: New American Library, 1966.

Murray, John Tucker. *English Dramatic Companies, 1558–1642*. 2 vols. 1910. Vol. 1 repr. New York: Russell, 1963.

Ozment, Stephen. *When Fathers Ruled: Family Life in Reformation Europe*. Cambridge, MA: Harvard University Press, 1983.

Pendleton, Thomas A. "Shakespeare's Children." *Mid-Hudson Language Studies* 3 (1980): 39–55.

Pollock, Linda A. *Forgotten Children: Parent-Child Relations from 1500 to 1900*. Cambridge: Cambridge University Press, 1983.

Ringler, William A., Jr. "The Number of Actors in Shakespeare's Early Plays." In *The Seventeenth-Century Stage*, ed. Gerald E. Bentley, 110–34. Chicago: University of Chicago Press, 1968.

Saccio, Peter. *Shakespeare's English Kings: History, Chronicle, and Drama*. London: Oxford University Press, 1977.

Schwartz, Murray, and Coppelia Kahn, eds. *Representing Shakespeare: New Psychoanalytic Essays*. Baltimore: Johns Hopkins University Press, 1980.

Shakespeare, William. *The Complete Signet Classic Shakespeare*. Gen. ed. Sylvan Barnet. San Diego: Harcourt, 1972.

———. *King John*. New York: British Broadcasting Company, 1983, videocassette.

Shapiro, Michael. *Children of the Revels: The Boy Companies of Shakespeare's Time and Their Plays*. New York: Columbia University Press, 1977.

Spilka, Mark. "On the Enrichment of Poor Monkeys by Myth and Dream; or, How Dickens Rousseausticated and Pre-Freudianized Victorian Views of Childhood." *Texas Studies in Literature and Language* 27 (1984): 171–179.

Thomson, Peter. *Shakespeare's Theatre*. London: Routledge, 1983.

The Troublesome Raigne of John, King of England. Ed. J. W. Sider. New York and London: Garland, 1979.

White, R. S. *Innocent Victims: Poetic Injustice in Shakespearean Tragedy*. London: Athlone, 1986.

Wooden, Warren W. *Children's Literature of the English Renaissance*. Ed. Jeanie Watson. Lexington: University Press of Kentucky, 1986.

Wrightson, Keith. *English Society 1580–1680*. New Brunswick: Rutgers University Press, 1982.

The Child-Reader of Children's Bibles, 1656–1753

Ruth B. Bottigheimer

W hen "the child" in "child-reader" is treated in contemporary scholarship, that historical child usually appears as the incarnation of one of two polar opposites: an innocent Romantic babe trailing clouds of glory or a guilt-laden Puritan predecessor. "Innocence" and sinful "knowledge" have provided the conceptual framework within which the identity of long-dead children has been sought, and rightly so, for those are the terms within which children were described in past centuries.

In this essay I will examine these concepts within a body of literature, children's Bibles, that pre-dates the emergence of belletristic children's literature. In the forewords and texts of children's Bibles between 1656 and 1753 we witness a profound shift in identity attributed to children by their elders. There we find the notion of an innocent child expressed with reference to distinctive and distinguishing issues: modes of unknowing, unknowing populations, and confessional identity. The concept of childhood innocence that emerged from the forms of innocence postulated within each of these categories, generally associated with the name of John Locke, precipitated internally coherent narrative strategies in Bible stories prepared for the young of different confessions.

INNOCENCE AND IGNORANCE

In studies of childhood innocence in children's literature, scholars have focussed on fiction written for children between 1750 and 1900, a period during which the concept of childhood innocence had become a cultural and literary trope. In writings about children, the concept of innocence has now become entangled with sexual knowledge, and in conjunction with the history of children's literature, "innocent" has come to connote a pre-lapsarian state, one that Wordsworth made memorable in his "Ode on Intimations of Immortality" (1807). His "Ode," based on a Romantic view of the child as a still-uncorrupted being that embodied and expressed spiritual superiority, was a confessionally bounded religious understanding of innocence that must be put into perspective within early modern thought about innocence and the young.

The aspect of childhood innocence most familiar to contemporary scholars developed from John Locke's two revolutionary works, *An Essay Concerning Humane* [sic] *Understanding* (1690) and *Some Thoughts on Education* (1693). Locke contradicted the then reigning idea that the infant mind entered the world equipped with innate ideas; on the contrary, he concluded, only sensory experience could provide the necessary raw material to furnish the empty space of the untaught mind, while subsequent reflection on that experience was the prerequisite for human thought. Locke initially characterized the child's mind as an unfurnished cabinet, later as a blank slate, the *tabula rasa* often referred to by eighteenth-century writers.

For generations before Locke's essay on human understanding, authors had automatically classed children together with uneducated or unlettered adults, "simple" folk. At a stroke, however, Locke's discussion had ruptured that unity, for he implicitly distinguished qualitatively between two different states of unknowing. The cognitively blank slate that Locke outlined stood for a state ripe for education, a hopeful beginning point that the late seventeenth-century Frenchman François Fénelon and eighteenth-century German educational theorists addressed. "Ignorant," on the other hand, suggested a woeful end state. Consequently children were *innocent* in the sense of being cognitively blank or unknowing, but simple folk were *ignorant*, unlearned despite their years of experiencing life. The authors of children's literature noted Locke's distinctions with remarkable speed, cited his work, and integrated his conclusions into their literary productions (Pickering 1981; Summerfield 1984, 82). With little delay, the new definition of the child-mind as informationally unknowing and morally untutored came to dominate European views of children.

A second stage in the redefinition of the child-mind, and also of the nature of the child-reader, developed in the train of Locke's works. In the forewords of children's Bibles, authors intimated that both children and the simple were equally blank in their cognitive ignorance, but they concluded that children and the simple differed measurably in terms of their social knowledge. Although uneducated, a simple adult was nonetheless personally acquainted with a broad range of human emotion and social experience, whereas children had yet to supply their empty cabinet with the images and sensations that such experiences would generate.

The new distinctions between children and the simple brought about a radical boundary shift in the readings offered to each group, a culturally transforming, mental and social reconfiguration of the first order. Early eighteenth-century children's literature reflected this new set of readership markers. The newly formulated child-reader was assumed to have limited social experience but to harbor boundless educable capacity.[1] For this reader belletristic children's literature began to be produced. Simple adult readers, on the other hand, who knew the world and its ways, at least within the limited sphere of the ignorant, continued to read simplified chapbooks that ranged from the piously monitory to the brawlingly violent (Schenda 1970, 1976).

CHILDREN'S BIBLES

We can follow the fundamental shift in attitudes towards the child-reader in children's Bible stories, a little-studied but rich body of European narrative literature for children that flourished in the decades before the mid-eighteenth-century emergence of children's fiction. Bible story collections were the largest single genre of narrative literature directed continuously at children in early modern Europe. Children's Bibles reveal as much, and sometimes more, about real attitudes toward children and childhood than any other single source, because their authors incorporated their, and society's, views into the design and content of these small books. Their agenda was neither to describe young children nor to produce a set of idealized, prescriptive behavioral concepts, as in a manual of manners, but to save the souls of their young readers. The singlemindedness with which children's Bible authors pursued their project made them express themselves unconsciously, a fact that gives twentieth-century readers relatively unimpeded access to their attitudes about children's nature.

Part of a body of devotional literature that included catechisms, prayers, Janeway's exhortations to piety, and Bunyan's examples of selfless virtue, vernacular Bible stories took on their modern form in German in the sixteenth century[2] (Brüggemann and Brunken I:143–526, 2:59–306) and in France in the seventeenth century. The genre began its modern expansion in the late seventeenth century in both Germany and France, in the early eighteenth century in England, and a few decades later in the United States. (Only in the mid-twentieth century did Bible story collections become a significant phenomenon in southern Europe [Bottigheimer 1991c, 1991b]). Developed for home and school use, Bible story collections reached a far greater proportion of European child-readers than any other single genre of narrative writing in the early modern period. As the product of a very early stage in the development of literature for children, children's Bibles offer an opportunity to observe the gestation and birth of the idea of childhood innocence at the end of the seventeenth and beginning of the eighteenth century.

Modern children's Bibles have titles like *The Children's Bible*, *La Bible des Enfans*, *Kinderbibel*, *La Bibbia del Bambino*, *La Biblia contada a los Niños*. In the seventeenth and eighteenth centuries, an age whose languages did not distinguish between "story" and "history,"[3] they were called *The History of Genesis*, *L'Histoire du Vieux et du Nouveau Testament*, and *Kleine Historische Bibel* or *Biblische Geschichte*. Their heroes and heroines were vividly drawn characters who always excited God's partisan passions and who sometimes elicited readers' penned response in the margins. In these stories children encountered not only adult transgressions, but also—more wrenching for the young reader—numerous child horrors: one brother murdered another (Cain and Abel), other brothers sold their sibling into slavery (Joseph), a bonny babe was consigned to the Nile (Moses), a bear devoured forty-two boys (Elisha), Herod ordered all boy babies killed, and a grandmother murdered all her grandsons but one (Athaliah). In some cases, children's Bibles intensified the canonical Bible's narrative drama by threatening a child's life with ever-greater devastation.

Children's Bibles rarely let children speak. Here and there the young Benjamin raised a fraternal voice to defend Joseph against his brothers' murderous intentions, but the most regularly heard infant words were Isaac's, formulated as a consenting question, as he and his father approached the hilltop sacrificial altar where he was to die. The parents, teachers, and preachers who composed children's Bibles wanted willing and silent compliance in response to their powerfully normative intentions.

LITERACY LEVELS AND THE CHILD-READER

The earliest collections of Protestant Bible stories lumped children together with simple folks (Rihel 1540, in Reu 58), because in their authors' eyes, the two groups of readers shared identical qualities. Both children and the simple, said Martin Luther, retained stories better via allegory, parable, and image; events impressed them more than dogma; and pictured events offered them the strongest possible impressions (Luther, *Passional* in *Betbüchlin*, Preface, n.p.; Bottigheimer 1990, 154). The familiar equation of "simple" and "young" had continued to issue easily from the pens of seventeenth-century German Protestant Bible story authors (Glassius [1654?]; Gesenius 1656, 1684; Weissmann 1684; Zeidler 1691), for in Protestant Germany in the sixteenth and seventeenth centuries readership groupings had been understood, and hence determined, solely by levels of literacy, not by differences in innocence or ignorance.

The nature of the stories that children's Bible authors included gives the clearest indication of their implicit assessment of the state of the mind and soul of the child-reader. A comparison of two German children's Bibles demonstrates the vast change in Protestant children's Bible authors' views of children's nature between 1656 and 1753, approximately half a century before and half a century after John Locke's seminal writings. The first example is Justus Gesenius's *Biblische Historien Altes und Neues Testaments/ Der Jugend und den Einfältigen zusammen gebracht* (Bible Histories of the Old and New Testament, Collected for the Use of Children and the Simple, 1656; see Reents 33–37); the second, Johann Peter Miller's *Erbauliche Erzählungen der vornehmsten biblischen Geschichten* (Devotional Stories of the Principal Bible Histories, 1753; see (Brüggemann and Brunken 2:230, 231, 242, 248, 1308–10).

47

Justus Gesenius exposed his readers to the entire array of stories that literate and book-reading young Lutherans might have been familiar with in the century since the appearance of Hartmann Beyer's Bible stories in 1555. They included troubling tales like Noah's drunken nakedness, the rape of Dinah, the story of Joseph and Potiphar's wife in all its adulterous detail, Jael's heroic murder of Sisera, and a graphic description of David's adultery with Bathsheba along with an account of his treacherous murder of her husband Uriah. Gesenius's Bible stories assume observant and knowing children, as aware of sexual assault and felonious battery as their elders. His child-reader was one of a household that included other simple, but adult, listeners, the servants and laborers who were an integral part of property-owning households in the early modern period. Its long baroque title said as much a little further on, "children and domestic servants" (Kinder und Gesinde). Although Gesenius, himself an educator, harbored the hope that his book would be adopted in elementary schools (Knaben und Mägdenschulen), his instructions were manifestly for home use. Gesenius's goal was that his readers (and listeners) remember the Bible's content in the words of Luther's translation so that they could better understand Sunday sermons and catechism sessions. They would learn in a physical manner, he said, with story readings interspersed with song and interrogation. What they missed should be beaten into them (einbleuen) until they had memorized the material (Gesenius Preface). His emphasis on memorizing the specific words of Luther's translation was characteristic of post-Reformation Lutheran rhetoric; his inclusion of numerous negative behavioral examples in his tales was consistent with most seventeenth-century educational theory and practice.

Johann Peter Miller's children's Bible (1753) exemplified post-Enlightenment and post-Lockean attitudes and consequently differed in nearly every respect from Gesenius's. When Miller composed his collection of Bible stories, he omitted Noah's nakedness, Dinah's rape, the sexual details of the story of Joseph and Potiphar's wife, and Jael's brutal heroism. He mentioned David's adultery and his murder of Uriah, but embedded them in extravagant praise of the Hebrew king's general goodness and limited his criticism to noting that David might not have been sufficiently on guard against his own inclinations.[4] Miller's pattern of omissions was consistent with a general expurgation of problematic texts from the pages of Protestant children's Bibles in the course of the eighteenth century. He did not openly advert to the innocence of his eighteenth-century child-reader; indeed, he accepted the contemporaneous Lutheran view that the child was a creature fallen at birth because of the effects of original sin (Reents 100). Nevertheless, the secular pedagogical concept of childhood experiential innocence as a natural concomitant of informational unknowing penetrated Miller's children's Bible, as is evident from his deletion of sexual episodes and paternal wrong-doing. Rector of the Helmstedt school (Peter-Perret 110–25, esp. 111), he meant his collection not for home but for school use, and designed it with a teacher-friendly format, including small-type directions for its use. Miller said he assumed that his young pupils owned a Bible where Luther's words could be found and, he continued plainly, he meant to use Bible stories not to etch Luther's words onto the child's memory, but to teach morality and to inculcate acceptable social behavior. The child-readers he envisioned would acquire knowledge in layers, deepening their comprehension of the Bible story by means of appended "Teachings," while the stories themselves would offer positive, rather than negative, examples. In Miller's eyes, child-readers' educability was simply the obverse of their state of informational unknowing. He distinguished between children's lack of school-mediated knowledge (a state to be actively remedied) and the absence of carnal knowledge (a state to be firmly maintained).

Changes of this magnitude in the genre of Bible stories do not reflect confessional differences (both Gesenius and Miller were Lutheran educators), but rather the inception, formulation, and the effective dissemination of new ideas about children. This revolutionary change in the history of writing for children caused a radical reformulation of the *nature* of the implied reader of Bible stories.

In 1693, John Locke addressed the issue of children's Bibles (Pickering 183), calling for the composition of a collection of Bible stories for children. Locke had probably been moved by the appearance in England's luxury book market of a remarkable two-volume illustrated folio, *The History of the Old Testament* and *The History of the New Testament* (1690, 1688) or perhaps by the children's book, *The History of Genesis* (1690). The original for both was Nicolas Fontaine's *L'Histoire du vieux et du Nouveau Testament*, written and published for children in Paris in 1670, with most of the blood and gore of the canonical Old Testament intact. However, it was not this sort of Bible story collection that Locke wanted, but rather a selection for the child's "Instruction" (Locke 1693, 187) that would exemplify Christian truths: "What you would have others do unto you, do you the Same unto them; and such other easy and plain moral Rules" (188). It would be "a good History of the Bible for young People to read, wherein every thing, that is fit to be put into it, being laid down in its due Order of Time, and several things omitted, which were suited only to riper Age, [so that] that Confusion, which is usually produced by promiscuous reading of the Scripture, as it lies now bound up in our Bibles, would be avoided. . . . Of this History of the Bible, I think too it would be well if there were a short and plain Epitome made, containing the chief and most material Heads, for Children to be conversant in as soon as they can read" (226–27). This children's Bible would include the "Story of Joseph and his Brethren, of David and Goliath, of David and Jonathan, etc." (187).

Locke was not the only educator to have been troubled by the contents of existing children's Bibles. Change in the meaning of childhood innocence and ignorance was widespread in the 1680s and 1690s. Six years before, in 1687, François Fénelon had published his essay on the education of girls. There he listed the titles of Bible stories he believed were appropriate for young readers in wording that suggests he was leafing through Fontaine's Bible.[5] Like Locke, Fénelon recommended excising sexuality, though *his* ideal set of Bible stories retained a few tales of violence.

Fénelon was French, tutor to the dauphin, yet his French Catholic views could be found in Germany in children's Bibles both Catholic and Reformed, that is, Calvinist. These attitudes can be followed and analyzed in the content of two children's Bibles, Johannes Melchior's Reformed *Kinder-Bibel* (1688) and Christoff Weigel's Catholic *Biblia Ectypa* (1695 et seq.). Melchior's children's Bible exhibited an "omission of brutal texts as well as a cautious depiction of sexual transgressions [that] point towards an adjustment of Biblical texts in a direction suitable for children" (Trocha 1991, 44). Melchior's was a short-lived work, but Weigel's work went through several editions. Weigel wrote his Bible book only a few years after Fénelon's *Education des Filles* (1687) and at virtually the same time as Locke's *Thoughts on Education* (1693). Because neither Fénelon's nor Locke's works appeared immediately in German translation, there is little likelihood that either influenced Weigel's editing. Initially he wrote for adults, but subsequently he purged his pictorial and textual histories for a child-readership. This act was a direct response to the purificatory mandates of the late sixteenth-century Council of Trent, as Weigel himself said in his preface (1695, n.p.).[6]

RADICAL REFORMATION OF CHILDREN'S BIBLES

The radical reformulation of children's Bibles all over Western Europe at the end of the seventeenth and beginning of the eighteenth centuries would appear to represent a simple expurgation of vexatious and corrupting examples of unacceptable behavior, like David's unbridled sexual desire for Bathsheba. This, at least, is consistent with the changes evident in the tables of contents, from our Protestant and Catholic German examples from 1656, 1695, and 1753. Their alterations seem to embody a mandate to maintain innocence. What, however, was the nature of "innocence" in this context? The word begins to take on an altogether new set of meanings when we re-examine the content changes in Miller's children's Bible, no longer standing solely for the absence of sexual knowledge on the child's part.

The recommendations of an educational theorist like Locke did not coincide neatly with the contents of post-1700 children's Bibles in Protestant England and Germany. These Bibles did not remove *all* examples of sexual transgression. On the contrary, when Protestant Bible story editors initially sought to establish innocence, they first exonerated the patriarchs (Bottigheimer forthcoming, chapter 9), but kept the sins of the wives and daughters, whom they roundly blamed. For example, in the broad variety of eighteenth-century tellings of Joseph and Potiphar's wife, Potiphar's wife's "lustful heart" and "despicable caresses" (here, Miller 33) were retained long after corresponding sexual excesses by male sinners had been erased. It seemed necessary to maintain her evil inclinations in order to highlight Joseph's virtue. Several generations would pass before this story came into conformity with Fénelon's and Locke's design for a children's Bible that included "Joseph and his Brothers" rather than Joseph and Potiphar's wife, and during this period Joseph became increasingly virtuous (in adjective choice and narrative action), while Potiphar's wife was steadily shorn of all justification for her ardor.

The patriarch's innocence of wrongdoing in the Joseph story was a phenomenon that eventually characterized all narratives of fathers and children in Protestant children's Bibles. Part of an apparently conscious re-ordering of gender values around 1700, the new order moved the father to the spotlit center stage, banished the mother to the shadows of the wings, and made the sexually innocent child the product of guiltless paternal rather than, as formerly, joint parental instruction. This may seem a sweeping generalization, but evidence internal to children's Bibles bears it out. Before 1700, the forewords of children's Bibles were addressed to both parents, and often specifically to "Mothers and Fathers," as in Gesenius's title and preface; after 1700, children's Bible authors turned exclusively toward fathers in the language of prefaces and forewords.[7] In this context it is useful to remember that on the continent in the eighteenth century, women underwent a parallel form of conceptual erasure, with the idealized mid-eighteenth-century wife a creature who knew only what her husband had taught her, a person like Rousseau's Sophie, who was "created especially to please man" (4:5) and was maintained untutored and untaught by her parents. "L'écoliere" to Émile's "maître" (4:256), she would learn philosophy, physics, mathematics, and history, "in a word, everything" (4:255), from her future husband. She was not to be a teacher, but a pupil. This gender-driven view had for many Bible readers a Scriptural basis in the story of Adam and Eve. A foundational narrative both in the canonical Bible and in children's Bibles, it unswervingly guided gender perceptions and social definitions for generations (Miles; Bottigheimer 1991a, 1991c).[8] In this story, a woman mediated fatal knowledge of good and evil, and, according to the overwhelming majority of thinkers and theologians, had plunged humanity into sin and thereby introduced death into the world. In the Edenic classroom, *female* mediation had been disastrous, and as alien as it may seem to modern ears, it was the consequences of Eve's "teaching" that were cited in early prohibitions forbidding women to teach. This evidence about the changing gender of domestic teachers and the shifting locus of sin expands the concept of childhood innocence asserted by Locke and others and places it within a broad early modern re-ordering of gender.

CONCLUSION

The reformulation of childhood innocence in the eighteenth century was a complex process: first, children were defined all over Europe as both informationally unknowing and experientially innocent, and then, in Protestant Europe, the inculpating actions of father-figures were edited to make men the gender exemplars of desirable conduct. Given the expressed views on sexuality of the French Catholic Fénelon and the publishing acts of the German Catholic Weigel, we would expect similar Bible story content in Catholic Europe. That, however, was not the case. Catholic children in eighteenth-century Europe were reared with a recognizably different set of expectations. Catholic children's Bibles between 1670 and 1770, which in practice meant Fontaine's *Histoire* or its English, Italian, German, and Portuguese translations, considered the question of childhood innocence, but ignored the Protestant solution of exculpating the fathers. The Catholic father, whether domestic or scriptural, needed the Church to save his soul every bit as much as did the Catholic mother, sister, and daughter. Hence in Catholic children's Bibles during most of the eighteenth century, David remained a wicked adulterer, Potiphar's wife expressed her illicit passion, and the child-reader was not protected from knowledge of the sins of the flesh. For Catholic child-readers of Bible stories, that purifying process began in the course of the nineteenth century, three or four generations later than it had for Protestant child-readers of Bible stories. Fénelon's eloquently expressed concerns did not alter the course of French Catholic children's Bibles, which had been established by Fontaine in 1670. Fontaine's pre-Lockean views eclipsed Weigel's and maintained a different set of expectations about the child-reader among Catholic children's Bible authors in the early modern period.

This discussion of the child-reader confirms the broad circulation of ideas about childhood innocence and demonstrates that these ideas were already finding expression in writing for children in Europe in the decade before John Locke's epoch-making delineation of the *tabula rasa*. Further, eighteenth-century writers for children (Fontaine was a *seventeenth*-century writer), both Catholic and Protestant, subscribed to and expressed shared assumptions about the existence of childhood innocence, although their assumptions took different textual forms. Eighteenth-century Protestant authors of children's Bibles generally understood children's unknowing innocence in Lockean terms, and as a result innocence in their view served as a prescription to create and maintain a view of the patriarchs as sexually innocent; Catholic authors of children's Bibles like Weigel, on the other hand, accepted childhood "unknowing" as a mandate to describe examples of human fallibility in graphic terms, for these flaws would and did require the benevolent intervention of the church.

The results of this study of European children's Bibles at the end of the seventeenth and beginning of the eighteenth centuries suggest that caution is necessary in discussions of the history of childhood, child-reading, or the child-reader. Children in the seventeenth and eighteenth centuries grew up in an age of pronounced confessional distinctions, and their Protestant or Catholic educators inculcated a confession-specific consciousness of sin, self, and sexual identity. It is not enough to speak of "the child" or of the "child-reader" in any century. Instead of a unitary "innocence," like that expressed in the "Ode on Intimations of Immortality," several different concepts of childhood innocence were in the process of formation as children's literature emerged during the eighteenth century. Class and confession each played a major role in conditioning attitudes towards childhood innocence; and the authors of children's Bibles, in turn, deployed carefully crafted religious narratives to shape and mold the child-reader's sense of self through Bible story collections for the young. How we imagine children to have responded to the literature their elders gave them, or to the books they themselves sought out, depends in large part on information about class and confession, which has been largely unused or unspecified in studies of children. We need to know more about these real, historical children who once wore soft velvet dresses or coarse linsey-woolsey smocks, who accepted or resisted the norms laid gently, or heavily, on their shoulders, and who skipped lightly to their nurseries or trudged wearily to their workshops. Class and confession are beginning points in understanding them, their world, and their response to that world.

NOTES

1. It is worth noting at this point that an early eighteenth-century child-reader was, in the overwhelming majority of cases, the child of a family of means. The economic gulf between such a child and the simple adult was so evident to contemporary writers and their readers that it was unnecessary to acknowledge or even to allude to it. But we contemporary readers, with democratized expectations, need to be reminded of that easily missed fact.

2. Before the age of print, Bible stories were widespread in Europe in Petrus Comestor's *Historia Scholastica*, which existed as luxury manuscripts for adult readers and as schoolbooks, usually in Latin but occasionally in the vernacular, for medieval schoolboys.

3. The German "Geschichte" and the French "histoire" signify both "story" and "history." English had two words, but in this context used them interchangeably.

4. Neither Gesenius nor Miller included the grisly tale of the rape-murder of the Levite's wife, which had formed part of Beyer's Bible stories collection.

5. I have compared Fénelon's list with the story titles of a second children's Bible, written by Claude Oronce Finé de Brianville (Paris: Charles de Sercy, 1670 et seq.) and have concluded that it is more likely that Fénelon had Fontaine's than Finé's book in his hand.

6. Similar tendencies were also evident in popular literature printed for a broad and barely literate readership of simple folk; their readings were also heavily censored, though with a different purpose, namely, to conserve political and social stability (Schenda 1970, 91–141).

7. The single exception to this pattern that I have encountered was in Zurich. When children's Bibles emerged there in the late eighteenth century, their verbose forewords were addressed to mothers and fathers. There are several possible explana-

tions for this fact, which I explore in chapter 2, "The History of the Bible for Children," in *The Bible for Children*.

8. The immense bibliography on Eve's role in the fall from grace, both primary and secondary, has been augmented in the 1980s and 1990s by thoughtful considerations of the phenomenon of gender skewing in theological exegesis by women scholars of religion, theology, and literature. For an extensive bibliography see Miles.

WORKS CITED

Primary Literature

[Brunfels, Otto]. *Catechesis puerorum, in fide, literis & moribus. Ex probatissimus quibusq; Authoribus, Per Othonem Brunfelsium.* Francofvrti: Apud Christianum Egenolphum, [1531].

Bunyan, John. *Book for Boys and Girls; or, Country Rhimes for Children.* London: n.p., 1686.

Fénelon, François de Salignac de la Mothe. *Education des filles.* Paris: Pierre au Bouin, Pierre Emery, et Charles Clousier, 1687.

Finé de Brianville, Claude Oronce. *Histoire Sacrée en tableaux, pour Monsieur le Dauphin, Avec leur Explication suivant le texte de l'Ecriture.* Paris: Charles de Sercy, 1670.

Fontaine, Nicolas. *L'Histoire du Vieux et du Nouveau Testament.* Paris: Pierre le Petit, 1670.

[Fontaine, Nicolas]. *The History of Genesis. Being an Account of the Holy Lives and Actions of the Patriarchs.* 1690. London: Andrew Bell, 1708.

———. *The History of the New Testament.* London: Richard Blome, 1688.

———. *The History of the Old Testament.* London: Richard Blome, 1690.

Gesenius, Justus. *Biblische Historien Altes und Neues Testaments / . . . Anitzo auf Begehren zum andernmahl mit Figuren gedruckt / und vormahls herfür gegeben.* Braunschweig: Christoph Friedrich Zilliger, 1684.

———. *Biblische Historien Altes und Neues Testaments / Der Jugend und den Einfältigen zusammen gebracht / und in zwey Theile / jedes Theil aber in vier und funffzig Lectiones zu dem Ende abgetheilet / damit Christliche Hausväter oder Haussmütter bey ihrer Christlichen Feyre und Sabbaths-Heiligung beide Theile alle Jahr gantz durch und zu Ende bringen / und ohne Mühe ihren Kindern und Gesinde (vermittelst deutlicher und verständlicher Vorlesung) bekant machen können: Samt einem Bericht oder Vorrede an den Leser wie diss Buch nützlich zu gebrauchen.* Braunschweig: Christoph Friederich Zilliger, 1656.

Glassius, Salomon. *Biblisches Handbüchlein.* Nürnberg: n.p., [1654?].

Janeway, James. *A Token for Children: Being An Exact Account of the Conversion, Holy and Exemplary Lives of Joyful Deaths of several Young Children.* 1672; London: T. Norris, 1709.

Locke, John. *An Essay on Humane Understanding.* London: Thomas Basset, 1690.

———. *Some Thoughts concerning Education.* London: A. & J. Churchill, 1693.

Luther, Martin. *Ein Betbüchlein mit Kalender und Passional. Wittenberg 1529.* Ed. Frieder Schulz. Kassel: Johannes Stauda, 1982.

———. *Parvvs catechismus pro pveris in Schola.* Wittenberg: Georg Rhau, 1529.

Miller, Johann Peter. *Erbauliche Erzählungen.* Leipzig: Weygand, 1973.

————. *Erbauliche Erzählungen der vornehmsten biblischen Geschichten zur Erweckung eines lebendigen Glaubens und der wahren Gottseligkeit in der Jugend.* Leipzig: Weygand, 1753.

Petrus Comester. *Historia Scholastica.* Köln: Conrad winters, 1479.

Reu, Johann Michael, ed. *Quellen zur Geschichte des kirchlichen Unterrichts in der evangelischen Kirche Deutschlands zwischen 1530 und 1600. Part II.* 1906; Hildesheim: Georg Olms, 1976.

Rousseau, Jean-Jacques. *Emile, ou de l'éducation.* A la Haye: Chez Jean Néaulm, Libraire, 1762. [Paris: Duchesne, 1762].

[Weigel, Christoph]. *Biblia Ectypa. Bildnussen auf Heilige Schrift dess Alt- und Neuen Testaments.* Augsburg: Weigel, 1695.

————. *Biblische Augen- und Seelen-Lust, das ist Die Heilige Geschichte alten Testaments . . . Der christlichen Jugend zu Erbaulicher Ergebung herausgegeben.* Augsburg: Christoph Weigel, 1696.

————. Title page missing. = a later, small, derivative edition. [Th. bibl. 1166/54 rara University Library: Göttingen].

————. Title page missing. = another later, slightly larger, derivative edition. [KK1288 Zentral Bibliothek: Zurich].

————. *Historiae Celebriores Veteris Testamenti Iconibus repraesentatae et Ad excitandas bonas meditationes selectis Epigrammatibus exornatae in lucem datae à Christophoro Weigelio.* Nürnberg: n.p., 1708.

Weissmann, Ehrnreich. *Kinder-Bibel.* Stuttgart: Johann Gottfried Zubrodt, 1684.

Zeidler, Johann Gottfried. *Bilder-Büchlein.* Magdeburg: Johann Daniel Müller, 1691.

Secondary Literature

Bottigheimer, Ruth B. "An Alternative Eve." *Children's Literature Quarterly* (1991a): 73–78.

————. "Kinderbibeln in Deutschland und Europa—geschichtlicher Überblick." In *Die Bibel als Kinderbuch,* ed. Roswitha Cordes, 85–93. Schuserte: Katholischen Akademie Schwerte, 1991b.

————. "Martin Luther's Children's Bible." *Wolfenbütteler Notizen zur Buchgeschichte* 15.2 (1990): 152–61.

————. "Religion for the Young in Bible Story Collections." *Fabula* 32 (1991c): 19–32.

Brüggemann, Theodor, and Otto Brunken. *Handbuch zur Kinder- und Jugendliteratur. 1570–1750.* Stuttgart: Metzler, 1991.

————. *The Bible for Children from the Age of Gutenberg to the Present.* Forthcoming.

————. *Handbuch zur Kinder- und Jugendliteratur. Vom Beginn des Buchdrucks bis 1570.* Stuttgart: Metzler, 1987.

Brüggemann, Theodor, and Hans-Heino Ewers. *Handbuch zur Kinder-und Jugendliteratur. Von 1750 bis 1800.* Stuttgart: Metzler, 1982.

Jackson, Mary V. *Engines of Instruction, Mischief, and Magic: Children's Literature in England from Its Beginnings to 1839.* Lincoln: University of Nebraska Press, 1989.

Miles, Margaret R. *Carnal Knowing.* Boston: Beacon, 1989.

Ozment, Steven. *When Fathers Ruled: Family Life in Reformation Europe.* Cambridge: Harvard University Press, 1983.

Peter-Perret, Sybille. *Biblische Geschichten für die Jugend erzählt. Eine Studie zur religiösen Kinder- und Jugendliteratur des 18. Jahrhunderts.* = Pädagogik und Psychologie 2.

Pickering, Samuel. *John Locke and Children's Books in Eighteenth-Century England.* Knoxville: University of Tennessee Press, 1981.

Reents, Christine. *Die Bibel als Schul- und Hausbuch für Kinder.* Göttingen: Vandenhoeck und Ruprecht, 1984.

Schenda, Rudolf. *Die Lesestoffe der kleinen Leute. Studien zur populären Literatur im 19. und 20. Jahrhundert.* Munich: Beck, 1976.

————. *Volk ohne Buch.* 1970; Munich: dtv, 1977.

Summerfield, Geoffrey. *Fantasy and Reason: Children's Literature in the Eighteenth Century.* Athens: University of Georgia Press, 1984.

Trocha, Jens. *Die Kinder-Bibel des Johannes Melchior.* Herborn: Herborn Theological Institute, 1991.

Reading Rosamond Reading:
Maria Edgeworth's "Wee-Wee Stories"
Interrogate the Canon

MITZI MYERS

> Someone asked Miss Edgeworth how she came
> to understand children as she did, what charm
> she used to win them. "I don't know . . . I lie
> down and let them crawl over me."
> —Anne Thackeray, *A Book of Sibyls,* 1883

> She wrote always in the library, heedless of any
> noise, even of the romps of children.
> —S. C. Hall, *A Book of Memories,* 1877

> Since none of us is a coherent subject, we are
> always *beside* ourselves, in multiple senses.
> —Linda Kaufmann, *Gender and Theory,* 1989

Like Sir Walter Scott's Abbotsford, Edgeworthstown, Ireland, was a routine stop for tourists in pursuit of literary lions. Modern histories marginalize Maria Edgeworth (1768–1849) as a pioneering regional novelist who anticipated and influenced Scott. If you know her at all, it is probably as the author of the first Anglo-Irish novel, *Castle Rackrent* (1800), a dramatic monologue narrated by Thady, the naive old family retainer who tells more than he knows. Or perhaps you've encountered *Belinda* (1801), the feminocentric fiction which impressed Jane Austen with its rational heroine, witty dialogue, and ironic comedy of manners. But once upon a time Edgeworth was more than an aside in literary history.[1] Not only the early nineteenth century's most popular and influential female novelist for adults, far outranking Austen, she was also renowned as a pioneering educator and writer for children, the prolific literary mother of several ongoing series of juvenile tales she always playfully calls "wee-wee stories."[2] Every tourist with a literary or educational bent wanted to see the famous author, the real children who were the models and first audience for her tales, and the family library where those children played and the author wrote—at the same time. Like their tiny creator, who had an uncanny ability to be in two places at once, simultaneously child and adult, Maria Edgeworth's "wee-wee stories" invite dual readings. They vividly represent the child's voice and point of view and they intelligently question the cultural systems of value—both past and present—which occlude the juvenile standpoint.

Visual aids are the harried primary teacher's godsend—and the historical scholar's too. The portraits with which I begin show iconographically the bilingual story I tell; the visual anecdotes embody my essay's theoretic arguments about the child-adult relationship and its multiple meanings in literary and cultural history. Mrs. S. C. Hall's *Pilgrimages to English Shrines* pictures the writer at home in 1842, all the more revealingly because Edgeworth was an old woman by then, still "full of vitality; unresting without being at all restless" (91). Christian and encomiastic, the Halls are much concerned to Victorianize a foremother they revere. They prefer sentimental piety to intellectual inquiry and aren't attuned to late-eighteenth-century educational experimentation, especially when it shows more interest in understanding children's acquisition of language and literature than in teaching them to pray. But the Halls are shrewd observers all the same, and their various pen-portraits and accompanying engraving of Maria Edgeworth at work amid the household verify the author's own vivid letters and stories.[3] "*We are all one and the same,*" Maria told the Halls, but they were still startled to experience the Edgeworth menage. Everybody around the library's big oblong table talked, the children of Francis, a much younger brother born in 1809, played at will, and the author herself sat on a corner of the sofa, writing at her miniature desk. "Miss Edgeworth's abstractedness, and yet power of attention to what was going on,—the one not seeming to interfere with the other,—puzzled us exceedingly." While the whole multitudinous family moved about and chatted, she remained "wrapt up, to all appearance, in her subject"; yet "knowing by a sort of instinct" exactly when the children or the conversation needed her, she would pause, clear up the difficulties, fetch the toy or book, or find the perfect illustrative passage in a volume, and then resume her pen and writing "in less space of time than we have taken to write it." She "never seemed to be in *her own head,* as it were," Mrs. Hall writes of Edgeworth's relational psychic habits (1853, 99, 105). "Incessant and yet genial activity was a marked feature of her nature," adds Mr. Hall: "She seemed to be as nearly ubiquitous as a human creature can be" (1883, 360).

The Halls' verbal sketches of the Edgeworth domestic establishment are supplemented by a rare illustration of the library with Maria at her desk, first published in the *Art-Journal* for 1849.[4] The Halls' illustrator captures a paradigm of creative activity, getting the communal setting right but leaving out the children. It's the children, however, who take center stage in the 1789 Adam Buck water color of the Edgeworths: this, the only authentic representation of Maria Edgeworth before the Halls', is a family portrait. Buck's lively pastel is also the scene of a woman's coming to writing, a crowded family table that's the subject, first audience, and emotional center of Edgeworth's work. Maria and her father sit at opposite ends of the table, a heap of papers between them. Children of every age jostle round the library table, emblem of interactive learning, some looking away, some participating. The conventional name for this kind of portrait is, fittingly, "conversation piece," but Buck's egalitarian disarray contravenes norms of decorum and hierarchy.[5] The 1789 and 1842 images that thus bracket Maria Edgeworth's long literary career also incarnate a discursive space. A literary site that simultaneously textualizes the child and invents the woman writer, Edgeworth's educational and juvenile writing is a conversation piece that keeps child and adult in dialogic interplay. Virginia Woolf made it *de rigueur* to deplore the lot of the woman who writes in the common sitting room (69); Edgeworth's pattern of literary endeavor as collaborative creativity suggests otherwise.[6]

The Buck portrait and the Halls' sketches embody the interplay of language, gender, and childhood which generates Maria Edgeworth's narration of her stories and herself. The illustrations also frame the problematic intersections which Edgeworth's writings attest: between women's and children's literature; between the woman writer and the canon; between the adult author and her child characters (often autobiographical); between adult language and literature and the child moving from her own talk to different literacies; between alternative constructions of the child and children's literature; between—in the most comprehensive sense— fathers and daughters and the kinds of languages and ways of knowing that Western culture makes gender-specific. Richard Lovell Edgeworth had twenty-two children by four wives; Maria, the eldest daughter and oldest surviving child of his first marriage, is stereotyped in literary history as daddy's girl, an affectionate daughter obediently producing educational texts. Critics still argue about whether her work was victimized or empowered by her influential, scientific-minded father, though both sides see the adult as determining the child's voice and read the daughter's books as rational, realistic mirrors of the paternal heritage. Although the father-daughter dyad offers a concrete referent for multiple relationships between the "canonical" and the "marginal," my concern is not psychobiography, but lability, the gift of being in two places at once that the woman writer for children enjoys, and transvaluation, our need to rethink her in rethinking the ways in which children and their languages have been constructed by our cultural and literary history. At once rational and reactive, adult and juvenile, this woman writer speaks for, to, and as a child; she occupies what theorists term multiple discursive positionalities.[7] In writing the child, she rewrites her cultural fathers and writes herself as well.

My essay addresses history's erasure of literary mothers like Edgeworth through considering the multivocal contributions that she makes to our recovery of the child and her language. The "wee-wee" story that's my focus, "The Bee and the Cow" from Edgeworth's 1814 *Continuation of Early Lessons*, stars her autobiographical child character, Rosamond. Midway in the series which traces Rosamond's progression from tot to teenager, the tale is, appropriately, a conversation among children about language and literacy. Through the youngsters' own dialogues, the tale shows us how literature means for children and how children matter for literary history. I'll glance at the fascination with actual children's voices which is the origin of Edgeworth's manual for enlightened mothers: the adult instructor as the apprentice of the conversations she records. But here I'm less interested in Edgeworth the rational educator, the coach participating in children's entrance into language, than in Edgeworth the comic story-teller, simultaneously the teacher who registers and the pupil who experiences a more advanced juvenile entrance into cultural literacy.[8] Edgeworth constitutes the child both as a rational object of empathic inquiry and as an emotional, experiencing subject with whom she and her readers identify. For Edgeworth, the juvenile protagonist Rosamond is still part of the mature writing self—she likes to joke about herself as "Rosamond at sixty," and even in her eighties the Rosamond voice shapes her most charming letters (1867, 2: 279). Neither the child as alien Other nor the nostalgically embalmed "best Philosopher" of Wordsworth's "Immortality Ode," Rosamond is a recuperative and restorative site, a place to which one can return; the perennial voice of the wit and nonsense Edgeworth delights in, Rosamond playfully tests canonical sense. The autobiographical Rosamond's misadventures with the masculine literary canon emblematize much more than a child's vocabulary and perspective at odds with accepted adult masterpieces. In interrogating the canon, the irrepressible Rosamond also interrogates the conventional narratives through which literary history manages awkward intersections.

Maria Edgeworth's educational advice, pedagogic fictions, and literary career provide an exemplary case for challenging outdated notions of historical children's literature and for problematizing child talk. She is acknowledged as the creator of the first "real" children in English literary history, children who see from a juvenile perspective, who speak in a juvenile voice. Edgeworth was not only tremendously influential in her own right—her works went through countless editions and were widely used for more than a century—but she thus established mimetic patterns that remain normative for the "realistic" family story. Edgeworth's juvenile stories are innovative because they are naturalistically observed and mimetically grounded; her parental guide is strikingly "modernist" because it tries to listen to the child's voice, rather than making it the vehicle for rote memorization, as was the more typical practice Hester Lynch Thrale records in her "Family Book," a mother's account begun not long before the first Edgeworth child register.[9] Edgeworth's *Practical Education* (1798), a progressive manual for parents coauthored with her father, Richard Lovell, interweaves actual child study entries from the family notebooks with every chapter and concludes with "Notes, Containing Conversations and Anecdotes of Children." These parent-child dialogues and glimpses of the way the juvenile mind construes reality are sometimes scientific object lessons but just as often whimsical reportage, quite free of adult intentionality.

Alike invested with authentic children's voices and actions, Edgeworth's tracts and tales evidence a sophisticated developmental philosophy grounded in juvenile

conversation and anecdote—the pupil teaching the teachers. Yet talk is not just the factual proof the manual points to or the selling point for the stories—see, these youngsters are just like yours or, see, this character is just like you. Rather, dialogue determines literary form; the conversational interchange is always Edgeworth's basic structural unit, and in the stories she explicitly terms *Lessons*, what happens is what's said. Talk constitutes pedagogic method as well: "From conversation, if properly managed, children may learn with ease, expedition, and delight, a variety of knowledge; and a skillful preceptor can apply in conversation all the principles that we have laboriously endeavoured to make intelligible in a quarto volume." Educators need to listen rather than lecture: "Since words have such power . . . over ideas, we must in education attend to the language of children as a means of judging of the state of their minds" (1798, 775, 247). This linguistic turn in child study that now seems a matter of course strikingly demonstrates more than the Edgeworths' modernity. It evinces late eighteenth-century attitudes toward the child and toward the representation of colloquial, nonstandard language quite different from Romantic literary history's clichés, which stigmatize pre-Wordsworthian childhood as arid and authoritarian.[10]

Edgeworth's literary children were every nineteenth-century youngster's imaginary playmates, as letters and memoirs so often record, but the autobiographical Rosamond is always a "most distinguished favorite" of girls—and boys too.[11] In successive series published over some twenty-five years, perpetually fallible Rosamond grows from early childhood to adolescence. A witty lover of words, she's usually wise too late. "Miss Edgeworth's naughty girl" provides an alternative comic identity for other adult women writers of the time besides her creator.[12] She's also the endearing exception invariably embraced by children's literary historians constrained to glance at Georgian tales before they reach the Romantic genres they prefer. Rosamond means well, but she continually misconstrues language, literature, and life. She loses her needles, hates getting up on cold mornings, and never runs out of ingenious self-justifications for her lapses. Her imagination, emotions, and curiosity run away with her; reading signs as realities, she precipitately talks and acts before she stops to think. She bursts into juvenile literary history in 1796 with the first and most famous story about her, "The Purple Jar," in which Rosamond at seven falls in love with an apothecary's sparkling window display: "O mother! oh! . . . Look, look! blue, green, red, yellow, and purple! O mamma, what beautiful things!" (9).[13] When she pours out the smelly liquid that produces the plain glass jar's seductive purple sign, she recognizes too late that she should—as her rational mother advises—pause to reflect. She's still leaping at life in the 1821 final sequel. She acquires greater power over her own mind—"not *great* resolution, maybe; but great for me, for a little girl like me"—but she never, significantly, finishes growing up (135). She never stops talking and questioning, either. She keeps up a running commentary on everything she does, sees, feels, and reads, from playing Zenobia, queen of the East, with a helmet of rushes and a bow of sallow, to regaling every listener in range with the "Wonders" of cheese mites, hunting spiders, and snowflakes from Dr. Hooke's discoveries via the microscope (123–31). Mimetically accurate and rhetorically resonant, Rosamond's voice is unforgettable, with its exuberant "Hey, mamma!" and its rueful "I am sure—no, not quite sure—but I hope I shall be wiser another time" (13).[14] It echoes through the nineteenth century, appropriated by almost everybody from novelists for the nursery now obscure to recognized geniuses like Louisa May Alcott and E. Nesbit.

Rosamond's vivacious fictional presence always takes shape within a fully realized family setting. We see what life was like for a comfortably situated Georgian household, from breakfast routines and morning visits to outings on the river and visits to cotton manufactories. We watch them at study and play; we learn how they think and what books they own. It's a world where literacy and literature are inwoven with family life, not creatures of the classroom. Parents read aloud, children eagerly consult books to find out more about whatever they've just encountered, and everybody's interested in how literature and science work, since scientific knowledge isn't yet bracketed off from literary culture or professionalized as an exclusive masculine preserve. That doesn't mean, though, that little girls and boys view spinning jennies or choose favorite poems with one androgynous voice. We hear Rosamond's reflective mother; her scientific-minded father; her obliging older brother Orlando; her sister Laura, a "Graveairs" as restrained as Rosamond is exuberant; and her closest brother, Godfrey. Rosamond's playmate and plague, he teases her, takes care of her, and never stops ridiculing her faults— "O Rosamond! what a coward you are!"—and her excuses—"I will lay any wager you please, that no day passes for a week to come without your making half a hundred at least" (185, 41, 66). Lively and vividly realized, Godfrey is a patronizing masculinist as well as an affectionate charmer. He's always pluming himself on his superior age, knowledge, and sex—and he's always getting his comeuppance. Godfrey and Rosamond's ongoing interplay miniaturizes a comic critique of masculinist discourse, modes of relating, and habits of selfhood.[15] As deftly as she expands the horizon for girls' rationality or moves from adult to child, Edgeworth distinguishes the two children's socially gendered grammars of language and feeling. In "The Bee and the Cow," the little parable about reading practices and cultural literacy that is my exemplary story, Edgeworth shows too how the classed experience of the barely literate working child resembles yet differs from that of her protagonists, for whom literature is a necessity of life, constituting and expressing their developing subjectivities.

Edgeworth's centering of domestic dialogue and the trivia of juvenile experience sutures educational ideology and literary form, making the what and how of representation one. By situating literature within the everyday lives of children and by delineating children within a democratized system of literary representation, the fiction foregrounds the meaning of literature for children and the meaning of children for literature. In his history of teaching English, Ian Michael distinguishes Richard Lovell's explications of verse for child readers and parent teachers as the "first . . . sustained attempt to 'teach' a poem," an effort to make accepted master-pieces rationally accessible that also recognizes the young reader's difficulties with poetic diction, elision, and allusion (211).[16] Still more innovative, Maria's lesson stories like "The Bee and the Cow" explore such verbal and cognitive difficulties from the child's perspective in the child's language. Almost entirely unmediated conversation, the tale's form literalizes the story's subject; rather than speaking for the children, it lets them speak for themselves, "invent" or imagine for themselves, and teach one another. Edgeworth's tales, like her life history, are structured around pedagogic relationships. Given her own predilection for a wise parent, it's striking how often she represents children as educational agents, teaching one another and themselves. As much about subversion as socialization, "The Bee and the Cow" foregrounds child talk and thinking, democratizes knowledge, and questions cultural canons and hierarchies. It brings popular juvenile works within the same frame of reference as acknowledged masterpieces, affirms childhood's own world of allusion and affectivity, and depicts in some detail how children interact with what they read. Within the lesson stories she designs as formative experiences for her child readers, Edgeworth embeds further stories of reading as formative experience, a maker of society and selves.

Edgeworth's storying of practical education always leaves room for those qualities culturally devalued as juvenile, feminine, nonsensical. Exploiting the salu-tary slippage between child and adult inherent in children's literature, "The Bee and the Cow" demonstrates Edgeworth's knack for being simultaneously present in multiple literary locales. Frolicking in her childship, she deftly identifies with the young readers inside and outside the story; at the same time, she speaks through the tale's adult educators to constitute the story as a parable for the parents who buy the book and may also read it to their children. The tale packs manifest and latent lessons into small space, and it has a hidden curriculum, a psychic agenda, too. Without theoretical pyrotechnics, Edgeworth's fictional embodiment of a child learning to read literature and her culture deconstructs its society's hierarchal and masculinist assumptions about literacy and literature, sense and nonsense. "The Bee and the Cow" thematizes the semiotic and cultural entan-glements of signifier and signified, child and adult, emergent juvenile literacy and the patriarchal politics of the adult canon (not to mention the ways that reading practices are shaped by gender and class). It's funny, based on a real incident, sophisticated about language and learning, and closely related to instructional texts: the specific canonical works like Pope's and Gray's that the children in the story are learning to read (and to question) are discussed in the Edgeworths' how-to-teach manuals, too. In Edgeworth's dual position as teacher and autobiographi-cal subject there is also a quite literal embodiment of the multiple voices we always have to process in historicizing the juvenile writers and readers of the past—a reminder that affective association and lived experience shape literary creation and cognitive processing as much as the purposive rationality that the Edgeworths are best known for recommending.

To that end, the story begins with the linguistic joke encoded in the title. Edgeworth's aesthetic practice is the formal equivalent of her child-centered educational innovation. She dramatizes pedagogic relations as juvenile dialogues, the children helping one another along: the tales are like overheard conversations, and this one opens *in medias res*. Godfrey, Rosamond's loving but masculinist brother, first bursts out: "A girl, who mistook a bee for a cow! She must have been an idiot!" The working-class child in question, being taught to read in the intervals of her work, has revealed to her teacher that she can't make sense of a story about a girl's being stung by a bee. Yes, she responds, she has seen a bee. Asked what it's like, she answers: "Ma'am, it is like a cow" (106).

Godfrey, Rosamond, and even their sage sister Laura—always as rational as Rosamond is emotional—puzzle themselves to account for so strange an idea, and in the process demonstrate Edgeworth's sensitivity to the pitfalls and pratfalls that accompany the acquisition of literacy and literature. It takes a bit of sleuthing to uncover the semiotic mystery of the tale's title. The children struggle with "guessing or inventing the reason," but make little progress until their father tells them how youngsters of the "poorer class" learn the alphabet: from picture books joining a letter with an illustration, as "A" for apple.[17] The joke turns out to be as much on Godfrey's enlightened scorn as the little girl's equation of "B" and cow. Rosamond's empathetic desire to prove that "the poor girl was not an idiot" helps her comprehend instantly what Godfrey barely grasps. By now, you, like Rosamond, may have figured out the story's title, the confusion of signifier and signified resulting from the picture alphabet the little factory girl had used to learn her letters. Chapbook ABC's like *The Silver Penny, for the Amusement and Instruction of Good Children* label a suitably bovine representation, "B Bull, b."[18] Taken aback by the child's effeminized bull, Godfrey still maintains that she must have been "uncommonly silly to make such a mistake," even though Laura recalls from her reading that urban factory children don't even know the words for hog or calf when the animals are shown them, much less their sex (106–7). For Rosamond, the affective quickens knowledge. Blinkered by androcentric privilege and disembodied logic, Godfrey can't recognize the power relations embedded in language that the little girl's experience emblematizes; he can't see, as students used to say, where she's coming from.[19]

Edgeworth's tale about the linguistic and literary education of young children is, at the simplest level, a lesson for adult educators in how and how not to transmit culture. The mother's story within the story about the lady who teaches the little working girl to read words, only to discover that the dislocated child has no lexicon of cultural meanings she can attach to the names she calls, is at once amusing and painful. Without sentimentalizing the linguistic gap between the two nations, Edgeworth dramatizes the failure of nominal literacy to effect community, a fact David Vincent and other historians of the reading process document. There's no connection between the child's everyday language and working world in the cotton factory and the sounds she pronounces aloud. Reciting what adult culture assigns to her without participating in a heritage that has no meaning for her life, she opens the tale by embodying a regurgitation model of learning that "The Bee and the Cow" works against at multiple levels. Like the manufactory child, the little middle-class readers also demonstrate the strange mistakes young-sters make when signifier and signified get entangled, when rote knowledge takes the place of lived understanding. The slippages of signs that plague the little factory girl trip more privileged readers too. Even the superior Godfrey—who has conveniently forgotten—is reminded by Rosamond that he once thought there must be two worlds since America was a new one. Even the ever-wise Laura has to confess how she misinterpreted the sentence, "Leonora walked on, her head a little higher than usual," into a grotesque image of a young heroine striding atop her own head (108). Like the account of the girl and the bee that confuses the factory child, the sentence Laura refers to comes from a story written specially for children. The anecdote of Lucy, the bee-stung girl, derives from the first part of "Harry and Lucy" in Edgeworth's own *Early Lessons* (1801), the initial installment of the lesson series also containing "The Purple Jar" and other early Rosamond stories; Leonora comes from "The Bracelets" in *The Parent's Assistant* (1796; 1800). Edgeworth's tongue-in-cheek reference to her own fictions within this fiction isn't just a family joke, for any contemporary child readers would get the allusions.[20] They'd find the opening mixup of bees and bulls even funnier than we do, because little Lucy has the bee in her hand with a bunch of flowers when it stings her—a grotesque image indeed! Consonant with the period's animal thematics, the fic-tional protagonist is more concerned about resuscitating the mashed bee than about her own bite: no wonder the factory child is puzzled about a little girl's worrying over a "bull" she's crushed in her hand.

It's appropriate that a tale about textual control, power, and productivity dramatizes reading as problematic negotiation, not just for the barely literate but for everyone. The juvenile conversation humorously explores what kinds of changes are produced in children when they enter a world of popular or canonical texts. Stimulated by the opening anecdote, Rosamond, Godfrey, and Laura go on to recount their own misadventures in processing the masterpieces of the adult male canon, so that the story emerges as a synecdoche for the acculturative process itself, literalizing and miniaturizing the historical acquisition of cultural literacy—and interrogating it too. Thomas Gray's "Elegy Written in a Country Church-Yard" and "The Bard," Alexander Pope's Homer and "The Rape of the Lock," and William Collins's "Ode to Evening," Georgian classics though they are, comi-cally exemplify in turn what happens when a simple transmission model of cultural knowledge governs pedagogy. List-based curricula and rote memorization produce ludicrous results. But Edgeworth's textual articulation of reading methodologies goes much farther than insisting that children have to comprehend what they read or illustrating that "learning by heart"—an odd phrase for rote learning divorced from context, if one thinks about it—simply won't do, even though these were both progressive positions at the time. "The Bee and the Cow" also specifies how gender identities are put together and cultural meanings evolve. When the Rosamond sequence's ongoing "trial of power between Godfrey and me" (199) takes a literary form in "The Bee and the Cow," the loving battle between brother and sister miniaturizes larger contests between the "canonical" and the "marginal."

The story's democratized representation of how children construe literature and themselves teases us into rethinking our notions of cultural masterpieces and autonomous meanings. Rosamond's slips and successes aren't, as Godfrey assumes, just a matter of knowing the objective meaning of certain words or the right schoolboy cribs to consult. Unlike most of their contemporaries, Edgeworth's characters have never been "forced to learn by rote poetry which we did not understand," but that doesn't mean they haven't memorized poetry they like (108).[21] Rosamond loves "pretty" lines, and besides, Laura already had Gray's "Elegy" by heart. Laura protests that she didn't learn the verses until she understood them and that she couldn't understand them until they were explained to her, but Godfrey eggs Rosamond on to recite what she has insisted on memorizing. He lets her get out exactly one line before he pounces, adamant that she define "curfew," "tolls," "knell," and "parting day."[22] With all the zest of a prosecuting attorney cross-examining a befuddled witness, Godfrey as masculinist philosopher codifies cognition. He appropriates what he supposes to be the objective workings of reason and the impersonal laws of language; he acts the universalist knower who thinks that there is a single valid meaning and that he owns it. Rosamond responds with, "Godfrey, I cannot tell the meaning of every word; but I know the general meaning. . . . Now let me go on." "Go on," he chortles, glorying in his privileged access to "heraldry," Hampden, Milton, and Cromwell: "You! who have not come to Cromwell yet in the history of England!"[23] Overwhelmed by his reduction of her "pretty" lines to an androcentric lexicon of detached meanings, Rosamond gives up in defeat; at least she knows what the poem's "twitt'ring" swallow is. "Oh, I grant you the swallow, but not the 'cock's shrill *clarion.*'" Godfrey is dumbfounded to find that Rosamond recognizes a rooster's exultant trumpeting; the reader isn't (110). Godfrey's appropriation of Gray's poem as literally a cultural *masterwork* and Rosamond's difficulties in assimilating it within her own frame of reference amusingly parallel their real-life juvenile contemporary, Marjory Fleming. She remarks in her journal, "I get my poetry now out of grey & I thin it beautiful & Majestick but I am sorry to say that I thi it is very Difficult to get by heart but we mus bear it well," adding tellingly that "Greys Elegey in a contry Church yard" is "excelent & much spoke of by both sex particulary by the men."[24]

Female readers may well agree with the little girl whose mother wrote Edgeworth that the child "thought Godfrey was allowed to be too *provoking* and too little considerate of the wishes of Rosamond, for a boy so well and so wisely educated," but Godfrey's schoolboy arrogance soon takes a tumble.[25] Like his severity to his sister, what he chooses to recite and explicate shows his identification of symbolic systems with men's mastery. He dramatizes language and literature as dominance and control, knowledge to be brandished over others, invariant meanings to be checked out in authoritative sources. He begins with Pope's translation of Sarpedon's speech to Glaucus—"Admired as heroes, and as gods obeyed"—the fantasy of every eighteenth-century schoolboy brought up on Homer.[26] Elated with one success, Godfrey proceeds triumphantly to "The Bard"; having fortified himself with Mason's notes on Gray, he shows off his knowledge of all the English and French kings and all the poem's historical allusions. But then comes "a passage where his historical notes gave him no assistance," an emotional incantation he "could not make any sense of." The father's inquisition forces Godfrey to own up that he's not much better off than Rosamond. "The Bard"'s speaker and subject is the inspired poet, but, revealingly, Godfrey is shaky on literary affect, however much he likes Gray's heroic references and grisly imagery. The irreproachable Laura likewise confesses that she learned Collins's "Ode to Evening," sure that "chaste Eve" was Adam's wife (111–12). "The Bee and the Cow" shows how important rational cognition is for children's language and literacy, but Edgeworth's fictional solution to failures in reading strategy involves more than understanding the meanings of words and matching them up with the right things and ideas.

The story raises questions not just of how young readers construe or misconstrue texts, but also of how texts construct readers. It depicts reading as an interactive process between text and reader, a process sometimes most fulfilling when it bypasses great traditions for lesser literatures with personal meaning. Although Rosamond puzzles herself terribly over Gray's "Elegy," she thoroughly grasps her "favorite little poem," which isn't canonical but a personal choice. It's an anonymous poem, often reprinted in juvenile anthologies and relevant to any child, especially to Rosamond who, like the redbreast in "The Robin's Petition" and like Maria Edgeworth herself in writing her stories, exercises literary skills to achieve love and a home.[27] Traditionally associated with juvenility, femininity, and nurturance, the robin, like Rosamond, is a dramatic and domestic performer: "Take me in by the side of your fire; / And when I am warmed and fed, / I'll whistle without other hire. / . . . I shall die if you drive me away."[28] "I am sure I understand all this," Rosamond pronounces with satisfaction, "and 'The poor Piedmontese and his Marmot'" by Lucy Aikin (108–9). Unhoused like the robin, the marmot—a cute, bushy-tailed rodent, rather like a woodchuck—performs to earn affection and sanctuary. He was caught by the Piedmontese who teaches him to dance and lives off his earnings, and now both "pine for their home," urging the audience to donate and speed them back to their distant mountains.[29] Such verses appeal because they connect to the little girl's own experience, because they incorporate her needs and express her own subjectivity, not because they've achieved the conventional status of unquestioned masterpiece.

Edgeworth's insertion of children's favorites, like her own "wee-wee" stories, Rosamond's anonymous bird poem, and Lucy Aikin's marmot verses from *Poetry for Children* (1801), focalizes child readership, language, and affectivity, valuing children's emotional literacy as well as their rational comprehension. "The Bee and the Cow" allows children's literature on the same narrative plane as canonical masterpieces, permitting youngsters to identify with Rosamond's beloved poems about needy robins and pet performing marmots, which are likely to be their choices too. It gives them, at a level they can enjoy, those pleasures of intertextuality and allusion that adult poetry, as Richard Lovell points out, often pitches too high for them to relish. The Edgeworths never fetishize book knowledge, but Maria's literary referentiality nevertheless delicately underlines how stories and lives are built out of other stories, understood or misunderstood, how what languages we know furnish what subjectivities we inhabit. Rosamond's favorites clarify how reading practices are always mixed up with contingent lives, how real life and read life interpenetrate. What she knows via storying is subjective, situated knowledge, the embedded kind of knowing culturally ascribed to women and children. Literary texts don't function for her as restatements of a verifiable reality, but as imaginative interpretations of her own subjectivity, expressing and defining her sense of herself. She hasn't arrived at her understandings through the commonsensical interpretive procedures and sequential thinking that practical education recommends, however necessary the story shows these to be. (Neither has Godfrey; his boyish assumption of majoritarian interpretive authority is hardly dispassionate.)

Edgeworth distances herself from masculine Romanticism's claims to a mysterious, essentialized child self—like the infant "best Philosopher" of Wordsworth's "Immortality Ode"—to show juvenile subjectivities in the process of construction, shaped by the linguistic cultures and literary experiences they encounter. In rejecting rote memorization and encouraging children to think and feel for themselves, Edgeworth isn't merely discarding a pedagogy founded on regurgitation. She also knows that different educational methodologies imply different subjectivities. In learning to read her culture, the story says, Rosamond is also learning to read herself; in learning literary languages she has also learned patterns for organizing the world—and so has Godfrey. The children's choices make legible the kinds of characters they are coming to be, as in Godfrey's passion for manly poems of war and rebellion and Laura's preference for Pope's celebrated lines on female good humor and merit from "The Rape of the Lock." But the story isn't just saying you are what you read. In textualizing reading practices in action, it also raises important questions of cognitive and affective development, of how we get a fix on the world and verify the "reality" of the representation we've constructed. Edgeworth is always glossed as the woman writer who stands for the father's common sense, dignifying daughters with access to masculine rationality and endorsing Enlightenment science's claim to universal, objective truths. But her juvenile stories, like this dialogue between children and the canon, locate Edgeworth somewhere else too, aside from both Enlightened masculinity and masculine Romanticism.[30] Children, especially little girls, need access to the Enlightenment understanding that construes the world via penetrating observation and orderly analysis. To grow up as women, daughters must learn to think like fathers. But enlightened women who can read their culture's master narrative aren't limited to the ways of knowing ascribed to masculine rationality. As a woman writer for children, Edgeworth enacts a double gesture of appropriation; she can use her reason and tweak it too. Clear thinking is survival strategy, but emotional responsiveness matters as much as precise observation and sequential investigation. Maria's tales for the young are far more than a fictionalized instructional system, however positive; they simultaneously enact and transgress *Practical Education*'s commonsensical plot of rational development and orderly acculturation. Their polyphonic discourses of child and adult embody an argument for multiple literacies.

Delicately underlining the interdependence of cognitive and affective knowing, the conclusion of "The Bee and the Cow" rewrites its origin, taking us back to the cotton manufactory the parents and children recently visited in their travels. The narrative about the factory, "The Silver Cup," comes just before this tale. Because Rosamond belongs to a family that understands how literacy and community are interdependent, she has intellectual and emotional resources the little factory girl lacks. Because she has just seen the machinery, she now has a context within which she can decode the descriptive verses her father repeats to her. As he concludes with, "And slowly circumvolves the labouring wheel below," she cries out gleefully, "the cotton machine, papa!" (113). The passage about the spinning jenny comes from Erasmus Darwin's *Botanic Garden*.[31] Almost as well known in his day as his grandson was later, famous for his vivid and accurate versification of contemporary science, Darwin covers everything from the production of cotton to botanical reproduction, graphically (and rather luridly) detailing all the "Loves of the Plants" in the section quoted. Maria was more skeptical about his aesthetic merits than her father, but she likes to quote him because he so tidily collapses the boundaries between scientific and literary ways of knowing. Darwin is a happy choice not just because he chances to describe a cotton factory, but because he stands for the dialogic interplay and situated knowing that Edgeworth makes central to her enactments of learning. He was a physician, philosopher, medical researcher, and a long-time friend who urged the Edgeworths in the nineties to return to educational writing. He was also, it is important to notice, a popular poet of the day, who made learning science fun, but Edgeworth knew he was unlikely to join the culture's canonical literary fathers like Homer and Pope. The "Loves of the Triangles," the devastating parody of his learned style and iconoclastic subject by the conservative satirists of the *Anti-Jacobin*, was probably even better known than Darwin himself. As Maria points out in the chapter on parody which (along with the introduction) she wrote for her father's *Readings on Poetry*, the burlesque is as good as its original, and it permanently associated Darwin's already rather bizarre literary reputation with a joke.[32] Like the juvenile poems and stories and the anonymous "Robin's Petition" in "The Bee and the Cow," Darwin's work is enjoyed not because of transcendent literary merit, but because he connects with a child's and her creator's experience. Despite his learning and his robust masculinity, Darwin figures with the marginal bees rather than the authoritative bulls of the literary canon.

In triumphantly appropriating Darwin's once popular, now obscure lines as her own, intellectually apprehended and emotionally appreciated, Rosamond weaves together the story's lessons. Edgeworth's final bit of intertextuality works to "release the tangled knots, and smooth the ravell'd fleece" (113) of her title's jeu d'esprit on child language and literacy. Like the rest of the tale, the conversational conclusion instructs both juvenile readers and adult educators, each carrying away rational *and* affective knowledge for use in later formative experiences. Children learn a lot about making reading work for them. Their parents and literary historians learn a lot about the making of children, for the tale also shows how the identities of young protagonists and adult authors simultaneously take shape through the juvenile storying of both. In appropriating the child's voice and place to write herself, Edgeworth is textualizing feminine as well as juvenile subjectivity. Rosamond's lessons portray a child accessing the adult universe of discourse; they simultaneously embody the experience of a grown-up writing as her father's daughter, yet also negotiating a complex stance toward hegemonical culture and language. Framing the world and her fictions in terms of common sense, Edgeworth's miniature narratives and child heroine simultaneously traverse rational rules to perpetuate nourishing nonsense. Her textually hybrid story lessons preach sense, but—refusing to inhabit a single identity—they also privilege the reactive and relational values she associates with nonsense, with the twinned subjects of children and linguistic play. Edgeworth speaks as a child in a tricky sense then; she writes to please her own father, to be the good girl, but her stories concurrently problematize rational morals and masculine masterpieces. She manages her delicate balancing act between child and adult, socialization and subversion, rational sense and playful nonsense, through her mastery of the juvenile dialogue. Edgeworth's multiple tongues inform the weary genre with gendered significance. Her child character Rosamond's comic encounters with language and literature function figuratively as well as pragmatically. As Edgeworth teaches children how talk works in the world, how it makes things happen and brings selves into being, her representations of Rosamond's ebullient voice trope her own literary career and psychic strategies as well. Moving easily between child and adult, pupil and teacher, "masculine" rationality and "feminine" caring, Maria Edgeworth shows us that she "sees with two pairs of eyes."[33] Literary history needs to view her with the same generosity.

Notes

This essay draws on a longer study of Maria Edgeworth and literary childhood: an interdisciplinary reassessment of her achievement in literature and educational theory focussing on her fiction for children, her pedagogical work, and the uses of children's literature for the woman writer. I'd like to thank the American Philosophical Society, the American Council of Learned Societies, and the John Simon Guggenheim Memorial Foundation for funding research incorporated in this essay.

1. Those who write about Maria Edgeworth usually call her "Maria" and refer to her father, Richard Lovell Edgeworth, as "Edgeworth." As a feminist critic, I will customarily refer to the daughter as "Edgeworth"; when readers might be puzzled, I'll use first names.

2. For Edgeworth's recurrent characterization of her tales, see *A Memoir of Maria Edgeworth* I: 21, 84, 105. Sometimes she begs her favorite cousin not to "call my little stories by the sublime title of 'my works,' I shall else be ashamed when the little mouse comes forth" (I: 73).

3. Anna Maria Hall was an Irish regionalist and Victorian children's writer of some repute. Despite her worshipful attitude, Mrs. Hall shows how Romantic connoisseurs of the child's imagination and spirituality misread their Enlightenment predecessors, substituting adult poetic images for experientially based children's voices.

4. Fairholt's 1842 sketch for the Halls wasn't published until after Edgeworth's death; it appears on the page preceding Mrs. Hall's 1849 essay and again in the 1866 article by the Halls, where it is accompanied by a bad copy of the Buck portrait (see note 5, this chapter).

5. The 1789 Buck portrait has been reproduced many times. It appears in *The Black Book of Edgeworthstown*, ed. Harriet Jessie Butler and Harold Edgeworth Butler, facing page 166; this family memoir also contains a later picture of the library, facing page 210. The Buck portrait is also the frontispiece to Marilyn Butler's 1972 literary biography, where it is misdated 1787. I am grateful to Mrs. Christina Colvin, Edgeworth's descendant, for microscopic examination of the date: only 1789 matches the number of children depicted.

6. The Edgeworthstown house had no drawing room; the library's use literalizes the notion of living with children that the Edgeworths stand for. Although Woolf's equation of separate writing space and creative activity is a modernist paradigm of the isolated artist, it animates countless feminist essays. Only recently has it become possible to question the modernist story of writing that Woolf's image emblematizes; recent examples exploring writing as socially situated and collaborative include Linda Brodkey's *Academic Writing as Social Practice*, especially ch. 3, "Picturing Writing: Writers in the Modern World"; and Jack Stillinger's *Multiple Authorship and the Myth of Solitary Genius*.

7. Adopting Michel Foucault's work on discursive systems and power relations, Teresa de Lauretis exemplifies this current feminist interest in "the understanding of the interrelatedness of discourses and social practices, and of the multiplicity of positionalities concurrently available in the social field seen as a field of forces: not a single system of power dominating the powerless but a tangle of distinct and variable relations of power and points of resistance" (131). The woman writer may discover such "points of resistance" in the contrapuntal voices of the reflective Georgian mother and the reactive child.

8. I examine Edgeworth's experientially-based teaching methodology and its implications for contemporary literacy studies more fully in my forthcoming book, *Romancing the Family: Maria Edgeworth and the Scene of Instruction.*

9. For Thrale as a managing mother, see Felicity A. Nussbaum, *Autobiographical Subject*, ch. 9.

10. Interest in child talk can be historically situated within a bourgeois and democratic reconceptualization of language as more than the property of a literary elite; see John Barrell, ch. 2, "The Language Properly So-Called: The Authority of Common Usage," in *English Literature in History*. Ian Michael's *The Teaching of English* analyzes concomitant changes in language and literary instruction; the Edgeworths are specially cited for their child-centered pedagogy (208–11). Other historical studies noticing mother-teachers' contributions to primary education and emergent national literacy include the essays of Renée Balibar, Lionel Gossman, and Paul M. Zall.

11. Like many other mothers of the period, Lady Anne Romilly, wife of the distinguished legal reformer, corresponded with Edgeworth about children and education. The author always asked for her juvenile readers' responses; Lady Romilly reported that Rosamond was "most distinguished" because "they feel a sympathy with her faults and feel that they resemble her in many things" (83). Lady Romilly remarks that "one amongst the innumerable excellent things I have learnt from Practical Education is to consider what is passing in the child's mind at the moment, and I am sure this is a thing which is seldom if ever attended to" (99; for further juvenile tributes, see 95–97).

12. See, for example, the best-selling poet Felicia Hemans's amusing representation of herself as "little better than a grown-up Rosamond . . . who constantly lie in bed till it is too late to get up early, break my needles, (when I use any,) leave my keys among my necklaces, answer all my amusing letters first and leave the others to their fate; in short, regularly commit small sins enough every day, to roll up into one great, immense, *frightful* one at the end of it!" (Chorley I: 261).

13. For more about "The Purple Jar," see my essays on "Socializing Rosamond: Educational Ideology and Fictional Form" and "'A Taste for Truth and Realities': Early Advice to Mothers on Books for Girls."

14. "The Purple Jar" was first published in the 1796 edition of *Parent's Assistant,* a collection of tales separate from the story series with recurring characters. It was revised and expanded in 1800. When Rosamond developed into the heroine of an ongoing sequence, "The Purple Jar" was shifted to the 1801 *Early Lessons;* further installments appear in the *Continuation of Early Lessons* for older children in 1814. Edgeworth is a pioneer in age-graded reading, and she's careful to specify what reader her tales are intended for, the audience developing along with the characters. Harry and Lucy's and Frank's stories are also part of these first two lessons series; Edgeworth published separate multi-volume finales for all three sets of characters in the 1820s. The 1821 *Rosamond: a Sequel* concludes the juvenile stories about Rosamond, but the same character, this time on the verge of marriage, also appears in the 1814 adult novel *Patronage.* Interestingly, Edgeworth (who never cares much for the standard

courtship plot of the woman's novel) promptly returned Rosamond to childhood in the post-*Patronage Early Lessons* of 1814. Edgeworth leaves Rosamond perpetually on the verge of adolescence in 1821, perhaps because the adult novel's conventional closure in marriage signals the death of the sprightly child heroine. The lessons series were often collected and reprinted in various combinations, as in volume 11 of the 1825 *Works* (confusingly subtitled *Early Lessons* but containing all of *Rosamond*). Often, too, the stories are presented as enjoyable fiction without the prefaces framing them as educational experiment, as in the edition I cite in the text, a nineteenth-century *Rosamond: With Other Tales* published by Harper I am lucky enough to own. Page numbers for all the Rosamond stories incorporated into the text refer to this edition.

15. Edgeworth's general fascination with dialects and linguistic habits informs her child speech too. There's not one single child language in her large body of work, but many, delicately discriminated by nationality, class, age, and gender, as well as individual character. Edgeworth's stories about very young children for beginning readers still work; "The Little Dog Trusty; or, The Liar and the Boy of Truth" and other first stories from *Early Lessons* were among the most widely reprinted. Even the playful satire of masculine and feminine linguistic styles she's fond of is modified by specific characterizations: Frank and Mary and Harry and Lucy, the other pairs in the lessons series, don't just recycle the Godfrey-Rosamond pattern. Since the Harry and Lucy sequence is intended to teach science, Richard Lovell was most involved with it; in the volumes published after his death, Harry and Lucy's very different verbal and cognitive styles emerge as a revelatory autobiographical statement advocating the father's scientific objectivity and laughing at it too.

16. Ian Michael is referring to the preface to Richard Lovell Edgeworth's 1802 *Poetry Explained for the Use of Young People*, which observes that poetic pleasure often depends on "remote allusions or metaphoric language" rapidly processed by adult sensibilities. Even when children master the "laborious process" of understanding fine poetry, the "pleasure escapes," so that they mostly remain content with "melodious sounds which are to them destitute of meaning" (iii–iv). In 1816, Maria and Richard Lovell together produced another book on teaching literature, *Readings on Poetry*, which develops the pedagogic theories underwriting "The Bee and the Cow."

17. Illustrated alphabets have probably provided more fun for later adult bibliophiles and more information for later social historians than pedagogic help for their original juvenile users. Some integrate learning to read with acquiring information about the world, but because they isolate signs from the context that gives them meaning, they're likely to derail users (like the factory child). Contemporary researchers like Ian Michael follow the Edgeworths in finding them pedagogically useless at best. For reproductions and collectors' appreciations, see Joyce Irene Whalley, *Cobwebs to Catch Flies: Illustrated Books for the Nursery and Schoolroom 1700–1900*, ch. 2; Iona Opie and Peter Opie, *A Nursery Companion*; and Iona Opie, Robert Opie, and Brian Alderson, *The Treasures of Childhood: Books, Toys, and Games from the Opie Collection*. The last is an unusually rich visual display of all the ways children are initiated into culture which illustrates bibliophilic enthusiasm as well as charming artifacts.

18. Printed by James Kendrew of York, *The Silver Penny* is reproduced in facsimile with other nineteenth-century examples in *Chapbook ABC's*, ed. Peter Stockham; for the bull as "B," see 45.

19. The little girl's "cow" for "bull" cuts two ways. If her irreverence for the stronger sex shocks Godfrey, her gender bender also reminds us how sexual (and class) positionings permeate the language that children learn. "He-cow" for "bull" has often been a feminine and juvenile euphemism. For recent theorizing of Western rationality as a gendered hierarchy that privileges abstract reason and devalues the affective as a source of knowledge, see Genevieve Lloyd's *The Man of Reason*; Victor Seidler's *Rediscovering Masculinity*; and Nancy C. M. Hartsock's *Money, Sex, and Power*, especially ch. 10 on abstract masculinity and feminist standpoint theory.

20. Edgeworth heard the story, one of many "anecdotes of children" which spice her letters, during the 1813 family visit to England; like Rosamond in the story preceding "The Bee and the Cow," Edgeworth had just been on a tour of the Strutt family's famous cotton mills. The original anecdote just has "some story about a bee"; Edgeworth elaborates the bare fact into a much better dialogue and makes a point of the literary allusion (1971, 31).

21. Marjory Fleming was even younger than Rosamond is in this story when she notes in her journal that memorizing male greats is a part of her education: "Doctor Swifts works are very funny & amusing & I get some by hart." Marjory kept her journal for about two years just before her death at almost nine.

22. Writing in the 1890s of children oppressed with explanatory notes to poems, Agnes Repplier waxes indignant over Rosamond's recitation: "Who can forget the pathetic scene . . . when Godfrey, whom I always thought, and still think, a very disagreeable boy, interrupts her ruthlessly" (55–57).

23. It is relevant to notice that Richard Lovell's explication of the "Elegy" in *Poetry Explained for the Use of Young People* (1802) also proceeds through the poem line by line, rationally glossing individual difficulties; he evinces concern when he finds a stanza which "interrupts the reasoning of the poem" (19). Since he thinks of poetry as primarily "a kind of painting in words" (11), he has little to say about the affective elements that would attract readers like Rosamond and the even younger Marjory Fleming.

24. Fleming 61, 127. Although Edgeworth couldn't read Marjory Fleming, the child author who died before she was nine, Marjory read Edgeworth with enjoyment, both her works for children and adults. Marjory's journals, published long after her death, document a range of reading interests that supports Edgeworth's representation of the period's literary childhood. Marjory's reading enjoyment was much more precocious than her writing skills. John Guillory's *Cultural Capital: The Problem of Literary Canon Formation* explains comprehensively how Gray's poem became simultaneously canonical and the perfect poem for introducing schoolchildren to the study of English literature (see ch. 2, "Mute Inglorious Miltons: Gray, Wordsworth, and the Vernacular Canon"). As Nancy Armstrong reminds us in "Literature as Women's History": "Today few of us realize that many of the features of our standard humanities curricu-

lum came from a curriculum designed specifically for educating polite young women who were not of the ruling class, or that the teaching of native British literature developed as a means of socializing children, the poor, and foreigners before we became a masculine profession" (367).

25. MacDonald 46. Rachel Mordecai Lazarus, who passed on this 1823 comment, was one of many mothers who corresponded with Edgeworth about their children. The author habitually asked for the responses of real children and tried to follow them. She also got quite a few letters from children themselves. The little girl's remark is important for literary historians who typically assume, as she does, that Edgeworth always intends to produce exemplary children. The book's continual deflation of Godfrey's masculine pretensions is one of its charms.

26. Appropriately, Pope was a teenager himself when he translated this episode from Homer; see the "Translations and Paraphrases Done in Youth" in John Butt's edition of *The Poems of Alexander Pope* (60–65).

27. "The Robin's Petition" was, incidentally, a big favorite of Edgeworth's. Recurring frequently in her unpublished letters, the verses became almost a code for relational love and domestic performance, an image of Edgeworth herself as family artist.

28. "The Robin's Petition" refers to a general literary tradition specifically appropriated by children and juvenile authors; the version Edgeworth uses is reprinted in E. V. Lucas 73–74.

29. Aikin 41–42. Lucy Aikin's anthology is composed mostly of snippets by other poets; "The Piedmontese and His Marmot," which Rosamond favors, is one of her few original contributions. Another of her own poems is a robin poem, and she includes one by another writer too. Edgeworth owned Aikin's book.

30. My understanding of Rosamond as subjective juvenile reader and of Edgeworth as situated female knower links two important bodies of scholarship: on children's and women's ways of knowing. Revisionist researchers in child development and feminist cultural critics similarly explore how marginal groups become, in the broadest sense, culturally literate, how their relationships with language and expression differ from the masculinist cognitive patterns normative since the Enlightenment, and how subjectivity is always multiple and understood through relations with others. Both groups stress connected, contextual, and narrative constructions of reality rather than more traditional "rational" and "objective" epistemology: they critique traditional Western knowledge systems and validate lived experience as a source of knowledge. See, for example, the work of David Bleich; Nicholas C. Burbules and Suzanne Rice; Jerome Bruner; Henry A. Giroux; Sandra Harding; Donna J. Haraway, especially ch. 9, "Situated Knowledges: The Science Question in Feminism and the Privilege of Partial Perspective"; Elizabeth D. Harvey and Kathleen Okruhlik; Mary Leach and Bronwyn Davies; Andrea A. Lunsford, Helene Moglen, and James Slevin; Jay L. Robinson et al.; Patrocinio P. Schweickart; and Kathleen Weiler.

31. Darwin 2: 83–84. The lines Edgeworth quotes are from Part 2, "The Loves

of the Plants" (canto 2: ll. 95–104); the reference in the text is to the two-volume 1799 fourth edition of *The Botanic Garden*.

32. For "The Loves of the Triangles: A Mathematical and Philosophical Poem" written in ridicule of Darwin, see Charles Edmonds's *Poetry of the Anti-Jacobin*, which identifies the authors (150–77). The Edgeworths, accustomed to the give and take of family criticism, actually read the parody to the target; unsurprisingly, Darwin felt "some pain" as well as "high admiration," Maria notes (1816 208–9).

33. Noddings 70. Although she does not address the children's writer in her provocative analysis of *Caring*, Nel Noddings's work on feminine ethics and moral education is especially relevant to juvenile authors, who must always embody the reciprocity of caring and being cared for that she investigates.

Works Cited

Aikin, Lucy. *Poetry for Children: Consisting of Short Pieces, to be Committed to Memory*. London: R. Phillips and B. Tabart, 1801.

Armstrong, Nancy. "Literature as Women's History." Genre 19.4 (winter 1986): 347–69.

Balibar, Renée. "National Language, Education, Literature." In *Literature, Politics, and Theory: Papers from the Essex Conference 1976–84*, ed. Francis Barker, Peter Hulme, Margaret Iversen, and Diana Loxley, 126–47. London and New York: Methuen, 1986.

Barrell, John. *English Literature in History 1730–80: An Equal, Wide Survey*. London: Hutchinson, 1983.

Bleich, David. *The Double Perspective: Language, Literacy, and Social Relations*. New York and Oxford: Oxford University Press, 1988.

Brodkey, Linda. *Academic Writing as Social Practice*. Philadelphia: Temple University Press, 1987.

Bruner, Jerome. "The Narrative Construction of Reality." *Critical Inquiry* 18.1 (autumn 1991): 1–21.

Burbules, Nicholas C., and Suzanne Rice. "Dialogue across Differences: Continuing the Conversation." *Harvard Educational Review* 61.4 (November 1991): 393–416.

Butler, Harriet Jessie, and Harold Edgeworth Butler. *The Black Book of Edgeworthstown and Other Edgeworth Memories 1585–1817*. London: Faber and Gwyer, 1927.

Butler, Marilyn. *Maria Edgeworth: A Literary Biography*. Oxford: Clarendon Press, 1972.

Chorley, Henry F., ed. *Memorials of Mrs. [Felicia] Hemans With Illustrations of Her Literary Character from Her Private Correspondence*. 2 vols. London: Saunders and Otley, 1836.

Darwin, Erasmus. *The Botanic Garden, A Poem: In Two Parts*. 1789–91. 4th ed. 2 vols. London: J[oseph] Johnson, 1799.

de Lauretis, Teresa. "Eccentric Subjects: Feminist Theory and Historical Consciousness." *Feminist Studies* 16.1 (spring 1990): 115–50.

Edgeworth, Maria, and Richard Lovell Edgeworth. *Practical Education*. London: J[oseph] Johnson, 1798.

Edgeworth, Maria. *Continuation of Early Lessons*. 2 vols. London: J[oseph] Johnson, 1814a.

———. *Early Lessons*. 10 pts. London: J[oseph] Johnson, 1801.

———. *Maria Edgeworth: Letters from England 1813–1844*. Ed. Christina Colvin. Oxford: Clarendon Press, 1971.

———. *A Memoir of Maria Edgeworth, with a Selection from Her Letters by the Late Mrs. [Frances] Edgeworth*. Ed. by Her Children. 3 vols. London: Privately printed Joseph Masters and Son, 1867.

———. *The Parent's Assistant*. 2 vols. London: J[oseph] Johnson, 1796.

———. *The Parent's Assistant*. 1800. 3rd ed. 6 vols. in 2. Classics of Children's Literature, 1621–1932. New York and London: Garland, 1976.

———. *Patronage*. 2nd ed. 4 vols. London: J[oseph] Johnson, 1814b.

———. *Rosamond: A Sequel to Early Lessons*. 2 vols. London: R. Hunter; and Baldwin, Craddock, and Joy, 1821.

———. *Rosamond: With Other Tales*. New York: Harper, n.d.

———. *Works of Maria Edgeworth*. 13 vols. Boston: Parker, 1825 [Vol. 11: *Early Lessons*, contains all of *Rosamond*; not the same as 1801 *Early Lessons*].

Edgeworth, Richard Lovell, and Maria Edgeworth. *Readings on Poetry*. London: R. Hunter, 1816.

Edgeworth, R[ichard] L[ovell]. *Poetry Explained for the Use of Young People*. London: J[oseph] Johnson, 1802.

Edmonds, Charles, ed. *Poetry of the Anti-Jacobin: Comprising the Celebrated Political and Satirical Poems*. New York: Putnam; London: Sampson Low, 1890.

Fleming, Marjory. *The Complete Marjory Fleming: Her Journals, Letters, and Verses*. Ed. Frank Sidgwick. London: Sidgwick and Jackson, 1934.

Giroux, Henry A. "Literacy, Pedagogy, and the Politics of Difference." *College Literature* 19.1 (February 1992): 1–11.

Gossman, Lionel. "Literature and Education." *New Literary History* 13.2 (winter 1982): 341–71.

Guillory, John. *Cultural Capital: The Problem of Literary Canon Formation*. Chicago: University of Chicago Press, 1993.

Hall, Mrs. S[amuel] C[arter] (Anna Maria). "Edgeworthstown, Memories of Maria Edgeworth." *Art-Journal* 11 (1849): 224–29.

———. *Pilgrimages to English Shrines*. 2nd ser. London: Arthur Hall, Virtue, 1853.

Hall, S[amuel] C[arter]. *A Book of Memories of Great Men and Women of the Age, from Personal Acquaintance*. 2nd ed. London: Virtue, 1877.

———. *Retrospect of A Long Life: From 1815 to 1883*. New York: Appleton, 1883.

Hall, S[amuel] C[arter], and Mrs. S. C. Hall. "Memories of the Authors of the Age: A Series of Written Portraits (from Personal Acquaintance) of Great Men and Women of the Epoch. Maria Edgeworth." *Art-Journal* 28 (1866): 345–49.

Haraway, Donna J. *Simians, Cyborgs, and Women: The Reinvention of Nature.* New York: Routledge, 1991.

Harding, Sandra. *The Science Question in Feminism.* Ithaca, NY, and London: Cornell University Press, 1986.

————. *Whose Science? Whose Knowledge? Thinking from Women's Lives.* Ithaca, NY: Cornell University Press, 1991.

Hartsock, Nancy C. M. *Money, Sex, and Power: Toward a Feminist Historical Materialism.* Longman Series in Feminist Theory. New York and London: Longman, 1983.

Harvey, Elizabeth D., and Kathleen Okruhlik, eds. *Women and Reason.* Ann Arbor: University of Michigan Press, 1992.

Kauffman, Linda. Introduction. In her *Gender and Theory: Dialogues on Feminist Criticism,* 1–8. Oxford: Basil Blackwell, 1989.

Leach, Mary, and Bronwyn Davies. "Crossing the Boundaries: Educational Thought and Gender Equity." *Educational Theory* 40.3 (summer 1990): 321–32.

Lloyd, Genevieve. *The Man of Reason: "Male" and "Female" in Western Philosophy.* Minneapolis: University of Minnesota Press, 1984.

Lucas, E[dward] V[erall], ed. *Another Book of Verses for Children.* 1907. New York: Macmillan, 1925.

Lunsford, Andrea A., Helene Moglen, and James Slevin, eds. *The Right to Literacy.* New York: Modern Language Association, 1990.

MacDonald, Edgar E. *The Education of the Heart: The Correspondence of Rachel Mordecai Lazarus and Maria Edgeworth.* Chapel Hill: University of North Carolina Press, 1977.

Michael, Ian. *The Teaching of English from the Sixteenth Century to 1870.* Cambridge: Cambridge University Press, 1987.

Myers, Mitzi. "Socializing Rosamond: Educational Ideology and Fictional Form." *Children's Literature Association Quarterly* 14.2 (summer 1989): 52–58.

————. " 'A Taste for Truth and Realities': Early Advice to Mothers on Books for Girls." *Children's Literature Association Quarterly* 12.3 (fall 1987): 118–24.

Noddings, Nel. *Caring: A Feminine Approach to Ethics and Moral Education.* Berkeley: University of California Press, 1984.

Nussbaum, Felicity A. *The Autobiographical Subject: Gender and Ideology in Eighteenth-Century England.* Baltimore and London: Johns Hopkins University Press, 1989.

Opie, Iona, and Peter Opie. *A Nursery Companion.* Oxford: Oxford University Press, 1980.

Opie, Iona, Robert Opie, and Brian Alderson. *The Treasures of Childhood: Books, Toys, and Games from the Opie Collection.* New York: Arcade/Little, Brown, 1989.

Pope, Alexander. *The Poems of Alexander Pope.* Ed. John Butt. New Haven: Yale University Press, 1963.

Repplier, Agnes. *Essays in Miniature.* Boston and New York: Houghton Mifflin; Cambridge: Riverside Press, 1895.

Robinson, Jay L., with Cathy Fleischer, Carol Lea Winkelmann, Patricia Lambert Stock, and Maxine Greene. *Conversations on the Written Word: Essays on Language and Literacy.* Portsmouth, NH: Boynton/Cook, Heinemann, 1990.

Romilly, Samuel Henry, ed. *Romilly-Edgeworth Letters 1813–1818*. London: John Murray, 1936.

Schweickart, Patrocinio P. "Reading, Teaching, and the Ethic of Care." In *Gender in the Classroom: Power and Pedagogy*, ed. Susan L. Gabriel and Isaiah Smithson, 78–95. Urbana and Chicago: University of Illinois Press, 1990.

Seidler, Victor J. *Rediscovering Masculinity: Reason, Language, and Sexuality*. New York: Routledge, Chapman, and Hall, 1989.

Stillinger, Jack. *Multiple Authorship and the Myth of Solitary Genius*. New York and Oxford: Oxford University Press, 1991.

Stockham, Peter, ed. *Chapbook ABC's: Reprints of Five Rare and Charming Early Juveniles*. New York: Dover, 1974.

Thackeray, Miss [Anne]. (Mrs. Richmond Ritchie). *A Book of Sibyls: Mrs. Barbauld, Miss Edgeworth, Mrs. Opie, Miss Austen*. London: Smith, Elder, 1883.

Vincent, David. *Literacy and Popular Culture: England 1750–1914*. Cambridge Studies in Oral and Literate Culture 19. Cambridge: Cambridge University Press, 1989.

Weiler, Kathleen. "Freire and a Feminist Pedagogy of Difference." *Harvard Educational Review* 61.4 (Nov. 1991): 449–74.

Whalley, Joyce Irene. *Cobwebs to Catch Flies: Illustrated Books for the Nursery and Schoolroom 1700–1900*. Berkeley and Los Angeles: University of California Press, 1975.

Woolf, Virginia. *A Room of One's Own*. 1929. New York: Harcourt, Brace, and World; Harbinger Books, 1957.

Zall, Paul M. "The Cool World of Samuel Taylor Coleridge: Mrs. Barbauld's Crew and the Building of a Mass Reading Class." *The Wordsworth Circle* 2.3 (summer 1971): 74–79.

The Drama of Imagination:
Marjory Fleming and Her Diaries

ALEXANDRA JOHNSON

I confess that I have been
more like a little young
Devil then a creature for
when Isabella went up
to stairs to teach me religion and my multi-
plication and to be good
and all my other lessons
I stamped my feet
and threw my new hat
which she made on the
ground and was sulky an
was dreadfully
passionate. (Sidgwick 40–41)

At first glance, the very columnar shape of the extract above suggests two
possibilities: poetry or a sampler—some printer of homilies sewn during
long winter nights. Yet after reading its text, the reader is still puzzled. To know
that it was part of a diary written between 1810 and 1811 does little to suggest
the author's identity. There are clues in the contents themselves—the misspellings
and multiplication tables. But together with the spirited behavior these could be
that of, say, a barely literate servant, for example, trying to improve herself. Or, as
was to become increasingly common later in the century, from Ruskin to Glad-
stone to Pre-Raphaelite Holman Hunt, a young woman being improved by someone else.[1]

The author of the diary was seven-year-old Marjory Fleming. Since its first
publication in 1858, it is a diary that Victorian writers from Swinburne to Robert
Louis Stevenson to Leslie Stephen numbered among their favorite diaries. Its
uniqueness lies not just in what it reveals about diaries, but, specifically, because
it is one kept by a child, a young girl. For the modern reader, Fleming's diary is

an illuminating record charting a child's inner drives and the social and cultural prohibitions at work against them. Indeed, one is hard-pressed to find a child's diary where genre and gender and the development of literary voice and skill combine so revealingly. The diary, so long the approved forum for a girl's creativity, is here both shelter and straightjacket for her linguistic, psychological, and literary development.

All the classic elements of a diary are present in the above excerpt: confession, drive for self-improvement, fear of authority and the rebellion against it. So, too, the syntax of received opinion; the use of "dreadfully" before "passionate" is not, one feels, just a casual adverb, but a predigested judgment hinting darkly at the rumors of sexuality and adult feeling to follow. Yet beyond the literal tutoring of Fleming's multiplication tables is its far more subtle corollary—the multiplication tables of her moral maturity, the shaping of a child's consciousness. Far more than the literal shaping of language, Fleming's diaries reveal the shaping of a child's— and future woman's—consciousness.

The youngest entry in the *Dictionary of National Biography*, the Scottish-bred Fleming was born in Kirkcaldy, Fife on January 15, 1803. The third child of James Fleming, a well-to-do accountant, Marjory was born into a culturally prominent family, descended from ministers on her father's side and Edinburgh surgeons on her mother's. The Raes, Marjory's maternal relatives, moved in Edinburgh's cultural circles, which included Sir Walter Scott, a distant relation who, as we shall see later, played an important if controversial role in her posthumous reputation. Fleming's literary precocity was sparked not so much by the family's well-stocked library at her disposal, but by a more significant event in her life, one that by the end of the nineteenth century would destine countless household libraries to stock her own story. Just before Marjory's sixth birthday, her seventeen-year-old cousin, Isabella (Isa) Keith, secured the Flemings's permission to take Marjory the dozen-mile journey to Edinburgh.[2] There, alternating between the Keith home at 1 North Charlotte Street and summers at nearby Ravelston and Braehead, Marjory spent the sixth through eighth years of her life in an atmosphere, as she wrote, of "rurel [*sic*] quiet friendship books" (Sidgwick, 23). However seemingly carefree her stay, it would become for Marjory a kind of astonishing tutorial of the self.

Under her aunt's supervision and Isabella's tutelage, Marjory Fleming honed the gifts that had impressed Isabella during her visit to the Fleming household earlier, in 1808. On Isabella's insistence, Marjory began keeping a diary from the age of nearly seven. True to its Latin root, she kept her diary daily, a practice encouraged and monitored by her older cousin. Recording not only her readings but their effects on her imagination, Fleming kept her diary for almost two full years, until her death a month shy of her ninth birthday from meningitis, a complication from measles. In 1858, excerpts from her diary were published by H. B. Farnie, the first of several Victorian editors who not only annotated Fleming's entries but actually deleted text, substituting their own more pious commentary.[3]

Fleming, the child, became Fleming, the text, something others felt their literal and literary right to shape. Isabella's earlier corrections of spellings and grammar became, in time, larger, more serious annotations of spirit and person. Corrections of language were, from the start, corrections of identity. Yet what fascinates any reader of Marjory Fleming's diaries is how Fleming the child—restive, rebellious, curious, learning—does constant battle with the world of adult authority. In a sense, Fleming's Victorian editors merely enlarged the socialization process Isabella and others had begun.

As Mary Jane Moffat and Charlotte Painter note in *Revelations* (1974), their anthology of women's diaries, Fleming "wrote of the difficulties of achieving an ideal of feminine goodness even before she learned to punctuate" (21). While a child's large handwriting automatically splintered lines in a small diary book, where Marjory opted for specific syntax—ellipses, parenthesis, fragments—is of particular psychological import. There's a raw poetry to the diary. Indeed, many lines in Fleming's diary work forcibly like poetry—the sharp splintering of line, the enjambments. Perhaps not surprisingly, the contents of Fleming's three diaries—comprised of notations and poems—were only gradually revealed during successive editions. It wasn't until Sidgwick and Jackson's 1934 line-by-line edition that the pious barnacles encrusted by the Victorians were finally taken off.[4] Indeed, to read Fleming's unedited diaries is to understand even more clearly Mark Twain's praise for this creature "made out of thunderstorms and sunshine."[5]

The inevitable work of separating the child from the legend is particularly complicated in Fleming's case. To do so requires examining the cultural phenomenon Fleming became, as well as placing her diary within its historical literary context in order to shed light on what engendered that cultural phenomenon. Since Arundell Esdaile's 1934 facsimile edition of Fleming's diaries, the task of both the reader and scholar has been not only to give Marjory back her words, but to scrape away those which a century after her death still prevented readers from seeing her own clearly. While the Victorian editing of Fleming's diaries will be discussed in detail later in this essay, for the moment it is necessary to take a brief look at the history of her diary as it passed from the private realm of her family to the public area of editors. In 1858, Farnie, a London journalist and opera librettist, gained access to Marjory's diaries. With the family's approval he published *Pet Marjorie: A Story of Child Life Fifty Years Ago*. The critical success of Marjory's story led John Brown, a Scottish physician and children's writer, to publish "Pet Marjorie: A Sketch," which, like Farnie earlier, used excerpts from Fleming's diaries to anchor his own narrative of her brief life. Brown's 1863 article in the *The North British Review*, though, was the first to propagate the account that dogged Fleming until our own century, namely, the link to Scott. (The evidence for and repercussions of that link are addressed later in this essay.) In Brown, as in all successive editions based on him, including Farnie's revised 1864 reissue, Marjory was seen as a child prodigy declaiming Shakespeare at Scott's knee. The legend, together with the precocity of the actual excerpts, won Fleming the praise of writers from Swinburne to Robert Louis Stevenson, and culminated in her enshrinement in the pantheon of the *Dictionary of National Biography*, the entry written by Sir Leslie Stephen, the book's editor, himself.[6] For the next half century, it was impossible to speak of Fleming without also mentioning those who had given the seal of approval on her fame: the *patri familias* of the Victorian literary establishment. It was her fate, it seems, never to have had creativity quite by herself.

In our own age, Fleming's literary fate has suffered an even more curious turn. While Marjory was known to twentieth-century readers from Arthur Ponsonby's popular *Scottish and Irish Diaries from the Sixteenth to the Nineteenth Century* (1927) and Arundell Esdaile's 1934 collotype of her diary, her fame was soon eclipsed. Between the First and Second World Wars, that slender period Robert Graves called the Long Weekend, the reading public's taste shifted. War diaries, not children's diaries, were now celebrated. The deeper reason for Fleming's decline was that most readers still knew of her largely through *other* people's words. For the better part of our own century, Fleming was dogged by the sentimental legacy of her Victorian editors. While Oriel Malet's 1946 novel, *Pet Marjorie*, sought to redress the historical inaccuracies in Fleming's life, most readers still associated her with Scott's "Pet," the child their Victorian parents or grandparents knew from either Farnie's or Brown's editions of her diaries. The irony, of course, is that Fleming herself was notoriously unsentimental; it was her editors who imposed the sentimental notion of children on her text. Despite Arundell Esdaile and Frank Sidgwick's editions of her unexpurgated diaries, for many readers Fleming was still the "child author" in Kate Wiley's 1909 *Pet Marjorie and Sir Walter Scott* (13). What modern reader would go beyond Wiley's opening line, "In this simple record of Marjorie Fleming's few bright years on earth" (Preface). What modern reader would be convinced that the "winsome little friend of Sir Walter Scott" (13) had produced diaries which, in the words of her third editor, Lachlan Macbean, "have been classed with the wonders of the world" (Preface).

The child who had enjoyed fame in the company of eminent Victorians now shared a solitary literary fate as a footnote. From 1957 on, Fleming appeared mostly as a spirited entry in compendiums such as *Treasury of Great Diaries* (Dunaway and Evans 181–85). Since the 1970s, the burgeoning interest in diaries in general has given us works such as Robert Fothergill's scholarly *Private Chronicles: A Study of English Diaries* (1974), Thomas Mallon's popular *A Book of One's Own: People and Their Diaries* (1984), Simon Brett's *The Faber Book of Diaries* (1987) and Ronald Blythe's *The Pleasure of Diaries: Four Centuries of Private Writing* (1989). Of these, only Fothergill mentions Fleming. It wasn't until 1974, when Charlotte Painter and Mary Jane Moffat published excerpts of Fleming's diaries in their anthology, *Revelations: Diaries of Women*, that many contemporary readers first learned of the precocious Fleming. It was the first time in over nearly half a century that readers knew her by her own words. (Interestingly, even in Patricia Havlice's 1987

And So to Bed: A Bibliography of Diaries Published in English, Fleming's precocity is still prized as she "repeated adult conversation"; 88.)

While feminist scholars such as Margaret Homans and Anne K. Mellor have written authoritatively on the primacy of language and female literary experience, even feminists have tended to overlook literary children like Fleming. In two of the finest studies on women's diaries so far, Harriet Blodgett's *Centuries of Female Days: Englishwomen's Private Diaries* (1988) and Judy Simons's *Diaries and Journals of Literary Women from Fanny Burney to Virginia Woolf* (1990), Fleming is never mentioned. The truth is that since the appearance of Margaret Willey's *Three Women Diarists* in 1964, most authors have chosen to focus on adult female diarists. Thus, in 1990 Fleming is again relegated to footnote status in comprehensive works such as Yale University Press' *The Feminist Companion to Literature in English* (Blain, Grundy, and Clements 379). There is a terrible irony at work here. If, as a genre, diaries have been considered footnotes to larger literature, so, in turn, have children often assumed secondary status to their adult literary counterparts. Yet if Marjory Fleming's diary teaches us anything, it is the literary potency of the diary and the wonders of the child who kept it. The hope of this essay is that it will bring readers once again to this remarkable diary, one that captivated Victorians and in our own century is only recently again coming to light.

To understand the legacy of Fleming's Victorian popularity, it is necessary to frame it within its historical literary context. By the late 1860s, the English reading public was increasingly familiar with the emerging literature of child protagonists. From *Jane Eyre* (1847) to *Mill on the Floss* (1860), novels examining the inner lives of children signaled a fascination in the national psyche for what, later in the century, would become the Victorian cult of the child, a complex embracing of childhood exemplified by the literary and photographic works of Lewis Carroll. The successive publication of Fleming's diaries, it must be stressed, coincided with the most famous and celebrated of that genre, specifically, the final wave of Dickens's novels, the late mature works from *Little Dorrit* (1855–57) to *Great Expectations* (1860–61). The prototype of child as innocent *and* moral being, the agent of his own salvation through work, had already been firmly established in two earlier Dickens novels, *David Copperfield* and *Bleak House* (Fanger 81–91). If they depicted a world of orphans and wards, the dangerous marginality of childhood, its abuses and threats in an increasingly industrialized society, then the real-life Fleming with her rural, nurturing family served as a reassuring icon to the Victorian public. While the sheer industry of her diary satisfied their notion of "Duty," more significantly, through her diary they glimpsed their own childhood before its loss and socialization.

Like Dickens's child protagonists withstanding the false maturity of adult society, its rules and social rigidities, the Victorian reading public found in Fleming's diaries the unselfconscious pluck of childhood itself. Indeed, the timeless appeal of Fleming's diaries, as her third editor, Lachlan Macbean, noted is that "we watch that mind, unconscious of its own immaturity, passing fearless judgments from the standpoint it has for the moment gained" (11). Yet like Pepys's injunctions to be kinder to his long-suffering wife or Dr. Johnson's diary notations to rise earlier, Marjory's almost superstitious vows to be good, to behave better, to read sermons and not novels are similarly doomed. We find her fidgety in church, covetous of a pack of cards, forgetful of her prayers, unabashed in enjoying her own talents. In short, acting much as the world expects a child of seven to act. The reader applauds Marjory Fleming's mettle much as one might the spontaneous outbursts of the very young Jane Eyre. Yet unlike Bronte's fictional character, Fleming didn't live long enough to complete her education in moral self-restraint. The power—and delight—of her diaries is witnessing a child in the process of self-expression, both personal and literary, while resisting the stuttering corrections of self-consciousness.

Few could argue with Macbean's observation that "she is not so much a child of genius as the genius of childhood" (22). Yet how many children's journals boast 9000 words, 560 lines of poetry, including a 208-line historically accurate poem on the life of Mary Queen of Scots? This is no ordinary child's diary. Fleming's diary is a focussed record of creative and personal expression. Its interests are books and drama, its passions, a mind concentrating itself on self-expression through literature and love. From start to finish, Marjory thought of herself as an author. However inchoate those attempts, on her death bed her final jotting was a poem, written on a slate and dedicated to Isabella, "Address to dear Isabella on the Author's Recovery." To the end, the *a* in author is uppercased. Fleming's diary is, above all, a living record of the forces that shaped or stunted the powers of her self-expression.

In this essay I will examine three crucial aspects of the single theme that emerges from reading Fleming's diaries: the drama of her imagination—in this case literally, as we shall see, the child who eschewed dolls, who preferred the thundering drama of the Old Testament to the sanguine moral judgments of the New, the drama of acting out, of testing limits. Drama here also translates into a literary penchant for plays, the drama less of acting out than *acting*, the intensively imaginative exercise through reading and writing of *imagining* oneself as someone else: in short, the start of a fledgling literary consciousness. Secondly, in her diaries one glimpses the unique situation that shaped both aspects of the drama of imagination, the sympathetic mentor relation with a non (primary) family member, a situation which both freed and focussed Fleming's imagination. Third, in the collaborative nature of that creativity, one sees how writing as self-expression was also used as both reward and punishment, a lure to love. To read Fleming's diary is to watch before our eyes the process and price of socialization around the links of literature and love, and how they intertwined in Marjory Fleming's consciousness. If, as Bruno Bettelheim posits, a child's chief tasks are to master his or her immediate world and to practice love, then Marjory Fleming's diaries chart the causal relation between them through literary self-expression. Lastly, I will examine how these three strands of argument combine to fashion a portrait of female literary creativity at its very earliest stages.

2

> Many people are hanged for Highway
> robbery Housebreking Murder &c &c (3)

So begins the diary of a nearly seven-year-old Marjory Fleming. No "Dear diary," none of the mawkish confession or learned piety one might expect from a child reared in the Calvinist climate of 1810 Scotland. Literally from the first, Marjory displays an instinct for drama in subject matter and the need not to disguise it. It is the hallmark of her diary. Its material is absorbed from her immediate world—stories of Trafalgar, of her childhood, of local murders and prison escapes. She records them as dutifully, if selectively, as she does the hanging of Haman from the Book of Esther or the demise of Mary Queen of Scots. If the diary attests to her keen powers as a listener, able to use what she overhears in the drawing room, it also shows other important awarenesses on her part. Consider the following passages selected from the very first few pages of her diary. Together with the preceding excerpt they form a pattern that endures throughout, a leitmotiv necessary to understand before any analysis of Fleming's diaries.[7]

> Isabella teaches me everything I know

> and I am much indebted to her

> Isabella campels me
> to sit down & not rise till this page
> is done

> We should get the better of our pas
> -ssion & not let them get the bet. (4–5)

These four citations characterize Marjory's diary and our experience of it: the pattern of drama and expressed feeling followed by a homily. If at the onset of the diary almost every spontaneous feeling or observation is followed intermittently by a borrowed homily, by the end of her diary those homilies are omnipresent and, increasingly, internalized. The opening two lines, as stated previously, catch the dramatic tenor of her imagination. From the second and third citations, it is equally clear that her imagination has been put to use within the set discipline of writing. From the final citation—a disguised echo of the second—it is already evident that writing is linked to behavior and, more significantly that, in the use of "we," behavior is contingent on her relation to others. While for all children the development of "I" is always linked to "we," what makes Fleming's case so compelling is that it is through her own sense and use of *language* that Marjory achieves her necessary separateness, her own sense of self.

From Marjory's diaries—and Isabella's letters—we glean the details of her diary keeping and its attendant activities. In April, 1810, two months shy of the duly noted celebration of George III's birthday, Marjory began keeping a record of her thoughts and reading, and, quite often, her misbehaving. The diary was kept in three exercises or "copy books," lined by Isabella and all but the final one paginated by her as well. Intended as part of Marjory's education, initially the diary became a convenient forum for the practice of penmanship and punctuation, "simecolings" and "commoes" (16). Working together, usually from 11 A.M. to 2 P.M., Isabella tutored Marjory in a variety of subjects—French, math, history, the Bible. Yet her great love, as her diaries chronicle from the onset, is literature. Her reading is varied and precocious: Gray, Swift, Fielding, Addison. So too the helter-skelter charm of a child's taste: Shakespeare and Mother Goose, Scott and Maria Edgeworth, Robert Morehead's sermons (ignored) and the *Newgate Calendar* (pored over).[8]

For a moment, let's look beyond these literal facts to examine a far more interesting truth implicit here about the nature of the diary itself. The cited passages underline the tacit assumption that the subject (and object) of the diary, namely Fleming herself, was a fully approved one. However numerous the homilies intended to check that, the diary was nonetheless an approved forum for her own opinions, opinions on literature, preferring Pope to other poets, say, or thinking Gray's "Elegy" "excellent" (*sic*) (127). Unlike most children's diaries, hers is one intended from the start not only to shape language, but specifically language learned (and often borrowed) from great literature. We have only to recall Southey's reply to the young Charlotte Brontë on how writing, and, by implication, contemplation of oneself, was not a proper sphere for female activity. "Literature," the poet laureate wrote her, "cannot be the business of a woman's life, and ought not to be. The more she is engaged in her proper duties, the less leisure she will have for it, even as an accomplishment and a recreation" (cited in Gaskell 173). While that cultural prohibition was so strong that, with the exception of Jane Austen, many nineteenth-century women first published under male pseudonyms, in the case of their early literary expression we find an interesting double standard. In the Brontës, for example, early diary keeping and juvenilia were encouraged by their father, not in spite of but, as we shall see later, *because* it was in the realm of a child—the language not valued or valuable. A child's written words never threaten to achieve the permanence of an adult's.[9]

What makes Fleming's diary unique then is that it breaks the cardinal rule of diaries, especially ones kept by little girls, namely, to keep self-expression private. A diary's secrecy, of course, is its guarantee of safety, essential for many a young girl as it's the one place, often the *only* place, she might express herself freely, especially on questions of those two forbidden fruits: love and literature. Yet from its inception Fleming's diary was public—not only to Isabella but, in lieu of letters home, to the family itself. This public dimension to her diary sparked the notion of performance. The diary became the stage for the drama of Marjory Fleming's imagination and language its performance. Moreover, since that language was fully shaped under the approving eyes of Isabella, it introduces here an important element: the notion of audience. From the start, Marjory Fleming wrote knowing she would be read. From the start, she was an author with a guaranteed audience. While that might tempt a kind of show-off behavior, in Fleming, moral goodness, as we shall see shortly, was too linked to behavior for language not to be taken seriously. Increasingly throughout her diary, she makes the connection between her talents and squandering them through dramatically bad behavior.

"She continues her journal every day entirely by herself," Isabella wrote the Flemings (Sidgwick 179). What began ostensibly in lieu of letters home, and then as a forum for lessons in spelling and penmanship, quickly transformed itself into an important forum for her own development. The diary served as the literal and figurative property of her imagination, which is why the overlay and tampering by her Victorian editors makes Fleming's legacy so revealing as it relates to children. While they all extol her keen intelligence, none underlines the link to how the notion of being read, of being an author, sharpened her already considerable imitative powers.

> I get my poetry now
> out of grey & I thin[k]
> it beautiful (61)

That mimetic talent paid off. On page 10 of Diary One, for example, she mentions for the first time her love of Gray. By page 18, the diary begins being written in long sections of verse. Yet the impact of Fleming's daily reading and practice of language shows more subtly in shifts in style itself. Perhaps ironically, the single book Isabella hoped would influence Marjory the most, namely the Bible, did just that. It became less an agent of her moral behavior than one of her sense and use of language. The very thing meant to discipline her became, in the end, the source that liberated her. Misspelled and ungrammatical as it often is, her prose is full of the rhythmic cadences of Ecclesiastes, the conscious repetitions of Psalms. If by the end of the diary the Bible's moral precepts are increasingly internalized, then her powers of direct observation, her delight in the daily world, are still undiminished by them. To the end, her meditations on the lyrical specificity of God's world far outnumber abstract paeans to Him. In her diaries we witness a child delighting in the shape of yew trees, the slant of light in an afternoon garden, the nimble movements of a pet monkey in the Keith household. In two typical early examples of how direct observation and imitative prose blend, she writes:

I like loud Mirement & laugh
-ter.—I love to walk in lonely solitude
& leave the bustel of the nosey town
behind me & while I look on noth-
-ing but what strikes the eye (12)

and:

The hedges are green the trees are green
& every thing bears a pleasure to the
eye when we look on them. (27)

Here we need to examine a crucial point central to any discussion of the development of a child's voice, namely how that voice evolves out of the interactions between adult discourse and the child's own vocal self-assertions. Fleming's diary illustrates the slow but shaping influence of Isabella's thoughts and opinions on Marjory's experiments with self-expression. The tension of the diary reveals itself most keenly through language, notably, the child's instinct for specificity—part of her mastering her immediate world—but also her own spontaneous cele-bration of it before she learns the "correct" way to experience it through the approved abstractions of language. Fleming's diary is all immediacy. The immedi-acy of her mastering her own world, of practicing love, of finding her own words to do so while resisting many imposed on her instead. In these three diaries we find no vocabulary lists, but the living language of her feelings. And her pleasure in this is considerable. Writing how she worked in passages of her favorite poem, Scott's "Helvellyn," incorporating them into her diary along with her own obser-vations on nature, she notes:

this address
I composed myself & no-
-body assisted me I am sure. (120)

Here we need to examine a subtler point implicit in the diary passages exam-ined so far. With the notion of audience comes the less obvious dividend for any author: the censor. Marjory's imagination and its drama were to have a resident critic. Most illuminating, though, is how the critic progressively shifts from exter-nal—Isabella—to Marjory herself. Consider the following excerpts selected from each diary. Diary One, begun April, 1810:

Into a bed where Isa lies
And to my questions she replies
Corrects my faults improves my mi[nd]. (26)

By Diary Two, begun July, 1810, what began as underlined misspellings and corrections of grammar shifts to an awareness of her own prose:

I acknowledge that this page is
far from being well written. (55)

Midway through that same diary comes a new element—the appearance of an editorial voice:

Isabella bids me give you
a note of the sarmon
preached by Mr
Bonner (81)

By Diary Three, kept between March and April, 1811, we now hear in that editorial voice both Marjory *and* Isabella:

I am sure of it indeed I like
the old testament better
then the new but the new
is far more instructive. (118)

We can almost hear the conversation on which it's based, Marjory's opinion tempered by Isabella's gentle correction. Within a year's time she has incorporated what she *should* feel (i.e., what others tell her is important) with what she in fact feels. By the end of Diary Three her sentences often automatically anticipate others' responses. On something as simple as predicting that it is going to rain, she now hesitates:

but it is
only my opinion which is
not always correct. (114)

However intrusive or inhibiting Isabella's looking over her shoulder, it also allowed Marjory to feel that her diary, and, by implication, her own powers of self-expression, were important. If Isabella functioned critically as a mentor, for Marjory she also became a muse. And here we need to examine an important element in our discussion of the shaping of Marjory's voice, namely, how her living with Isabella holds important parallels in the lives and literature of the major nineteenth-century English women writers: Austen, Eliot, the Bronte sisters. Early in life, each spent lengthy stays in the household of a relative or important non-family member: Eliot in the Bray family, Austen in the Leigh Perrot's home in Bath, Charlotte Bronte in the Nussey household.[10] From *Mansfield Park* to *Jane*

Eyre to *Middlemarch*, this legacy is detailed in the fiction itself: the many months in another home wherein the female protagonist undergoes some important sea change of the self. In literature, each writer revealed an important truth she had found in her own life: to step outside the safe boundaries of immediate family life is, inevitably, to discover new perimeters of the self, a territory now charted through language—diary form in youth, novels in adulthood.

What makes Fleming's diary so important in this regard is that it serves as one of the earliest models of female literary creativity we have. It is an undisturbed record of a child literally and figuratively finding her voice. Fleming's life bears none of the early psychological abrasions and upheavals suffered by Eliot and the Brontes (the first death she knew would be her own). Her intimate, circumscribed world is closer to Austen's, the writer whose wit and penchant for social caricature Fleming as a child most resembles. Yet, what Fleming and these other writers share is their experience of sympathetic companionship outside the immediate family and its stimulus to the imagination (Nestor chs. 5, 6). Out of that world came the single requirement for authentic self-expression, the very thing denied Dickens's child protagonists: safety. The safety to express themselves freely as children or young adults is usually granted them only at the resolution of their moral journey. The stuttering Smike in *Nicholas Nickleby*, for example, is choked less by breath than by the constrictions of survival. But the tics of his tongue are less narrative devices than powerful metaphors for the relation between language, self-expression and safety. For many of Dickens's characters unselfconscious speech is a luxury. They aren't speech-impaired so much as life-impaired.

No wonder then that the Victorian public found Marjory Fleming's diary so reassuring. It was a respite from Dickens's orphans and wards, the social and psychological misfits social historians like Mayhew showed to be much closer to the real life casualties of the seismic upheavals in Victorian life. Yet, deeper, Fleming's diary was tangible proof of safety, a child experiencing herself and the world through the learned stability of language. Indeed, what her diary illustrates so profoundly is how the process of language and a sense of self are vitally shaped by a safe environment. And, as in Dickens's novels, that process often is collaborative but not necessarily familial. If the fictional Smike had his Nicholas Nickleby, then in real life Fleming had Isabella as a shaping presence.

Here we come to the second crucial aspect in any discussion of Fleming and her diaries: the sympathetic mentor relation with an adult and its influence on the development of the child's voice. However exacting Isabella's tutelage, it was responsible not only for encouraging Marjory's burgeoning power of self-expression, but also, in some deep way, of making it possible in the first place. Isabella may not have given birth to Marjory, but she helped Marjory give birth to herself. For a moment we need to examine the notion of muse as mother and how it relates to a child's power to develop a language of the self. If, as psychologist Jessica Benjamin cogently argues in *The Bonds of Love* (1988), most children's earliest sense of self is shaped by their mother, it is significant that almost every woman who grew up to be a major writer either lost her mother young (Eliot, the Brontes) or had an important primary relation with a sister or sisters (Austen, the Brontes). Had Fleming stayed at home, her precocity would undoubtedly have been recognized but not necessarily used. Unquestionably, it was her nearly three-year tutelage *away* from home which disciplined that intelligence and inspired the writing of the diary that made her famous.[11] The Flemings, by all accounts, were an affectionate family and Marjory a cherished child. Yet while the shores of Kirkcaldy were visible by telescope across the Firth from Edinburgh, and while family members visited her at the Keiths, with the exception of three letters appended to her diary, there is hardly any mention of her family in the diaries. While this may be explained, in part, by arguing that Marjory knew her diaries would be sent home eventually, after Marjory's death Isabella, not the Flemings, still had them as her cherished property, and sent them on reluctantly (Sidgwick, 182).

Isabella was an important mother surrogate for Marjory, a bond reinforced by the fact that Isabella was also the namesake of Marjory's own other and older sister. Thus three important nurturing figures were conveniently combined into one person. On her return to Kirkcaldy in July of 1811, Marjory addressed letters to Isabella as: "My Dear little Mama" and "My Dear Mother" (166, 169). Whatever the primary bond, the Keith household held another key element in Marjory's developing self-expression. As a member of a *visiting* household, Marjory sensed her own specialness, which was constantly reinforced. The diary that might have languished on a windowseat in her immediate family, unnoticed by a mother too busy with other children, became the conscious focus for Fleming and her larger audience, the Keith household. In this regard, Marjory's stay was auspicious in other ways. While she occasionally fought with her older cousins, there was no real sibling rivalry to speak of to distract or distort her own developing powers of language. Moreover, there was no stern father or authority figure, as in the case of Eliot and the Brontes, to dismiss or forbid that self-expression (Sadoff chs. 2, 3).

Marjory's acknowledgment of Isabella's crucial role in her developing sense of language makes one of the most revealing entries in the diary:

I can never repay
Isabella for what
she has done but by
good behave-our. (83)

Behave-our. While closer to the British spelling of behaviour, it nonetheless betrays an unerring serendipity of meaning that stems from a child's supple experiments with language. Within this misspelling rests an unconscious truth: the collaborative nature of creativity between Isabella and Marjory. Her gratitude to Isabella as the catalyst for that self-expression is immense. It informs her diary from its first page to the very final words she wrote:

O Isa pain did visit me
I was at the last extremity
How often did I think of you (176)

For Marjory, language became the way of showing Isabella her constant gratitude. To be good, then, meant being good with words; to please meant pleasing
with words. Marjory ingeniously acknowledges this even in the topography of her
diary. An early entry, for example, describing herself sleeping at the foot of Isabella's bed is playfully written upside down and then rights itself when she goes on
to another topic (24). In one of the diaries' most inspired passages, Marjory
describes literally awakening her own muse. Fleming's diaries crackle with accidents of language: newly coined words, breathtakingly apt puns. Here is one of
the most delicious, an early one which, as her second editor John Brown suggests,
refers to the Venus de Medici in the Uffizi Gallery in Florence (Brown, 22).

I went into Isabellas bed to make her smile
like the Genius Demedicus the statute in an-
-cient Greece but she fell asleep in my very fa[ce]
at which my anger broke forth so that
I awoke her from a very comfortable nap. (8)

Genius Demedicus. How rich the sheer pleasure of its associations: linking the object
of her love to art (the Uffizi statue), but also to Venus, goddess of love. The
combined effect of the passage is a portrait of genius awakening—not Isabella,
but Marjory and her keen awareness of the pleasures of self-expression. Marjory's
subsequent tantrum at being thwarted seems no different from centuries of writers
or artists whose human muses—models or mistresses—have momentarily failed
them. But muse Isabella was. Fleming's diaries are an encoded valentine to her,
and language a slowly crafted arrow to capture the object of her love. To read
them in order is to see how, for Fleming, love was inextricably linked in her
consciousness to self-expression. To lose one was to risk losing the other. Increasingly in her diaries it was a link she well understood, the causal relation between
behavior and the bestowal of love.

As the final lines of the Genius Demedicus passage attest, though, Isabella
had her hands full. Not unaware of this Marjory writes:

My religion is greatly
falling off . . .
but as for reganing my
carecter I despare. (80)

The diary is an index to Marjory's naughtiness, studded with transgressions of
polite behavior. Yet as the diary seesaws between temper and remorse, Marjory's

deepening powers of self-expression provide her with a confidence her misbehavings would otherwise rob her of. She literally always has the last word on her own affairs. As early as age seven, Fleming began to learn through her diary what all adult writers know: language is a way of controlling the unbridled imagination, of stilling action so as to concentrate it into work. Isabella capitalized on this by using writing to channel what Marjory might otherwise risk saying to someone's face. Consider Marjory's sassily candid description of a woman discussing Marjory's aunt. It was written shortly after her arrival in Edinburgh:

> This horid
> fat Simpliton says
> that my Aunt is
> beautifull which is intire
> -ly impossible for that
> is not her nature.— (160)

But even in writing her diary, control wasn't always easy for the seven-year-old child. Marjory's self-confessed "passions" were so intense at times that, as is visible in Arundell Esdaile's 1934 collotype facsimile of the journals, her actual penmanship steadily deteriorates while recording them, and pages are torn, ripped off at the bottom.

Here we come to the final conjugation in the drama of Marjory's imagination, namely her conscious self-assertion with, and often against, adult authority. By Diary Two, so important had Marjory understood her diary to be that she chose it as the arena of her behavioral battles:

> Last night I behaved extre-
> mely ill and threw my
> work in the stairs and
> would not pick it up
> which was very wrong. (51–52)

And twenty-one pages later:

> I am going to tell you
> that in all my life I
> never behaved so ill for
> when Isa bid me go out
> of the room I would not
> go & when Isa came to
> the room I threw my book at her in a dreadful
> passion & she did not lick
> me (73–74)

Instinctively, Isabella also understood it as a means of corrective punishment. Consider Marjory's notation:

> To Day I have ben very
> ungrateful and bad and
> disobedient Isabella gave
> me my writing I wrote
> so ill that she took it
> away and located it up
> in her desk where I
> stood trying to open
> it till she made me come
> and read my bible
> but I was in a bad honor
> and red it so Carelessly. (43–44)

While seemingly penitent, Marjory's words here can't disguise her deeper feelings: bad humor written as bad honor, red for having to read, the uncharacteristic lowercasing of *b* in Bible.

Between Diary Two and Three we witness an important shift in expressive consciousness. Marjory's internalized censor castigates her for wasting the talents that, with Isabella's help, she's happily discovered. The following citation is typical of many throughout Diary Two and Three. (Note the capitalization of the verb Improve below.)

> I am
> thinking how I should Impr[ove]
> the many talents I have.
> I am very sory I have
> threwn them away (53)

Perhaps no excerpt is more revealing than the following passage from Diary Two in which both aspects of the drama of Marjory's imagination—and the inevitable conflict over them—come together. Marjory records reading a book about:

> A man [who] went into
> a house & he saw
> a sack & he went &
> look into it & he saw
> a dead body in it. (87–88)

Directly underneath, Isabella writes: "Marjory must write no more journal till she writes better" (88). What follows for two full pages, presumably to practice penmanship, are words that can hardly be accidental in their choice: "Communications," "Expectations," "forwardness."

Despite Isabella's stylistic and behavioral corrections, Marjory's sense of drama not only continued unabated but she actively made the literal leap to *writing* about drama. Increasingly, her wish is to read and write about historical drama. Of all the written forms, drama is the most concrete, an element essential to a child in the process of developing language: the action verbs of her own life. Indeed, the central question of her identity with language increasingly centers on drama, its capacity to act on—and at times to act out—her feelings. If at night Marjory's imagination was fired by her reading of the *Arabian Nights* and Mrs. Radcliffe's *The Mysteries of Udolpho*, through the daily discipline of the diary, Isabella found a suitable vehicle to focus and harness her charge's dramatic imagination. The diaries chart the shift from dramatic acting out to a love of drama itself. Marjory's literal penchant for acting was noted as early as her arrival in Edinburgh. In a letter to her sister written in 1809, Marjory writes:

> Miss
> Potune a Lady of my
> acquaintance praises me
> dreadfully.—I repeated
> something out of De[a]n
> Sw[i]ft and she said
> I was fit for the Stage. (158–59)

What others saw only reinforced the direction into which Marjory's imagination gravitated naturally. As early as page 9 of Diary One she writes:

> I should like to see a play very much
> for I never saw one in all my life &
> don't believe I ever shall but I hope
> I can be content without going to one. (9)

By reflexively couching it as something that won't happen, Marjory begins to acknowledge a subconscious truth: drama is somehow unacceptable for a young girl. "I hope I can be content," already anticipates the disappointment. She was right. The penultimate line of her diary is:

> King John is
> a beautiful play & so is King Rich-
> ard the 3 I never saw a play acted in
> my life. (131)

Unable to watch or act out plays, she did the next best thing: write her own in the form of epic verse. Absorbing stories around her—tales of Trafalgar of her infancy, reports from Corunna—or from her reading, she worked the drama of her imagination through verse. Like the Brontes's, her juvenilia was rooted in national and local history. Just as Charlotte Bronte found in Wellington and Byron the twins of her own creative imagination, so in Mary Queen of Scots Fleming found the heroine of hers (Moglen 99). Soon after her arrival at 1 North Charlotte Street, Marjory began reading the history of Scotland. Within two years she had skillfully translated the facts of Mary Queen of Scots's and King James's lives into metered verse.

In Marjory's mastery of her 208-line poem to Mary Queen of Scots we witness an interesting paradox, one that relates directly to diary keeping by young girls. While the journals testify to Marjory's capacity for language, they proportionately demonstrate her conflicted and, at times, diminished sense of being female. To read Fleming's diary is to witness Marjory's unconscious and later acknowledged understanding that while she might read or write about a heroine, in polite society it wasn't necessarily possible to be one. In terms of writing and language, there's a deeper implication: what is possible to express in the juvenilia of a diary might not be deemed acceptable in adult writing. And here we find the paradox of diary keeping for a young girl. By definition and design, a diary involves two simultaneous if contradictory processes: the emergence of a concrete language of feelings and the learned overlay of censorship through socialization. Language, the vehicle of self-expression, also becomes in time an instrument of self-censorship. This tension between confession and censorship in the diary underlines the eroding effects of socialization on talent and identity. Consider the following excerpts selected from each of the diaries. As early as page 6 of Diary One Marjory writes of herself:

> I am very
> strong & robust & not of the delicate sex
> not of the fair but of the deficent in look. (6)

This bold certainty of identity is still as yet unselfconscious. Yet in Diary Two she writes:

> I would rather have
> a man dog than a
> women dog because they
> do not bear like women
> dogs, it is a hard case (55)

Writing, that genderless realm of expression for a child, allowed her production and accomplishment. Literary precocity was the approved arena where as a child she could shine. Thus, while by page 29 of Diary One she begins a poem on a turkey, "Dedicated to Mrs. H. Crawfurd by the author MF," by Diary Two she defaults:

> I will never again trust in
> my own pow[e]r (82)

By Diary Three, it's not her own literary efforts but her outside reading that confronts her with restrictive portraits of women. She acknowledges:

> Fighting is what ladies is not qua
> lyfied for they would not make a good
> figure in battle or in a dual Alas we fe-
> males are of little use to our country. (125)

Despite the literal split in fe/male in the third and fourth lines, Marjory then advances an ingenious *deus ex machina* of an argument, discrediting a story about women:

> but it is only a story out of Mo-
> thers Gooses Fary tales so I do not give
> it cridit, that is to say I do not belive
> the truth of it (126)

Marjory here underlines a keen but sad truth: since it's only a *child's* tale, it should not be taken seriously. Fleming the child neatly pulls the rug out from under the world of adult final opinion.

At this point we begin to see how the drama of Fleming's imagination finds its final and inevitable source of authority: literature. Whether reading or writing it, literature is for Marjory the link throughout all the diaries, the single thread that binds her drama of love and language. She constantly tests her own experience of those two realities against her reading. While in *Northanger Abbey* (1818), Jane Austen lampoons the effects Mrs. Radcliffe's gothic narrative had on young girls' imaginations, for Marjory in Diary One it becomes an introduction to the drama of love:

> I am reading the Mysteries of udolpho
> & am much interested in the fate of poor
> poor Emily. (24)

If in Diaries One and Two Marjory masters a language of feeling about herself and Isabella, then in Diary Three, with her reading of Fielding, she experiences love outside the immediate family. In Diary Three Marjory discovers men. With this comes not only whole new possibilities of feeling but repressions of language around those newfound feelings. By Diary Three the full effect of socialization, the increased conflict between Marjory's expressed feelings and Isabella's censuring of them, find their final drama. Consider:

In the love novels all
the heroins are very des-
-perate Isabella will not
alow me to speak about lovers
& heroins & tis too refined for
my taste a lodestone is a cu
-rous thing indeed it is true
Heroick love doth win disgra[ce]
is my maxium & I will
follow it for ever &. (103)

If novels have been her introduction to adult love, her diary becomes a guileless way to record a child flirting:

Yesterday
a marrade [man] named Mr
John Balfour Esq offered
to kiss me, & offered to marry
me though the man was es-
pused, & his wife was prsent, &
said he must ask her per
-mision but he did not I
think he was ashamed or con-
founded before 3 gentelman. (101)

As Diary Three makes clear, love is still tied to literary expression and its immediate model of Isabella.

Isabella is always reading &
writing in her room, & does not
come down for long & I wish every
body would follow her example
& be as good as pious & virtious as
she is & they would get husban
soon enough, love is a very
papithatick thinhg as well as
troubelsom & tiresome but O
Isabella forbid me to speak a-
-bout it. (109)

Here Marjory makes conscious the connection that has long been implicit in her diaries, namely, the link between love and language, between reading and writing and the approbations of behavior. As the previous three citations suggest, she experiences a new conflict of identity concerning language: its expression beyond the immediate object of her affection—Isabella—to men.

While we might infer from the preceding passage that Isabella was experiencing her own romantic problems, her steady censoring of Marjory on the subject of love suggests a deeper source. It is the recognition on Isabella's part that in the initiation into love for the opposite sex Marjory was no longer a child. The future woman beckoned. Words about love were now charged with a different meaning—less perhaps for Marjory than for Isabella. The diary here comes too close to adult feeling, the words no longer part of the safe genderless realm of children's writing. Passions are no longer synonymous with childish tantrums but real sexual feeling. Significantly, directly after the John Balfour notation Marjory writes:

> Isabella teaches me to read my
> bible & tells me to be good and
> say my prayers, and every
> thing that is nesary for a
> good carecter and a good con
> -science. (101)

Despite Isabella's insistence on censuring Marjory's expressions of love, the diarist continues:

> A sailor called heree to say
> farewell, it must be dread-
> full to leave his native country
> where he might get a wife
> or perhaps me, for I love
> very much & wth
> all my heart, but O I
> forgot Isabella forbid me to
> speak of love. (108)

The diary, originally intended as a forum to express herself fully, is now one to repress certain feelings. Late in Diary Three the language dramatically mirrors this fragmented internal process: feeling and guilt, desire and doubt. Perhaps no passage more clearly illustrates where self-expression and socialization are at odds than the following. Joined haphazardly by dashes, the punctuation stitches together the homilies. Unlike notations in Diary One, every spontaneous observation is now cautioned and contradicted by a learned homily. The effect is a kind of ricocheting not just of language but of the very self who selects it:

> I composed myself & no
> -body assisted me I am sure
> I get acquainted with boys & girls
> almost every day.—wickedness
> and vice makes one miserable &
> unhappy as well as concousness
> of guilt on our mind.—Doctor
> Swifts works are very funny
> & amusing & I get some by hart.—
> Vanity is a great folly and some-
> -times leads to a great sin disimu-
> -lation I think is worse. This was
> a bad day but now is a bad one. Selfe-
> -denial is a good thing and a vir-
> tue. (120–21)

And what has the virtue of self-denial wrought? Its legacy is already buried in Diary Two:

> I will never again trust in
> my own pow[e]r. for I see
> that I cannot be good with-
> -out Gods assistence, I will
> trust in my selfe & it
>   Isas health will be
> quite ruined by
> me it will indeed; (82–83)

This passage marks a turning point in Marjory Fleming's diary: a splitting of the self. Notice how Marjory artificially stunts the first sentence with a period. Is there ever a more poignant and defiant period than the one recording her disbelief in her own power? The homily that follows it, the received opinion of goodness somehow outside the child's self, outside Fleming's own creative nature, is separated and added on. It reads like a run-on sentence, a child's breathless confession. Fleming's guilt over the bad (i.e., spontaneous) behavior that tried Isabella's patience is evident. Yet it is Isabella, not Marjory, whom she puts in the syntactical doghouse of indentation. But Isabella literally has the last word. In lines five and six where Marjory had written "I will / trust in my selfe," Isabella's correction adds "never" before trust. The adult voice literally and figuratively corrects the child's. Note how Fleming uses the familiar "Isa" when she feels bad about something she's done, but uses "Isabella," as elsewhere in the diary, when she's being punished. The psychological distance of punishment is reflected in the instinctive use of the formal. More telling, from this point on in her diary, Marjory Fleming splits the word "my selfe" whenever she has to refer to herself.

3

That split was exploited in a deeper sense by Fleming's Victorian editors who began their careers nearly a half century after the above passage was written. If her diaries attest to Marjory's self-discovery through language, then, posthumously, they also chart the curious history of her diary's discovery and distortion by others. In his popular six-penny book, H. B. Farnie, Fleming's first editor, accurately portrays Marjory's two final acts: quoting Burns on her deathbed and penning a poem on a slate to Isabella. Yet, as his subtitle "*A Story of Child Life Fifty Years Ago*" suggests, his is less a portrait of a child writer than an opportunity for an adult writer to idealize childhood. In 1858 Marjory the child became Marjorie the text. Farnie's most obvious and egregious tampering with the text of her life is his literal changing of her name from Marjory to Marjorie. Not only did he change the spelling to suit (presumably) a more childlike spelling, but coined the sugary epithet "Pet" to precede it. (Surviving documents show her known in both the Keith and Fleming households as Maidie, Muff, or Madgie—but never Pet.) So lasting was this sobriquet associated with her fame, though, that even her modern tombstone in Abbotshall churchyard now bears both the pseudonym and misspelling "Pet Marjorie."

Marjory fared little better with her second editor. While in 1864 John Brown and Farnie were to engage in bitter—and public—literary battles over who was the more scrupulous editor of Marjory's diaries, Brown, though a careful transcriber of her manuscript, also proved unreliable. Until his own fifth edition he kept Farnie's misspelling and adopted the "Pet" epithet. More seriously, he was responsible for promulgating the Scott legend. The evidence for that link is tenuous. A relative by marriage on the Keith side, Scott spent his Christmases at Ravelston, and he and Marjory might have met in that large company. Brown's evidence for the Scott link comes from a letter Marjory's younger surviving sister, Elizabeth, wrote Brown in 1863 in which she claims that Scott had inscribed Maria Edgeworth's *Rosamund* and *Harry and Lucy* to Marjory. "I regret to say," Elizabeth Fleming wrote Brown, "these little volumes have disappeared" (Sidgwick 184). Given that Marjory's Bible survives with her place still marked at David's lament for Jonathan, it's hard to imagine that two books inscribed by Scott himself could have been mislaid. The evidence argues strenuously against their meeting. Not only is there no mention in Scott's journals of Marjory; just as significantly, the only reference to Scott in hers is that he is the author of her favorite poem. To read Fleming's diaries is to encounter a keenly aware child, one noting everything from gooseberries that make her "teath water" to missing the married Mr. Balfour whom she fears she'll never see again (Sidgwick 77). If she detailed her feelings for Balfour—as well as for the visiting sailor—she no doubt would have noted her meetings with her literary idol Scott.

Fame, if not of one's own making, can still be had by association with others. And there is no easier (and safer) source than the dead. This, most likely, is the case with Elizabeth Fleming, who innocently extended Marjory's (and therefore her own) fame by the familial link to Scott. Brown himself capitalized on this. While later known as the author of the popular children's tale *Rab and His Friends*, it was as the editor of Marjory's diaries that he secured his own reputation. In his elegy on Brown, Swinburne wrote that the author was now in, "Some happier isle in the Elysian sea / Where Rab may lick the hand of Marjorie" (Sidgwick xix). Whatever the reality of the Scott connection, Brown wrote an astonishing account from the slender evidence based on his correspondence with Elizabeth Fleming. In a typical example from his *Pet Marjorie*, he writes: "Sir Walter was in that house almost every day, and had a key, so in he and the hound went, shaking themselves in the lobby. 'Marjorie! Marjorie!' shouted her friend, 'where are ye, my bonnie wee croodlin doo?' In a moment a bright, eager child of seven was in his arms, and he was kissing her all over" (Sidgwick xvii). What Frank Sidgwick charitably calls Brown's "highly coloured opening" nonetheless prevailed as all subsequent editions of Marjory Fleming's diaries, including Farnie's quickly revised 1864 edition, were based on Brown's tale of "Pet Marjorie."[12]

It is worth considering for a moment a contemporary review of the "Pet Marjorie" booklet to examine attitudes about children writers. In a characteristic review of Farnie's 1864 edition, a critic for *The London Review* wrote: "She was the delight of Walter Scott, who was so much attached to her that when he was weary with literary toil he would send for his favourite to amuse him. He said that her repeating passages from Shakespeare overpowered him as nothing else did. Many of the extracts from her diary shew a wonderful precocity."[13] Here, true to her epithet, "Pet Marjorie" is suggestive of the literary child as trained family animal, domesticated. Adorable on cue. There to "amuse him." More significantly, here her diaries are literally commented upon as an afterthought. Now Marjorie's behavior, not her language, is what's at stake. And with this the irony of diary writing for a child comes full circle. The diary reverts to its original use: a forum for self-improvement, not of language. It is no longer her own words but the language of socialization that is applauded. Yet there is a deeper implication in the Scott link: that a child, especially a girl, wasn't quite allowed to achieve literary fame alone. She needed to be linked to a famous literary authority figure, Scott in this case (and later Stevenson, Twain, Stephens). Implicit in this supervised alliance is that, as a child, she shouldn't be allowed out alone, unescorted through her own literary consciousness. Artistic genius, as Judith Rowbotham argues in her study of Victorian girlhood and fiction, was only viable "where a self-sacrificing woman could do good, by bringing 'beautiful feeling,' if not (to) the absolute genius of men, (then) to a work of art or a performance" (242).

Fleming herself, no doubt, had little idea how prophetic her words would become when she wrote:

> A great many authors have expressed
> themselfes too sentimentaly I am stu-
> dying what I like. (105)

So, it seems, were the editors of her own diaries. While each successive editor provided more of her actual text—Farnie 1150 words of prose, 150 of verse; Brown 2380 prose, 100 verse; Macbean (in 1904) 8900 prose, 560 verse—it was still overshadowed by the "Pet" legend (Sidgwick xxi). In 1894, Robert Louis Stevenson wrote: "Marjorie [*sic*] Fleming . . . was possibly—no, I take back possibly—she was one of the noblest works of God."[14] Yet since many of her own words had been changed, how was he to know? While Macbean's only transgression was altering her columns into paragraph form, many of the textual errors resulted from accurately transcribing Brown's manuscript. Brown only selectively kept Marjory's childish misspellings, altering and lowercasing "devil," for example, in this essay's opening passage. In short, he kept her to sounding as adults *expect* a child to sound. While, like Farnie, Victorian propriety forced Brown to omit "my bottom" from the opening of Marjory's first letter: "I now sit down on my bottom to answer," other changes were far less innocent (Sidgwick 157). By deleting lines in Marjory's turkey poem, Brown made omissions which, as Frank Sidgwick notes, "conceal the fact that Marjory's best-known couplet is really a triplet" (189). More disturbing is Brown's coy assertion "And here is some more of her prattle" (22). But even her "prattle" is often changed. In her poem on Mary Queen of Scots, for example, what read "And I do think she gained a prise" becomes in Brown a hesitation: "I supposed she has gained" (147). Marjory's slipping into bed, "And with great care I myself keep" is rewritten as "And with great care within I creep." Brown's literal rewritings often suggest subtler aims: "the delight of my heart" becomes "the delight of my soul." Thus the concrete language (and organ) of feeling is supplanted by foggy Victorian metaphysics.

As John Pfeiffer argues in *The Child in Nineteenth Century British Fiction and Thought* (1969), no symbol more exemplified that metaphysic than a child: the emblem of innocence, untainted by sexuality. Here we need to look at the much deeper question underlying what Farnie referred to in his introduction as "baby literature" (x). The Victorians, one suspects, not only tolerated Fleming's literary precocity but actively sentimentalized it because she had obeyed a most cherished notion reinforced by many of Dickens's female characters: the good die young. It's as if Little Nell had left a diary. As Alexander Welsh discusses in his chapter "Two Angels of Death" in *The City of Dickens* (1971), underlining the Victorian notion of work is the celebration of sacrifice, especially by women and children. What could be more attractive, then, than a precocious diary kept by a child who died young? Fleming's juvenilia, unlike the Brontes's, never threatened to become adult (and female) literature. Passion never erupted into the threat of womanliness; the child is forever preserved in literary amber. Passion here is a child's temper tantrum, not its darker foreboding of sexuality. "The problems for the good girl, and for the author," Judith Rowbotham notes, "came when she stepped outside her natural sphere, whether voluntarily or involuntarily" (266).

Indeed, it's not Fleming per se who's implicitly being trained in her diary, but her social role. To read her diaries is to see that it's less Fleming the child than Fleming the future producer of children who is being so carefully shaped. Fleming's diaries then are primers for that favorite word of women from Queen Victoria and George Eliot: duty. As J. S. Bratton notes in *The Impact of Victorian Children's Fiction* (1981), the tidal wave of didactic fiction written for children between 1800 and 1850 focussed on shaping girls into "the unselfish woman, the potentially happy and successful helpmeet" (184). In her diaries, we watch Marjory Fleming literally learning the language of duty and, with it, that literature is incompatible with that end. One wonders if, in time, Fleming's restive intelligence would have dulled, her ambitions defeated by Calvinist homilies. Or if the columns of her diary would have literally flattened into prose recorded in perfect penmanship. If, in short, the diary would have become less like defiant raw poetry than a sampler stitched on long Scottish winter nights. Luckily, only Fleming the child answers back from her own pages.

Of all her editors, Farnie came closest to raising the single most thoughtful issue had Fleming lived. Towards the end of his narrative he writes:

> I have often mused on the probable destiny of Pet, if she had been permitted to live, and have arrived at the conclusion that she would have essayed literature in some branch or other. . . . If such, then, was the likely path over which she would have wended, had she lived, how merciful may have been the decree which had said she might not reach her womanhood. I have an idea, that the woman who has written books worthy of the world's reading—who has penned the emotions of a noble female soul—I think that every such one has lived in sadness and anxiety. . . . Who shall doubt this who has read the sad inner-life of Charlotte Bronte. . . . *Destiny* called Charlotte Bronte from solitude, from un-opportunity, from sorrow . . .—called her to write. And she did write—she could not help it. So do I think that had Pet lived, her career might have been the same. (60–61)

Yet let us consider this for a moment. Born five years after Marjory Fleming's death, Charlotte Bronte could roughly be considered a contemporary. The more fitting comparison, perhaps, is Isabella Keith herself. She is the important subtext in the Fleming narrative. Implicit in her shaping of her literary protégée is Keith's own ambitions. Marjory merely *does* everything that Isabella, now as a young woman of marriageable age, must do covertly: read, write, instruct. Wait for marriage. Literary ambition, as Deirdre David notes in *Intellectual Women and the Victorian*

Patriarchy (1987), is something most adult women often needed to legitimize *through* someone else, a child in this case. In this sense, Fleming's journals are a paradigm of female literary ambitions and realities: what is an acceptable activity for a child is later something she must sacrifice through or to others. And Isabella's fate? In 1824 she married the zoologist James Wilson, a naturalist and writer, and became *his* literary helpmate. She died in 1837. Her fate is summed up by her husband's biographer, who wrote of her: "Of human helps, the first and greatest undoubtedly was his excellent wife, and the consolations to which he was introduced under her gentle kindness became unspeakably precious when he was left again in the home of his pilgrimage" (cited in Macbean 127–28). "Of human helps," "consolations," "gentle kindness," these are the words of elegies. And here the elegy is literary. Unlike Charlotte Bronte, Keith followed Southey's advice: marriage, children, husband's career. These were the proper language of a life, the learned language in which Virginia Woolf's "Angel in the House" was fluent. The uniqueness of Marjory Fleming's diaries is that childhood and its original language of ambition are both preserved for posterity. The slow socialization of talent is still incomplete. In her sheer pluck then Fleming is closer to another precocious Scot—the clever Jane Carlyle who also showed all the promise of literary drive. Yet, as Phyllis Rose suggests in *Parallel Lives* (1983), despite or because of Carlyle's stormy brilliant marriage and its passport for her into London's literary circles, she was never able to break out of the forum of her diary and letters (243–59). Would Marjory Fleming have been any different?

In the end, whatever their errors in censorship and mythmaking, Fleming's editors—H. B. Farnie, Dr. John Brown, Lachlan Macbean—ironically helped preserve Fleming's diaries by keeping them firmly in the public eye. Yet if the public eye was where writers from Twain to Sir Leslie Stephen felt was the right place for her diaries, it isn't, one feels, where Marjory herself would be had she lived. Southey's admonition to Charlotte Bronte was far too prevalent a cultural belief. In our own age, one suspects, Marjory Fleming would have become an actress or possibly a playwright. The dramatic language of her diaries is too forceful not to find its expressive channel. Safeguarding that authenticity of voice, so prized by diary writers today, would be the order of the day. Yet Fleming lived in her century, not ours. In the end, Isa, the determined monitor, would have prevailed. Duty would have been done. Her diary and the writing of poetry in time would have become, in Southey's phrase, an accomplishment or recreation. If pressed why, Fleming probably would have recited from I Corinthians 13:11, lines that had supplanted her own: "When I was a child, I spake as a child, I understood as a child, I thought as a child; but when I became a (wo) man, I put away childish things."

NOTES

1. See Gay Daly, *Pre-Raphaelites in Love* (New York: Ticknor & Fields, 1989).
2. Since Isabella Keith's birth date was not recorded, she was estimated to be at least 11 years Marjory's senior. See Sidgwick xv.

3. Farnie's "Pet Marjorie" story appeared first in the *Fife Herald* in 1847 and was then published as a six-penny booklet in 1858. See Sidgwick xvii.

4. Arundell Esdaile of the British Museum published the first collotype facsimile of Fleming's manuscripts in 1934. His editor, Frank Sidgwick, transcribed and printed Fleming's work in a separate 1934 edition. Oxford University Press published Frank Sidgwick's edition in 1935.

5. Mark Twain's "Pet Marjorie" first appeared in *Harper's Bazaar*, 1909. See Moffat and Painter 21–22.

6. Leslie Stephen's 1889 entry reads, in part, "Her life is probably the shortest recorded in these volumes, and certainly she is one of the most charming characters" (281).

7. I have used the Sidgwick and Jackson 1934 text throughout, keeping all Marjory Fleming's misspellings and errors, and Isabella's corrections. Marjory's handwriting averaged six to ten words per line; I've kept the original columnar shape of the text.

8. For a discussion of nineteenth-century novels influenced by the notorious criminal recordings in the *Newgate Calendar*, see "The Newgate Novel" in *The Stanford Companion to Victorian Fiction*, ed. John Sutherland, 462–63. Palo Alto, CA: Stanford University Press, 1989.

9. See Sadoff, "Language and Mastery" chapter.

10. See Ruby V. Redinger, *George Eliot: The Emergent Self* (New York: Knopf, 1975); Winifred Gerin, *Charlotte Bronte: The Evolution of Genius* (New York: Oxford University Press, 1967); Brian Wilks, *Jane Austen* (London: Hamlyn, 1978).

11. See "Mothers and Children: The Relegated Roles," and "Self-Expression and Catharsis: The Role of Memoir," in Lynne Agress, *The Feminine Irony*. London: Associated University Presses, 1978.

12. Farnie published his revised edition in December, 1863, though, as Frank Sidgwick notes in his introduction, its British Museum title page is 1864 (xviii).

13. Quoted in "Opinions of the Press" in H. B. Farnie's 1864 edition of *Pet Marjorie: A Story of Child Life Fifty Years Ago*.

14. Robert Louis Stevenson's letter to W. Archer, March 27, 1894, quoted in Arundell Esdaile as an epigraph.

WORKS CITED

Benjamin, Jessica. *The Bonds of Love*. New York: Pantheon, 1988.

Bettelheim, Bruno, and Karen Zelar. *On Learning to Read: A Child's Fascination with Meaning*. New York: Knopf, 1972.

Blain, Vivian, Isobel Grundy, and Patricia Clements, eds. *The Feminist Companion to Literature in English*. New Haven: Yale University Press, 1990.

Blodgett, Harriet. *Centuries of Female Days: Englishwomen's Private Diaries*. New Brunswick, NJ: Rutgers University Press, 1988.

Blythe, Ronald, ed. *The Pleasure of Diaries: Four Centuries of Private Writing.* New York: Pantheon, 1989.

Bratton, J. S. *The Impact of Victorian Children's Fiction.* London: Croom Helm, 1981.

Brett, Simon, ed. *The Faber Book of Diaries.* London: Faber and Faber, 1987.

Brown, John. *Marjorie Fleming: A Sketch.* Edinburgh: David Douglas, 1893.

David, Deirdre. *Intellectual Women and the Victorian Patriarchy.* Ithaca, NY: Cornell University Press, 1987.

Dunaway, Phillip, and Mel Evans, eds. *Treasury of Great Diaries.* New York: Doubleday, 1957.

Esdaile, Arundell. *The Journals, Letters & Verse of Marjory Fleming.* London: Sidgwick and Jackson, 1934.

Fanger, Donald. *Dostoevsky and Romantic Realism: Balzac, Dickens and Gogol.* Chicago: University of Chicago Press, 1967.

Farnie, H. B. *Pet Marjorie: A Story of Child Life Fifty Years Ago.* Edinburgh: William P. Nimmo, 1864.

Fothergill, Robert. *Private Chronicles: A Study of English Diaries.* Oxford: Oxford University Press, 1974.

Gaskell, Elizabeth. *The Life of Charlotte Bronte.* London: Penguin Classic Edition, 1985.

Havlice, Patricia P. *And So To Bed: A Bibliography of Diaries Published in English.* London: Scarecrow Press, 1987.

Homans, Margaret. *Bearing the Word: Language and Female Experience in Nineteenth Century Women's Writing.* Chicago: University of Chicago Press, 1986.

Macbean, Lachlan, ed. *Pet Marjorie.* London: Simpkin, Marshall, Hamilton, Kent & Co., 1914.

Malet, Oriel. *Pet Marjorie.* London: Faber and Faber, 1946.

Mallon, Thomas. *A Book of One's Own: People and Their Diaries.* New York: Ticknor and Fields, 1984.

Mellor, Anne K. *Romanticism and Gender.* New York: Routledge, 1993.

Moffat, Mary Jane, and Charlotte Painter, eds. *Revelations: Diaries of Women.* New York: Random House, 1974.

Moglen, Helen. *Charlotte Bronte: The Self Conceived.* New York: Norton, 1976.

Nestor, Pauline. *Female Friendships and Communities: Charlotte Brontë, George Eliot, Elizabeth Gaskell.* New York: Oxford University Press, 1985.

Pfeiffer, John. *The Child in 19th-Century British Fiction and Thought: A Typology.* Louisville: The University of Kentucky Press, 1969.

Ponsonby, Arthur. *Scottish and Irish Diaries from the Sixteenth to Nineteenth Century.* London: Methuen, 1927.

Rose, Phyllis. *Parallel Lives.* New York: Knopf, 1983.

Rowbotham, Judith. *Good Girls Make Good Wives: Guidance for Girls in Victorian Fiction.* Oxford: Basil Blackwell, 1989.

Sadoff, Dianne E. *Monsters of Affection: Dickens, Eliot and Bronte on Fatherhood.* Baltimore: Johns Hopkins University Press, 1982.

Sidgwick, Frank, ed. *The Complete Marjory Fleming: Her Journals, Letters and Verses.* London: Sidgwick & Jackson, 1934.

Simons, Judy. *Diaries and Journals of Literary Women from Fanny Burney to Virginia Woolf.* London: Macmillan, 1990.

Stephen, Leslie, ed. *Dictionary of National Biography.* Vol. 19. London, 1889.

Welsh, Alexander. *The City of Dickens.* New York: Oxford University Press, 1971.

Wiley, Kate. *Pet Marjorie and Sir Walter Scott.* New York: Cochrane Publishing Company, 1909.

Willey, Margaret. *Three Women Diarists.* London: Longmans, 1964.

Narrating the Past:
The Role of Childhood and History
in Russian Literary Culture

ANDREW WACHTEL

The earliest Russian representations of childhood reflect one of the central tasks that modern Russian prose literature defined for itself at the beginning of the nineteenth century, the elaboration of an adequate means for expressing a new understanding of the past—that of the nation (history) and that of the individual (autobiography). This need was, of course, not unique to Russia, but it was particularly acute there. In Western Europe, the normative poetics of neo-classicism formulated in the seventeenth century disintegrated gradually in the course of the eighteenth. By the end of the eighteenth century, the prose experiments performed in the English and French novel gave writers the wherewithal to deal with the past in radically new ways. It is, perhaps, problematic to claim that new literary resources allowed for the consciousness of self that we find in Rousseau's *Confessions* or for the historical consciousness of the novels of Walter Scott rather than the reverse. But whatever the causality, the fact remains that autobiographical and historical expression of the kind pioneered by Rousseau and Scott would have been unimaginable in the framework of neoclassical poetics.

In Russia, neoclassical poetics were not assimilated until the mid-eighteenth century and they still held sway (despite some breakdowns) at the turn of the nineteenth century. Specifically, the influence of neoclassicism could still be felt in the almost complete absence of artistic prose in Russian literary culture at this period. Thus, when Russian writers encountered the literary practices of Rousseau (in particular *Julie, ou la nouvelle Héloïse* and *Confessions*) and Scott (the *Waverley* novels) and began to try to emulate them, they did so more with reference to European neoclassicism than to the English and French eighteenth-century novel. Not surprisingly, the Russian literary system proved incapable of dealing with new views of history and autobiography without radical modification. In order to assimilate these new forms, Russian literary culture needed to digest more than one hundred years of European development in little more than a generation, and the result was a strange set of deformations. Trends that had taken half a century to evolve in Europe were absorbed one on top of another, and literary models that were completely incompatible elsewhere frequently overlapped in Russia.

What does all of this have to do with historical and autobiographical narration? In Europe over the course of the first half of the nineteenth century a fairly rigid method of dealing with the past arose. In the area of history, the split between academic history writing (identified as nonfiction) and the historical novel (fiction) became canonized. As opposed to the eighteenth century, when writers like Voltaire and Schiller could produce works of history and of belles lettres, nineteenth-century novelists no longer produced nonfictional histories and historians did not dabble in fiction.[1] In the realm of personal history, an analogous split arose, here between the autobiography (nonfiction) and the usually third-person autobiographical novel (fiction).[2] Ultimately, in the spirit of the industrial age, these divisions (to a certain extent artificial ones, as we have come to realize) produced a seemingly rational division of labor between history and autobiography on the one hand and fictional genres on the other.

In Russia this neat division of labor never obtained. Unlike their European counterparts, Russian writers of belles lettres refused to allow themselves to be confined to the sphere of literature. They did not acquiesce to a sharp split between autobiography and fiction based on truth value and they continue to this day to combine history with fiction (see, for example, Alexander Solzhenitsyn's monumental cycle *The Red Wheel,* of which only the first volume, *August, 1914,* has been translated into English in its final form). Even more interesting, the hybrid forms they created to overcome the split between history and fiction and autobiography and fiction were analogous. In both cases, Russian authors produced a series of texts that display an ambiguous internal dialogue—texts of threshold literature that invite, indeed require, being interpreted as fiction and non-fiction simultaneously.[3]

Childhood descriptions came remarkably late to Russian literature. Indeed, the first full-scale description of childhood experience in Russian culture is Tolstoy's *Childhood* (1852). True, there had been a handful of fictional works in which child characters had appeared before the publication of Tolstoy's work, but for all intents and purposes childhood experience was not a literary fact in Russia before the 1850s.[4] Nor was childhood an autobiographical fact, at least as far as can be ascertained from published autobiographies. As opposed to the lavish amounts of space given over to descriptions of childhood experience in autobiographies from the latter half of the 19th century, autobiographies written before the 1850s rarely devote more than a couple of pages to the subject, and these are generally confined to setting out factual detail rather than attempting to recall the child's own perspective.

When Tolstoy came to consider how best to represent childhood—that is, the personal past—he evidently perceived the problem as related to that of how to relate the nation's past. The genre he chose to present the first detailed description of childhood experience in Russian—I call it the pseudo-autobiography—has clear structural analogies with the techniques Russian writers had already developed for dealing with history (and which Tolstoy himself would later perfect in *War and Peace*). It is, therefore, worthwhile to turn first to a brief look at the Russian literary approach to history.

Let us take as an example Alexander Pushkin's well-known historical novel *The Captain's Daughter* (1836). At first glance, this would seem to be an exemplary work of historical fiction, one that fits squarely in the tradition of Walter Scott's novels even as it modifies some of Scott's techniques. The story is narrated in the first person by Petr Grinev. Like Waverley, Grinev is an unremarkable person who, by some strange twists of fate, gets caught in the middle of an important historical conflict: that between the rebellious Cossack forces led by Emelian Pugachev in 1773–74 and the government of Catherine the Great. Like Waverley, Grinev has the opportunity to observe the conflict from both sides. And finally, as in Scott's novel, the hero of *The Captain's Daughter* is eventually reconnected with the government's victorious forces, cleared of suspicions of wrongdoing, and able to marry his sweetheart. The view of history expressed here is unoriginal.[5]

Unlike his great predecessor, however, Pushkin evidently did not consider the historical novel alone to be an adequate expression of history. Many readers must have been surprised by the novel's final paragraph: "The notes of Petr Andreevich Grinev break off here. . . . Petr Andreevich Grinev's manuscript was presented to us by one of his grandsons, who discovered that we were occupied with a work about the period described by his grandfather. With the permission of his relatives, we decided to publish it separately, choosing an appropriate epigraph for each chapter and permitting ourselves to change several names. The Editor" (8:374; translation mine). On one level, of course, this paragraph merely creates a frame that places the narrative in the venerable "found manuscript" tradition. For the Russian reader, however, it does a great deal more, for it points unmistakably to another text by Pushkin: the *History of the Pugachev Uprising* (1834). It is this narrative nonfictional history of the Pugachev rebellion to which Pushkin is alluding when he mentions being "occupied with a work about the period." That is, in the frame of his novel Pushkin reminds his readers of the existence of another text concerning the same period written by him but in an entirely different genre.

The *History* is a seemingly dispassionate third-person account of the rise and fall of the uprising, copiously documented and expressing a view of the historical process quite different from Grinev's. Whereas the novel emphasizes the perspective of an individual for whom accident and irony play a central role in history and for whom events are significant primarily insofar as they relate to his own life, the history has no room for an individual perspective. The historian does not see events in their unfolding presentness (as Grinev does), but rather looks back well after the fact on a finished sequence of events. The reader who recalls both texts is confronted with a paradox. Each presents what appears to be a monologic view of history. These views are quite distinct, yet they are produced by the same author. We realize eventually that this is the point—an adequate perception of history requires the observer (reader) to be aware of multiple potential modes of historical interpretation simultaneously, and it is precisely this awareness that is engendered by Pushkin's inter-generic dialogue of monologic works.[6]

The primary drawback of Pushkin's method of inter-generic dialogue is that readers cannot recognize its existence unless they know the two separate works and read them more or less in tandem. The obvious way to get around this weakness would be to combine fictional and historical narration in a single work, binding them in such a way that readers are no longer at liberty to ignore the presence of inter-generic dialogue. This is precisely what Lev Tolstoy does in *War and Peace*. In fact, he describes events of the Napoleonic period not from two but rather from three distinct monologic narrative positions. I call them the fictional, historical, and metahistorical voices.[7] The fictional and historical voices correspond, more or less, to the positions of Pushkin's fictional and historical narrators in *The Captain's Daughter* and the *History of Pugachev* respectively. The function of the metahistorical voice is to mediate the interaction of historical and fictional voices within a single text.[8]

In *War and Peace*, the historian's position is outside and a bit above the events he is considering, and after them in time. The historical narrative voice relates completed stories (usually, but not always involving nonfictional characters) with the full knowledge and analytical power that can only be achieved in hindsight. Tolstoy employs this voice in order to tell his readers what actually happened during the Napoleonic campaign, to set the record straight, as it were.[9] In contrast, the fictional narrator attempts to reproduce the experience of characters who know neither how specific situations will be resolved nor their own ultimate fate. The fictional narrator reproduces the perspective of the individual within the flow of history for whom a multitude of contingent possibilities exist. Although this narrative is grammatically in the past tense, it creates an illusion of presentness.[10] Ultimately, there is no way for readers to reconcile the two narrative approaches described here. They must instead realize that fictional and historical narration present different perspectives and different truths—equal perhaps, but separate, and shown here in dialogical contrast.

The formulation of the theoretical necessity of seeing events from multiple perspectives is provided in the epilogue to *War and Peace*. The metahistorian believes that in theory there must be laws governing history. At the same time, he realizes that no individual could survive thinking that life lacked any component of free will. The metahistorian in *War and Peace* is therefore obsessed with the question of how to reconcile human beings' belief that they can make free choices with the logical impossibility of this belief. This impasse cannot be resolved by Tolstoy on the level of philosophy. It can, however, be thematized on the level of narrative through the interaction of the historical and fictional voices in the text.

Turning back to literary descriptions of childhood, it becomes clear that Russian writers learned a great deal from the national tradition of inter-generic dialogue on historical themes. In the pseudo-autobiography, the author employs a first-person narration as in a standard autobiography. But the narrator does not possess the author's name. Instead, he is a fictional character who tells the story of his life, a life that within the Russian tradition at least has more than a little in common with that of the actual author. The pseudo-autobiography, therefore, allows in theory for a complex three-way interaction. The narration can issue from the point of view of the child, or from the point of view of the adult narrator who can modify, embellish, or correct the child's "memories," or from the point of view of the implied author who can lend his fictional characters as many or as few of his own memories as he chooses.[11] The problem of personal identity that is always present in any autobiography—that is, to what extent is the adult writer "the same person" as his or her childhood incarnation—is both complicated and simplified in the pseudo-autobiography. On the one hand, the ambiguous relation between author and narrator makes the problem of identity between author and child even more problematic. At the same time, the now-obvious fictionality of the child's perspective tends to make the question of identity seem less important.

From an author's point of view, the pseudo-autobiographical genre is ideal. By mimicking the form of the autobiography the narrative accrues many of its advantages—in particular, it encourages readers to indulge the irrational but common tendency to accept first-person narration as more true—perhaps because it evokes memories of what Philipe Lejeune has called the "autobiographical pact." At the same time, the author is not limited by actual memories, and is free to create a composite figure whose voice is not bound by the vagaries of memory. Because of the fictional nature of the narrative, the author need not worry that readers will question the accuracy of the child's perspective. We do not ask how the narrator could possibly remember details of his feelings, conversations, and observations at the age of two or three; instead of truth we demand only plausibility. The basis for the analogy between pseudo-autobiography and inter-generic dialogue on historical subjects is now clear. In both cases, authors choose to juxtapose the perspective of narration as if from the inside and in the unfolding specific present (the perspective of the fictional historical narrator or that of the child) to that of narration from hindsight and with full knowledge of the outcome of historical processes or childhood experiences being described. Neither perspective alone is considered adequate for a full portrayal of autobiographical or historical truth; instead, truth arises from the dialogic interaction of fictional and historical or fictional and autobiographical perspectives.

If we turn to *Childhood*, we can see just how the complicated orchestration of Tolstoy's three coexistent narrative voices works. The following passage concerns the feelings of the child observing the conduct of his mother's old nanny after his mother's death:

At the time I was amazed at the change from touching emotion, with which she spoke to me, to grumbling and trivial calculation. [The child's experience has been reproduced here: it does not analzye or seek to explain, but merely to present what happened. Of course the words "at the time" show that there is nevertheless a sense of lost time.] Thinking about it later, I understood that despite what was happening in her soul she still had enough spirit left to take care of her work. . . . Grief had affected her so strongly that she did not find it necessary to hide the fact that she could take care of other things: she wouldn't have even understood how such a thought could arise. [Here we are in the presence of the adult narrator who looks back on the raw material of the child's perception, interprets it and even tries to "correct" the child's impression.]

Vanity is the feeling most incompatible with true grief but, at the same time, the feeling is so deeply imbedded in human nature that it is very rare that even the strongest grief can drive it out. Vanity in grief is manifested in the desire to seem either afflicted or unhappy or firm. [This is the implied author's voice, which extrapolates from the story of the nanny and the child's reaction to it in order to show a general truth about mankind] (1:91; translation mine).

There is, of course, one more level on which the dialogue works—as readers we wonder whether this set of memories actually was Tolstoy's or whether it belongs only to his fictional creation, Nikolai Irten'ev. We cannot know this for sure, although we may suspect that since Tolstoy's own mother died when he was less than two, this particular scene is probably fictional. This suspicion does not, however, lessen the impact of the child's vivid memories, here or anywhere else in the text, nor does it mean that other sections of the book are not, in fact, autobiographical.

When later Russian writers chose to treat the theme of childhood, they frequently employed the pseudo-autobiographical model Tolstoy had provided. As opposed to Europe, where the pseudo-autobiography had no specific generic implications, in Russia it quickly became the vehicle of choice (indeed, practically the only viable genre) for literary descriptions of childhood.[12] By no means is this to imply that writers like Aksakov, Gorky, Belyi or Bunin merely repeated the Tolstoyan paradigm. As is often the case with the legacy of major writers, Tolstoy's model was modified and attacked even as certain features were borrowed.

Perhaps the best example of how far the pseudo-autobiography could be stretched while still remaining viable can be seen in Andrei Belyi's novel *Kotik Letaev* (finished 1916, published 1922). This work is also one of the most successful attempts in world literature at recreating the experiential world of a very young child and his earliest attempts at verbalization. The classic narrative situation of the pseudo-autobiography involves the presence of the perspectives of both an adult narrator (who is not supposed to be the author himself) and a child. This structure is retained throughout *Kotik Letaev*, and, considering the rapidity with which Belyi cuts back and forth between the two points of view, he can be said to develop this narrative technique to an extreme. The dual point of view, and hence the novel's connection with the pseudo-autobiographical tradition, is apparent from the first sentence: "Here, on the sheer-cutting brink,—I hurl long, mute glances into the past. . . . I am thirty five years old: self-consciousness has torn up my brain and cast itself into childhood" (9; all translations of this work are my own).

This is the perspective of the adult narrator who will illuminate his past incarnation(s) in the course of the novel. The image of the thirty-five-year-old narrator, who has reached the midpoint of his life amidst a mountain landscape, is undoubtedly connected to that of Dante at the beginning of the *Inferno.* Both narrators find themselves temporarily lost and in need of guidance to find their way again. For Dante, relief takes the form of a religious revelation which leads him on a long journey through hell, purgatory and heaven. For Belyi it lies within the self and takes the form of a mental journey back to the world of childhood and to the occult worlds which the child experienced before birth. In both cases the narrator's visions produce the work of art that is presented to the reader.

In earlier pseudo-autobiographies the narrative representation of childhood consciousness was generally quite simple. The narrative conceit was that the world should be described as a conscious but unsophisticated observer might have seen it. The adult narrator's perspective provided more complicated commentary, fleshing out the child's perspective. In Belyi's view, on the contrary, the child can see and experience things that adults can not. He possesses an inner vision to which the adult narrator is not privy. In this respect Belyi obviously drew heavily on the thought of Rudolph Steiner.[13] However, Steiner did not give Belyi any indication of how to express this philosophical/occult insight in a work of prose fiction. On the level of narrative Belyi had to find his own resolution. He solved the problem by reversing the traditional relation between the experiencing child and the experienced narrator. His solution manifests itself in the greater complexity of the child's "voice" (translated into words by the narrator) vis à vis the narrator's simple commentary. This, for example, is how the child's first memories are described:

> Here is my image of the entrance into life: a corridor, an archway and darkness; crawling things are chasing after me . . . —
> —this image is related to the one of striding along temple-like corridors in the company of a man with a bull's head who was holding a scepter.
> . . . .
> The voice of my mother cut through this:
> —"He's burning as if he were on fire!"
> Later on they told me that I was continuously sick (28)

Two possible interpretations of this memory are proposed. The child seems to have access to a world (the precise contents of which are not of primary importance) in which he is in touch with strange beings: a world filled with complicated imagery, often based on neologistic word use and paronomasiac or rhythmic connections between words. At the same time, the adult narrator proposes a rather mundane physiological explanation for the mythological world: the child had a high fever and was merely hallucinating. The latter explanation is not sufficient, however, for it fails to explain how the child could have visualized images which he had never seen or heard of. As a result, the adult's explanation does not cancel out the child's occult perceptions. Instead, it indicates that the adult narrator, although he can, with great effort, recall and verbalize the experiences he had as a young child, cannot return to that state; still, his literary intuition is able to recapture and transmit images that his conscious mind cannot adequately explain. Like the quests of almost all the narrators of pseudo-autobiography, the older Kotik's search is nostalgic. The time when he could actively read the record of previously existing worlds has passed; it can only be recreated by crystallizing personal experience in a literary text.

Of course, one of the main tasks of the pseudo-autobiography had always been to represent the development of a child over time. Tolstoy's account begins on Irten'ev's tenth birthday, and so he does not deal with the earliest stages of development. But in *Kotik Letaev* it is precisely the earliest stages of life, when the child starts to understand the concreteness of the world around him and to be able to depict it in words, that form the core of the novel. At this early stage of development, images and the words used to describe them are not always connected. One could say that the child experiences ambiguity because of his inability to differentiate signified from signifier. For example, Kotik's first remembered conscious image is of a lion. He first sees the "lion" while he is playing in a sandbox. The section describing this encounter is written in an intentionally confusing manner which, for a number of pages, prevents the reader from realizing that the "lion" was actually a Saint Bernard. Presumably the infant knows what a lion is because of some occult understanding of the concept "lion." However, this occult knowledge is inapplicable in the adult world where this preverbal lion turned out not to have been a lion after all.

As a child he never understood his mistake and it was only twenty years later, according to the narrator, that an aquaintance told him that "Lion" was the name of a Saint Bernard that had lived in their neighborhood. As was the case with the physiological explanation of the child's hallucinations, a realistic decoding of the childhood vision is not entirely satisfactory. In the narrator's present tense (that is, at the time of writing the novel) he knows that the lion was a dog, but he continues to assert that it was a real lion insofar as the word has the power to create its own reality. "Clearly there was no dog. There were exclamations: 'Lion is coming!' and a lion came" (48). The child's experience and the narrator's perspective are, therefore, in competition—depending on which point of view we wish to observe the story from, either of them could be correct. Most likely, Belyi seems to be saying, both are.

Thus far I have only discussed the dialogue between narrator and child in *Kotik Letaev*. But it is important to remember the constant presence of the implied author as well. In *Childhood*, the implied author appeared through his generalizing statements. In *Kotik Letaev* he is not present in the text itself, but rather in the text's penumbra. Belyi was an intensely autobiographical writer—many of his works have obvious autobiographical subtexts, including his "Second Symphony" (1902), the novel *Petersburg* (1916), the long poem "First Encounter" (1921), and the novel *The Baptized Chinaman* (1922, a sequel to *Kotik Letaev*), not to mention his trio of autobiographies from the 1930s. As a result, any reader of Belyi's texts is conditioned to expect the possibility that the author's presence hovers over a specific work. In this case, the fact that Kotik's father is a mathematician (as was Belyi's), and the conflicts between Kotik's parents (which echo those between Belyi's, as described elsewhere) make the autobiographical connection unmistakable.

That Belyi wished his readers to recognize the distinction between the narrator of *Kotik Letaev* and himself (and thereby to appreciate the dialogue between implied author and narrator as well as that between the adult and childhood perspectives of the narrator) can be seen in the remarks he made in his autobiography *At the Turn of the Century* (1930) about the relationship of his novel to the Russian pseudo-autobiographical tradition:

> Tolstoy and others took the later stages of a youngster's life; and they took it under different conditions; that is why they worked out a different language for memories; a linguistic tradition grew up; "Belyi" did not have a tradition for the notation of earlier events which were experienced in special conditions, about which we will speak later; thus "Belyi's" different language issues from different circumstances; thus, one shouldn't chide him for linguistic preciosity but instead ask the question, is it necessary to study the different circumstances of Belyi's naturalism? (165–66; translation mine)

In the Russian pseudo-autobiographical tradition the lost world of childhood, the happiest time of life, could be reentered only through memory. For Belyi there are two roads to childhood: one backward through the creative force of memory, the other forward, through death, which will physically bring him back to the world of "memory of memories."[14] The myth of childhood (in this case earliest childhood) as a kind of earthly paradise is still present in *Kotik Letaev*. But the content of childhood paradise is radically modified in accordance with the teachings of Steiner and with Belyi's private mythology.

According to Steiner, the child loses his ability to travel freely into pre-existing worlds sometime between his second and third year of life. In *Kotik Letaev* the loss of free access to previous incarnations is marked, and made up for to some extent, by the four-year-old's increasing ability to perceive new experiences in the physical world. In this regard, the sections describing young Kotik's first memories of the countryside are illuminating. For the young child, the entire universe had initially encompassed only his nursery. It gradually expanded to include his apartment, with a view onto the street and then to all of Moscow.

When the child is transported from the safe haven of his urban universe into the countryside, he feels as if his whole world has collapsed. It should be noted that in the Russian tradition of childhood autobiography (wherein childhood is almost always spent on an estate in the countryside) arrival in the city frequently put an end to many of the child's previous assumptions about life. Young Kotik's disorientation is the result of a journey in the opposite direction, but it is equally strong. He thinks of "the loss of old masses" and "the collapsed cosmos." Gradually he begins to explore the world around him, conversing with a chicken, discovering mushrooms in the grass, and so forth.

When he was very young, Kotik's understanding of self was fluid and abstract. Now his expanding consciousness even allows him to comprehend his own image, when he sees his reflection in a pond. At first he does not recognize himself and thinks he is seeing another "little boy" but, slightly later, when a surfacing fish breaks up the mirror image, he remarks: "Akh, the fishy destroyed him: I am the 'little boy'; it's me, akh, me that she has destroyed" (157). Thus, very gradually, the child's identification of himself with various pre-existing figures and worlds weakens, and the idea of a unique self, which emerges both from those previous selves and from the specific life situation of Kotik, takes form.

Ultimately, the way in which the narrator shows the child creating his own world, by concretizing external stimuli in a highly personal idiom, makes *Kotik Letaev* the spiritual history of a modernist. Whereas Realist writers accepted the existence of the phenomenal world and strove to show their younger incarnation's development in that world, Belyi's narrator both grows within the real world and creates (or rediscovers) other worlds in the process of writing. Belyi's experimentation bends the Russian pseudo-autobiographical tradition almost to the breaking point, but *Kotik Letaev* remains a recognizable member of its genre.

For Russian writers on childhood of the nineteenth and twentieth centuries, the consciousness of the child was fundamentally different from that of the adult. Consequently, the autobiography, which tends to favor the adult perspective, was only infrequently used. At the same time, fiction alone was also not seen as acceptable, presumably because Russian writers refused to give up the truth claims associated with nonfictional writing; instead, on the analogy of their inter-generic dialogues on historical themes, they created a hybrid genre that allowed for the virtually simultaneous expression of the experiencing, present-tense voice of the child and the past-tense, analytic perspective of the adult voice. These two voices were balanced by the actual or implied presence of an author, whose biography served as the material for the pseudo-autobiographical novel. In recent decades, postmodernist writers and critics in the United States and Western Europe have been striving to dismantle the boundaries between history and fiction and between autobiography and fiction. As they succeed, they may begin to realize what Russian culture knew all along—the most powerful way to present the past is through the dialogic interaction of different narrative perspectives. As far as descriptions of childhood go, this means that at least part of the truth must indeed come from the mouths of babes.

NOTES

1. "In the course of the 19th century historians withdrew more and more to the university, to be followed by historians of literature and literary critics; and thus history, like literary scholarship, passed from the hands of the poet and man of letters into those of the professor. . . . The old common ground of history and literature—the idea of mimesis, and the central importance of rhetoric—has thus been gradually vacated by both (Gossman 230–31).

2. It is true, of course, that some theorists of autobiography have attempted to extend the concept to include practically all works of fiction with autobiographical content (cf. Spengemann). Most critics, however, do draw a line between works of autobiographical fiction and autobiographies proper on the basis of the truth claims of the latter works (cf. Pascal, and especially Lejeune).

3. The term "threshold literature" was coined by Gary Saul Morson, who wrote that such works are intentionally created by their authors so that "it is uncertain which of two mutually exclusive sets of conventions governs a work. When this kind of ambivalence obtains, it is possible to read the work according to different hermeneutical procedures and hence, all other things being equal, to derive contradictory interpretations. Doubly decodable, the same text becomes, in effect, two different works" (48–50).

4. Karamzin's fragment "A Knight of Our Time" (1802), the first significant work of Russian fiction with a child protagonist, had no immediate influence. Goncharov's fragment "Oblomov's Dream" (1848) is the only other important fictional description of a child in Russia before the appearance of Tolstoy's work.

5. According to Lukács, "He [Pushkin] creates an historical novel of an aesthetically higher type than his master. We stress the word 'aesthetically' advisedly. For in the interpretation of history itself, Pushkin continues along Scott's path; he applies the latter's method of Russian history" (72–73). I am entirely in agreement with Lukács on this latter point.

6. The term "inter-generic dialogue" is, of course, ultimately derived from Bakhtin, but it was coined by Morson. He suggests the possibility (which is indeed the case here) that an entire tradition "may also be constituted by *inter*-generic dialogues with neighboring genres regarded as hostile to its core philosophical assumptions" (79, and for more 81–84).

7. For a fuller discussion of the interaction of these three voice positions, see Wachtel, *An Obsession with History*, ch. 4.

8. Ultimately, a reading of *War and Peace* in this context derives its authority from Tolstoy's own idea of his narrative method—for in his drafts for the depiction of the battle of Austerlitz, he spoke of his need to portray the battle "from the point of view

of military history [the historian's voice], from the point of view of epic poetry [the fictional voice], and from our point of view [the philosopher of history]" (cited in Zaidenshnur 348).

9. It has long been recognized, of course, that Tolstoy willfully ignored all historical facts that did not fit his interpretation of events. While a knowledge of this may undercut the reader's belief in the accuracy of Tolstoy's interpretation, it does not affect the balance between the historical and fictional voices in *War and Peace*, because their different perspectives are achieved not on the basis of the truth value of their statements but rather on their approach to telling stories.

10. Käte Hamburger first analyzed this narrative mode (which she calls the "epic preterite") in her classic study *The Logic of Literature* (see 64–81).

11. This form was not unique to Russia, nor was it invented by Tolstoy. Claudio Guillen uses the term pseudo-autobiography to describe a feature of Spanish picaresque novels, though these works are not, in fact, autobiographical at all. In my sense of the term, an autobiographical component is necessary. Some European works that fit this stricter definition include Constant's *Adolphe* (1816) and de Musset's *La confession d'un enfant du siècle* (1836). Perhaps the most famous European example is *David Copperfield* (1849–50, translated into Russian, 1851), which undoubtedly influenced the young Tolstoy.

12. Tolstoy's *Childhood* also served as the point of departure for the mythologization of childhood in general in Russia. Major pseudo-autobiographies devoted to childhood in Russia include Sergei Aksakov's *The Childhood Years of Bagrov's Grandson* (1858), Maksim Gorky's *Childhood* (1913), Andrei Belyi's *Kotik Letaev* (1916), and Ivan Bunin's *Life of Arsen'ev* (1932–33). For a full description of the development and workings of this genre and of the myths of childhood in Russian culture, see Wachtel, 1990.

13. Steiner believed that the very young child still had access to the spirit world, access that gradually disappears as the adult's consciousness develops. For a detailed discussion of the importance for Belyi's work of anthroposophical thought in general and Steiner in particular, see Alexandrov.

14. The epilogue of *Kotik Letaev* is constructed on the opposition of forward moving time and space with a Steinerian-influenced mythical belief in eternal return. The narrator repeats the stages in which the world opened out before him: "My eyes widen; and with an unseeing glance I look into space; events spring up like a village or the seasons of the year; the noises of time await me" (290). The widening of consciousness leads ultimately to death (crucifixion, in this case). After death, however, the narrator sees the promise of resurrection into the world he knew as an infant.

WORKS CITED

Alexandrov, Vladimir. *Andrey Bely: The Major Symbolist Fiction.* Cambridge, MA: Harvard University Press, 1985.

Belyi, A. *Kotik Letaev.* Munich: Eidos Verlag, 1964.

————. *Na rubezhe dvukh stoletii* (At the Turn of the Century). Letchworth, Hertfordshire: Bradda Books, 1966.

Gossman, Lionel. *Between History and Literature.* Cambridge, MA: Harvard University Press, 1990.

Guillen, Claudio. *Literature as a System: Essays Toward the Theory of Literary History.* Princeton: Princeton University Press, 1971.

Hamburger, Käte. *The Logic of Literature.* Trans. Marilynn J. Rose. Bloomington: Indiana University Press, 1973.

Lejeune, Philippe. *Le pacte autobiographique.* Paris; Editons Seuil, 1975.

Lukács, Georg. *The Historical Novel.* Lincoln: University of Nebraska Press, 1983.

Morson, Gary Saul. *The Boundaries of Genre.* Austin: University of Texas Press, 1981.

Pascal, Roy. "The Autobiographical Novel and The Autobiography." *Essays in Criticism* 9.2 (April, 1959): 134–50.

Pushkin, A. S. *Polnoe sobranie sochinenii.* 14 vols. Moscow, 1937–41.

Spengemann, William C. *The Forms of Autobiography: Episodes in the History of a Literary Genre.* New Haven, CT: Yale University Press, 1980.

Tolstoy, L. N. *Polnoe sobranie sochinenii.* 90 vols. Moscow, 1928–58.

Wachtel, Andrew. *The Battle for Childhood: Creation of a Russian Myth.* Stanford: Stanford University Press, 1990.

————. *An Obsession with History: Russian Writers Confront the Past.* Stanford: Stanford University Press, 1994.

Zaidenshnur, E. V. *"Voina i mir" L. N. Tolstogo* (L. N. Tolstoy's *War and Peace*). Moscow, 1966.

Pip as "Infant Tongue"
and as Adult Narrator
in Chapter One of *Great Expectations*

MARY GALBRAITH

Like autobiographers, fictional narrators may recount their childhood experiences from a number of different vantage points. As Dorrit Cohn points out in a review of retrospective techniques, there is a wide spectrum from "the enlightened and knowing narrator who elucidates his mental confusions of earlier days" to "a narrator who closely identifies with his past self" (143). In addition to this axis of identification/dissociation, a retrospective narrator also may "enter into" his or her lived experience as a child to a greater or lesser degree, from a "reliving" or phenomenological orientation to a conventional narrative distance focussing on external events and behavior.

Three of Charles Dickens's novels are modeled as biographies, beginning with the birth or childhood of the protagonist: *Oliver Twist, David Copperfield,* and *Great Expectations* all represent traumatic early experiences of the boy protagonist and the ways in which these events shape his growth and life. Narration in the first two novels defines rather simply the extremes of Cohn's spectrum: *Oliver Twist* is a child character whose thoughts are presented through a highly sardonic, evaluative, unidentified third-person narrator, while *David Copperfield* is his own narrator and makes a determined effort to re-enter faithfully his earlier self as child and to relive his early life.

In *Great Expectations,* however, while narrator and child overtly share the first-person pronoun and the name of Philip Pirrip, the overlapping of their experience and knowledge is more complex in terms of both axes—identification/dissociation and subjective immediacy/narrative distancing—compared to the earlier novels. The shifting relations between adult narrator and experiencing child are particularly striking in chapter I of the novel, and an analysis of this chapter illustrates how a "linguistics of consciousness" may elucidate issues of narrator-character relations in general as well as some of the ways in which a child's understanding

123

may be depicted in fiction. By a "linguistics of consciousness" is meant the study not only of traditional point of view ("Who speaks?" "Who sees?") but, more broadly, what levels and qualities of consciousness, feeling, and epistemology are represented in the NOW of the storyworld.[1]

I have divided the chapter into three sections, each of which roughly encompasses a different narrator-child relation: in the first section, the narrator separates himself from the child, but probes deeply into the child's experience; in the second, the narrator identifies with the child, but recounts events from a dramatic, rather than a psychological, position; and in the third, the narrator identifies with the child and enters into the child's lived experience. These three sections also correspond to the development of self-consciousness in the child: before, during, and after Pip's encounter with the frightening man later identified as Magwitch. That encounter marks a moment crucial to the formation of identity for both child *and* adult, as Dickens's multilayered, shifting narrative viewpoint suggests.

SECTION ONE:

My father's family name being Pirrip, and my Christian name Philip, my infant tongue could make of both names nothing larger or more explicit than Pip. So I called myself Pip, and came to be called Pip.

I give Pirrip as my father's family name on the authority of his tombstone and my sister—Mrs. Joe Gargery, who married the blacksmith. As I never saw my father or my mother, and never saw any likeness of either of them (for their days were long before the days of photographs), my first fancies regarding what they were like were unreasonably derived from their tombstones. The shape of the letters on my father's gave me an odd idea that he was a square, stout, dark man, with curly black hair. From the character and turn of the inscription, *"Also Georgiana Wife of the Above,"* I drew a childish conclusion that my mother was freckled and sickly. To five little stone lozenges, each about a foot and a half long, which were arranged in a neat row beside their grave, and were sacred to the memory of five little brothers of mine—who gave up trying to get a living exceedingly early in that universal struggle—I am indebted for a belief I religiously entertained that they had all been born on their backs with their hands in their trousers pockets, and had never taken them out in this state of existence.

Ours was the marsh country, down by the river, within, as the river wound, twenty miles of sea. My first most vivid and broad impression of the identity of things seems to me to have been gained on a memorable raw afternoon towards evening. At such a time I found out for certain that this bleak place overgrown with nettles was the churchyard; and that Philip Pirrip, late of this Parish, and Also Georgiana Wife of the Above, were dead and buried; and that Alexander, Bartholomew, Abraham, Tobias, and Roger, infant children of the aforesaid, were also dead and buried; and that the dark flat wilderness beyond the churchyard, intersected with dikes and mounds and gates, with scattered cattle feeding on it, was the marshes; and that the low leaden line beyond was the river; and that the distant savage lair from which the wind was rushing was the sea; and that the small bundle of shivers growing afraid of it all and beginning to cry was Pip. (9–10)

Great Expectations has a first-person main character. It also has an overt narrator "I." Although these two "I's" are the same person in the broad sense, they do not share the same knowledge and they do not share the same time and space. In the first few paragraphs of the novel, the distance between these two "I's" is of particular significance. In paragraph 1, for example, the narrator "I" refers to "my infant tongue," thus distinguishing his body parts into different existences between "then" and "now." But the word pronounced by this infant tongue, "Pip," may be accepted as the name for both "I's." The question is raised as to which parts of Pip's childhood experience are definitive for his whole life, and in what sense the narrator still "has" the experience of the child. What relation does the narrator bear to his own past tense?

Paragraph 2 begins in the present tense and directly refers to the "I" as narrator: "I give Pirrip as my father's family name. . . ." While describing his childhood worldview in the following sentences, the narrator puts an adult disclaimer before each belief he held as a child. His first fancies were "unreasonably derived"; the letters on his father's tombstone "gave me an odd idea"; while from his mother's inscription, which is directly quoted and italicized, he "drew a childish conclusion." Finally come the five gravestones of his brothers, which gave him "a belief I religiously entertained." The description of the five deceased brothers and his ideas about them is related in the register of making a living, producing a comical incongruity that distances the narrator from his childhood perception.

Paragraphs 1 and 2 thus introduce the reader to the child Pip as a thinking, perceiving, and speaking being, a member of a particular family, mostly dead, a child whose consciousness is ambiguously distinguished from, owned by, and disclaimed by the adult narrator. In one clause, for example, there is tense ambiguity about the persistence of an old (i.e., childish) belief: "I am indebted for a belief I religiously entertained. . . ." The present tense of the first verb, "am indebted," is discordant with the completed aspect of the second verb, "entertained." Does he still hold the belief or not?

Paragraph 2 reports childhood beliefs and perceptions, but its expressive elements belong mostly to the adult Pip. The content of the reported perceptions and beliefs is not, however, cancelled by the adult narrator's evaluative commentary. The sobriety and longing which any reader will attribute to the child in the situation described—that is, looking at and reading the tombstones of his parents and brothers and picturing his family from "clues" provided by these representations—is called upon without direct expression by the child. The child's consciousness is thus described, though not mimetically reproduced, and this consciousness haunts the paragraph "behind" the comic style of the adult narrator.

The impressions the child Pip creates of his family are entirely subjective and private, extrapolated as they are from the only physical evidence he has of them: their tombstones and epitaphs. He reads this symbolic evidence as icon and index—as direct resemblance and imprint, rather than as arbitrary sign (Peirce 2.274–3.03). But in a meaningful sense these signs thereby *become* his parents and his brothers, so reading is not empty. That is, these stones and their "characters" become, *for him,* equivalent to parents and brothers, and his perception of the stones is entirely colored by his equivalence (later in chapter I, Pip will point at a tombstone and say, "There, sir! . . . Also Georgiana. That's my mother," thereby startling his listener who is led to expect a living person). The nearness of the stones, both in actual proximity and in felt connection, to the bodies of his kin creates the only family intimacy Pip can have. This imaginative act of the child endows the stones with the power of existential relation and the power of identity.[2]

Paragraph 3 begins with the promising word "ours," which bespeaks group consciousness and affiliation. The past tense of "Ours was the marsh country" indicates once again the lack of continuity between the adult narrator and the child character; if the narrator were still living in the marsh country or still identified himself with the referent of "ours," he would use the present tense here. Still, this "ours" posits some kind of kinship identity for the child Pip. This first sentence of paragraph 3 also promises a sentimental description of native place. The preposing of "ours" gives a lofty, biblical syntax to the sentence, and the mention of marsh, river, and sea raises expectations for a traditional description to follow, praising one's home soil as the source of life, beauty, and value. The preposing of "ours" also topicalizes the possessive pronoun, since it constitutes a stylistic inversion (freestanding possessive pronouns are normally found only after the verb).

But the hopefulness of the word "ours" is completely dashed by the rest of the paragraph. The second sentence seems to ignore the first. In fact, the second sentence is the theme sentence of the paragraph that follows, since it introduces the scene to come, which in no way fulfills the optimism of the first sentence. The second sentence sets up the referential moment about to be described, the "memorable raw afternoon" when Pip gains his "first vivid and broad impression of the identity of things."

The expressive and stylistic effects of the third sentence of paragraph 3 are attributable to both the child Pip and to the narrator. "At such a time" suggests that the scene to be described is oddly both singular and normative, experienced once by the child yet generalized by the adult narrator. The words naively quoted from the tombstone are attributable to the child Pip, but these in turn are recounted by the narrator as an amusing (if poignant) mistake. The legal register of the terms "late," "the above," and "aforesaid" seems rather dry for a tombstone, but they are evidently taken by the child directly and without irony. Again, there is a big difference between the ignorant but profound directness with which the child "takes" his environment and the expectation at the level of narration that readers will see the admittedly black humor of using legal terms to refer to this devastating situation. However, in this sentence the child's own perception is not subordinated to the narrator's commentary as it was in the second paragraph ("childish," "unreasonable"). The most salient stylistic feature of the sentence is its set of equivalences:

actual perception	reassuring name
bleak, overgrown, nettles	= churchyard
dark, flat, scattered	= marshes
low leaden line	= river
distant savage lair	= sea
small bundle, shivers, afraid, cry	= Pip

On the right are conventionally hopeful terms of place and identity, while on the left is the bleak reality of the child's actual present experience. The child has learned to put some hope in the conventional connotations of words, but in this moment of realization he names objects as they exist *for him*, and perceives the inescapability of his situation. Words cannot protect him from the facticity of the universe, nor from the particularity of his own case. For him, home, parents, and native place are THIS: dead people, a bleak landscape, no nurturance or protection. The promise of the words "mother," "father," "brother," and "home" are not to be fulfilled for him. Hope has no power over this landscape. All of this is told in one long, poignant sentence, in which the child's perception is largely deferred to by the narrator, as indicated by the unshifted deictic "this" of "this bleak place." The child's "first most vivid and broad impression of the identity of things" is depicted not only as a first impression, but by inference as the forging of a template by which all conventional representations will be hereafter imprinted.

In this passage the child Pip is not deluding himself. His realization is the opposite of solipsism in its delusional sense; he is facing the difficult truth that "the world is not what I think but what I live through" (Merleau-Ponty, xvii). But the historical, factual world has imposed upon him a solitude from which there seems to be no escape, and in that sense Pip is trapped in the private world of his own thoughts and perceptions. With the exception of the ironic reproduction of the words from the tombstones, the narrator in this paragraph does not undercut the child's experience, but allows it to "fill up" the entire narrative frame.

THE MIDDLE SECTION

"Hold your noise!" cried a terrible voice, as a man started up from among the graves at the side of the church porch. "Keep still, you little devil, or I'll cut your throat!"

A fearful man, all in coarse grey, with a great iron on his leg. A man with no hat, and with broken shoes, and with an old rag tied round his head. A man who had been soaked in water, and smothered in mud, and lamed by stones, and cut by flints, and stung by nettles, and torn by briars; who limped, and shivered, and glared, and growled; and whose teeth chattered in his head, as he seized me by the chin.

"Oh! Don't cut my throat, sir," I pleaded in terror. "Pray don't do it, sir."

"Tell us your name!" said the man. "Quick!"

"Pip, sir."

"Once more," said the man, staring at me. "Give it mouth!"

"Pip. Pip, sir."

"Show us where you live," said the man. "Pint out the place!"

I pointed to where our village lay, on the flat inshore among the alder-trees and pollards, a mile or more from the church.

The man, after looking at me for a moment, turned me upside down, and emptied my pockets. There was nothing in them but a piece of bread. When the church came to itself—for he was so sudden and strong that he made it go head over heels before me, and I saw the steeple under my feet—when the church came to itself, I say, I was seated on a high tombstone, trembling, while he ate the bread ravenously.

"You young dog," said the man, licking his lips, "what fat cheeks you ha' got." I believe they were fat, though I was at that time undersized, for my years, and not strong.

"Darn me if I couldn't eat 'em," said the man, with a threatening shake of his head, "and if I han't half a mind to't!"

I earnestly expressed my hope that he wouldn't and held tighter to the tombstone on which he had put me; partly to keep myself upon it; partly to keep myself from crying.

"Now lookee here!" said the man. "Where's your mother?"

"There, sir!" said I.

He started, made a short run, and stopped and looked over his shoulder.

"There, sir!" I timidly explained. "Also Georgiana. That's my mother."

"Oh!" said he, coming back. "And is that your father alonger your mother?"

"Yes, sir," said I; "him too; late of this parish."

"Ha!" he muttered then, considering. "Who d'ye live with—supposin' ye're kindly let to live, which I han't made up my mind about?"

"My sister, sir—Mrs. Joe Gargery—wife of Joe Gargery, the blacksmith, sir."

"Blacksmith, eh?" said he. And looked down at his leg.

After darkly looking at his leg and at me several times, he came closer to my tombstone, took me by both arms, and tilted me back as far as he could hold me, so that his eyes looked most powerfully down into mine, and mine looked most helplessly up into his.

"Now lookee here," he said, "the question being whether you're to be let to live. You know what a file is?"

"Yes, sir."

"And you know what wittles is?"

"Yes, sir."

After each question he tilted me over a little more, so as to give me a greater sense of helplessness and danger.

"You get me a file." He tilted me again. "And you get me wittles." He tilted me again. "You bring 'em both to me." He tilted me again. "Or I'll have your heart and liver out." He tilted me again.

I was dreadfully frightened, and so giddy that I clung to him with both hands, and said, "If you would kindly please to let me keep upright, sir, perhaps I shouldn't be sick, and perhaps I could attend more."

He gave me a most tremendous dip and roll, so that the church jumped over its own weathercock. Then he held me by the arms in an upright position on the top of the stone, and went on in these fearful terms:

"You bring me, to-morrow morning early, that file and them wittles. You bring the lot to me at that old battery over yonder. You do it, and you never dare to say a word or dare to make a sign concerning your having seen such a person as me, or any person sumever, and you shall be let to live. You fail, or you go from my words in any partickler, no matter how small it is, and your heart and your liver shall be tore out, roasted, and ate. Now, I ain't alone, as you may think I am. There's a young man hid with me, in comparison with which young man I am a angel. That young man hears the words I speak. That young man has a secret way Pecooliar to himself of getting at a boy, and at his heart, and at his liver. It is in wain for a boy to attempt to hide himself from that young man. A boy may lock his door, may be warm in bed, may tuck himself up, may draw the clothes over his head, may think himself comfortable and safe, but that young man will softly creep and creep his way to him and tear him open. I am a-keeping that young man from harming of you at the present moment with great difficulty. I find it very hard to hold that young man off of your inside. Now, what do you say?"

I said that I would get him the file, and I would get him what broken bits of food I could, and I would come to him at the battery, early in the morning.

"Say, Lord strike you dead if you don't!" said the man.

I said so, and he took me down.

"Now," he pursued, "you remember what you've undertook, and you remember that young man, and you get home!"

"Goo-good night, sir," I faltered.

"Much of that!" said he, glancing about him over the cold wet flat. "I wish I was a frog. Or a eel!" (10–13)

Between paragraphs 3 and 4, a strange transition takes place. Paragraph 3 takes place almost in dream time, completely subjective and solitary. But suddenly: "'Hold your noise!' cried a terrible voice." The change of ontological realm, from sublime subjectivity to interpersonal emergency, is quite a jolt. This is heightened by the positioning of the directly quoted exclamation at the beginning of the sentence, without preface, so that the intrusion is not mediated by narrative preparation. This positioning "enacts" (Chatman 32) the child Pip's immediate experience as he is forcefully startled from one realm to another. For the reader as well as for Pip, the shout is a quintessential indexical sign in that "it is simply intended to act upon the hearer's nervous system and to rouse him" (Peirce 2.3).

"'Hold your noise!'" not only heralds a change of ontological realm in what follows; it calls into question many of the representations of the previous paragraph. It refers to noise being made, and the obvious inference is that the noise being made is the sound of the child Pip crying in the churchyard, at the time when the previous paragraph left off. If this is the case, then the temporal vagueness indicated by "at such a time" is contradicted. The exclamation, and the story which follows, also calls for a reinterpretation of the word "memorable." Paragraph 3 leads us to believe that the memorability of the occasion described was due to Pip's solitary realization, and that therefore his consciousness is the sole cause of the afternoon's specialness. He has put two and two together by himself, and come to a kind of mournful inspiration. But with the intrusion of the man we come later to know as Magwitch, this day's significance takes on a whole new meaning. The shock of Pip's encounter with Magwitch seems far more likely to be the source of both the memorability of the afternoon and the conclusions drawn by Pip as to his situation in life. Thus, instead of narrating a discrete moment of consciousness in the child Pip, paragraph 3 may be foreshadowing and summarizing the episode about to be recounted in the remainder of chapter I. In this case, "'Hold your noise!'" might *not* refer back to the child crying in the previous paragraph but would rather be the beginning of the story qua story. This reading is supported by the words "found out" in paragraph 3 which imply that Pip's realization came about as the result of new information provided by some event, and nothing happens in paragraph 3 that could be characterized as providing new information.

Magwitch's entrance is violent and sensational, both at the narrative level and at the story level, but after his outburst and threat to slit Pip's throat, a paragraph intervenes, entirely devoted to a description of the man, largely made up of relative clause sentence fragments. Since sentence fragments are themselves expressive of subjectivity (Banfield 39) they too draw attention to a subjective presence. But whose? Pip is a plucky and observant child, but it strains credibility that he would notice that the man has been "cut by flints, and stung by nettles" while the man is seizing the child by the chin. The obvious alternative is that the adult narrator inserts this descriptive passage as both a dramatic device and as a help to the reader in picturing the scene. However, the expressive effects of these sentence fragments seem more those of an embellishing storyteller than the elaborations of an adult Pip. They call to mind a virtuoso authorial figure rather than a "contained" narrator.

Further, the case relationship between the man and the violent verbs in the sentence is primarily one of patient (victim) rather than agent (attacker). He has been soaked, smothered, lamed, cut, stung, and torn. This makes the description all the more inappropriate as a rendering of the child's perception, and makes the "me" who is seized in the last clause of the sentence seem to be a very different consciousness from that expressed by the style of the sentence.

The complexity of narrative consciousness in this section is evident in another intervening description just after Matwitch comments hungrily on the child's fat cheeks. Here the adult Pip *is* the source of the subsequent affirmation of Magwitch's observation, and his present belief that his cheeks *were* fat evinces a tone of pride in the fact when the sentence is read aloud. While the child presumably felt threatened then, the narrator feels satisfied now, and it is only his present reaction that is explicitly expressed in the paragraph, as if he, rather than the child, were responding to Magwitch.

With the appearance of a second actor into the story, the chapter becomes dramatized. During the interaction between Magwitch and Pip, Pip's beliefs, thoughts, and perceptions are not reported as they were in the first three paragraphs; instead the narrative gives descriptions of actions and events, quoted dialogue, and adjectives and adverbs to tell Pip's state of mind--in short, something close to a nonpsychological traditional narrative. The only "inner" image in this section is the upside down church, which appears twice. But this image is literally aspectual: it does not contain the kind of creative perception that we saw earlier in Pip's vision.

The child Pip's expression in this section is limited to directly quoted speech, in which the child is constrained to extreme deference, obedience, and repression of impulses. Of course this lack of opportunity for uncensored expression corresponds to the reality of a situation in which one's life is threatened, but the narrative goes further in suppressing Pip's expression by converting some of the child's speech to indirect discourse. Magwitch's speech is never converted to an indirect report, but Pip's speech is indirectly reported or referred to three times during the conversation. On one occasion this indirect rendering appears to be fairly faithful to the actual words spoken: "I said that I would get him the file, and I would get him what broken bits of food I could, and I would come to him at the battery early in the morning." With the exception of "broken bits of food," the words could be a simple transformation from direct to indirect speech.

But on the other two occasions, significant expression is excised by covering direct quotation with paraphrase. The first is Pip's reply to Magwitch's stated desire to eat Pip's cheeks: "I earnestly expressed my hope that he wouldn't." One is reminded by the register here of the closing sentiments of a formal letter, and the use of this register to report the desperate cries of a small boy produces a distance once again between the attitude expressed by the narrative style and the existential position of the child. We know already (and will know much better in the next few chapters) that this small boy is capable of remarkable self-control, but the irony evinced here must be attributed to a higher narrative level than that of the character Pip. At the same time, the child is demonstrating on a muscular level the same capacity for dual attitudes: "I earnestly expressed my hope that he wouldn't, and held tighter to the tombstone on which he had put me; partly to keep myself upon it; partly to keep myself from crying." Thus the distanced style of the narrative and the child's muscular self-control are of a piece here; they each make possible the inhibition of "childish" expression.

The second instance in which indirect discourse covers significant expression occurs when Magwitch commands Pip to swear an oath:

> "Say, Lord strike you dead if you don't!" said the man.
> I said so, and he took me down.

The rationale for excluding Pip's expression here by substituting the proform "so" for his actual words might be that his actual words would merely repeat Magwitch's, with a change of pronoun. But this substitution does eliminate from direct expression an utterance which for the child Pip is freighted with momentous, personalized significance. The effect of excluding this utterance is to de-emphasize the personalized sense of occasion Pip must feel when he utters this awful oath. This de-emphasis is seconded by the conjoining of "I said so" with "he took me down," which effectively speeds us by the act of the oath to what happens next.

Magwitch's speech to Pip consists of demands for information, instructions for Pip to act, and threats as to what he (or his "young man") will do to Pip if Pip fails to comply. Magwitch's seizure of the child puts Pip on the spot; he is commanded to speak and act even as he is terrorized and constrained. He is forced to give account of himself clearly and boldly (" 'Give it mouth!' ") while completely under the domination of a man who literally turns him upside down. The effect of this on Pip must be both to shrink and enlarge him: he shrinks in fear, but he also takes on a new and important role as the addressee of all this wild attention. Someone is definitely noticing him and caring about what he has to say. Magwitch's threats are indications of his need for Pip to speak truly and to act according to his words. In other words, the relationship between Pip's words and their referents matters desperately to Magwitch. This is demonstrated when Pip answers Magwitch's question, " 'Where is your mother?' " by saying " 'There sir!' " presumably pointing to the nearby tombstone. In response to Pip's gesture, Magwitch starts to run away in fright.

The effects of Magwitch's presence on Pip are dramatized or reported rather than expressed by the child. Pip is not allowed by Magwitch to express his feelings in free action or speech, nor even in thought or perception by the narrator. This prohibition is forcefully expressed by Magwitch in his first words: "Hold your noise! . . . Keep still, you little devil, or I'll cut your throat!" By preventing Pip from crying out or moving, Magwitch completely cuts Pip off from spontaneous expression. The suppression of Pip's muscles and affect is imperfect—he trembles and stutters—but it is surprisingly well-accomplished; Pip is able to speak articulately and politely in order to save his own life. He even manages to make a skillful and rhetorically subtle speech at a moment when he ought to be incoherent: "I was dreadfully frightened, and so giddy that I clung to him with both hands, and said, 'If you would kindly please to let me keep upright, sir, perhaps I shouldn't be sick, and perhaps I could attend more'" (12).

The actions which take place while Pip and Magwitch talk are full of violent body contact. Magwitch grabs Pip by the chin, turns Pip upside down, tilts Pip again and again while putting his face close to the boy's face, and holds him by the arms. Pip's experience of Magwitch's handling is described as "terror" and "helplessness," leaving him "frightened" and "giddy," and the actions attributed to Magwitch give plenty of reason for Pip to feel these emotions and sensations. But we are given no evidence of how Magwitch's grip actually feels. Granted, such description is difficult, but it is not impossible: in *David Copperfield*, for example, the narrator remembers "the touch of Peggotty's forefinger as she used to hold it out to me, and . . . its being roughened by needlework, like a pocket nutmeg-grater" (61).

Only two descriptions of perception and feeling in this section may be unambiguously attributed to the child Pip's own consciousness. The first, already mentioned, is the reason given for Pip's holding tight to the tombstone: "partly, to keep myself from crying." The second perception from the child's point of view is the upside-down church. In the first mention of the upside-down church the narrator provides an explanation in an aside set off by dashes which serves to explain this unusual image to a projected listener/reader. The second mention of the upside-down church omits these narratorial helps, since the reader is now presumed to understand the odd reference: "He gave me a most tremendous dip and roll, so that the church jumped over its weathercock." This description uses Pip's own body as the source of stillness with respect to which other objects are judged to move. Still, the subjectivity the reader must inhabit in order to understand the image of the upside-down church is primarily physical rather than psychological, unlike the creative "vision" of the child in paragraphs 2 and 3.

In this middle section, a third character is introduced into the drama: the "young man" Magwitch uses as a further threat to induce Pip to obey. Pip never sees the young man (at least in this chapter), and knows of him solely through Magwitch's vividly frightening description. Yet the characterization "young man" is an odd one for such a monster as Magwitch describes; Magwitch's own appearance as described sounds a good deal more intimidating. Of course, the "young man" is later connected by Pip with the other convict who mysteriously disppears into the mist when the boy brings food and file to Magwitch. Most profoundly, the "young man" seems a magical allusion to the ambitions that Pip will later develop. Each sentence Magwitch utters here takes on new meaning when read as referring to the adolescent snob latent in Pip (e.g., "That young man has a secret way . . . of getting at a boy, and at his heart, and at his liver"), so that Magwitch's words may be seen as a magical oracle that only the adult narrator understands, and only in retrospect.

At the same time, he hugged his shuddering body in both his arms—clasping himself, as if to hold himself together—and limped towards the low church wall. As I saw him go, picking his way among the nettles, and among the brambles that bound the green mounds, he looked in my eyes as if he were eluding the hands of the dead people, stretching up cautiously out of their graves to get a twist upon his ankle and pull him in.

When he came to the low church wall, he got over it like a man whose legs were numbed and stiff, and then turned round to look for me. When I saw him turning, I set my face towards home, and made the best use of my legs. But presently I looked over my shoulder, and saw him going on again towards the river, still hugging himself in both arms, and picking his way with his sore feet among the great stones dropped into the marshes here and there for stepping-places when the rains were heavy, or the tide was in.

The marshes were just a long black horizontal line then, as I stopped to look after him; and the river was just another horizontal line, not nearly so broad nor yet so black; and the sky was just a row of long angry red lines and dense black lines intermixed. On the edge of the river I could faintly make out the only two black things in all the prospect that seemed to be standing upright; one of these was the beacon by which the sailors steered—like an unhooped cask upon a pole—an ugly thing when you were near it; the other a gibbet, with some chains hanging to it which had once held a pirate. The man was limping on toward this latter, as if he were the pirate come to life and come down, and going back to hook himself up again. It gave me a terrible turn when I thought so, and as I saw the cattle lifting their heads to gaze after him, I wondered whether they thought so, too. I looked all around for the horrible young man, and could see no signs of him. But now I was frightened again, and ran home without stopping. (13)

In the last section of chapter I, after Magwitch takes his leave, Pip's perception as projected or deepened consciousness returns to dominate the scene. We are reintroduced to the child Pip's body as the origin not only of his visual field but of his perception in the deepest sense: the imagination and creativity which gave Pip's "infant tongue" the ability to "call" himself and gave his young vision the ability to produce parental images from letters on tombstones is here reactivated within the frame, "in my young eyes." Other than this one framing qualifier, which is less judgmental than those found in the first section quoted, the last three paragraphs of chapter I do not contain distancing commentary by the adult narrator.

This last section is almost entirely devoted to representing Pip's psychological process and perception through psycho-narration and represented perception. Psycho-narration (Cohn 28–57) is the reporting of inner states of a character as propositions subordinated to psychological verbs such as "he thought" or "he felt." Represented perception (Banfield 183–223) is verbal capturing of nonverbal experiencing, such as the example from Virginia Woolf used by Banfield: "She sat up in bed and looked out through the slit of the blind. Through the gap she could see a slice of the sky; then roofs; then the tree in the garden; then the backs of the houses opposite standing in a long row" (Woolf 141, quoted in Banfield 201). As such, the *words* used in psycho-narration and represented perception, unlike those of represented speech and reflective thought, are not attributable to the character, even though the *sense* of the words recreates the character's own experience.[3] On the other hand, the words here do not call attention to a narrator's separate consciousness either. Framing verbs of consciousness and perception ("I saw," "I looked," "I thought," "I wondered") are here neutral and objective. Furthermore, the evaluative elements found in these last three paragraphs—"just" repeated three times in the first sentence of the last paragraph, "angry," "ugly," "terrible," and "horrible" applied to the landscape—are attributable (as experiences, not words) to the child's own consciousness.[4]

The last three paragraphs of chapter I, then, offer themselves as a faithful verbalization of the child Pip's perception, without discordant intrusion by the narrator. Of course, a completely faithful translation of experience into words is not possible: verbalization must transform experience. But there are degrees of faithfulness, dependent on the felt proximity of language to perceptual and bodily experience. As C. S. Peirce comments when describing the faculties necessary for phenomenology, there is a profound difference between an artist's (and the child's!) perception of the immediacy of a landscape and the casual observer's (or ordinary adult's) "stereotypic" view of the same landscape:

Where the ground is covered by snow on which the sun shines brightly except where shadows fall, if you ask any ordinary man what its color appears to be, he will tell you white, pure white, whiter in the sunlight, a little grayish in the shadow. But that is not what is before his eyes that he is describing; it is his theory of what *ought* to be seen. The artist will tell him that the shadows are not grey but a dull blue and that the snow in the sunshine is of a rich yellow. (5.42)

Similarly, in the first sentence of the final paragraph of chapter I, the landscape is described not as a composition of conventionally recognizable objects but as a composition of black and red lines which are linked to conventional, basic-level nouns.

conventional name		actual perception
marshes	just	long black horizontal line
river	just	horizontal line, not nearly so broad nor yet so black
sky	just	row of long angry red lines and dense black lines intermixed

The repeated word "just" between each equivalence has both emotional and conceptual import, expressing a direct experience of deprivation and a conceptual knowledge of how marsh, river, and sky are *supposed* to look. Similarly, the word "angry," which attributes intentionality to lines in the sky, expresses both a directly felt threat and an aesthetic, "as if" sensibility. Dividing up these directly felt experiences and conceptual characterizations between the consciousness of the child and the consciousness of the narrator is a matter for conjecture. We can be sure that the child felt the deprivation and the threat, and we can be sure that the narrator knows about perceptual and aesthetic convention. But how much the child knows, and how much the narrator feels, is unclear in a fruitful way. The lines of past and present become blurred and intertwined.

As the table above suggests, there is a strong relationship between the last paragraph in the chapter and paragraph 3. The two paragraphs share a psychologically loaded landscape of sky, marsh, cattle, river, and sea, and both paragraphs contain lists of equivalences between conventionally positive terms and existentially negative phenomena. In both paragraphs the verb "to be" is used repeatedly to link these two incommensurable but nevertheless inseparable universes: the conventional social world and the immediate experience of one's own predicament. Both paragraphs end with the naming and dramatizing of fear, fear aroused by a landscape whose appearance both constitutes and reflects the child's distress.

The question arises, then: are the two paragraphs "about" the same event? Is the situation in the last paragraph, influenced as it is by all that has happened in the middle section between Pip and Magwitch, the occasion of the realization described in paragraph 3? If it is, then it would be necessary to use psychoanalytic narrative logic to explain the differences between the two accounts: the repression of Magwitch's role in the account in paragraph 3, the re-emergence of Magwitch through abreactive memory in the middle section, and his restoration into the landscape in the last section. This sort of logic, though, would recast the chapter as a case study of the adult narrator, which is not the way it presents itself.

In terms of story-level motivation rather than the narrator's psychology, the two paragraphs reflect the difference in the child Pip's perception and existential situation before and after Magwitch's appearance on the scene. In the earlier landscape, nature is a flat wasteland and people are dead and buried, hence horizontal and invisible, without actual effect and conjurable only by a creative imagination. In the later landscape, after Pip's brutal encounter with Magwitch, nature becomes further abstracted and actively hostile, and human presence, in the form of things which stand upright, comes alive on the horizon. The later scene contains a man walking, drawing attention to the vertical and intentional. In addition, there is an unlit beacon and a gibbet, which duplicate the vertical attitude of the man and conventionally symbolize his hopes and nightmares. Like other conventionally positive terms in this chapter, the beacon does not fulfill such a role—it is not lit, and it is ugly. But the negative connotations of the gibbet are powerfully fulfilled; it not only resonates with fear but is brought into active service by Pip's imagination: he sees Magwitch walking toward the gibbet "as if" he were a hanged man who had left the scene of his execution and now returned to hang himself up again. Despite the "as if," the effect of this perception is somatic and immediate: "It gave me a terrible turn when I thought so, and as I saw the cattle lifting their heads to gaze after him, I wondered whether they thought so, too." This singular thought indicates both the strength of the child Pip's imagination and his uncertainty about the source of his imaginative experience. The cattle are reacting, in some sense, to the same stimulus which has gripped Pip. They notice the man walking near them, and raise their heads to look at him, thus affirming his intersubjective reality. At what point do Pip's perception of the man and that of the cattle diverge? For Pip, this is an open question. The possibility that the cattle may be "in on" the "as if" possibilities of the scene is both fascinating and frightening; fascinating because this would reduce the alienation of the landscape, and frightening because it would mean that Pip's vision is not a private fiction but a horrifying creation out of his control. Before his encounter with Magwitch, the landscape has been grim and dead, but mappable; after his encounter with Magwitch, the world comes alive, but its life is unpredictable and uncaring, a consciousness capable of retribution but not guidance.

Pip's fantasy of the hands reaching out of the graves and his wondering whether the cows share his perception both raise the question of the motivation behind his perceptions: does he see in this way as a fulfillment of his own desire, or as a clairvoyant glimpse of the reality behind outward appearances? If his own unconscious desire is the cause of these images, and if these images have some direct effect on reality, then his fantasies are dangerous both to himself and to others. This possibility suggests that the story to come may be influenced by the hero's fantasies, even if he does nothing to realize them.[5] This kind of plot logic is not forbidden, but it is not realistic. It recalls, instead, the "primary process" narrative logic of fairy tales and dreams, in which wishes magically become events. Belief in magical thinking may be "childish" and "unreasonably derived," but it cannot be argued away.

Neither can the facticity of Magwitch be argued away. He is not merely a dream figure or a plot device. His presence as a bodily character is at first overwhelmingly, brutally Other and strange to Pip. It is only when he is at a safe distance, walking away, that Pip can safely imagine him as a fictional character. In his actual encounter with Magwitch Pip's isolation is completely disrupted. "Hold your noise!" is a world-shattering surprise.

Unlike *David Copperfield*, *Great Expectations* is not a memoir. The reports of Pip as narrator about Pip as character are not given in the language of memory, but retain for the most part the traditional epistemological separation between narrator and third-person character. By contrast, in the "first impression" section of the earlier novel, David the narrator looks "far back, into the blank of my infancy," where "I have an impression on my mind which I cannot distinguish from actual remembrance," and enters the past but retains the present tense as he relives it: "There comes out of the cloud, our house—not new to me, but quite familiar, in its earliest remembrance. On the ground floor is Pegotty's kitchen. . . . There is one cock who . . . seems to take particular notice of me as I look at him through the kitchen window, who makes me shiver, he is so fierce" (62). The distance between the now of speaking and the now of the narrated event is collapsed. In Karl Bühler's phrase, Mohammad has gone to the mountain—the narrator has transported himself to the place/time of which he speaks (28).

By contrast, the distance between the narrator and the child is never completely collapsed in the recounting of the child Pip's first impressions, despite one instance of a proximal deictic ("*this* bleak place").[6] Instead, the narrator either distances himself from the child or he disappears, leaving the field to the child. He has access to the child's consciousness, but he does not frame this access as "memory." In short, he behaves as an extradiegetic or a witness narrator rather than as a memoirist.

In each of the three sections of the chapter—before Magwitch's appearance, the encounter with Magwitch, and his going away—there are significant differences in the adult narrator's role with regard to the child character. In the first section, the narrator reports past events accompanied by an overt marking of his own differences from the child's perspective. He evaluates the child's beliefs and takes an ironic position that contrasts strongly with the child's own immersion in his situation, a stance reminiscent of the opening pages of *Oliver Twist*, in which breathing is referred to as a "troublesome practice, but one which custom has rendered necessary to our easy existence" (23–24). The effect is comical understatement, but the narrative register of the later work is far more richly child-centered and variable.

Indeed, in the second section, the narrator virtually disappears. The evaluative adjectives and adverbs here—"terrible," "fearful," "helplessly," "dreadfully"—do not draw a line between the narrator's and the child's experience as they did in the first section ("unreasonably," "odd," "childish"). But the narrative does not enter strongly into the child's experience either, except to the limited extent of presenting the child's angle of vision when he is upside down and naming the child's feelings as fear, helplessness, terror, and giddiness. The orientational center shifts in the middle section from the child's consciousness and the narrator's judgment to a more free-standing dramatic position. One way of illustrating this is to imaginatively convert the chapter into a film representation. The first section could not be presented faithfully without a narrative voice-over, nor without at least one impressionistic shot meant to convey the character's psychologically colored vision. The second section, on the other hand, demands a presentation without narrative voice-over and without a subjective point of view except for the angle-of-vision change for the upside-down church.

Continuing this imaginative filming, the third section would have to be shot entirely as a subjective, impressionistic sequence. A narrative voice-over would destroy the force of these last paragraphs, in which narration is devoted whole-heartedly to the child Pip's perspective, as the child's perception re-emerges to dominate the scene. The look and feel of the landscape, the hands reaching up out of graves, the pirate going to hook himself on the gibbet, and the wondering cows are inaccessible except through the child Pip's consciousness, not only as a visual point of view, but as creative projections of his desire, vulnerability, imagi-nation, and insight. This last section, then, comes close to a modernist rendition of subjectivity as a complex fusion of inner and outer events. The syntax, verb tense, and word choice of the passage are not directly expressive of the child's consciousness; the style is not stream-of-consciousness or internal monologue. But the passage uses subjective narrative techniques which capture the child's percep-tual and reasoning processes without the distancing imposition of adult evalua-tions, and thus qualifies as what Chatman calls "perceptual internal monologue," which he defines as "the communication by conventional verbal transformation, . . . of the character's unarticulated sense impressions (without a narrator's internal analysis)" (188).

Without limiting itself to mimetic reproduction of the boy Pip's articula-tions, therefore, the chapter richly conveys the experience of being a child. More-over, because the mediating adult narrator seems variously present and absent, the interchange between child and adult consciousness is more fluid than in *Oliver Twist*, where the narrator is disassociated from the subject, or in *David Copperfield*, where the immediacy of childhood experience depends upon effacing the adult through the fictive summoning of memory. That the adult has retained the name Pip—the "infant tongue" 's foreshortened sign of his own identity—suggests that chapter 1 does not simply narrate the past experience of a child but recovers the source of the adult's continuing identity. As a moment of origin, the encounter with Magwitch is shown to have provoked the subject's first awareness of his own place in the universe and the logic for the life story that will make up the rest of *Great Expectations*.

Dramatically speaking, the chapter moves from a scene of developmentally motivated perception, to a scene of externally imposed action, to a scene of dra-matically charged perception. Each scene has its own kind of subjectivity, and when the complexities of the narrator are added, the result is a dense interaction of ontological realms and possibilities: subjectivity as bodily and intellectual un-folding, as biography, as memory, as lofty perspective, as suffering, as imagining, as feeling, as holding on, as speaking, as appearing, as fantasizing, as wanting. But the primal moment of subjectivity, and the one which colors all the others to come, is suffered by the "bundle of shivers" whose cries of human need go either unanswered or are answered with a bellowing "Hold your noise!"

NOTES

1. For approaches to a "linguistics of subjectivity," see Banfield, Kuroda, Gal-braith, Li, and Wiebe.

139

2. Using Searle's notions of word-to-world fit and world-to-word fit, Pip's relations to the stones can be described as follows: Pip takes the characters and shapes of the tombstones as signs with a word-to-world fit, that is, as signs which mean because they refer to and faithfully describe a reality beyond and before them. By his belief, he *creates* a world which from a non-believer's standpoint has a world-to-word fit, as a "reality" conjured to fit the meaning of the signs as he interprets them.

3. With Banfield, I consider that the presence of words not attributable to a character does not "prove" the existence of a narrator (in the sense of a fictional persona "telling the story"), since according to the conventions of fiction, language may be completely objective (that is, fictional sentences may simply declare that a state of affairs exists without being anyone's argument or assertion). Even though there is definitely a narrator in *Great Expectations,* this narrator is realized to differing degrees according to specific linguistic signs of his presence, as this analysis of chapter I illustrates.

4. One possible exception is the aside about the beacon, "—an ugly thing when you were near it," which contains both an evaluation and an informal use of the second-person pronoun in its sense of "one," but really meaning "I." This use indicates a "reliving" of repeated childhood experience with the beacon, and thus constitutes the only example in this chapter of the narrator entering into felt-relations with the world of the story.

5. That magical thinking plays a part in the plot of *Great Expectations* has been well argued by Julian Moynahan in his essay, "The Hero's Guilt." As he points out, the apparent discrepancy later in the novel between Pip's sense of guilt and his actual wrongdoing can only be explained by positing a causal connection between Pip's mind and events in the novel. Events in which Pip seems to have no hand, like the bludgeoning of his sister and the burning of Miss Havisham, can be read as the translation into reality of his revenge fantasies.

6. In the reliving form of narrative that opens *David Copperfield,* deictics are not shifted, even though the events spoken of are in the past. "Here" does not become "there," "now" does not become "then," as they do in chapter I of *Great Expectations.*

Works Cited

Banfield, Ann. *Unspeakable Sentences.* London: Routledge and Kegan Paul, 1982.

Bühler, Karl. "The Deictic Field of Language and Deictic Words." Trans. R. Jarvella and W. Klein. In *Speech, Place and Action: Studies in Deixis and Related Topics,* ed. R. Jarvella and W. Klein. Chichester: John Wiley and Sons, 1982.

Chatman, Seymour. *Story and Discourse.* Ithaca, NY: Cornell University Press, 1975.

Cohn, Dorrit. *Transparent Minds.* Princeton: Princeton University Press, 1978.

Dickens, Charles. *Great Expectations.* New York: Signet, 1980.

———. *Oliver Twist.* New York: Signet, 1980.

———. *The Personal History of David Copperfield.* Baltimore/Middlesex: Penguin, 1966.

Galbraith, Mary. "Subjectivity in the Novel. Diss.", SUNY Buffalo, 1990.

Genette, Gerard. *Narrative Discourse.* Trans. Jane E. Lewin. Ithaca, NY: Cornell University Press, 1986.

Kuroda, S. Y. "Where Epistemology, Style, and Grammar Meet: A Case Study from Japanese." In *A Festschrift for Morris Halle,* ed. P. Kiparsky and S. Anderson, 377–91. New York: Holt, Rinehart and Winston.

Lakoff, George. *Women, Fire, and Dangerous Things: What Categories Reveal about the Mind.* Chicago: University of Chicago Press, 1987.

Li, Naicong. "Perspective-taking in Mandarin Discourse." Diss., SUNY Buffalo, 1991.

Merleau-Ponty, Maurice. *Phenomenology of Perception.* Trans. Colin Smith. London: Routledge and Kegan Paul, 1962.

Moynahan, Julian. "The Hero's Guilt: The Case of *Great Expectations.*" In *Victorian Literature,* ed. Robert O. Preyer. New York: Harper and Row, 1967.

Peirce, Charles S. *Collected Papers of Charles Sanders Peirce.* 8 vols. Vols. 1–6 ed. Charles Hartshorne and Paul Weiss. Vols. 7–8 ed. Arthur W. Burks. Cambridge: Harvard University Press, 1931–1958.

Searle, John. *Intentionality.* Cambridge: Cambridge University Press, 1983.

Wiebe, Janyce M. "Recognizing Subjective Sentences: A Computational Investigation of Narrative Text." Technical Report 90–03. Buffalo: SUNY Buffalo Dept. of Computer Science, 1990.

Woolf, Virginia. *The Years.* London: Hogarth Press, 1990.

"Vers l'Une, Vers l'Autre, Verlaine":
Rimbaud and the Riddle of the Sphinx

Michael Lastinger

Few writers have been the object of more wild speculation and extravagant interpretation than Arthur Rimbaud (1854–1891), the French poet who, despite having ended his literary career by the time he was twenty years of age, is considered by many to be one of the most influential and revolutionary writers of modern times. Depending on the critic, Rimbaud is a fountain of political, historical, religious, psychological, mystical, or metaphysical meaning. Again, depending on the critic, the sources of Rimbaud's inspiration can be traced to his involvement in the Paris Commune of 1871, his reading of the Bible, or his study of alchemy and the kabbala. Whatever ultimate significance scholars attribute to Rimbaud's work, most agree that the poet's childhood is both a source of inspiration and a constant theme throughout his short literary career. Some have even argued that it is in fact Rimbaud's proximity to his own childhood during the brief years of his literary activity that gives his poetry its unique quality. As Wallace Fowlie queries and then suggests of Rimbaud, "Was he a prophet? genius? mythical figure? He was a poet, but not an ordinary poet. He was a child expressing himself in the language of a man" (5).

The nature of Rimbaud's poetic language will be the primary object of this study, but intricately woven into the extravagant beliefs concerning Rimbaud's poetic work are the equally extravagant stories of Rimbaud's life itself. It has been more than a quarter century now since Etiemble tried in his monumental *Le Mythe de Rimbaud* (The Myth of Rimbaud) to squelch the rumors and speculations surrounding the life and work of a person who is considered almost universally to be one of the world's greatest poets. Etiemble has made a great contribution to our understanding of Rimbaud in a more "realistic" light, but he has hardly succeeded in reducing the fascination of the Rimbaud legend.

It is of course Rimbaud's stature as one of our foremost poets that contributes in large part to the myths and stories surrounding him. But perhaps even more important is the strange mixture of what we do and do not know about him. We do know that he was born in 1854 in a small, provincial town in northern France and that he spent his earliest years in the bosom of a family that had as little interest in poetry as the townsfolk milling around the local market-place. We know that Rimbaud produced his greatest work beginning at the age of fourteen and that soon after his twentieth year he abandoned literature forever. We know that he ran away from home on several occasions as a boy and that he continued his wanderings throughout a life of adventure that would lead him to places like Paris, London, Stockholm, Stuttgart, and Java, and through the deserts of Abyssinia. Rimbaud was the first European to tread many of the paths he followed, and where there were no paths he blazed new ones both geographically and artistically. We know of Rimbaud's emotionally turbulent, socially scandalous, and sometimes physically violent relationship with the equally important poet Paul Verlaine (1844–1896)—a relationship that ended in 1873 in a scene involving gun shots that sent Rimbaud to a Brussels hospital and Verlaine to a Belgian prison. We do indeed know many details concerning these and other significant moments of Rimbaud's life.

But alongside the intriguing facts of Rimbaud's life and the powerful poetic works that are unmistakably connected to that life are the great gaps to which Rimbaud's readers seem so irresistibly drawn. This is hardly surprising given that, as we shall see, some of the most extravagant stories date from the poet's earliest infancy and were probably propagated by his mother. In addition, many of Rimbaud's public pranks seem calculated to upset the bourgeois values of his contemporaries and to invite conjecture as to his private behavior. It is only natural, then, that the speculation about the relation between Rimbaud's life and his work is part of a tradition that dates back to the poet's earliest biographers and continues to flourish even today. One thinks, for example, of the contemporary American novelist Kathy Acker's recent work, *In Memoriam to Identity*, which begins with her own rewriting of Rimbaud's early years and his adventures with Verlaine, or of the Oliver Stone film, *The Doors*, in which Jim Morrison cites Rimbaud's "Voyant" letters as he explains his life and his work to a hostile journalist.

The purpose of the present study is, therefore, to explore the relation between Rimbaud's poetic language and the manner in which that language seems to be determined by the poet's childhood experience of the world. I hope to show that one of the keys to understanding Rimbaud's poetic voice is a recognition of the degree to which this boy genius is a rare, if not unique, example of the literary *infans loquens*. As both the oxymoron and Fowlie's remark suggest, Rimbaud is a child speaking, but a child speaking an "adult" language that is, for reasons that will become evident as I proceed, all but completely closed off to him. Central to my exploration of Rimbaud's poetry as that of "a child expressing himself as a man" will be a consideration of recent psychoanalytical findings which link certain

143

forms of childhood trauma, including both emotional and sexual abuse, to their manifestations in the language and "mythology" of the survivor.

A first step in this exploration must obviously involve a brief consideration of Rimbaud's age during the years of his poetic production. In contemporary terms those years, from the age of fourteen to twenty, cover those of the modern day adolescent. The French historian Philippe Ariès points out however that the idea of adolescence is a very recent one, gaining full hold only in the years after World War I (48–51).[1] Strictly speaking, nineteenth-century France recognized only ritual passages that led directly from childhood to adulthood, typically such things as marriage, joining the army, and completing an education or vocational training. Rimbaud's poetic career spans the years when one might have expected one of these passages to have occurred. The conspicuous absence of any such ritual from these years of Rimbaud's life suggests that in one major sense he remained a child some time past the time he should have become a "man." As we shall see, Rimbaud's traumatic relationships with the adults he knew from his earliest years on are perhaps most responsible both for this confusion of boundaries and for some of Rimbaud's most profound poetic innovations. In any case— and the thematics of his poetry shows this as clearly as his cultural circumstance— Rimbaud had at his disposal only the two radically incompatible categories of child and adult.

Now, it is precisely the otherness of the adult language to which the child poet must have recourse that makes for the disappropriation of the poetic self which characterizes Rimbaud's revolutionary work; as he says himself in one of his best remembered phrases, "je est un autre," I is someone else (304, 305).[2] It is my contention that Rimbaud's work is part of an effort to overcome this radical alienation through a poetic quest that leads him, both figuratively and literally, to explore revolutionary new grounds. In other words, Rimbaud's poetry is a reflection of a quest that seeks at once a language and a place that would allow him to disclose an experience of childhood that is fated by the nature of our culture and our language to remain all but "unspeakable." Unspeakable in that much in Rimbaud's radically new poetic voice points to a precocious genius that was enkindled (or perhaps "enkindered") by the most traumatic forms of emotional, verbal, and sexual contact with the adult world.

It is for this reason that the mysteries and legends surrounding Rimbaud's childhood take on a particular importance for those wishing to explore the radical poetic novelty of Rimbaud's writings. Unfortunately, as is the case with the other legends of Rimbaud's life and work, those involving his early years are centered upon some of the greatest gaps in our factual knowledge about Rimbaud. In fact, we know even less about the poet's earliest childhood than we do about his last years in the depths of Abyssinia. What we do know, nevertheless, points to an early series of traumatic experiences, only a few of which are clearly documented. We are fairly certain, for example, that the marriage between his parents Captain Frédéric Rimbaud and Vitalie Cuif was a rocky one. As Enid Starkie points out,

Rimbaud's "earliest recollection was of a quarrel between his father and mother, in which each in turn had seized a silver bowl . . . and had flung it on the floor with an echoing noise that . . . had terrified the children" (31). Little Arthur was only six years old when his father definitively abandoned his family. Madame Rimbaud's reputation as a cold, harsh disciplinarian is by now one of the stock features of the Rimbaud legend.

Yves Bonnefoy, who has carefully studied Rimbaud's relationship with his mother, is convinced that, at least as far as Arthur is concerned, Madame Rimbaud's emotional withdrawal came soon after the Captain's departure, just as the boy was reaching the age of seven. Bonnefoy bases his conclusion in part on the important early piece "Les Poètes de sept ans" (Seven-Year-Old Poets 74–78). Rimbaud included this in a letter to Paul Demeny in June, 1871, but it was possibly written around the time of the poet's sixteenth birthday (October, 1870) and soon after he received a harsh letter from Madame Rimbaud in which she called him "un petit drôle," a little brat. Whatever the date of composition, however, the poem clearly points to a critical moment in the poet's childhood, one in which the protective parent suddenly and brutally becomes a frightful figure of malevolent aggression. The abrupt change in attitude of the parent toward her child is one of the signs of a general pattern of emotional cruelty that seems to be a key to Rimbaud's relation to language in general. Bonnefoy suggests as much, writing that:

> I almost wonder if it is not often from the mother's behavior that the child— *infans*, one who is still unable to speak properly, who has yet to learn the true potential of words—derives the wonder, or doubt, that henceforward set him forever reflecting on the mystery of signs, on the enigma of their weakness but also on the hope of their inherent powers. (1989, 77)

The "mystery of signs" to which Bonnefoy refers as being one of the key elements of Rimbaud's poetic voice is of course related to the other mysteries surrounding this poet's life.

It is, as Bonnefoy suggests, first and foremost in the figure of Madame Rimbaud that we find clues to this link between Rimbaud's life and his poetic language, but we also see signs of it in the other figures of adult authority we know to have influenced the poet's life and work. What I am suggesting here is a series of transferences beginning with Rimbaud's traumatic relationship with his mother, passing then to Rimbaud's schoolmaster Georges Izambard, and finally fixing on the master poet Paul Verlaine. Relations with all three figures are characterized by an early period of intimate and admiring affection that is followed by disillusion, hostility, and flights of abandonment. Most important, of course, is the fact that each of these relationships reigns over a different period of poetic productivity and innovation. In essence, Rimbaud's poetic voice, his effort to "speak," evolves following each new effort to establish a meaningful relation between himself and the adult to whom he addresses his emotional needs. And, as Leonard Shengold points out, "Because of the compulsion to repeat, traumata in childhood lead to reenactments—usually with people not originally involved" (97). Always with the same needs, always with the same results, Rimbaud the boy poet turned first toward Madame Rimbaud, then to Georges Izambard, and finally to Paul Verlaine—"Vers l'Une, Vers l'Autre, Verlaine."[3] In the end, with no one left to love and nothing left to say, Rimbaud abandoned friends, family, and poetry for a life of literal wandering in the desert.

As we explore some of Rimbaud's texts and their relation to the adults in the poet's life, we should be aware of a trap laid by the texts themselves. Insofar as these writings often show signs of a transference of the poet's hostile feelings onto different figures of the adult world, it is important that we as readers of Rimbaud not fix our own hostilities on the figures involved—something of which many critics have been guilty, particularly in the case of Madame Rimbaud[4] and to a lesser degree that of Verlaine. It is certain that some of Rimbaud's critics echo, perhaps unwittingly, the poet's own emotional assessment of the adults in his life. The reasons for the highly emotional content of much that is written about Rimbaud stem quite possibly from the fact that much in his life and in his writing suggests that his earliest relations with the adult world were characterized by something far more traumatic than the rigorous discipline imposed upon him in his mother's house. In short, it seems quite likely that Rimbaud as a child was abused emotionally and, almost surely, sexually, to the point that his view of the adult world and indeed language itself were profoundly affected.

A suspicion of some form of abuse is implicit in much that has been written about Rimbaud's life and work, but no one to my knowledge has explored the "true" nature of this abuse nor the degree to which it influenced the young poet's brief career. The reasons for this silence are many, not the least of which is our lack of factual information about the poet's earliest years—a lacuna that is perhaps a symptom in itself. The last thing we can look for is, of course, a direct avowal on the part of the object of child abuse. In addition to the fact that the child does not yet have the "language" necessary for such revelations, almost everything in the social and psychological world in which we live makes it more difficult to speak of child abuse than to listen to direct accounts of it. This is particularly true when it is suggested that such abuse has occurred in a house of such ostentatiously moral rectitude as Madame Rimbaud's. But, as Sándor Ferenczi pointed out long ago, "even children of very respectable, sincerely puritanical families, fall victim to real violence or rape much more often than one had dared to suppose" (227).

In some of Rimbaud's writing one nevertheless comes across direct expositions of sexual encounters, either fantasized or real, between a young child resembling Rimbaud himself and an older person. In one of his earliest prose poems, for example, we find a scene that takes place in the "maison rustique de mes parents," the rustic house of my parents:

146

Moi j'étais abandonné dans cette maison de campagne sans fin. . . . J'étais dans une chambre très sombre: que faisais-je? Une servante vint près de moi: je puis dire que c'était un petit chien: quoiqu'elle fût belle, et d'une noblesse maternelle inexprimable pour moi: pure, connue, toute charmante! Elle me pinça le bras. . . . Je la renversai dans une corbeille de coussins et de toiles de navire, en un coin noir. Je ne me rappelle plus que son pantalon à dentelles blanches.

I was abandoned in this vast country house. . . . I was in a very dark room: what was I doing? A servant girl came near me: I can say she was a little dog: although she was beautiful, of an inexpressible maternal nobility for me: pure, known, totally charming! She pinched my arm. . . . I took her in a basket of cushions and ship canvases, in a dark corner. I remember only her white lace panties. (288–91)

No doubt this poem seems more like an innocent erotic fantasy than any real sexual encounter, and ironically, this is so perhaps chiefly because of its relatively direct exposition of the event and the fairly explicit identification of the sexual partner as a servant girl (or a dog?). Was Rimbaud seduced as a young child by a household servant? That is a possibility, but certainly not the only one. It could be that some other trusted member of the household was the perpetrator of the abuse. One thinks immediately of the boy's unsavory uncles, one of whom, for reasons unknown, was banned from the house by Madame Rimbaud. Captain Rimbaud himself left the family when young Arthur was only six, also for reasons that are still not entirely clear. Yet it appears far more likely that it is Madame Rimbaud herself who, at least symptomatically, is the agent of an incestuous relationship with her son. As we shall see, the textual evidence of sexual abuse is ample, and much of it points specifically to Madame Rimbaud at least as the figure on whom the resultant confusion and hostility were fixed.

Among the principal signs of this traumatic relationship between parent and child are the images of the terrible mother one finds so often in Rimbaud. In many regards the poet's portraits of his mother related her to what Shengold calls the "parent of Sphinx," a particularly frightening image of the primal or soul-murdering parent.[5] Shengold also points out the essential "analogy between Jocasta and the monstrous Sphinx that figures in the Oedipus legend" (41), suggesting that both are conflicting images of the same parental figure who is perceived at times as loving and affectionate and at times frightful and menacing. Take, for example, the case of maternal seduction of a child in which "the mother's facial expression would completely change—she would suddenly 'stare through' him with no sign of recognition. . . . Sometimes baring and offering her breast, she would use her finger as a penetrative organ to invade the child's anus" (Shengold 42). This icy, sphinx-like stare is strikingly similar to the one to which the child poet is subjected in "les Poètes de sept ans" where the terrible mother appears before her child and, "l'ayant surpris à des pitiés immondes," (catching) him in actions of filthy pity, she fixes upon him that icy, "blue regard,—qui ment," The blue glance—that lies (76, 77).

This deceitful, lying gaze evokes the "acres hypocrisies," bitter hypocrisy (76, 77), mentioned earlier in the poem and attributed to the poet-narrator himself. This sort of identification between the child and his adult abuser is typical of incestuous relationships and is underlined throughout the poem. In the first quatrain, for example, it is the boy himself who has blue eyes like those later attributed to the "lying" mother. It is also the mother who in the first line holds "le livre du devoir," the exercise book (74, 75),[6] only later to be replaced with the poet himself, who has shifted from the first person "je" to the third person "il" who now sits reading the Bible.[7] Thus both mother and child hide behind an open book, but a book whose secret message is far different from that announced on the cover. The apparent confusion of identities in this poem is but one more sign of profound trauma, for as Shengold suggests, "most frequently a really traumatic experience is avoided by identification with the aggressor" (97). Rimbaud's "I" is indeed already an "other."

But just as important as the displaced and unstable identities in Rimbaud's poetry is the theme of hypocrisy itself, the "great lie" which in cases of childhood trauma is often indicative not so much of personal or religious insincerity as of the trauma brought on by the primal parent as sphinx. Shengold makes the point that "mendacity has been described as a characteristic of the 'primal parent' " (46). This is so largely because the emotional and sexual abuse to which the primal parent subjects the child necessitates both deception on the part of the adult and denial on the part of the child. In Rimbaud's case, as in many other cases of adult seduction of male children, the "lie" appears to center on anal erogeneity. In fact, the relatively overt thematization of anality in Rimbaud's work is evidence of an attempt to achieve what Shengold calls "anal defense," which is attained through "becoming able to control the anal sphincter" on both the physical and emotional levels (77). He goes on to suggest that "The overuse of the emotional sphincter makes for a kind of anal-sadistic universe with all the contradictions that this entails" (77–78). Elsewhere, Shengold points out the etymological relation between the words "sphinx" ("Strangler" in Greek) and "sphincter" (41), a relation which, in Rimbaud's case, has more than merely semantic implications.

In this light, the link between the boy-poet in "Les Poètes de sept ans," a child who confuses his own identity with that of his mother while letting himself be caught enjoying his "pitiés immondes," and the hero of "le Châtiment de Tartufe" (Tartufe's Punishment 38, 39) is striking. In the latter poem the pious hypocrite is introduced "Tisonnant, tisonnant son coeur amoureux sous / Sa chaste robe noire, heureux, la main gantée," Raking, raking his amorous heart under / His chaste black robe, happy, his hand gloved.[8] Then along comes the "Méchant," wicked fellow, who grabs the hypocrite's robe and literally defrocks him, thus exposing his "long chapelet des pèchès pardonnés," long rosary of pardoned sins, and leaving him "nu du haut jusques en bas!" naked from top to bottom. Rimbaud's imagery here seems specifically designed to conflate the religious code outwardly espoused by Madame Rimbaud with veiled references to lewd bodily exhibition. This tendency is continued in "Accroupissements" (Squattings 72–75), a poem Rimbaud describes as "un chant pieux," a pious hymn, in which the good Friar Milotus's visit to the latrine is described in unsparingly vivid detail.

One might then wonder about the abrupt evocation of "Vénus au ciel profond," Venus in the deep sky, which ends this poem, but only until one rereads the piece entitled "Vénus Anadyomène" (Venus Anadyomene 40–41). In this poem we are witness to the bath of a corpulent woman whose hair is "fortement pommadés," heavily pommaded (as is the poet's in "les Poètes de sept ans"). As she stands out of her tub, attention is drawn to the fact that, "Les reins portent deux mots gravés: CLARA VÉNUS; / Et tout ce corps remue et tend sa large croupe / Belle hideusement d'un ulcère à l'anus," The buttocks bear two engraved words: CLARA VENUS; /—And that whole body moves and extends its broad rump / Hideously beautiful with an ulcer on the anus.

These scatological portraits of religious figures suggest deep resentment toward a moral code held by a person whose private conduct Rimbaud knows to be far different from what outside appearances and behavior would lead us to believe. Such images seem at the very least to be part of a general assault on the kind of conspicuous piety that characterized the household Rimbaud knew as a child. Madame Rimbaud's coldly puritanical demeanor itself may be read as a sign of something far different from what we often believe about her. As Ferenzci writes of cases of sexual relations with children:

> Almost always the perpetrator behaves as though nothing has happened, and consoles himself with the thought: "Oh, it is only a child, he does not know anything, he will forget it all." Not infrequently after such events, the seducer becomes over-moralistic or religious and endeavors to save the soul of the child by severity. (228)

If there is anything in the legend or Rimbaud's childhood that stands out it is the image of Madame Rimbaud clad in black from head to toe sanctimoniously marching her children through the streets of Charleville on their way to High Mass. It might seem uncalled for to question the sincerity of Madame Rimbaud's religious practices, but Rimbaud's work itself clearly invites the query: what is the truth that lies behind that blue gaze?

If the early poems I have just drawn upon suggest premature sexual experience and a fixation on anality, there is one poem that seems at once to evoke anal sex directly and to mark a radical new step in the development of Rimbaud's poetry. In "Le Coeur volé" (The Stolen Heart, 80–83) the reader is witness to a scene that seems to describe an episode of Rimbaud's visit to Paris during the Commune of 1871. One of the stanzas explains why "Mon triste coeur bave à la poupe," My sad heart slobbers at the poop:

Ithyphalliques et pioupiesques
Leurs insultes l'ont dépravé!
A la vesprée ils font des fresques
Ithyphalliques et pioupiesques.
O flots abracadabrantesques,
Prenez mon coeur, qu'il soit lavé;
Ithyphalliques et pioupiesques
Leurs insultes l'ont dépravé!

Ithyphallic and soldierish,
Their jeerings have depraved it!
On the rudder you see frescoes
Ithyphallic and soldierish.
O abracadabratic waves,
Take my heart, let it be washed!
Ithyphallic and solderish,
Their jeerings have depraved it.

Many of Rimbaud's biographers believe that on this trip to Paris, one of his early flights from home undertaken when he was sixteen and during which he fell in among a rough group of soldiers taking part in the Commune, Rimbaud was violently sodomized by those whom he had hoped to join as brothers in revolution. Enid Starkie writes, for example, that it was during this hopeful visit to the French capital that Rimbaud

> received his first initiation into sex and in so brutal and unexpected a manner that he was startled and outraged, and that his whole nature recoiled from it with fascinated disgust. . . . It was a sudden and blinding revelation of what sex really was, of what it could do to him, and it showed him how false had been all his imagined emotions. (80–81)

It seems quite probable, though, that rather than an initial introduction to sex, this incident served as a harsh reminder of a sexuality he had already known.[9] This would explain the image of the slobbering "poop" that dominates the first stanza, a stanza that otherwise has nothing to do with the sea. It is from the rear that the heart has been violated. But at the same time there are images of the heart being devoured: "J'aurai des sursauts stomachiques / Si mon triste coeur est ravalé," I will have stomach retchings, / If my heart is [swallowed up].[10] Along the same lines Shengold observes that "the anal and perianal area of erogeneity seems to be the principal intrapsychic site for the overwhelming stimulation (experienced as being eaten into and eaten up) that can lead to ego dissolution" (87). It is exactly this kind of disorientation ("Comment agir, ô coeur volé?" How will I act, O stolen heart?)[11] that is now going to guide Rimbaud's work.

The early traits that typify Rimbaud's genius are accentuated and in a sense (de-)systemized soon after the composition of this poem, which is one of those enclosed in the important letter of May 13, 1871 (302–35). It is in this letter, addressed to his schoolmaster, fellow poet, and close friend Georges Izambard, that Rimbaud first formulates his now famous "voyant," seer, theory of the poet's visionary and social mission. (That letter is of course soon to be followed by the longer one on the same subject sent to Paul Demeny on May 15; 304–11). One of the more interesting points about the May letter to Izambard is the scornful tone Rimbaud uses throughout. This tone seems to take specific aim at the moral code Izambard has now apparently begun to preach:

> On se doit à la Société, m'avez-vous dit; vous faites partie des corps enseignants: vous roulez dans la bonne ornière. . . . Mais vous finirez toujours comme un satisfait qui n'a rien fait, n'ayant rien voulu faire. Sans compter que votre poésie subjective sera toujours horriblement fadasse. . . . Vous n'êtes pas *enseignant* pour moi.

> You have told me we owe a duty to Society. You belong to the teaching body: you move along in the right track. . . . But you will always end up a self-satisfied man who has done nothing because he wanted to do nothing. Not to mention that your subjective poetry will always be horribly insipid. . . . You are not a teacher for me.

The temper here is particularly striking if one compares it to the letter Rimbaud wrote to Izambard only a few months earlier (November 2, 1870; 300–3):

> La reconnaissance que je vous ai, je ne saurais pas vous l'exprimer aujourd'-hui plus que l'autre jour. Je vous le prouverai! Il s'agirait de faire quelque chose pour vous, que je mourrais pour le faire,—je vous en donne ma parole.
> J'ai encore un tas de choses à dire . . . [Rimbaud's ellipsis]

> The gratitude I feel for you, I could not express today any more than any other day. I will prove it to you! If it were a question of doing something for you, I would die in order to do it. I give you my word.
> I still have many things to say . . .

Despite the obvious differences in these two letters, they do nevertheless have several essential similarities. Primary among these are the explicit references to the problem of self-expression. In the November 1870 letter Rimbaud obviously attempts to say something he cannot express. One can hardly help querying as to the nature of the "word" Rimbaud gives in this letter and, most particularly, of those "many things" he leaves unsaid as he closes. In the later farewell letter to Izambard, Rimbaud makes a remark on the (non-)meaning of "Le Coeur volé" that strikes a very similar chord. As we have seen, this poem comes very close to saying something quite explicit. But the young Rimbaud underlines this fact in a most indirect fashion, saying of the piece, "Ça ne veut pas rien dire," This does not mean nothing.[12] Once again Rimbaud is evoking the problems of failed communication and flight from the adult figure to whom that communication is addressed—and also from whom it is concealed—that we earlier saw centered on his mother. This time, of course, Izambard is the adult on whom Rimbaud fixates his anguish. It is at once to him that the boy poet addresses a desperate cry and from him that he flees in bitter and final disappointment.

As we turn our attention to the theoretical content of the two "voyant" letters written in May 1871, we might remember that they are the product of a sixteen-year-old boy whose first attempt to cross the threshold of manhood, the rush to Paris to join the "army" of the Commune, has met with the gravest of humiliations.[13] Certainly the most widely cited phrase from these treatises on "objective poetry" is the poet's claim that "*Je est un autre*," *I* is an other. If we relate this statement and the general tone and content of the "voyant" letters (including the poems "Le Coeur volé" and "Accroupissements" that accompany them) to what Maud Mannoni says of the abused child in analysis we see striking parallels. In her comments regarding Sammy, whose mother saw him even before his birth as destined to be her "persecuting object" (52), Mannoni states:

> The child enters the analysis with the *I* of a discourse where he poses a question concerning the desire of the Other, but, failing to communicate, through this relationship with the Other, the themes that preoccupy him (theme of death, anxiety of being devoured), he soon places himself in an impersonal discourse (myth) or takes refuge in a learned discourse which is that of the adult. (53)

As is typical of his writing, Rimbaud also seems to have his language both ways, joining the impersonal "I" of his objective poetry to the learned discourse that earned him the reputation of child prodigy. But in both cases what seems at first to be a "refuge" is also a form of exile, the exile of a child into a strange world of words made by and for adults. Surely no single poem illustrates this point better than Rimbaud's most widely read—and in some ways most enigmatic—piece "Le Bateau ivre" (The Drunken Boat 114–21). Like "Le Coeur volé," it too was written in the critical year of 1871. As Antoine Adam points out, "the two poems, however different in expression, have at their origin the same feeling of disgust, the same need of purification" (918). The kinship of the two poems is also evident on the level of the marine imagery which otherwise appears to be so out of place in "Le Coeur volé." "Le Bateau ivre" represents perhaps an effort to provide an answer to the unresolved question "Comment agir?"—How will I act?—that closes the slightly earlier poem. Part of that effort is evident, for example, in the link now established between the themes of tortured wanderlust and that of lost innocence, both of which center on the images of a child lost in a hostile world, a world not without love but whose love on every occasion has turned exceedingly bitter. "Je regrette l'Europe aux anciens parapets!" [I] miss Europe with its ancient parapets! says the little rudderless boat lost at sea. And he continues his plaint:

> L'âcre amour m'a goflé de torpeurs enivrantes.
> O que ma quille éclate! O que j'aille à la mer!
> Si je désire une eau d'Europe, c'est la flache
> Noire et froide où vers le crépuscule embaumé
> Un enfant accroupi plein de tristesses, lâche
> Un bateau frêle comme un papillon de mai.

> Acrid love has swollen me with intoxicating torpor.
> O let my keel burst! O let me go into the sea!
> If I want a water of Europe, it is the black
> Cold puddle where in the sweet-smelling twilight
> A squatting child full of sadness releases
> A boat as fragile as a May butterfly.

The "voyant" letters, "Le Coeur volé," and "Le Bateau ivre" clearly mark a new turn in the young poet's career, but one that is really an intensification of patterns already apparent in his work. Their underlying themes of "acrid love," innocent suffering, and loss of identity, when considered in the light of their relation to Rimbaud's rude sexual encounter in Paris, seem only further to confirm the hypotheses I have put forward about his early childhood and his precocious genius that reached new heights in 1871. Rimbaud's revolutionary poetic voice is indeed the product of genius, but that genius, which is one of language itself, also seems to be the product of a child's traumatic experience of the world. That such an experience is unspeakable in the language society ordinarily accords to children only intensifies the imperative Rimbaud invokes in his second "voyant" letter: "Trouver une langue," A language must be found.

Unable to speak directly of the conflicting feelings that result from the violation of society's strictest taboo, it is hardly surprising that this child poet resorts to the language of the adult Other. Nor is it surprising that in doing so he breaks the referential constraints in a manner that reflects the violation of social and familial constraints to which he has been subjected.

In fact, the rapid development in Rimbaud's poetic genius that occurred in 1871 can itself be seen as a symptom of the very kind of traumatic sexual experience I suspect in Rimbaud's case. Ferenczi writes, for example:

One is justified—in contradistinction to the familiar regression [associated with sexual abuse]—to speak of a *traumatic progression*, of a *precocious maturity*. It is natural to compare this with the precocious maturity of the fruit that was injured by a bird or insect. Not only emotionally, but also *intellectually*, can the trauma bring to maturity a part of the person. (229; Ferenczi's emphasis)

But Ferenczi recognizes alongside this rapid development of intellectual and emotional powers a potential crisis in other parts of the child's being: "When the child recovers from such an attack, he feels enormously confused, in fact split—innocent and culpable at the same time—and his confidence in the testimony of his own senses is broken" (228). Ferenczi here evokes two other characteristics of Rimbaud's "voyant" period, and not coincidentally the problems of the physical and the moral senses are as closely associated in Rimbaud's letter as in Ferenczi's paper:

Le Poëte se fait *voyant* par un long, immense et raisonné *dérèglement* de *tous les sens.* Toutes les formes d'amour, de souffrance, de folie; il cherche lui-même, il épuise en lui tous les poisons, pour n'en garder que les quintessences. Ineffable torture où il a besoin de toute la foi, de toute la force surhumaine, où il devient entre tous le grand malade, le grand criminel, le grand maudit—et le suprême Savant!—Car il arrive à l'*inconnu*! [Rimbaud's emphasis]

The Poet makes himself a *seer* by a long, gigantic and rational *derangement of all the senses.* All forms of love, suffering, and madness. He searches himself. He exhausts all poisons in himself and keeps only their quintessences. Unspeakable torture where he needs all his faith, all his superhuman strength, where he becomes among all men the great patient, the great criminal, the one accursed—and the supreme Scholar!—Because he reaches the *unknown*! (306–7)

Rimbaud thus prescribes the systematic derangement of the senses through which the *voyant* becomes "le grand malade," not so much a patient to be healed as one who basks in his own illness. It is this suffering individual alone who may find the language of the *unknown*. This vision of pathology as a source of salvation parallels closely what Mannoni says of the child whose voice is effectively squelched by the adult social and familial norms of communication: "If the child has the impression that every access to true speech is blocked, he can in certain cases search out through illness a possibility of expression" (63).

The new cultivation of illness must also be accompanied by a rejection of all the social norms that are responsible for blocking the Poet's access to true language. He thus must become "le grand criminel, le grand maudit," the great criminal, the one accursed, by the normal world. Yet in the very letter where Rimbaud tries to set himself free from the constraints of conventional morality he further burdens himself with an apparently unbearable responsibility. As he says of the poet he hopes to be: "Il est chargé de l'humanité, des *animaux* même. . . ," He is responsible for humanity, even for the *animals* (308–9). Here we see evidence of what Shengold calls a "moral chameleon," a person who feels himself "entitled to everything," "above all laws," and who at the same time lives under the constant threat of being "crushed and annihilated" (54–55). This again is symptomatic of incestuous sexual relations which, in Shengold's words, are often responsible for the survivor's strong sense of being "the privileged and entitled child of Fortune (in part because of having transgressed the sternest human proscription, having like the gods committed parricide and lived in incest), and yet feeling the need for punishment (banishment, blindness, castration, annihilation)" (53). During the months and years following May 1871, Rimbaud would indeed live a life above the law, and to such a conspicuous degree that it is hard to imagine he was not secretly wishing for the severest of chastisements.

But at the heart of the quest upon which Rimbaud set himself lies (all puns intended) "le langage universel," the universal language, through which he sincerely hoped to attain "la vraie vie," true life. Such naive faith in the limitless possibilities of a language he had not yet mastered is but one more sign of a childlike being experiencing a traumatic crisis of identity: "Cette langue sera de l'âme pour l'âme, résumant tout, parfums, sons, couleurs, de la pensée accrochant la pensée et tirant. . . . Enormité devenant norme, absorbée par tous, il [le poète] serait vraiment *un multiplicateur de progrès!*" This language will be of the soul for the soul, containing everything, smells, sounds, colors, thought holding on to thought and pulling. . . . Enormity becoming normal, absorbed by all, he would really be *a multiplier of progress!* (308–9). As Mannoni suggests, "What the child in a state of profound confusion (through the abrupt loss of all points of identificatory reference) *demands* is the exact word, that 'master word' that he invokes in a state of crisis, so that through it a form of self-mastery might be acquired" (28).

This mastery will always remain beyond Rimbaud's reach, but his violent struggle to attain it has left us expressions of human desire whose power and mysterious beauty have rarely been equaled. In this case that language happens to be that of a child (albeit one standing at the threshold of the adult world), a child who not only still believes in the possibility of an all-encompassing "master word," but who also recognizes that that word is not yet his own. Although now reaching the pinnacle of his poetic career, Rimbaud still sees himself as *infans*, not yet in possession of anything that approaches real language. He still conceives of the true poet in the future ("perfect") tense—and this of necessity, for Rimbaud continues to see every other tense as indeed imperfect.

The question of a language yet to be acquired leads us directly to the next important adult figure in Rimbaud's life—Paul Verlaine. As Mannoni reminds us, it is Freud himself in his essay on *Dreams and Occultism* who underlined the belief of the child in search of identity in "the Omnipotence of adult thought" (45). In this light, one of the more interesting elements of Rimbaud's second "voyant" letter is the list of those great poets he believes to be possessed with the gift of "voyance," that is, those adults who have mastered the word. The last name on that list is that of someone Rimbaud would soon know in person: "Paul Verlaine, un vrai Poète," Paul Verlaine, a real poet.

Rimbaud's most productive and original period of creation, the one beginning with the "voyant" letters and soon to be dominated by his turbulent relation with Verlaine, is characterized by many of the previously mentioned symptoms of childhood seduction, and which are often intensified by this new adult relation.

Here again, much of what we see in this relationship reflects the transference of Rimbaud's ambiguous feelings toward the adults in his life to the figure of Verlaine. For example, his early admiration for Verlaine's poetic gift fits in with the general scope of the "voyant" letters. Aside from the purely literary association of these two poets, though, the most widely known aspect of their relationship is of course their fiery friendship, a friendship that begins with Rimbaud's plea for the guiding hand of an adult as he begins his entry into Parisian literary circles and which soon turns into a passionate sexual liaison. Once again, this experience with a figure of authority seems to intensify Rimbaud's confusion about his place in relation to the adult world. Verlaine is drawn into the dual role of parental protector and adult seducer, and soon the pair's exploits come to typify what Shengold observes in clinical cases to be:

> a kind of public performance that is frequently indulged in by homosexuals (in whom it can also conceivably stem from childhood seduction): compulsive activities in public toilets, subway trains, and parks, which can express and "play with" the wish to be caught and punished, and simultaneously assert that one can get away with anything. (58)

This behavior will become a constant in Rimbaud's relation with Verlaine until the latter, having finished his term in prison for firing upon and wounding his young companion, undergoes a radical moral conversion of the type described by Ferenczi: "Not infrequently after such events, the seducer becomes over-moralistic or religious and endeavors to save the soul of the child by severity" (228). Verlaine thus undergoes a radical, if temporary, spiritual conversion and becomes, as he wrote to his young friend on December 12, 1875, "Religieux, strictement, parce que c'est la seule chose intelligente et bonne" (1972, 300–31), Religious, strictly, because that is the only intelligent and good thing (my translation). He then tries desperately to end the child's "errant" ways and bring him back onto the path of the straight and narrow: "Ce m'est un si grand chagrin de te voir en des voies idiotes, toi si intelligent, si prêt . . ." (1972, 301), It gives me such great sorrow to see you on such idiotic paths, you [who are] so intelligent, so ready . . . (my translation). Like Madame Rimbaud, who turns to the strictest of religious practices, like Izambard, who as Rimbaud scathingly points out in his "voyant" letter preaches "duty to Society" and follows "the right track," now Paul Verlaine tries to put his young friend on the high road of moral rectitude.

For us, though, far more important than Rimbaud's public defiance of the moral code is his revolutionary search for a true language. This search for a language, that position from which to speak through to an adult world that in the child's eyes seems surely to be one of physical power and metaphysical presence, was of necessity carried out from a perspective of alienation. And that alienation is one that comes across both in the way Rimbaud led his life and in the way he revolutionized not only the literary landscape of France but also that of the world. From the French Symbolists like Stéfane Mallarmé who first would appreciate his greatness to the Austrian Hugo von Hofmannsthal, to the German Rainer Maria Rilke, to the Irishmen William Butler Yeats and James Joyce, to the (also homeless) Americans Gertrude Stein and T. S. Eliot, from the spiritually inspired Paul Claudel to the "systematically" irrational Surrealists to the sensually explicit Henry Miller, to the brooding hedonism of Jim Morrison (another poet who would end his days in a fugue to a foreign land,)[14] all would claim Rimbaud as a forerunner. It seems a mystery how one poet whose career spans so short a time and whose body of work is so small could have such impact on nearly every literary movement of the twentieth century. The key, however, surely lies in this young poet's special insight into the realities, both sublime and horrifying, of human experience. "The centre cannot hold," as Yeats once said, but before him Rimbaud had already witnessed a decentered world and created a language to express it, a language whose very lack of center at once deprives it of any directly accessible surface "meaning" and infuses it with spiritual and sensual qualities that touch the depths of our being. Rimbaud uses adult words, but he opens those words up and he breaks them down so that they speak mysteriously but surely to the loving and suffering child in all of us.

This explains in part why this boy poet who had no country to call home soon was to have them all. Rimbaud wrote in the "Avertissement" to a piece he was, perhaps appropriately, never to write but whose preface is applicable to almost everything he did produce:

> Ces écritures-ci sont d'un jeune, tout jeune *homme*, dont la vie s'est développée n'importe où; sans mère, sans pays, insoucieux de tout ce qu'on connaît, fuyant toute force morale, comme furent déjà plusieurs pitoyables jeunes hommes. Mais, lui, si ennuyé et si troublé, qu'il ne fit que s'amener à la mort comme à une pudeur terrible et fatale. N'ayant pas aimé de femmes—quoique plein de sang!—il eut son âme et son coeur, toute sa force, élevés en des erreurs étranges et tristes . . . . Mais, cette bizarre souffrance possédant une autorité inquiétante, il faut sincèrement désirer que cetter âme, égarée parmi nous tous, et qui veut la mort, ce semble, rencontre en cet instant-là des consolations sérieuses et soit digne.

> These writings are of a young, a very young *man*, whose life evolved in no particular place; without a mother, without a country, indifferent to everything that is familiar, avoiding all moral pressure, just like several other pitiful young men. But this fellow was so bored and disturbed that he led himself to death as to some terrible and fatal bashfulness. Not having loved women—although passionate!—his soul and his heart and all his strength were trained in strange, sad errors. . . . But this unusual suffering possessing a troublesome authority, one must sincerely hope that this Soul, wandering about among us all, and who, it would seem, wants death, will encounter at that moment serious consolations and be worthy. ("Les Déserts de l'amour," Deserts of Love, 286–87)

"Without a mother, without a country," Rimbaud writes, and he wanders. That (m)other, that homeland—the person and the place—Rimbaud seeks so desperately through his ceaseless fugues and his intoxicating poems are of course to elude him forever. Yet even in the preliminary farewell to poetry (and to Verlaine) that is *Une Saison en enfer* (*A Season in Hell*), he still believes in the preeminent power of a voice, and oracle, somewhere *out there*. But more than ever the "true" language he seeks to master is beyond his grasp: "Nous allons à l'*Esprit*. C'est très-certain, c'est oracle, ce que je dis. Je comprends, et ne sachant m'expliquer sans paroles païennes, je voudrais me taire," We are moving toward the *Spirit*. I tell you it is very certain, oracular. I understand, and not knowing how to explain this without using pagan words, I prefer to be silent (176–77).

Rimbaud does make one last effort to "speak" in *Illuminations*, but this is the last of his poetic works. Rimbaud is not yet twenty, he is about to become a "man" and "put away childish things." One of the greatest poetic voices of the modern world will now be forever silent.

In conclusion I will briefly examine an aspect of Rimbaud's life that parallels his poetic career and appears to play an essential role in his abandonment of it. Just as the adults in his young poet's life mark different periods of development in his poetry, so do the travels he undertakes, beginning at the age of fifteen when he first runs away to Paris, and which take on ever greater importance as he grows older.

It seems significant therefore that as Rimbaud puts away his childhood, he still does not go through any of the rites of transition his society expected of him, those to which I referred earlier as being absent from the most productive years of his literary career. He neither marries nor finishes the studies he had so brilliantly begun, although he does ask his friend Ernest Delahaye about the requirements for a secondary degree in the sciences, "le 'bachot' ès sciences" (October 14, 1875; 1972, 299). In 1876 he also joins the Dutch colonial army, but soon after arriving at his station on the island of Java he deserts and returns to his mother's home in Charleville.[15] But his stays at home are ever briefer, and they too are about to come to an end. On the verge of becoming a man, Rimbaud evidently finds it more and more impossible to live under the watchful gaze of the sphinx, and it is though his travels that he now more than ever seeks to escape her.

There is, of course, more to the sphinx than her gaze. Shengold, who, it will be remembered, sees the sphinx and Jocasta of the Oedipus myth as two faces of the same primal mother, reminds us that it was Jocasta who pinned her son's feet together before abandoning him, thus leaving him crippled for life (46). He also points out that in the original story, Oedipus's answer to the sphinx's riddle about the creature who walks on four limbs in the morning, two at noon, and three in the evening involves his finding the key to "locomotion—the ability to move away from the mother—and in answering it Oedipus establishes his separate identity and manhood" (44). The riddle of the sphinx reveals precisely the greatest fear of the sphinx-like parent: "It is the child's standing up and walking away, out of the symbiotic unit, that these potentially soul-murdering mothers cannot tolerate" (Shengold 44).

There is indeed some evidence that Madame Rimbaud suffered from this very anxiety. One of the oldest stories of the Rimbaud legend, first related by Paterne Berrichon, holds that immediately after his birth the nurse bathed the infant and "laid him down on a cushion while she left the room to fetch the swaddling clothes. When she returned, however, she found . . . that the infant no longer lay where she had deposited him, that he had rolled on to the floor and was crawling to the door, to begin his life of wandering" (Starkie 30). It is also said that at barely eight months old he was already able to walk without the slightest assistance ("il marchait sans aide aucune," cited in Etiemble 261). These stories, though related by a succession of different biographers until they took on an air of historical fact, could surely have had but one source. And no matter their dubious relation to reality, they indicate great anxiety on the part of the sphinx-like parent, who obviously kept them alive until the biographers picked up on them. Rimbaud himself surely seized upon this fear in his mother and played upon it as one of his chief means of revenge. Rimbaud knew the answer to the riddle and thus how to slay the sphinx. Oedipus walks away and the sphinx dies. Rimbaud's lifelong fugues and wanderings can thus be traced directly to his feelings of hostility toward his mother. Walking away is not as easy as it may seem, however, for Oedipus has bad feet—the name itself means swollen or wounded foot. Rimbaud, at least early on in his life, is somewhat luckier, hindered, as he notes in one of his most famous and touching pieces, "Ma Bohème" (My Bohemian Life 62–64) merely by "mes souliers blessés," my wounded shoes. Once again we see one of the ironies of the *infans* as prodigious genius: he cannot speak and his language touches the depths of the universe; he cannot walk and his footsteps cover the face of earth. And in both cases what he says and what he flees must surely center upon a deep and terrible secret. Such is the riddle of the Sphinx.

Rimbaud thus could do no other than try to flee the frightful image of the primal parent, though he would never fully escape her blue gaze. Just as he could not find the words to solve the riddle, neither could he find the legs strong enough to walk away. Thus his life and his work reflect an endless series of discoveries and disappointments, of departures and returns. But it would take much more than a pair of "wounded shoes" to stop this modern Oedipus. On May 27, 1891, Arthur Rimbaud goes under the surgeon's knife and loses not his shoe or his foot, but his swollen, cancerous leg. The following November 10, he dies.

It is surely no mere coincidence that one of Rimbaud's peripatetic adventures seems to have led him to the Upper Egyptian temples of Luxor (see Borer 234–36). There, about eight feet above the floor of one of the ancient sanctuaries, we see still today, chiseled into the stone in building-block capital letters, the name of the poet: RIMBAUD. The entry to this temple, as one might almost expect, is protected by the alley of the sphinxes. It is they who now stand a timeless watch over the name of a child, a maker of rhyme who might at last have found, if not his true language, at least his place.

NOTES

I would like to thank the Radiological Consultants Association of West Virginia for the grant that allowed me to complete this paper.

1. Interestingly, Ariès considers the earliest example of a modern adolescent to be Wagner's Siegfried, a work completed in 1869, just as Rimbaud was beginning his most creative years (49).

2. Literally, "*I* is an other." Unless otherwise indicated, all translations of Rimbaud will be Fowlie's and those from other works in French will refer, where possible, to extant English language editions. To Fowlie's translations I have also restored emphasis to words originally emphasized in Rimbaud's writings. Double page numbers in citations to Fowlie indicate French original and English translation on opposite facing page. I have provided all translations from the French for Mannoni and Adam.

3. Literally, Toward the One, Toward the Other, [Toward] Verlaine. Upon reading this formula for Rimbaud's search for a meaningful relationship with an adult, my colleague and spouse Valérie Crétaux Lastinger suggested, quite appropriately, the spelling "Vers l'aine"—Toward the crotch—as an alternative designation for the third phase of the quest. In any case, the reference here is first to Madame Rimbaud as mother, then to Georges Izambard as Other, and finally to Verlaine as lover and master poet.

4. Bonnefoy gives us ample warning when he points to his own mistake in this regard: "In my earlier essay, a long time ago, I wrote that Vitalie Cuif was 'a being full of obstinacy, avarice, concealed hatred and aridity,' and I have somewhat regretted since then that I painted her in such black colors" (1989, 68).

5. In defining the term "soul murder," Shengold writes: "Soul murder is my dramatic designation for a certain category of traumatic experience: instances of repetitive and chronic overstimulation, alternating with emotional deprivation, that are deliberately brought about by another individual" (16–17). He goes on to write that "in individuals, psychic murder is founded on the relations between hostile, cruel, indifferent, psychotic, or psychopathic parents and the child prisoners in their charge" (19).

6. The word "devoir," particularly in the singular, means not only "exercise" but, perhaps more properly, "duty" or "obligation" and carries in French very heavy moral and religious connotations.

7. The role of the open books in this poem is perhaps also related to the incestuous relationship, particularly since the book is the Bible, which Rimbaud associates with the moral rectitude of his mother. Shengold relates a case in which a patient dreamt repeatedly of the reading of a newspaper and "falsely insisted on [the] 'good' character of the mother." Shengold observes, after Freud, that "The newspaper

is symbolic—paper, derived from wood and material, symbolizes woman and mother
. . .—and the opening of a newspaper and its perusal represent C.'s conflict-filled, scoptophilic, terrified 'enjoyment' of his mother's spread thighs and genitals during her exhibitionistic displays" (56).

8. The verb "tisonner" might also be translated as "to poke" as in "to poke a fire": a "tisonnier," the instrument used for this purpose, is known in English as a "poker," for example. As we will see in "Le Coeur volé," the heart ("le coeur") in Rimbaud seems often to be associated with anal sexuality. In that light, the verb "tisonner" used here becomes strongly evocative.

9. Suzanne Briet has pointed out that Rimbaud associated the word "abracadabrantesques" with memories of his early childhood and believed it to be a magical means to "préserver de la fièvre," protecting one from fever (quoted in Adam 891 n 9). The poem seems therefore to evoke at once a fairly recent event and one more distant in the past. One sees here also the germ of Rimbaud's burgeoning fascination with the kabbala and mysticism in general.

10. Fowlie translates "ravalé" as "degraded," a reading that is correct but not complete. The verb "ravaler" literally means "to swallow again." Its use in the passive voice here suggests a feeling of being devoured and the prefix "r-" (re-) indicates that this is perhaps a repetition of some previous event. "Ravaler" also means to repress what one feels and would like to express, as in the English "to swallow one's words." Of course, all of these connotations enter into Rimbaud's poetic usage of the word.

11. Note that Rimbaud uses the infinitive of the verb "agir" ("to act"). The "I" that Fowlie supplies is already dissipated.

12. My translation. Fowlie seems to be thrown off here by a grammatical "error" on Rimbaud's part. Consciously or unconsciously, he corrects the poet's syntax by eliminating the negative "pas" and gives the French as being "Ça ne veut rien dire." He then translates this new sentence as "This means nothing." Rimbaud's original sentence is "Ça ne veut pas rien dire" (1972, 249), and it contains a double negative, which in itself is perfectly acceptable in French but in this case would require another "ne" for the second negative "rien," nothing. Antoine Adam explains that Rimbaud surely meant to write "Cela ne veut pas ne rien dire," This does not mean nothing. Adam suggests: "If Rimbaud's historians wished to look the truth in the face, they would say that in this month of May 1871 he ceases to manipulate the French language with the mastery that he has possessed up till then and that he would soon recover" (1074). All this suggests an effort to cry out for help in response to a situation that makes the cry all but indecipherable and is typical of the sort of ego dissolution that can result from violent anal overstimulation. The fact that the word "coeur," which from "Le Châtiment of Tartuffe" to "Le Coeur volé" seems to be associated with anality, appears so conspicuously in the final salutations of these two May 1871 letters only seems to confirm this hypothesis.

13. Another sign of this desire to cross over into manhood is the new name Rimbaud uses and the lie he tells concerning his age in his August 15, 1871 letter to the solidly successful poet Théodore de Banville (312, 313). In that letter, which is

signed "Alcide Bava" and which accompanies a sampling of Rimbaud's most recent work, the young poet claims to be eighteen years old. In truth he has not yet turned seventeen. He further reminds Banville of the poems he had sent him the previous year when he was "only seventeen." (At that time he was in fact just over fifteen and a half.) It is interesting to note that in the May 24, 1870 letter introducing those first poems, Rimbaud refers to himself as an "enfant touché par le doigt de la Muse," a child touched by the finger of the Muse (1972, 236). Rimbaud concludes his 1871 letter by asking the master if he sees any progress over the work of a year earlier. This letter, with its new signature, its misrepresentation of the poet's age, and its apparent rejection of a youthful body of work, suggests a conscious effort on Rimbaud's part to seek confirmation of what he feels to be his new maturity.

14. Jim Morrison's body now lies in the Père-Lachaise cemetery in Paris.

15. Strangely, he claims to have deserted from the *French* army in a letter written in English to the Consul of the United States (May 14, 1877). Here he speaks of himself in the third person and asks "about the conditions on which he could conclude an immediate engagement in the American navy" (1972, 302–3). In that letter he claims also to have qualified as a "sailor in a Scotch bark," a reference to the boat on which he returned after deserting his post in Java. Obviously, Rimbaud is no respecter of countries.

WORKS CITED

Acker, Kathy. *In Memoriam to Identity*. New York: Grove Weidenfeld, 1990.

Adam, Antoine. Notices, notes et variantes. In *Oeuvres complètes*, by Arthur Rimbaud, 837–1213. Paris: Gallimard, 1972.

Ariès, Philippe. *L'Enfant et la vie familiale sous l'Ancien Régime*. Paris: Seuil, 1973.

Bonnefoy, Yves. "Madame Rimbaud." Trans. Jean Stewart. In *The Act and the Place of Poetry*, ed. John Naughton, 66–95. Chicago: University of Chicago Press, 1989.

———. *Rimbaud*. Trans. Paul Schmidt. New York: Harper and Row, 1973.

Borer, Alain. *Un Sieur Rimbaud: la terre et les pierres*. Paris: Lachenal et Ritter, 1984.

Briet, Suzanne. *Rimbaud notre prochain, avec des documents inédits*. Paris: Nouvelles éditions latines, 1956.

The Doors. Dir. Oliver Stone. Imagine Entertainment and Tri-Star Pictures, 1991. Film.

Etiemble, R. *Le Mythe de Rimbaud: Structure et mythe*. Paris: Gallimard, 1961.

Ferenczi, Sándor. "Confusion of Tongues between the Adult and the Child." *International Journal of Psychoanalysis* 30 (1949): 225–30.

Fowlie, Wallace. Introduction. In his *Rimbaud: Complete Works, Selected Letters*, by Arthur Rimbaud, 1–6. Chicago: University of Chicago Press, 1966.

Mannoni, Maud. *L'Enfant, sa "maladie" et les autres: le symptôme et la parole*. Paris: Seuil, 1967.

Rimbaud, Arthur. *Oeuvres Complètes*. Ed. Antoine Adam. Paris: Gallimard, 1972.

————. *Rimbaud: Complete Works, Selected Letters.* Ed. and trans. Wallace Fowlie. Chicago: University of Chicago Press, 1966.

Shengold, Leonard. *Soul Murder: The Effects of Childhood Abuse and Deprivation.* New Haven, CT: Yale University Press, 1989.

Starkie, Enid. *Arthur Rimbaud.* New York: New Directions, 1961.

Verlaine, Paul. *Royal Tastes: Erotic Writings.* Trans. Alan Stone. New York: Harmony Books, 1984.

A Womb of His Own:
Lawrence's Passional/Parental View of Childhood

Carol Sklenicka and Mark Spilka

> The youth walks up to the white horse, to put
> its halter on and the horse looks at him in
> silence.
> They are so silent, they are in another world.
> —D. H. Lawrence, "The White Horse"

I

In a long speculative essay called *Fantasia of the Unconscious* (1922), D. H. Lawrence quarrels with the adult habit of wanting children to draw as cameras photograph. Children's drawings are matters of vision and desire, he argues, not of accuracy or skill:

> When a boy of eight sees a horse, he doesn't see the correct biological object we intend him to see. He sees a big living presence of no particular shape with hair dangling from its neck and four legs. If he puts two eyes in the profile, he is quite right. Because he does *not* see with optical, photographic vision. . . . The optical image is just a mere vibrating blur to a child—and indeed, to a passionate adult. In this vibrating blur the soul sees its own true correspondent. (125–26)

Such imagining of and admiration for a childlike mode of consciousness marks Lawrence's own rendering of children in his fiction, poetry and essays. Through the idea of a "vibrating blur" he shows us not only how a child might see the world, but also how a "passionate adult" like himself might write about children. For Lawrence, certainly, photographic realism was not as important as seeing that "vibrating blur" and making it live in his fiction.

In his two speculative studies of psychological development, *Psychoanalysis and the Unconscious* (1921) and *Fantasia of the Unconscious* (published together in one volume, 1960), Lawrence tried to validate and mythicize the pristine child consciousness as an ideal for modern adults to preserve and emulate; and in *Fantasia* especially, he made a point of including the generation and guidance of children as adult male concerns—indeed, he stressed them as paternal functions. But in his early novels he had already staked out childhood as a creative dominion, and had drawn there some of the finest portraits of children in modern literature: William and Paul Morel and the young Miriam Leivers in *Sons and Lovers* (1913); Tom Brangwen, his stepdaughter Anna Lensky, and her daughter Ursula Brangwen in *The Rainbow* (1915); and the strange Hawthornian child, Winifred Crich, in *Women in Love* (1920). Early in *Women in Love*, moreover, he had made a point of connecting the child's pristine vision with his own developing mode of seeing and presenting passional experience. Thus, when the school inspector Rupert Birkin visits the classroom of his future wife, Ursula Brangwen, he offers a lesson in drawing catkins that prefigures the "vibrating blur" passage of *Fantasia*:

> Ursula stood in front of the class, leading the children by questions to understand the structure and the meaning of the catkins.
>
> A heavy, copper-coloured beam of light came in at the west window, gilding the outlines of the children's heads with red gold, and falling on the wall opposite in a rich, ruddy illumination. Ursula, however, was scarcely conscious of it. . . .
>
> She heard, but did not notice the click of the door. Suddenly she started. She saw, in the shaft of ruddy, copper-coloured light near her, the face of a man. It was gleaming like fire, watching her, waiting for her to be aware. . . .
>
> "Did I startle you?" said Birkin, shaking hands with her. "I thought you had heard me come in."
>
> "No," she faltered, scarcely able to speak. . . .
>
> "It is so dark," he said. "Shall we have the light?"
>
> And moving aside, he switched on the strong electric lights. The class-room was distinct and hard, a strange place after the soft dim magic that filled it before he came. . . .
>
> "You are doing catkins?" he asked, picking up a piece of hazel from a scholar's desk in front of him "Are they as far out as this? . . ."
>
> "The red ones too!" he said, looking at the flickers of crimson that came from the female bud. . . .
>
> Suddenly he lifted his face to her, and her heart quickened at the flicker of his voice.
>
> "Give them some crayons, won't you?" he said, "so that they can make the gynaecious flowers red, and the androgynous yellow. I'd chalk them in plain, chalk in nothing else, merely the red and the yellow. Outline scarcely matters in this case. . . . It's the fact you want to emphasize, not a subjective impression to record. What's the fact?—red little spiky stigmas of the female flower, dangling yellow male catkin, yellow pollen flying from one to another. Make a pictorial record of the fact, as a child does when drawing a face—two eyes, one nose, mouth with teeth—so— "And he drew a figure on the blackboard. (*Women in Love* 35–36)

At this point Hermione Roddice, Birkin's present lover, enters the classroom, and the discussion broadens to include the vexed modern issue of hyperconscious awareness, or that mentalization of passional experience, and of "subjective impressions," which is a decided hazard of the collusive love between Birkin and Hermione that Lawrence wants to criticize. Indeed, this schoolroom passage is very much like its Dickensian precedent in *Hard Times*, in which the childhood heroine Sissy Jupe is caught in a similar shaft of sunlight to emphasize her ruddy ways and their marked contrast with the albino scholar Bitzer. Thus, as the school's prize utilitarian pupil, the pale Bitzer knows that a horse is in utilitarian fact a "graminivorous quadruped" but does not see it as Sissy would, with a child's fancy and lustrous sense of color and fun. Similarly Lawrence asks us, in *Fantasia* as in *Women in Love*, to see as children see when they draw "pictorial records of fact," whereby faces become "two eyes, one nose, mouth with teeth—so," and catkins become colorful flickering flowers, and a horse becomes "a big living presence of no particular shape with hair dangling from its neck and four legs." For like Dickens, Lawrence too is attacking alternate views of mind and feeling which prevent us from seeing and knowing our world with a child's passional directness.

But his modern game, in *Women in Love*, is to give us the emotional facts of a child's way of seeing things by connecting the charged flow of feeling between Birkin and Ursula in that varied classroom light with the colorful flow of pollen between male and female flowers of the catkin plant. It is a complicated game, moreover, in that Birkin seems to echo Dickens's utilitarian spokesman, Thomas Gradgrind, from *Hard Times*, in his emphasis on "hard facts" here; while at the same time he rightly stresses the value of externalization in handling subjective impressions. But this may only be Lawrence's way of bringing out the harshness of Birkin's take-charge masculine manner in this chapter, as he turns on those magic-dispelling lights, then lectures away at both Ursula and Hermione with his own mentalized versions of emotional liberation—ignoring all the while the degree to which Ursula understands and perhaps even anticipates him in her more magical teaching ambience for sketching flowers. To capture such complicated feelings, at any rate, Lawrence himself emphasizes the emotionally loaded external scene; and he is ever-mindful of the danger of destroying or warping the subjective flow between his characters through mentalizing tactics like those Birkin evinces here in the hard electric light, and of which the even more hyperconscious Hermione will soon be accused.

The lesson in catkins is renewed, later in the novel, by the contrast between the child Winifred's respectful passional sense of her pet rabbit Bismarck as *"un mystere, ein Wunder,"* when he escapes from his hutch, and the obscene anticipations of erotic lacerations between future lovers Gudrun Brangwen and Gerald Crich as they willfully quell the stubborn Bismarck. These modern avatars of "northern ice-destruction," or the use of mind and will to exploit the emotions in a violent struggle for power, are Lawrence's sophisticated versions of mentalized eroticism, and the perverse interiorities of their obscene relations in the rabbit scene are captured more powerfully through external focus and control than any direct wallowing in the subjective niceties of sexual combat might convey. Or so Lawrence might argue. For it is on this point that he separates himself from such modern peers in the language of hyperconscious perversities as Mann, Joyce, or Proust.

As most of us would agree, when these moderns emphasize the excesses of refined consciousness, they exercise the artistic possibilities of controlled and difficult language with great skill; but Lawrence scores them nonetheless for wallowing in the very medium they depict. Indeed, he scoffs at the self-conscious anatomies and dissections that flourish in the experimental works of Joyce, Proust, and Dorothy Richardson: "You can hear the death-rattle in their throats," he argues. "They can hear it themselves. They are listening to it with acute interest." And he goes on to mock such "infantile" absorption in the fictional death-twinges of toes and the descriptive blending of death-bed odors like frankincense and bacon fat. Such extreme self-consciousness, such stripping of emotions "to the finest threads," seems "childish, after a certain age." It may be all right to be self-conscious at seventeen, he argues, even at twenty-seven: "but if we are going it strong at thirty-seven, then it is a sign of arrested development"; and of "senile precocity" after that (1985, 151–52).

But if his contemporaries seem either "senile" or "infantile" to Lawrence, some of them—notably Joyce, Proust, and Mann (whom he elsewhere dismisses on similar grounds)—found languages for the expression of childhood experience that most of us appreciate. How does Lawrence distinguish his own preoccupation with the "vibrating blur" of childhood vision from things infantile? As we have already seen, he not only appropriates such vision for the use of "passionate adults," he connects it also with his own parental functions, whether as foster parent or novelist. Thus, if he had no children of his own, he advises others how to raise them with perfect aplomb in *Fantasia*, chiefly by casting himself as an adept in how children think and feel. Similarly, in his fictions, where children are, as it were, his own parental creations, he functions as that "passionate adult" who preserves childlike vision by focussing for the most part on external and relational actions, and so avoiding that hyperconscious obsession with shredded subjectivities that characterizes, in his view, such mentalizing contemporaries as Joyce, Proust, and Mann.

Perhaps more interestingly, he preserves and enhances the childlike through his painterly affinities with the French impressionists. Their influence seems evident in his own amateur paintings of the 1920s; but it is also strongly and for some critics definitively evident in his early fictions. Thus Joseph Warren Beach argues in *The Twentieth Century Novel* that Lawrence was not concerned with the shape of a thing in his fiction, but with the living feel of it; indeed, he painted "shimmering protoplasm" in emulation of the French impressionists: "It is this shimmeriness which is the chief contribution of Lawrence to novelistic technique. . . . He is, in the novel, very little of the dramatist and very much of the poet" (384).

We may want to quarrel with the minimization of drama here, since Lawrence's fiction often has its own powerful emotional form; but the connection we are now able to make between "shimmering protoplasm" and the child's vision of vibrating life seems helpful, especially with regard to the painting of light and color which the impressionists stressed and which those ruddy lights and vivid colors in the schoolroom scene in *Women in Love* certainly recall. But Lawrence's sheer visual *élan* has been admired by many observers and needs no further documentation. What is interesting is its external reinforcement of the emotional and tactile force of his depictions of children, after the manner of the impressionists (e.g., Renoir, Cassatt), for whom children were often favored subjects.

The living feel of things, for children as for adults, begins to take on interesting contours, then, as we examine Lawrence's passional/paternal views. Ultimately, of course, we must connect his "vibrating blur" with the primitive indefinite, or with that particular romantic metaphysic of the relation between the human and nature which is almost his signature as the fictional creator of birds, beasts, and flowers. This is what Lawrence hints at in *Fantasia* when he speaks of the soul as finding its own true correspondent in the horse's "vibrating blur." The life-force in nature, as in ourselves, comes across through the childlike vision we share as "passionate adults." In his essays on the novel his sense of the relatedness of all things in fiction, and of its vitalistic function in portraying "live man and live woman," is a stylistic incorporation of his vision of the life-force in humankind and nature. Late in his career, in *Apocalypse* (1931), he would exhibit his awareness of the "mana" or "theos" concept in anthropology, which corresponds so obviously with fictional relatedness:

> To the ancient consciousness . . . the universe was a great complex activity of things existing and moving and having effect. . . . Everything was *theos*; but even so, not at the same moment. At the moment, whatever *struck* you was god. If it was a pool of water, the very watery pool might strike you: then that was god; or a faint vapour at evening rising might catch the imagination; then that was *theos*; or thirst might overcome you at the sight of the water; then the thirst itself was god; or you drank, and the delicious and indescribable slaking of thirst was the god; or you felt the sudden chill of the water as you touched it: and then another god came into being, "the cold": and this was not a quality, it was an existing entity, almost a creature, certainly a *theos*. (84–85)

Finally, then, it is this relational sense of living and moving within a field of religious force, this primitive consciousness of indefinite powers and forces working in nature and ourselves, which explains what Lawrence means by the "vibrational blur" of childhood vision; and what he alludes to through Winifred Crich in *Women in Love*, when that precocious child calls her pet rabbit Bismarck "*un mystere, ein Wunder.*"

With Lawrence, then, the primitive and the childhood consciousness are one, and the passional consciousness of adult observers like himself partakes of them.

That it partakes also of ordinary consciousness, or that the adult observer moves easily between the ordinary and the primitive, or better still, stands above them and moves between them as in Lawrence's favorite metaphor of the Holy Ghost, as it mediates between body and soul, must also be noted. For above all, it is the movement between forms of consciousness which accounts for Lawrence's curious blend of traditional and experimental styles in his major fictions, and for his fictional treatment of children. We begin to see this especially through his running quarrel with Freud, first in *Sons and Lovers*, then in his two books on the unconscious, as he works out his own peculiar version of passional development.

2

Though *Sons and Lovers* was perhaps the first treatment of the Oedipus complex in modern fiction, its Freudian borrowings are somewhat garbled. Instead of positing innately sensual love for the mother and hostile rivalry with the father in small children, Lawrence demonstrates parental imposition of such longings and hostilities when first William, then Paul, reach puberty. Indeed, he tells us that their mother, Gertrude Morel, "was a woman who waited for her children to grow up" before turning to them for the satisfactions her husband had denied her (68). Meanwhile she has given them life and warmth, bonded with them in sensual ways that Lawrence considers healthy, as when the ailing Paul sleeps with his mother and is healed through the warmth and security of her physical presence (67). Such healthy sensual and affectional parent-child relations become defiantly counter-Freudian doctrines by the time Lawrence writes *Fantasia* and its companion study of passional development. Indeed, the tactile bonds are so salutary that Lawrence gets into trouble with future critics by insisting that vigorous spankings are preferable to "guilt-trips" from disapproving parents; but once more his preference for the sensual and tactile over mentalized emotions suggests why Freud belongs, in his view, among the hyperconscious anatomists and shredders. He resists Freud's analytical approach to dreams and passions, his depiction of the unconscious as "a chamber of horrors," his denials of sensual and affectional vitality and warmth between parents and children. His own Rousseauistic scheme, whereby adult society either corrupts or nurtures the edenic realm of childhood consciousness, suggests the need for intelligent choices by responsible parents able to stand above and move between the known dimensions of ordinary consciousness and the unknown dimensions of passional being.

We can see in his fictions examples of pernicious and responsible behaviors, in this regard, among parental characters. In *Sons and Lovers*, for instance, the children are strikingly vulnerable to exploitation by their parents, Gertrude and Walter Morel; their minds are like embattled territories wherein these two powerful personalities and stronger souls struggle for influence in predominantly damaging (though sometimes nurturing) ways. This embattled quality appears in radical shifts of points of view and interpretation within the novel and in complex imagery that reveals the relations of Paul to his parents in childhood, and in later years to his lovers. In the following passages, for instance, Lawrence creates a diptych of interiorized portraits in which Gertrude and Paul consider each other. Each feels responsibility and guilt for the other's very existence. First Gertrude watches Paul, whose survival has defied her initial rejection of him:

> So after dinner he lay down on the sofa, on the warm chintz cushions the children loved. Then he fell into a kind of doze. That afternoon Mrs. Morel was ironing. She listened to the small, restless noise the boy made in his throat as she worked. Again rose in her heart the old, almost weary feeling towards him. She had never expected him to live. And yet he had a great vitality in his young body. Perhaps it would have been a little relief to her if he had died. She always felt a mixture of anguish in her love for him.

Then Paul watches his mother:

> He, in his semi-conscious sleep, was vaguely aware of the clatter of the iron on the iron-stand, of the faint thud, thud on the ironing-board. Once roused, he opened his eyes to see his mother standing on the hearthrug with the hot iron near her cheek, listening, as it were, to the heat. Her still face, with the mouth closed tight from suffering and disillusion and self-denial, and her nose the smallest bit to one side, and her blue eyes so young, quick, and warm, made his heart contract with love. When she was quiet, so, she looked brave and rich with life, but as if she had been done out of her rights. It hurt the boy keenly, this feeling about her that she had never had her life's fulfilment: and his own incapability to make up to her hurt him with a sense of impotence, yet made him patiently dogged inside. It was his childish aim. (105)

These two portraits epitomize the attitude toward childhood that prevails in *Sons and Lovers.* Though Lawrence does not use the Freudian word—guilt—a sense of guilty responsibility is present both in Gertrude's "weary feeling" towards Paul and in his "hurt" feeling because his mother has "never had her life's fulfilment." This guilt represents a possessive sentimentalizing, a distortion through overpersonalizing, of the relationship between parent and child. Lawrence later came to advise, speaking in the persona of a parent, that "there must be in me no departure from myself, lest I injure the pre-conscious dynamic relation" (1960b, 89). In the paragraphs just quoted there is more departure from the self than Lawrence would approve, and it causes a penumbra in the picture each makes of the other. The images are deceptively clear because of the realistic regard of places and things that surrounds the characters; but Paul's sentiments, and his childlike vision of the mouth, nose, and eyes of his suffering mother, seem precocious in their emotional distortions. A child would not ordinarily notice the youthful warmth and quickness of his mother's blue eyes, though an adolescent might.

Similarly, the regret about her unfulfillment is an adolescent's, though it seems obviously learned from the mother's frequent transmissions of her sufferings to her children at this point in the novel: indeed, however precociously, the passage records such a transmission. The re-creation of the mother's consciousness is more plausible, or more familiar, and in that sense more effective: we are used to the assumption that a mother departs from herself for her children, whatever her weariness toward them; and yet Lawrence's inclusion of that weariness prefigures his later aversion to sacrificial motherhood and intimates also his present sense of potential damage to her oddly wakeful son.

In his letter to his editor, Edward Garnett, describing his intentions in *Sons and Lovers*, Lawrence speaks to the novel's paradoxical mix of vitality and potential damage in parent-child relations:

> A woman of character and refinement goes into the lower class, and has no satisfaction in her own life. She has had a passion for her husband, so the children are born of passion, and have heaps of vitality. But as her sons grow up, she selects them as lovers—first the eldest, then the second. These sons are *urged* into life by their reciprocal love of their mother—urged on and on. But when they come to manhood, they can't love, because their mother is the strongest power in their lives, and holds them. (1979–89, I: 476–77)

The passage suggests the terrible imposition of the mother's need for satisfaction on her sons and its future consequences, while at the same time indicating the heritage of passional vitality and spiritual determination she bequeaths them. What it doesn't mention is the father's place in this mixed preparation for the future: *his* enormous sensual vitality and creative energy; *his* earthy gentleness with the children when he works at home and tells pit stories; *his* male default, finally, as he victimizes his wife through economic irresponsibility and drunken rages, squanderings and beatings. The problem of reclaiming and revising his mixed paternal heritage would take Lawrence a lifetime to resolve, but there is some evidence in this novel and the next one of the ideal of male nurture and male self-responsibility that would eventually emerge.

3

In his next novel, *The Rainbow*, Anna Lensky's stepfather, Tom Brangwen, is a case in point. The delicacy of Lawrence's treatment of their parent-child relation is one of the many rewarding aspects of that richly satisfying novel, and again he proceeds through a childlike vision of emotionally charged externals, as in the often cited scene in the barn when Tom comforts the child Anna, distraught by separation from her birthing mother, by taking her along in his arms while he feeds the cows. But even before that, Lawrence establishes the grounds for their close relation by external means. A comparison of his approach to the relatively healthy child Anna, who is virtually denied interior language, and his later approach to her daughter Ursula, who as the more modern child is subjected to unhealthy parental imposition and is accordingly almost flooded with interior language, will help to demonstrate some of the more crucial assumptions he was then able to make about parent-child relations and their effect on emotional development.

These differences in interiority are postulated upon a distinction Lawrence makes in *Fantasia* between a child's natural consciousness and his or her mental consciousness. Arguing that mental or objective consciousness emerges rather late in a child's development, he opposes any attempt to hurry it, and to that end he even proposes the delay of formal schooling until age ten (117–29). Thus Anna in *The Rainbow*, born about 1863, is represented without interior language. She utters brief lines of dialogue, particularly in exchanges with her stepfather, Tom Brangwen (who is also notably inarticulate); but her vibrant character is presented primarily through an external point of view in visual, tactile, and kinetic images. In the following scene, which establishes the direction of her new relation with Brangwen, Anna expresses her ambivalence about her mother's marriage through her anger at the farm geese and her wish for them to accept her.

> "You're naughty, you're naughty," cried Anna, tears of dismay and vexation in her eyes. And she stamped her slipper.
> "Why, what are they doing?" asked Brangwen.
> "They won't let me come in," she said, turning her flushed little face to him.
> "Yi, they will. You can go in if you want to," and he pushed open the gate for her.
> She stood irresolute, looking at the group of bluey-white geese standing monumental under the grey, cold day.
> "Go on," he said.
> She marched valiantly a few steps in. Her little body started convulsively at the sudden, derisive Can-cank-ank of the geese. A blankness spread over her. The geese trailed away with uplifted heads under the low grey sky.
> "They don't know you," said Brangwen. "You should tell 'em what your name is."
> "They're *naughty* to shout at me," she flashed.
> "They think you don't live here," he said.

The scene is completed when Tom overhears Anna, who does not know he is present:

> Later he found her at the gate calling shrilly and imperiously:
> "My name is Anna, Anna Lensky, and I live here, because Mr. Brangwen's my father now. He *is*, yes he *is*. And I live here."
> This pleased Brangwen very much. And gradually, without knowing it herself, she clung to him, in her lost, childish, desolate moments, when it was good to creep up to something big and warm, and bury her little self in his big,

unlimited being. Instinctively he was careful of her, careful to recognise her and to give himself to her disposal. (1989, 66)

Lawrence rarely veers from the above uses of surface description, dialogue, and shifting points of view in presenting Anna as a child; and if he pauses at the end now to define and summarize the passions of both characters from his own parental point of view, it is only to underscore the exemplary nature of the healthy exchange, the benign example of male nurture and its supportive consequences he has just pulled off. Meanwhile, the scene conveys that psychological event with perfect clarity. The episode of Anna and the geese adequately portrays the child-self in action; and when Anna Lensky tells the birds, "Mr. Brangwen's my father now," the reader is supposed to join with Brangwen in believing it. Lawrence goes one better, moreover, than the approved goal of Victorian educators, as reported by Anita Schorsch, of stimulating benevolence in children by exposing them to the quiet dependency of "ducks, chickens, and other barnyard animals" (123): he makes the encounter with the noisy geese into a trial from which Anna emerges with a new identity.

Anna's unfixed nature in childhood and Lawrence's understanding of family relationships require that she be seen externally from several perspectives and juxtaposed with other characters (e.g., her mother, the servant, Tilly, and Tom). Illuminated from this variety of angles, she becomes, as it were, a prism that creates the rainbow of her unformed energetic being. This prismatic style of characterization suggests still another way by which Lawrence preserves the childlike and avoids the infantile: it allows him, that is to say, to avoid a kind of sentimentality that inheres in the child's point of view in many first-person accounts of family disruption. In *Jane Eyre* or *David Copperfield*, for instance, the hostile aspect of the adult environment and the reader's sympathy for the child are effectively—and wonderfully—enhanced by the author's restriction to Jane's or David's perspective. But Lawrence's hope for the novel opposes the personal, particularly the personal that refers to the writer's "specific case," the precious and the exaggerated, in favor of what he sees as "genuine relationships—which are always *new*" (1985, 242). Thus Robert Langbaum, praising Lawrence for avoiding sentimentality in "the most beautiful account of father-daughter love [Tom and Anna's] and the most beautiful portrait of a child in the English novel," notes the quality of "energy" that Lawrence evokes in the creation of Anna. Lawrence avoids sentimentality, Langbaum argues, because he "pitches the child's life at the appropriate phase of identity; he treats her as a kind of energy. Sentimentality comes from treating as individual and rational emotions that are impersonal and generated by external forces" (308–9).

While the energy Anna exhibits is not personal in the sense of emanating from a well-defined ego, it is assuredly individual. This paradox of individual but impersonal being is supported by Lawrence's insistence, in *Psychoanalysis*, that individuality inheres in a child from before birth: "The nature of the infant does *not* follow from the natures of its parents. The nature of the infant is *not* just a new permutation-and-combination of elements contained in the natures of the parents. . . . There is in the nature of the infant something entirely new, underived, underivable, something which is *causeless*. And this something is the unanalysable, indefinable reality of individuality" (14).

Conversely, mental consciousness or personality (roughly, ego) is acquired later, a learned and therefore artificial construction. Lawrence's child, then, loses rather than finds her *self* as she matures, contrary to the model that prevails in much twentieth-century psychology. We see, in this light, that Lawrence avoids sentimentality in his portrait of Anna because of the definiteness of her separate individual being, which persists at her core at this stage, resisting sentimentalization *despite* the effects of external forces upon her. Langbaum's notion of Anna as a "kind of energy" also helps to explain the commensurate insistence and volubility of her presence. There is something impersonal about her emotions in that they exist at a level deeper than that of the social intercourse between personalities. Anna's adjustment to life at Marsh Farm emanates from her natural individuality, which is no longer stifled by her mother's emotional need: "Her little life settled on its own swivel. . . . She became more childish, not so abnormal, not charged with cares she could not understand. . . . The child was freed. She became an independent, forgetful little soul, loving from her own centre" (1989, 79).

The other girl in *The Rainbow*, Anna's daughter Ursula, is seen from the interior. Born about 1883, just two years before Lawrence, she seems to be a person with whom he strongly identifies and whose point of view he can readily assume through the last half of the novel. In her early years, when his authorial point of view is not residing within her consciousness, it is in her father's, exploring the dark and confined relationship of the young father to his first child. The interiority of Ursula's childhood derives also from the demands of intense individuality and modernity which Lawrence had already conceived as part of her character in his first draft of the later chapters of this novel and their extension into the events of *Women in Love*, which he then called "The Sisters." In inventing Ursula's childhood, then, Lawrence was providing an appropriate history, devising a myth of origins, for a modern independent woman who could participate in his study of "*the* problem of today, the establishment of a new relation, or the readjustment of the old one, between men and women" (1979–89, I:546). Thus, despite her links with previous generations, Ursula represents a modern conception of the child, one in which the unconscious and its manifestations are crucial. So crucial, in fact, as to seem almost paradoxical if traffic in things unconscious takes Lawrence toward that wallowing in perverse interiorities he elsewhere finds "infantile." Bear with us, then, as we approach and examine this paradoxical realm and its continued preservations of things childlike from such hazards.

Lawrence renders Ursula's psychological growth, as he did Paul Morel's in *Sons and Lovers*, from before birth. When Anna Lensky Brangwen tells her parents she is expecting her first child (Ursula), the unborn girl's implied participation in the scene borrows from the rhetoric of mythical and holy births. The context is entirely ordinary: a disagreement with her husband (her stepfather's nephew Will Brangwen) has prevented Anna from giving the news of her pregnancy to him and she has turned to her parents instead. When Will passes by their house, the family servant calls him in to join the group at the table:

> They talked of trivial things. Through the open door the level rays of sunset poured in, shining on the floor. A grey hen appeared stepping swiftly in the doorway, pecking, and the light through her comb and her wattles made an oriflamme tossed here and there, as she went[;] her grey body was like a ghost.
> Anna, watching, threw scraps of bread, and she felt the child flame within her. She seemed to remember again forgotten, burning, far-off things.
> "Where was I born, mother?" she asked. (1989, 164–65)

Oriflamme, or auriflamme, the term that connects these pending and forgotten births, was first employed to name the orange or red-orange flag of the Abbey of St. Denis, a flag that was used as an inspirational banner by early French kings. Associated now with the comb and wattles of an ordinary chicken, it becomes an image that transcends medieval quaintness and near ludicrousness to magnify and beautify the fowl. Lawrence reveals a certain holiness and grandeur in everyday life by sketching unmediated, myth-like connections between the evening light, the ghostly body of a hen, with its comb-like aureole, and the movement of Ursula in Anna's womb. The aura that Lawrence seems to impose on the scene with the flame imagery is felt by all those present, including the recalcitrant Will, and thus becomes a palpable force toward reconciliation of the family.

As they walk home hand in hand, however, the distance between Anna and Will suddenly widens when she tells him she is pregnant. Anna feels too glorified and set apart herself to sense the change: "The blaze of light on her heart was too beautiful and dazzling, from the conception in her womb." But Will, troubled by her happy absorption, suddenly feels cut off and frightened: "she seemed fulfilled and separate and sufficient in her half of the world. Why could he not always be one with her? It was he who had given her the child" (1989, 166). This conflict between the parents—between Anna's beatified sense of her pregnant self and Will's insecurely patriarchal desire to merge with his wife and possess the child—eventually lodges in Ursula's consciousness, which exhibits a unique combination of expansive psychic qualities (like Anna's) and analytical emotional qualities (like Will's). These qualities modify her innate individuality and force upon her a quest to forge her own being that will continue into adulthood. This dislodgement of and challenge to her being, and to its flaming sanction even before birth, makes her profoundly modern.

In the first version of his study of American literature, *The Symbolic Meaning* (1918–19), Lawrence declares of Pearl in Nathaniel Hawthorne's *Scarlet Letter:* "We cannot help regarding the phenomenon of Pearl with wonder, and fear, and amazement, and respect. . . . Nowhere in literature is the spirit of much of modern childhood so profoundly, almost magically revealed" (1964, 137). The character Pearl, Lawrence also notes, is more of a symbolic abstraction than a personality. Hawthorne's art neglects the character's "personal plane" in favor of the soul's "passional abstraction" (127). Likewise, in *The Rainbow*, Lawrence wishes to imagine his characters in a zone beyond that of realistic personal qualities. Much of the first part of *The Rainbow*, the part in which Anna (Ursula's mother) grows up, seems to take place on pre-conscious levels of being. The apparent incongruity of the objective portrayal of young Anna within this rather oceanic context is actually a technique by which Lawrence emphasizes the inaccessibility of the child's consciousness and enacts its development; at the same time, he asserts the mingling of the physical and the spiritual by representing Anna's psychic growth in terms of external events.

By contrast, one of Lawrence's problems in creating the story of Ursula is that her modernity requires that she awaken to mental consciousness at an early age. Lawrence assigns himself to write about the interchange between conscious and subconscious in a modern character without creating the kind of diabolical split that he criticizes in Pearl. Ursula is, like Pearl, a study in the interaction of the various impulses that make up the consciousness (for Lawrence this term includes the unconscious or "blood consciousness"). She is even more modern than Pearl: "Her father was the dawn wherein her consciousness woke up. But for him, she might have gone on like the other children . . . one with the flowers and insects and playthings, having no existence apart from the object of her attention. But her father came too near to her. The clasp of his hands and power of his breast woke up almost in pain from the transient unconsciousness of childhood" (1989, 205). As a child Ursula responds to this parental imposition by shifting rapidly from one mood to another; but she has also, from an early age, the ability to divide her consciousness into levels, retaining one feeling or response in secret while displaying another one to the world. It is this trait, displayed through interior views of her consciousness, that makes Ursula, along with Paul of "The Rocking-Horse Winner," especially modern among Lawrence's child characters. And it is another trait that links her with Hawthorne's Pearl. Lawrence's exposure of this self-consciousness and private consciousness makes Ursula entirely different, then, from the externally dramatized Anna. We can see this difference in an incident which occurs when she is four years old and which begins upon an external plane. Her father, shocked by "zigzagging lines of deep little footprints across his work," has shouted at her for trampling his seed beds:

> Her soul, her consciousness, seemed to die away. She became shut off and senseless, a little fixed creature whose soul had gone hard and unresponsive. The sense of her own unreality hardened her like a frost. She cared no longer. . . .
> Yet far away in her, the sobs were tearing her soul. And when he had gone,

she would go and creep under the parlour sofa, and lie clinched in the silent, hidden misery of childhood.

When she crawled out . . . she went rather stiffly to play. She willed to forget. She cut off her childish soul from memory, so that the pain, and the insult should not be real. (207–8)

Lawrence proceeds here through a kind of sympathetic discourse, a summarizing of the character's thoughts and feelings that allows him to economize on subjective exposition rather than exploit and anatomize its properties. It is this sympathetic mimicry, which enables him to enter and leave the realm of things interior as its sensitive register, and to mediate between it and things external from his parental point of view, that works to preserve things childlike. We have already seen its effects, for instance, in that previous summary passage following Anna's triumph with the geese; or, less plausibly, in the internal shifts of the ironing scene in *Sons and Lovers*. Nonetheless the language here implies a bifurcation of the self; it ascribes a remarkable degree of intention to the young girl's management of her own psyche and experience, and so describes her in terms that Lawrence usually reserves for adult characters and their more conscious dealings with the unconscious.

4

The Rainbow would seem to be the high-water mark of Lawrence's interest in representing children as characters in his novels. As we have seen, he would concentrate in his next novel, *Women in Love*, on the relation between childhood consciousness, as precariously represented by the strange modern child, Winifred Crich, and the needs of adult characters to preserve and nurture its equivalent in their own passional progress. But *Women in Love* is itself the high point of Lawrence's artistic development as a writer of major experimental fictions. In this novel about precarious modern times, he proceeds almost exclusively by symbolic and ritualistic scenes and the modulations of sympathetic mimicry to set his characters in passional relation to the life within and around themselves, and to explore thereby their movements toward or away from greater or lesser fullness of spontaneous being. In turning away from the richness of that achievement, and from the preoccupation with the growth and change of maturing children that preceded and made it possible, he would enter the troubled male leadership phase of his career, and would sacrifice the artistic and emotional richness of his early major novels for what he would himself call "thought-adventures" and "pollyanalytics," as if to emphasize the change in the level of his artistic seriousness. Only in his shorter novels and tales would he advance his artistic work with continuing seriousness.

The "thought-adventures" were *Aaron's Rod* (1922) and *Kangaroo* (1923), and

perhaps also—though with a renewed attempt at poetic and mythic enrichment—
The Plumed Serpent (1926). Children are present in these largely political novels only
briefly, and then as mere pawns, perhaps in keeping with the pessimistic view of
lost vitality which pervades them, and with their dubious attempts to restore that
vitality through personal and cultural forms of male supremacy. Meanwhile, in his
two long essays of psychological "pollyanalytics," Lawrence would summarize and
extend his earlier fictional findings about children's development and would shape
his own provocative view of adult male functions within that familiar domestic
context.

As Judith Ruderman points out (31–36), Lawrence's concern with male
leadership actually begins in *Fantasia*, where he first asserts that men must have a
goal in the world beyond that of an achieved relationship with women, whereas
women should subordinate their own self-assertions and support men's "passionate, purposive activity" (1960b, 156–57, 160). But within this announcement of
male missions to come, Lawrence asserts and explicates the paternal role in child-
rearing as if staking out for himself that most female of domains. He does so in
two related ways.

First, he emphasizes the role of the sperm—"the bright male germ"—in the
making of the individual child, which he connects with two other privileged subjects, the solar plexus and blood consciousness. This original germ "still lies sparkling and potent within the solar plexus." The physical connection of the child
to its mother is more obvious because of the navel, their relation seems accordingly
"more plausible and flagrant"; but, he asks, "is that any reason for supposing it
deeper, more vital, more intrinsic? . . . The smaller, brilliant male-spark . . . may
be even more vivid, even more intrinsic. So beware how you deny the father-quick
of yourself. You may be denying the most intrinsic quick of all" (1960b, 70).

Secondly, Lawrence insists upon the importance of the father in raising the
child because, in order to develop a proper balance and independence, the child
must grow "in the interplay of two great life-waves, the womanly and the male"
(1960b, 73). The role Lawrence recommends for fathers here is not necessarily
masculine in any stereotypical sense; if a mother is "too generally hard and indifferent, then it rests with the father to provide the delicate sympathy and the
refined discipline" (88). Whether the father is called upon to be sympathetic or
stern, he must "stand outside as the final authority and make the necessary adjust-
ments . . . to maintain some sort of equilibrium between the two modes of love
in his infant" (87).

A feminist reading of these sections of *Fantasia* might waver as to whether
Lawrence is trying to usurp female territory or to share it responsibly, to acknowledge, that is to say, the importance of child nurture for men as for women, and
to elevate it for men by removing its historic segregation by gender. While the
sagacity and unilateral authority he imputes to the father are plainly patriarchal,
his overall attitude evinces continuing respect for the child and a wary respect also
for the mother's biological being. During the 1920s, this wariness undergirds

many of Lawrence's misogynistic remarks about women and their roles. In these years he seems to substitute for his classic Oedipal desires a kind of womb-envy, a wish to possess what might well be called a womb of his own. Amidst her thoroughgoing analysis of Lawrence and matriarchy, for instance, Sandra Gilbert makes the startlingly right observation that for Lawrence "the phallus almost functions as a kind of substitute baby . . . miniature but autonomous" (154). If this is so, then even Lawrence's most privileged signifier, the phallus itself, becomes secondary to the signified, the human child; and Lawrence the male author becomes the androgynous mother/father to the children in his novels.

Lawrence's didactic approach to parenthood dominates *Fantasia*. He attempts to describe and prescribe the relations of children and parents. Thus fathers and mothers alike must never let an idealized notion of love replace a more essential respect between individuals: "Never forget your own honour as adult individual toward a small individual. It is a question of honour, not of love" (115). Indeed, without such honour, parental love may turn possessive and invasive: "Instead of leaving the child with its own limited but deep and incomprehensible feelings, the parent . . . stimulates the child into a consciousness which does not belong to it, on one plane, and robs it of its own spontaneous consciousness and freedom on the other plane" (151). Speaking earlier as a foster parent, Lawrence reminds his peers that children "are more sagacious than we are. They twig soon enough if there is a flaw in our intention and our own true spontaneity" (91). Therefore they must be treated honestly and directly, not bullied, patronized, or idealized. Nor can parents expect or teach a child to love them; rather they must "always remember that it is a single little soul by itself; and that the responsibility for the wise, warm relationship is yours, the adult's" (115). When, to the contrary, the child's natural individuality is invaded too early by the demands of mental consciousness, there is hell to pay. If the individual survives, it is through painful, symbolic rebirths like those at the closings of *Sons and Lovers* and *The Rainbow*, where both Paul Morel and Ursula Brangwen re-enact the pangs of original birth by moving respectively from the beckoning darkness of a mother's death toward the light of a "glowing town," and from potential marital bondage and the miscarriage of an unwanted pregnancy toward the rainbow's radiant promise.

Toward the end of the pessimistic leadership phase, and perhaps because of it, Lawrence wrote his only story about the death of a young child. Thus, in "The Rocking-Horse Winner" (1926), he treats the child as Dickens and James did before him in grim Victorian times: as a helpless victim of the wrongheaded values of the adult world. Yet the child is also a peculiarly active and in that sense a peculiarly modern victim. Whenever he rides his rocking-horse, for instance, he possesses uncanny powers and is able to predict the winners of horse races on which his friend Bassett, the family gardener, then places his secret bets. He is driven to this magical extreme by a parental imposition, a whisper running through the house expressing his mother's insatiable demand: *"There must be more money."* Ultimately he dies as he rides into feverish delirium while intuiting the winner of the next major race, winning eighty thousand pounds for the mother who survives him.

The story's rhetoric is also like that of a Dickensian fable or fairy-tale, as in the opening line ("[Once] there was a woman who was beautiful"), the haunting whispers just noted, the illustrative obsessions, and the closing moral precept. The precept illustrated, however, is a modern one like those we have already seen in *Fantasia*: adults should not twist a child's spirit to serve their own desires. Thus the Paul of this story is essentially another Paul Morel, whose mother transmits whispers of unfulfillment but who loves him too little, in this case, rather than too much. Because he feels the coldness of her heart, and because she tells him that his father had no luck, the boy tells her that he possesses luck. Then, when he learns about horse-racing from the gardener, he undertakes to prove himself and begins to intuit winners. When his clandestine deposits of his winnings in his mother's account only bring more creditors, Paul vows to earn more and more. But his quest for the wrong kind of knowledge kills him; the attempt to assume his father's role, and to hold himself responsible for satisfying his mother, is too much for him. His uncanny ability to articulate his mother's desire for hard cash has been substituted for his own desire to express filial love. The rocking-horse is, as it were, a corrupt substitute for healthy physical affection and the unmastered language of childhood.

Along with its Victorian leanings, "The Rocking-Horse Winner" combines the mimetic representation of a child that marks Lawrence's earlier fiction with the more symbolic presentation of themes in his later fiction. Thus Uncle Oscar's eulogy for his nephew—"poor devil, poor devil, he's best gone out of a life where he rides his rocking-horse to find a winner" (1961, 3:804)—may stand as Lawrence's general moral comment on the modern experience of doomed childhood in the period following World War I, in which "There are plenty of children, and no hope" (1979–89, 2: 635). Hope fails because the child's individuality is immediately perverted by modern thinking:

> We talk about education—leading forth the natural intelligence of a child. But ours is just the opposite of leading forth. It is a ramming in of brain facts through the head, and a consequent distortion, suffocation, and starvation of the primary centres of consciousness. . . . By the age of twenty-one our young people are helpless, hopeless, selfless, floundering mental entities, with nothing in front of them, because they have been starved from the roots, systematically, for twenty-one years, and fed through the head. (1960b, 128)

By 1928, however, Lawrence began to feel more sanguine. In *Lady Chatterley's Lover* he turned away from the pessimism and the dubious militancy of the leadership phase, and issued a call for a new novel, a whole new range of tender feelings, and new men and women to express them. Here his earlier notions about male nurture and life-responsibility would finally bear belated fruit, and his reclamation of the better possibilities of his paternal heritage, and of his own and his parents' marriages, would find fictional expression. Here, too, the conflict of worldly despair and personal salvation through sexual tenderness and mutual nurture would finally be resolved by the expectation of a child. Thus, as the novel moves toward its close, the gamekeeper lover of the title, Oliver Mellors, speaks to the lady in question of his fears and responds warmly to her reassuring command:

> "I've a dread of puttin' children i' th' world," he said. "I've such a dread o' th' future for 'em."
> "But you've put it into me. Be tender to it, and that will be its future already. Kiss it."
> He quivered because it was true. . . . He kissed her belly and her mound of Venus, to kiss close to the womb and the foetus within the womb. (291–92)

This unborn child seems to us to presage the desire in Lawrence's last work to reclaim the child from ordinary experience and the rhetoric of realistic fiction and to appropriate it for the myth of renewal in the flesh. In *The Escaped Cock* (1929), which rewrites the story of Christ in Lawrence's terms, the priestess of Isis is impregnated by a Lawrence/Christ figure who calls himself Osiris. As he escapes from the regions of her temple, where her mother's slaves have conspired to kill him, he says to himself and the reader: "I have sowed the seed of my life and my resurrection, and put my touch forever upon the choice woman of this day, and I carry her perfume in my flesh like essence of roses" (61). Within this mythic rhetoric, the figuration of resurrection obtains specificity as a child and is rooted in the particular time of "this day"—though the child is yet to be born and the time undated.

5

In this brief exposition of some of the varied means by which Lawrence offers a rhetoric for fictional childhood, we have tried to show that his understanding of and regard for the child is not a static concept, but rather one that evolves with and remains vital to the rest of his thought and art. Because Lawrence feels certain about the individual nature of the child by the middle of his career, he feels no occasion to adopt a particular style or language for the child's consciousness; nor does he attempt at any point to simulate directly the nature of childhood speech or thought as, for example, Joyce, Woolf, and Faulkner sometimes do. Instead he develops a variety of rhetorical strategies for expressing healthy or unhealthy states of childhood consciousness that respect the different life within each child. Thus, if some modes of mental discourse now seem to him more hazardous in this respect than others, more perilously perverse, even as the lives of children become more hazardous and perverse in modern times, he can still find healthy modes of discourse which will accommodate those hazards and honor the different possibilities of life within each child. Indeed, as we have tried throughout to suggest, Lawrence's success in the creation of child characters and the seriousness of his theory of child consciousness are of a piece with his desire to people literature with characters who are not so much realistic as they are, according to his lights, alive, and therefore to be valued for the life within them.

If, in the course of these remarks, our own preference for *The Rainbow* stands out, even as we trace new dimensions of the subject in his other works, it is because the girls Anna and Ursula seem to us Lawrence's most vibrant representations of childhood. Thus, even in their deeper purposes, our studies of his other works simply circle around our wonder at these two creations. A recent speculation from biographer Jeffrey Meyers that Lawrence was made sterile by a mumps-like disease at age sixteen suggests to us, in this light, an androgynous conceit: that these two girls are daughters Lawrence would have liked to have mothered forth, had gender and the mumps allowed him to be a mother, whereas poor Paul of "The Rocking-Horse Winner" is the boy for whose fate in the greedy world he would have feared and trembled, had he been able to be a father. By the vibrant light of this lustrous androgynous fancy, then, if not in literal or utilitarian fact, the novels function for Lawrence as a womb over which he presides as both mother and father.

WORKS CITED

Beach, Joseph Warren, *The Twentieth Century Novel: Studies in Technique.* New York: Appleton-Century-Crofts, 1932.

Dickens, Charles. *Hard Times.* Edited by George Ford and Sylvère Monod. New York: Norton Critical Edition, 1966.

Gilbert, Sandra. "Potent Griselda: 'The Ladybird' and the Great Mother." In *D. H. Lawrence: A Centenary Consideration,* ed. Peter Balbert and Phillip L. Marcus, 130–61. Ithaca, NY: Cornell University Press, 1985.

Langbaum, Robert. *The Mysteries of Identity: A Theme in Modern Literature.* New York: Oxford University Press, 1977.

Lawrence, D. H. *Apocalypse.* 1931. New York: Viking Press, 1932.

———. *The Complete Short Stories.* 1961. 3 vols. New York: Penguin, 1976a.

———. *The Escaped Cock.* Edited by Gerald M. Lacy. Santa Barbara, CA: Black Sparrow, 1976b.

———. *Lady Chatterley's Lover.* 1928. Harmondsworth: Penguin, 1960a.

———. *The Letters of D. H. Lawrence.* Edited by James T. Boulton, et al. 5 vols. to date. Cambridge: Cambridge University Press, 1979–89.

———. *Psychoanalysis and the Unconscious* and *Fantasia of the Unconscious.* 1921, 1922. New York: Viking, 1960b.

————. *The Rainbow.* 1915. Edited by Mark Kinkead-Weekes. Cambridge: Cambridge University Press, 1989.

————. *Sons and Lovers.* 1913. Edited by Keith Sagar. New York: Penguin, 1981.

————. *Study of Thomas Hardy and Other Essays.* Cambridge: Cambridge University Press, 1985.

————. *The Symbolic Meaning: The Uncollected Versions of Studies in Classic American Literature.* Edited by Armin Arnold. New York: Viking, 1964.

————. *Women in Love.* 1920. Edited by David Farmer, Lindeth Vasey, and John Worthen. Cambridge: Cambridge University Press, 1987.

Meyers, Jeffrey. *D. H. Lawrence: A Biography.* New York: Knopf, 1990.

Ruderman, Judith. *D. H. Lawrence and the Devouring Mother: The Search for a Patriarchal Ideal of Leadership.* Durham, NC: Duke University Press, 1984.

Schorsch, Anita. *Images of Childhood: An Illustrated Social History.* Pittstown, NJ: Main Street Press, 1985.

Sklenicka, Carol. *D. H. Lawrence and the Child.* Columbia, MO: University of Missouri Press, 1991.

Spilka, Mark. *The Love Ethic of D. H. Lawrence.* Bloomington: Indiana University Press, 1955.

"We Haven't the Words": The Silence of Children in the Novels of Virginia Woolf

ELIZABETH GOODENOUGH

The central drama of Virginia Woolf's fiction lies in the relation characters form with their pasts. In sketching some aspect of infancy, childhood, adolescence, or young adulthood, all her major works show how the early life of the individual gives rise to the multiple identities of the adult. Adult consciousness is thus conceived as an amalgam of the interchange between self and world, a process that originates with an individual's first sense impressions.

Woolf's development as a novelist suggests that as she found her own voice as an artist, she became more confident about the possibility of establishing a personal vision. However, she differs from other writers concerned with childhood and the emergence of identity by her romantic pessimism. Her fiction celebrates the consciousness of children: in their wonder and certainty they embody the purest kind of integrity a character can achieve. She portrays the individual's first impressions as the most distilled and authentic moments of life: a union of self and external world is achieved which epitomizes the self and can never be attained again. But according to the logic of her universe, the very intensities of early life invite their own curtailment: the child's reckless imagination and perfect self-absorption cannot survive the maturation process.

While childhood is fundamental to Woolf's response to and understanding of human life, it is remarkable how rarely children talk in her novels. Little juvenile dialogue is recorded and if children do speak, their speech is inarticulate or extremely simple. That children's language goes largely unrecorded does not indicate Woolf thought children were actually voiceless creatures, seen but not heard by their elders. Passionate in his desire, James Ramsay, age six, has presumably asked his mother more than once if he can go to the lighthouse. Yet the beginning of *To the Lighthouse* (1927) deletes his urgent childish question even as it propels the novel

184

into being. Only the mother's response is recorded: " 'Yes, of course, if it's fine tomorrow,' " said Mrs. Ramsay. 'But you'll have to be up with the lark' " (9).

At this critical juncture, like other moments when children appear in her fiction, Woolf calls attention to the interior being of children by her refusal to render their speech. For adults familiar with the repetitive "When can I?" formulations of children, reading James's actual words would inevitably reduce the level and significance of an experience Woolf respected as the symbol and germ of creative life. Instead, after the ellipsis of James's query—represented by the blank space from which the words of the text take their origin—the narrative moves inward toward an inexpressible reality, the intense visualizing and symbol-making process of early life:

> To her son these words conveyed an extraordinary joy, as if it were settled, and the expedition were bound to take place, and the wonder to which he had looked, for years and years it seemed, was, after a night's darkness and day's sail within touch. Since he belonged even at the age of six to that great clan which cannot keep this feeling separate from that, but must let future prospects, with their joys and sorrows, cloud what is actually at hand, since to such people even in earliest childhood any turn in the wheel of sensation has the power to crystallize and transfix the moment upon which its gloom or radiance rests, James Ramsay, sitting on the floor cutting out pictures from the illustrated catalogue of the Army and Navy Stores, endowed the picture of a refrigerator, as his mother spoke, with heavenly bliss. It was fringed with joy. (9)

When Woolf describes the "true romantic" in an essay on Richard Sheridan, she contrasts this being to the eighteenth-century playwright whose sentimental romanticism left him discontented with the actual world. But the true romantic, she asserts, "makes his past out of an intense joy in the present; it is the best of what he sees, caught up and set beyond the reach of change" (1977, 46). If "past" is replaced by "future," this definition applies admirably to James and the "great clan" of true romantics to which he belongs. The future prospect of the lighthouse, "the best of what he sees," is constructed from the sympathetic understanding of his mother. Powerless over the weather, James is a creature of such high hopes that he banishes the condition prefacing Mrs. Ramsay's response altogether. Instead, he seizes on her faith that he can meet the challenge of being "up with the lark," Shelley's image for a vision so charged it can only be intimated through soaring flight and song. By Mrs. Ramsay's affirmation of his hopefulness, James considers the ecstatic future a "settled" reality. And just as the glamour of the expedition arises from his mother's validation of him, the excitement of his prospect permeates the present, transfixing the moment and endowing the protected world he inhabits with "heavenly bliss."

Although the narrator explains James's train of thought and feeling—how he processes his mother's response, how time stops and a moment is eternalized in a mind brimming with anticipation—what James actually sees is only hinted at. But

185

the absolute authority and receptivity of the child's mind, transforming impressions in a unique configuration, symbolizes Woolf's highest ideal: the power and freedom of the unfettered imagination to create its own reality.

In her association of the child with the creative imagination, Woolf reflects the influence of Romanticism on her psychology and aesthetic philosophy. Believing, like Wordsworth, that "the impressions of childhood are those that last longest and cut deepest" (1966, 1:62), Woolf gained early in her own life a sense of mastery and autonomy through words. But she was attracted throughout her career to the possibilities for communication offered by sign and alternative languages. In her essay, "On Not Knowing Greek," Woolf discusses the variety of ways words can communicate and termed ambiguity "the mark of highest poetry" because "the meaning is just on the far side of language. It is the meaning which in moments of astonishing excitement we perceive in our minds without words" (1966, 1:7). In *Night and Day* (1919), Woolf's second novel, the young Katherine Hilbery secretly studies mathematics and astronomy because she prefers "the exactitude, the star-like impersonality of figures to the confusion, agitation, and vagueness of the finest prose" (40). Finally ambushed by "what other people call love" (472), she becomes aware of desire, emerging "wild, irrational, and unexplained, resembling something felt in childhood" (442).

Constantly wary of phrases, Woolf exhibited a primitivist tendency in her attempt to recapture preverbal experience, to return to the anonymity of a common beginning, to exorcise the civilization of the species as well as the individual. To convey significant realities she knew she had to think backwards, to start from scratch, to reorder language in a radical way. As Bernard, the frustrated writer, states at the end of *The Waves* (1931): "I need a little language such as lovers use, words of one syllable such as children speak when they come into the room and find their mother sewing and pick up some scrap of bright wool, a feather, a shred of chintz. I need a howl; a cry" (381). Children in Woolf's fiction, in their social nonconformity and isolation, are free to be silent. They resist the linear and reductive logic of sentences and resort to cries or monosyllabic exclamations to express what they see. But in their failure to share the generalizing talk and well-worn formulas of their elders, Woolf draws attention to a singularity of being she can only liken to heaven. Just as Shelley uses a skylark to symbolize the gyrating thrill of apprehending a transcendent world in song, Woolf in "Mr. Hudson's Childhood" describes her unorthodox sense of something beyond through the unspoken excitement of childhood epiphanies:

> Between or behind the dense and involved confusion which grown up life presented there appeared for moments chinks of pure daylight in which the simple, unmistakeable truth, the underlying reason, otherwise so overlaid and befogged was revealed. Such seasons, or more probably seconds, were of so intense a revelation that the wonder came to be how the truth could ever again be overcast, as it

certainly would be overcast directly this lantern-like illumination went out. (1965, 94)

In her emphasis on the receptivity of youth to moments of sensation and on selfhood as a hard outer construct, like a house or a room, Woolf recalls the epistemology of "brain-building" which Water Pater developed in his autobiographical essay "The Child in the House" and the bildungsroman *Marius the Epicurean* (1885). Like Pater, she stresses the formative role of memory and the transforming power of the child's visionary imagination. As he had indicated, "we see inwardly as children and thus create our own heaven out of whatever random piece of earth we inhabit. . . . the child finds for itself, and with unstinted delight, a difference for the sense, in those whites and reds through the smoke on very homely buildings, and in the gold of the dandelions at the road-side, just beyond the houses, where not a handful of earth is virgin and untouched, in the lack of better ministries to its desire of beauty" (175). The child's capacity to create such a heaven is at the core of Woolf's visual psychology. In her celebration of this primordial instinct, Woolf reflects "the respect shown in romantic and modern literature and in modern culture generally for the mental life of children, primitives and even animals," a respect Robert Langbaum relates to Freud's use of the Darwinian "legend" in his integration of biology, psychology and social history: "Freud traces our highest achievements back to the primeval ooze, showing that our thoughts like our bodies recapitulate the history of the species, and this imaginative appropriation of evolutionary biology awakens in us a sense of awe before the miracle of culture—as a flower growing out of the mud" (10).

The paradoxical extremes of this view are well represented in *Between the Acts* (1941), in which an iconoclastic rural pageant of English history is staged in a world on the brink of collapse. Among the shards of British civilization (as Woolf, fearing Hitler's invasion as she wrote, presents a day in June 1939) the speechless vulnerability of the very young child is related to his invincible powers of seeing. George Oliver, out for a stroll with his nurses, lags behind when a flower suddenly captures his eye: "It blazed a soft yellow, a lambent light under a film of velvet; it filled the caverns behind the eyes with light. All that inner darkness became a hall, leaf smelling, earth smelling, of inner light. And the tree was beyond the flower; the grass, the flower and the tree were complete" (12). The wholeness of the objects George beholds, each in succession complete in itself, results from the "level" of his experience—primitive as well as close to the ground. Grubbing in the grass, the toddler sees the flower up close and apprehends its individual concreteness. The boundaries of his being dissolve in a mystical revelation of perception and sensation: color, form, light, and smell all merge in the cathedral space behind his eyes.

The elder Mr. Oliver, a retired colonel, then terrifies his grandson in his private theater of rapture. Putting on a snout of newspaper and coming towards the child, he seems a "peaked eyeless monster moving on legs, brandishing arms."

When instructed by his nurses to say, "Good morning, sir," George stands speech-less, gaping at his grandfather, and then bursts out crying. In a grotesque parody of adult discourse, the colonel's afghan hound, who also reacts to the mayhem, is drilled like George in civil behavior: "Heel! heel, you brute" the colonel bawls before muttering about George "a crybaby—a crybaby" (13).

This fictional event, based on a moment in Woolf's late memoirs in which she analyzes the source of her own creative instincts, shows how the child's vision-ary process is threatened by the cruelties of adults, their conventional language, and conformity of outlook. In "A Sketch of the Past," Woolf's autobiographical writings, the author associates her early empowerment from seeing a flower whole with the later satisfaction of making something whole or real by "putting it into words" (1976, 72). The context of George's momentary illumination, however, reveals the horrifying blindness of ordinary adults, who impose on others the puppet responses which control them.

Between the Acts is full of such misapprehensions. The failure of Mr. Oliver to respect or even recognize George's inner vision shows how adults lose their own creative potential. Only the religious and impractical Lucy Swithin would under-stand that the significant drama played out within George occurs "behind the eyes; not on the lips" because "we haven't the words" (55). The adults gather in the countryside to gain some vision of themselves through dramatic art, but their pageant fails utterly to communicate what the author intended. Only through artistic efforts, however, can adults attempt to recover the original wholeness of inward vision Woolf saw in the child's spontaneous apprehension of nature.

In dramatizing the origins of creativity, the children in Woolf's fiction exhibit the paradoxical qualities of the Jungian archetype:

> The motifs of "insignificance," exposure, abandonment, danger, etc. try to show how precarious is the psychic possibility of wholeness, that is, the enormous difficulties to be met with in attaining this "highest good." They also signify the powerlessness and helplessness of the life-urge which subjects every growing thing to the law of maximum self-fulfillment, while at the same time the environmental influences place all sorts of insuperable obstacles in the way of individuation. (166)

George, "grubbing in the grass," epitomizes the more hopeful sign of Woolf's novels because he suggests the humble and universal origins of the creative instinct. Like the other characters in this village setting, the toddler takes part in a larger drama of animals, nature, and people, impelled by some irresistible force to seek revelation. Precisely because Woolf saw in the preverbal, unspoken, or not yet sayable insights of childhood the most intense experience and expression of life that she knew, she spent her literary career devising narrative strategies to commu-nicate the inchoate, striving to create what Terence Hewit in *The Voyage Out* (1915) aspires to write: a novel about Silence or the things people don't say (216).

Woolf's first three novels, written between the ages of twenty-five and forty, are all studies of young people approaching adulthood: two of the three protagonists die on the threshold of maturity. Yet death in *The Voyage Out* and *Jacob's Room* (1922) is viewed not as tragic waste but as escape from the corruption adult life implies. While Dickens portrayed small boys at the crossroads of destiny, Woolf's first two novels center on young women whose sheltered education has preserved them in an unformed, even infantile state. At twenty-four, Rachel Vinrace of *The Voyage Out* is hardly a child, but her upbringing, conducted by conservative aunts, "kindly doctors and gentle old professors" who discourage any seriousness of purpose, has left her inarticulate, awkward, and apathetic. She has grown into young adulthood accepting her alienation from the spoken word: "It appeared that nobody ever said a thing they meant, or ever talked of a feeling they felt" (37). In her shy diffidence Rachel symbolizes an isolate innocence that becomes, in progressive encounters with the world and its own profound realities, a vessel and a victim of the forces of life. But as Patricia Laurence points out, Rachel's nightmares, floating states of mind, and final delirium are not represented as "absences" (as Freud and Breuer labeled Anna O.'s bizarre states) but as a creative "presence" in the novel, a silence "infused with a new psychic life" (166–67). In representing Rachel's incipience as a rich interiority beyond verbalization, Woolf experimented with ways of rendering our unfinished selves, the zone where language and reason are too slow and limited to respond. She would later draw attention to this creative, inner space through child figures in *Jacob's Room, To the Lighthouse,* and *The Waves,* and the affinities of children to artists in *To the Lighthouse* and *Between the Acts,* and to the insane in *Mrs. Dalloway* (1925).

The image of the voyage, which inaugurates Rachel's journey inward as well as her sexual awakening, expresses the peculiar tropism of her personality. The strangeness of Rachel's "development" is its lack of transformation and apparent passivity, which leads her to feel "always unprepared and amazed and knowing nothing" and gives her a look of wonder, as if she were "dropping milk from a height as though to see what kind of drops it made" (925). Rachel's dumbness and impressibility, her willingness to follow the intuitional and irrational in a vague and non-directive way, are the source of her childlike freedom and creativity of consciousness.

The essential aspect of Rachel—her indeterminateness—cannot be conveyed objectively. Her background and the impression she makes on her elders, who are either irritated by her ineptitude, or overlook her altogether, characterize an individual too unformed and unreflecting to cast light upon herself. Woolf thus relies on the use of extended symbolic metaphors to convey the qualities of youth Rachel embodies. She is identified with the *Euphrosyne,* the ship which carries her, with an aunt and uncle, Helen and Ridley Ambrose, to an island off the coast of South America. Rachel thus embarks on a venture which ultimately brings her all the conditions of a sea voyage—separation from ordinary life, new ways of seeing, vast silence, and unexplored space:

When the ship was out of sight of land, it became plain that the people of England were completely mute. The disease attacked other parts of the earth; Europe shrank, Asia shrank, Africa and America shrank, until it seemed doubtful whether the ship would ever run against any of those wrinkled rocks again. But, on the other hand, an immense dignity had descended upon her; she was an inhabitant of the great world, which has so few inhabitants, travelling all day across an empty universe, with veils drawn before her and behind. She was more lonely than the caravan crossing the desert; she was infinitely more mysterious, moving by her own power and sustained by her own resources. The sea might give her death or some unexampled joy, and none would know of it. She was a bride going forth to her husband, a virgin unknown of men; in her vigour and purity she might be likened to all beautiful things, worshipped and felt as a symbol. (32)

The rich poetic language describing the *Euphrosyne* clearly applies to Rachel and the aura of suspense surrounding her destiny. Just as a ship at sea provokes the imagination and symbolizes unknown ports and possibilities, Rachel, who possesses unimpeded freedom to grow, has no identity nor identifiable destination. Her power, like that of a child, is pure potential; in her silence, remoteness, and lack of commitment she is self-sufficient. Over her anonymity hangs the same mystery and excitement conveyed by the ship at sea. But although the consummate beauty and dignity of this spectacle are conferred on Rachel, the passage celebrates precisely those qualities which are unknown to others. From the rather factual summary of the view those on land have of ships at sea, the description progresses to the incremental alterations of perception those on board ship have of the land. The final burst of sympathetic imagination which personifies the solitary ship offers a view of the voyager that could be seen by no observer: no one can witness or truly describe rites of passage.

Ironically commenting on the conventional bildungsroman or picaresque novel, Woolf's plot is thus strategically designed to frustrate expectations of progressive development into adult society or the achievement of a final destination. Rachel's experience does not integrate her with the social environment but in fact completes her isolation from it. After an expedition up the river to a remote native village where she and Hewet have a sexual encounter in the jungle, she becomes engaged and contracts a mysterious fever that causes her death two weeks later. Her maturation, after twenty-four years of seclusion, occurs with astonishing speed. Unfolding like a closed bud thrust into a hothouse environment, Rachel finds in eight months a meaning and pattern to her own life that satisfy and sustain her. But this inward realization, though precipitated by outward engagement with others, leads to nothing beyond itself. In fact, the deeper logic of this mock picaresque work is that the very forces which make Rachel aware of her being also threaten to confine and adulterate it. The tropical fever and delirium which suddenly strike extend the dreams and drifting thought stimulated by the voyage. Just as Neverland, Barrie's map of the child's unconscious, saves Peter Pan from growing up, death enables Rachel to preserve intact the purity, freedom, and wonder of her being.

This outcome is prefigured in the first part of the novel when Rachel meets Mr. Dalloway on board ship and through him glimpses a unifying principle opposed to the severed realities of her world—the depths of "what one saw and felt, but did not talk about" (37) and the mannered surface of her genteel existence. But the negative underside of their encounter, which climaxes in Dalloway's passionate kiss, leads her to see the elemental forces underlying social reality, a liberating but disturbing revelation that ultimately gives rise to her horror of the body. Rachel's subsequent quest does not endow her with a social identity but accentuates her tendency to merge with her surroundings and leads finally to the dissolution of her personality—a completely non-egoistic expansion of the self.

This aspect of Rachel's evolution (or descent) is associated with her probing the origins of uncivilized man as well as plumbing the sea like an amphibian for earlier stages of human development. Rachel's pull toward the primordial in nature enacts her inarticulate intuition with the Dalloways that "if one went back far enough, everything perhaps was intelligible; everything was in common; for the mammoths who pastured in the fields of Richmond High Street had turned into paving stones and boxes full of ribbon, and her aunts" (67). Rachel's affinity with unevolved, undifferentiated forms of life becomes more explicit as her erotic preference for the sea emerges. After her engagement to Hewet, when the two are wrestling, she suddenly evades his mastering grip by crying, "I'm a mermaid! I can swim . . . so the game's up" (298). A strange idea, more appealing to her than Hewet's embrace, takes over her imagination: "To be flung into the sea, to be washed hither and thither, and driven about the roots of the world—the idea was incoherently delightful" (298).

In the end *The Voyage Out* awards its heroine both extremes of experience—death as well as unexampled joy. Rachel thus remains a potent figure of ambiguity: her vulnerability as potential childbearer is only enhanced by the virgin crossing. The process of growth, while deepening Rachel's receptivity and engagement with the world, also accentuates her tendency to withdraw into a realm of her own creation. The passage which activates oscillations of consciousness inward and outward inaugurates a voyage back in time as well, a plumbing of the deepest level of consciousness. Presenting the unconscious as prehistory is, as Gillian Beer has noted, common to such other twentieth-century writers as Conrad and Eliot, but Rachel's affinity to water suggests that Woolf, like Darwin (who also lost his mother as a child), had a special need to establish "continuity with lost origins" through the sea, the womb of all life (111). In death, Rachel finally sinks to a state of undifferentiated being in which she "saw and heard nothing but a faint booming sound, which was the sound of the sea rolling over her head" (341).

On the surface *The Voyage Out* has the inevitable anguish of romantic tragedy: two young people on the threshold of life, eagerly plan their future together when suddenly, for no apparent reason, the couple is thwarted by death. Or perhaps the boldness of their aspiration angered the gods. Woolf believed that the cruelty of Attic drama, "which is quite unlike our British brutality," was conditioned by its performance in the open air and intense heat of Greece (1966, 2). Rachel's mysterious fever, like the typhoid Woolf's brother, Thoby Stephen, contracted in Greece, is somehow related to tropical conditions and her vulnerability to a foreign climate. Helen Ambrose's view of the treachery of nature makes her blame the couple for having gone on the expedition into the jungle, "for having ventured too far and exposed themselves" (286). The afternoon her niece falls ill is "so hot that the breaking of the waves" nearby sounds "like the repeated sigh of some exhausted creature" (326).

Another way to perceive Rachel's fate, however, is through the myth of Sabrina, the protector of virginity, invoked by Hewet's reading *Comus* to Rachel as she sickens. Just as the nymph of the "smooth Severn stream" rescues the Lady of Milton's masque from bestial enchantment, Rachel's illness saves her from the domination and deadening compromises of marriage. The mixture of defiance and evasion in Rachel's death enables her to remain "free, like the wind or the sea" (244), not "walled up in a warm firelit room" with a husband (241). The imprisonment of sexual identity is explicit when Hewet asks Rachel about her life:

"Why does it interest you?" she asked.
"Partly because you're a woman," he replied.
When he said this, Rachel who had become oblivious of anything, and had reverted to a childlike state of interest and pleasure, lost her freedom and became self-conscious. (215)

The freedom Rachel wants is anonymity: "walking alone, and knowing I don't matter a damn to anybody" (215).

It may seem strange that childhood is freer than womanhood, but this attitude inspires Woolf's celebration of the paradoxical power of Rachel. Echoing Shelley, whose Adonais also escaped "the contagion of the world's slow stain," Rachel rages at the veil of blue sky and sea, as if it were a curtain thwarting her: "all the things one wants are on the other side. . . . I hate these divisions, don't you, Terence?" (302). Like Milton's "Lady," whose role in the masque is enacted by a child, Woolf's heroine is a child in a woman's body. It makes dramatic sense in Milton's masque that a young girl would defend chastity, the virtue which preserves the soul intact until its return to a celestial origin. The innocence of Milton's Lady, however, is purely rational, and she defends a Platonic ideal. Woolf's virgin triumphs covertly through the instinctual life which initiates her quest, insures her integrity, and enables her to return to an original state of being. Although the pastoral is the redemptive mode in *Comus*, nature in this tropical setting is, like Shelley's west wind, both destroyer and preserver. On the one hand, the exotic and unknown of South American forests suggest a pastoral landscape, beautiful and untouched, beckoning and benevolent; on the other, they betoken a primitive and elemental reality that is treacherous, alien, and indifferent to human life. The primal state with which the faithful soul is reunited in Milton is a realm of perfect human virtue; ultimate reality in Woolf, however, involves a dissolution of the individual into the impersonal energies of nature. Milton's child implies the future life of the adult, but Rachel is saved by being the victim of her own sensations. The essential pessimism of Woolf's myth of virginity is that it centers on death.

Just as the seventeenth-century maiden who resists seduction in Milton's masque will presumably grow up and marry in actual life, changing her heroine's name from Cynthia to Rachel enabled Woolf to present the full potential of virginity. Instead of identifying her protagonist with the militant archetype of chastity, Woolf chose the Biblical figure of pathos who died in childbirth away from home. Woolf's heroine experiences the sensations of love and a taste of passion—enough to enlarge her vision of life—but she escapes the sexuality and socialization of marriage. Rachel, the wife of Jacob and mother of Benjamin, is not so fortunate. The prophet Jeremiah sees her standing by her grave, weeping for her children, the tribes of Israel, taken captive in Babylonia. His prophecy concerning Rachel is fulfilled in the New Testament account of the Slaughter of the Innocents. Unlike her Hebraic prototype, Woolf's Rachel does not live to bear the daughter she and Hewet dream of or to face the vulnerability of her own children's lives: "In Ramah there was a voice heard, lamentation, and weeping, and great mourning, Rachel weeping for her children and would not be comforted because they were not" (Matthew 2:18). This fate is reserved for Helen Ambrose, the older woman of experience in *The Voyage Out*, whose misery and fear for her children stand as an ominous warning in the opening chapter.

In this allegorical and indirect novel one can see the pessimism and contradictions of Virginia Stephen's own quest for autonomy in her twenties, which followed that of her step-sister, Stella Duckworth. Stella's bid for an independent life ended like Rachel's in unexpected death, when Virginia was fifteen, three months after Stella's wedding and the onset of pregnancy. Critics have complained of Woolf's extreme obliquity in portraying Rachel's sexual initiation, its displacement in erotic jungle images. But as Patricia Laurence suggests, "given Woolf's own manic-depressive states, her lifelong interest in illness and the 'material' aspects of the body, she may have been more captivated by dramatizing scenes of illness in *The Voyage Out* . . . than with the subject of love or sex, upon which she is often 'silent' " (166).

In her memoirs Woolf recalls that during her adolescence a verbal taboo like that about sex surrounded the subject of death:

> Mother's death and Stella's death kept us, I suppose, together. We never spoke of either of them; I can remember the awkwardness with which Thoby avoided saying "Stella" when a ship called *Stella* sank. (I remember when Thoby died, that

Adrian and I agreed to talk about him. "There are so many people that are dead now," we said.) But this silence was known to cover something. (1976, 107).

The final irony of *The Voyage Out* is that the sinking of Rachel, who goes forth like a ship to meet her destiny, enables the adults left behind to communicate through silence, not simply through words, which cover up reality.

In *Jacob's Room*, the novel in which Woolf said she had finally, at forty, discovered her own voice, the hero is almost entirely mute. The few monosyllabic words he does speak are alive for him like the objects he discovers. "Oh, a huge crab," the child murmurs, plunging his hand into the hollow of water at the top of a rock (9). Moments of vision in this novel are unlike Joyce's epiphanies: they are not instants of revelation which define stages of development and explain actions. Rather, they are seconds of intense visualization or pure sensation whose meaning is unclear and indefinable. The book itself is a rich accumulation of odds and ends like those found in Jacob's room—Sandra's letter, Lady Rocksbier's invitation, Jacob's old shoes (176)—brooded over by a strange presence which reports, suggests, but cannot conclude. The silence and mystery of Jacob Flanders, like the inconclusiveness of his life, tease the imagination and thwart expectations. But the truncation and impressionism of this work express the freshness and concentration of original apprehension, the unawareness and boundless possibility Woolf saw in early life.

"Intensity of life compared with immobility" (quoted in Zwerdling, 908)—this note written as Woolf was beginning *Jacob's Room* may illuminate the dialectic of youth and age which governs this novel's shifting point of view and the larger opposition between Woolf's first three studies of youth and the subsequent novels about maturity. Woolf's appreciation of the rapid unfolding of early life made her equally aware of its brevity. As she indicates in *Jacob's Room*, this magnificent rush inevitably entails its own exhaustion:

> Why, from the very windows, even in the dusk, you see a swelling run through the street, an aspiration, as with arms outstretched, eyes desiring, mouths agape. And then we peaceably subside. For if the exaltation lasted we should be blown like foam into the air. The stars would shine through us. We should go down the gale in salt drops—as sometimes happens. (120)

Such an experience does happen in *Mrs. Dalloway* to the shell-shocked Septimus Smith, who feels life so intensely that the earth seems to penetrate his body. He panics, however, because he cannot feel himself. Mrs. Dalloway, his counterpart in the novel, is defended from such dispersal by her capacity to experience herself as a specific person, although it is precisely because she is defined or pinned down by her identity that she may be said to have "peaceably subsided" into middle age. Her strategy for survival depends on the fundamental detachment of her personality and her periodic withdrawal from life. Like a nun she retreats to her attic room: "It was all over for her. The sheet was stretched and the bed narrow. She had gone up into the tower alone and left them blackberrying in the sun" (70).

By contrast, Septimus Smith and Elizabeth Dalloway, characters as unfused as the sensitive, anti-social Rachel and the silent Jacob, are set in contexts calculated to show how vulnerable and ephemeral is their special way of looking at the world. In her essay "On Being Ill" Woolf describes how influenza alters perception:

> That illusion of a world so shaped that it echoes every groan, . . . where however strange your experience other people have had it too, where however far you travel in your own mind someone has been there before you—is all an illusion. We do not know our own souls, let alone the souls of others. . . . There is a virgin forest in each; a snowfield where even the print of birds' feet is unknown. (1966, 4: 196)

Septimus in his illness sees the world as if for the first time; he commits suicide to preserve this untracked territory within himself. Like the child who makes up his meaning to explain what he sees, Septimus is perpetually engaged in interpreting his perceptions, which come upon him with terrifying truth. As surreal and disoriented as his vision becomes, his prophetic and paranoid insights have their own validity. People like Dr. Bradshaw are, in fact, out to get him because his dissociated perceptions are so resistant to the consensus and "genial pretense" (1966, 4: 196) on which society rests.

Septimus's visual deviance is powerfully relayed in the skywriting episode, which precipitates in him a revelation of cosmic unity reminiscent of the Romantic poets. An aeroplane, racing, swooping "exactly where it liked, swiftly, freely, like a skater" (30) as it spells out smoke letters behind it, has an ineffable life of its own that mesmerizes the crowd below. "And now, curving up and up, straight up, like something mounting in ecstasy, in pure delight, out from behind poured white smoke looping, writing a T, an O, an F" (42). Like Shelley's skylark, this aerial vision of technology communicates a message no one can fathom. Septimus, however, who has continued to write poetry in his madness, looks beyond the surface mystery to create a deeper one: he believes it is a beacon from the abode of the eternal ("Adonais" 55.9):

> So, thought Septimus, looking up, they are signalling to me. Not indeed in actual words; that is, he could not read the language yet; but it was plain enough, this exquisite beauty, and tears filled his eyes as he looked at the smoke words languishing and melting in the sky and bestowing upon him in their inexhaustible charity and laughing goodness one shape after another of unimaginable beauty and signalling their intention to provide for him, for nothing, for ever, for looking merely, with beauty, more beauty! Tears ran down his cheeks.
>
> It was toffee; they were advertising toffee, a nursemaid told Rezia. (31)

The anti-climax of these juxtaposed responses—the nursemaid's flat reality following the enthralling drama exploding like fireworks in Septimus's manic brain—commends as it undercuts his incommunicable delusion.

Hearing news of this young man's suicide at her party, Clarissa does not pity Septimus. She envisions his defiance, holding his "treasure" as he plunged, and compares his act with the deadening conversations and incremental diminishments exacted from all who grow old: "A thing there was that mattered; a thing, wreathed about with chatter, defaced, obscured in her own life, let drop every day in corruption, lies, chatter. This he had preserved" (280). The extraordinary excitement Clarissa still feels in life, finding it "absolutely absorbing" (11), is not simply an expression of enthusiastic self-regard. Rather, her exquisite pleasure in the moment derives from her continual awareness of the "icy claws" of death (54), the inexorable pressure of time, and her feeling always that "it was a very, very dangerous thing to live even one day" (11). Mrs. Dalloway expresses the same distrust of life as does *The Voyage Out* but articulates a counter response to it. Clarissa's capacity to say "nonsense!" to Shelley's pessimism depends on the complexity of what Phyllis Rose calls her "self-made image" (122). "A virginity preserved through childbirth which clung to her like a sheet" (46) means that Clarissa fails her husband sexually, but it also ensures that an adventuring imagination, the secret excitement of the child exploring, endures within her. Preserving this continuity with the past so defensively is the source of Mrs. Dalloway's sense of herself:

> For she was a child, throwing bread to the ducks, between her parents, and at the same time a grown woman coming to her parents who stood by the lake, holding her life in her arms which, as she neared them, grew larger and larger in her arms, until it became a whole life, a complete life, which she put down by them and said, "This is what I have made of it! This!" (64)

While Woolf's early protagonists escape the closure and compromise of adulthood by dying, characters in her later works liberate themselves from the emotional tyranny of adults simply by growing up. Although the open-ended future Elizabeth Dalloway imagines ("she would like to become a doctor, a farmer, possibly go into Parliament" [207]) will inevitably close, Woolf captures the brief moment when the cocooned anonymity of early adolescence makes all things seem available. The simple, open-ended sentences which register Elizabeth's thoughts the afternoon she strays into London are as stilted and unassuming as her manners: "It was quite different here from Westminster . . . It was so serious; it was so busy" (207). Her limited vocabulary and excessive qualifying cannot, however, communicate the totality of her experience. As if inspired by her inarticulateness, the narrator renders Elizabeth's becoming through "trailing clouds of glory" that are shorn of sentimental notions of childhood purity:

> For although the clouds were of mountainous white so that one could fancy hacking hard chips off with a hatchet . . . there was perpetual movement among

them. . . . Fixed though they seemed . . . nothing could be fresher, freer, more sensitive superficially than the snow-white or gold-kindled surface; to change, to go, to dismantle the solemn assemblage was immediately possible. (210, 211)

Billowing out like the clouds over the Strand, but not yet assuming final or finite shape, Elizabeth's molten state accentuates "how remorseless life is!" in what it makes one become (111). Whether one strolls by "dim, fat, blind, past everything . . . except self-esteem and comfort" like Hugh Whitbread (288) or is able, like Clarissa, "to sum it all up in the moment" she passes (264), the possibility "to change, to go, to dismantle" lasts only for a second. At the same time, by situating this girl in a jealous triangle—between her mother and tutor, Miss Kilman—both of whose vicarious needs Elizabeth is oblivious of, Woolf reveals the ugly struggle for power endemic to selfhood. That this disturbing reality grasps even at the roots of as detached and richly appreciative a personality as Mrs. Dalloway indicates how profoundly Woolf distrusted the adult ego.

In *To the Lighthouse*, the visionary intensities of the child are associated with the fierce struggle of the artist to create, a labor as solitary and overwhelming as giving birth. Needing the primitive courage and absorption of an exploring child, the painter Lily Briscoe must complete a passage "from conception to work as dreadful as any down a dark passage for a child" (73). The opening chapter of this novel, like that of *Jacob's Room*, juxtaposes a thwarted artist, an inexplicably sad mother, and children playing by the sea. In both works two painters struggle with their vision on canvas as the desire of small boys swells the narrative into movement. James's anticipated voyage, like Jacob's solitary ascent of a huge rock, generates "textual force" as Peter Brooks defines it—a "conjunction of the narrative of desire and the desire of the narrative." Like "that 'passion for (of) meaning' which Barthes found central to the reading of narrative," this force "motivates and energizes its reading" and "animates the combinatory play of sense-making" (48). In the violently expansive and exploratory rush of our common origin, Woolf locates the genesis of both narratives. The forward thrust of two little boys' visionary quests initiates rites of passage not completed until Jacob begins his ascent of the Acropolis and James finally reaches the lighthouse ten years after the start of the novel.

Mrs. Ramsay is right to imagine that her six-year-old will always remember his disappointment (95). As Bernard asserts in *The Waves*, the ordinary events of childhood "happen in one second and last forever" (342). The expedition to the lighthouse, which James has dreamed of making "for years and years it seemed" (9) is a symbol of frustration precisely because he is a child, and any postponement is not simply a matter of time—another day or week—but intensifies, in Frederick Buechner's words, "that exquisite impatience which is childhood itself" (39).

In this opening scene, however, James Ramsay, like Jacob Flanders, is characterized as almost entirely silent. Only Mrs. Ramsay intuits her children's buried "speechless feelings" (123) and "secret language" (9), but even she cannot fathom what they see. Watching Cam dash by, she ponders why her daughter is running: "It might be a vision—of a shell, of a wheelbarrow, of a fairy kingdom on the far side of the hedge; or it might be the glory of speed; no one knew" (84). Calling Cam to deliver a message to Mildred, the cook, she imagines her daughter an unreliable mouthpiece. She pictures her own words "dropped into a well, where, if the waters were clear, they were also so extraordinarily distorting that, even if they descended, one saw them twisting about to make Heaven knows what pattern on the floor of the child's mind." Woolf's irony, however, in scenes where children deliver the verbal communiqués of adults, is not directed toward the inadequacy of the messengers. With "parrot-like instinct" Cam picks up Mildred's words accurately and produces them for her mother "in colorless sing-song." But her mindless repetition of what she had heard conveys the thin, unoriginal quality of grown-up talk. She is impatient, "shifting from foot to foot" (85), to return to a fuller drama—the wordless freedom and sensation of her own play.

The Waves, Woolf's masterwork on the silence of becoming, demonstrates the power of original moments of sensation to determine the shape of life. By identifying the self entirely with its first sights or sounds, the book traces successive stages of life as they extend, elaborate, or refine some primary mode of apprehension. In the beginning, nursery age characters focus on objects which flood their consciousness: "I see a ring," said Bernard, "hanging above me. It quivers in a loop of light"; "I hear a sound," said Rhoda, "cheep, chirp; cheep, chirp; going up and down." (180). Such primary images in *The Waves* are progressively distanced from perceiving minds and finally come to epitomize the outlook and predisposition of the adults. Although the six characters in *The Waves* have known each other since early childhood and can thus intuit differences among their various ways of responding to the world, the interior monologues which articulate their development indicate—like Keats's vale of soul-making—that what is deepest and most essential about subjectivity occurs in a wordless and private domain that cannot be shared and in fact remains fundamentally inexpressible in art.

In contrast to the auditory sensations and linguistic playfulness of young Stephen Daedalus in *A Portrait of the Artist as a Young Man* (1916), the actual speech of Woolf's children is not recorded in *The Waves*. As a small child, Stephen composes a simple but acutely expressive poem ("Pull out his eyes, / Apologise . . .") that reveals his promise as a writer. But we must infer what childish diction Bernard, the story-teller and phrase-maker, might use since the vocabulary of the six extended monologues is uniform and highly sophisticated from infancy. Embedded in their perceptions, the six soliloquists apprehend words visually and tactilely. "Those are white words," said Susan, "like stones one picks up by the seashore" (188). In her focus on word and image as individuating agents, Woolf anticipates Jung's metaphor or archetypal symbol, created and pursued by the self in its quest for self-realization. Although this extended play-poem seems to bear out Bernard's assertion that "nobody . . . ever changes the attitude in which we saw them first" (365), the process of maturation in *The Waves* is inherently destructive of creativity. Time rather than the character's action or education is the agent of growth and forces changes in perception. As Bernard says in middle age, a shell forms gradually "upon the soft soul, nacrous, shiny, upon which sensations tap their beaks in vain" (353).

At the center of this mythopoetic bildungsroman is the mute but magnificent Percival, who challenges the notion of separate lives and the fidelity of language. Premature death at age twenty-five leaves him, as Forster described Jacob Flanders, "a closely sealed jar" (17). Although Woolf modeled both elusive characters on her brother, Thoby, who died in 1906, Percival's heroism, unlike Jacob's, is appreciated long before he is thrown off a horse in India. From childhood, when "little boys trooped after him across the playing-fields" copying his every gesture (260), this unreflecting youth is a kind of icon to his peers, the beauty and flower of civilization as the multiple resonances of his name suggest. The only character who never defines himself through verbal assertions, Percival sits silent at his farewell dinner just as he sat wordlessly as a boy, "among the tickling grasses when the breeze parted the clouds and they formed again." As Louis realizes in the egotism of young adulthood, Percival makes them "all aware that these attempts to say, I am this, I am that, which we make coming together, like separated parts of one body and soul, are false. Something has been left out from fear. Something has been altered, from vanity. We have tried to accentuate differences" (270). The more fundamental, impersonal reality of which all lives partake is likened by Woolf to the amorphous elements of clouds and waves. Bringing the group together, as he has since childhood, Percival enables the six to experience themselves as a single globe or flower, like the red carnation Bernard sees at Percival's farewell dinner: "a seven-sided flower, many-petalled . . . a whole flower to which every eye brings its own contribution" (263). The momentary energy of such a vision, like George's in *Between the Acts*, arises from its mythical dimension. Blake called his "giant forms" Albion, as Eric Warner notes, "a mythic representation of Mankind itself," and Woolf's effort to enlarge and unite her characters through the "conventional" hero, Percival, "moves in the same direction" (76). At the end of the novel, Bernard finally feels a rejuvenating desire rise within him; as if carried on the crest of a new wave, he confronts death through the power of everything Percival has meant to him: "It is death against whom I ride with my spear couched and my hair flying back like a young man's, like Percival's, when he galloped in India. I strike spurs into my horse. Against you I will fling myself, unvanquished and unyielding, O Death!" (383).

When Jacob Flanders "becomes a man," he talks—in extended sentences—for the first time in the novel. Speaking cant, pontificating on Greek culture, his voice becomes unspecific, manfully detached from immediate experience, just before he disappears in World War I. His passage into adult discourse occurs as the trajectory of his young life breaks like a wave against the hard, leveling world of fact and choice, male politics and war, where words are used like weapons or items of social exchange. There "words have been used too often; touched and turned, and left exposed to the dust of the street" (93). Jacob, too, merges at the end into his own civilization and loses himself in the act of growing up. As the narrator remarks, when Jacob is lolling in a Cambridge punt: "It is curious, lying in a boat, to watch the waves. Here are three coming regularly one after another, all much of a size. Then, hurrying after them comes a fourth, very large and menacing; it lifts the boat; on it goes; somehow merges without accomplishing anything; flattens itself out with the rest" (120). But Jacob's death in this mock bildungsroman is portrayed less as futile defeat than ironic victory, for the hero escapes adulthood. The illusion of promise which youth represents is preserved. And Woolf, through her refusal to capture or delineate this character, recovers the wonder and marvellous secrecy which children find inherent in life: "The words we seek hang close to the tree. We come at dawn and find them sweet beneath the leaf" (93).

Works Cited

Beer, Gillian. "Virginia Woolf and Pre-History." In *Virginia Woolf: A Centenary Perspective*, ed. Eric Warner, 99–123. New York: St. Martin's Press, 1984.

Brooks, Peter. *Reading for the Plot: Design and Intention in Narrative.* New York: Vintage, 1985.

Buechner, Frederick. *The Sacred Journey.* San Francisco: Harper, 1982.

Forster, E. M. *Two Cheers for Democracy.* New York: Harcourt Brace and World, 1942.

Joyce, James. *A Portrait of the Artist as a Young Man.* New York: Viking Press, 1972.

Jung, C. G. *Archetypes and the Collective Unconscious.* Princeton: Princeton University Press, 1969.

Langbaum, Robert. "Freud and Sociobiology." *The Word from Below: Essays on Modern Literature and Culture.* Madison: University of Wisconsin Press, 1987.

Laurence, Patricia Ondek. *The Reading of Silence: Virginia Woolf in the English Tradition.* Stanford: Stanford University Press, 1991.

Pater, Walter. *Miscellaneous Studies: A Series of Essays.* London: Macmillan, 1917.

Rose, Phyllis. *Virginia Woolf: Woman of Letters.* New York: Oxford University Press, 1978.

Schlack, Beverly Ann. *Continuing Presences: Virginia Woolf's Use of Literary Allusion.* University Park: Pennsylvania State University Press, 1979.

Warner, Eric. *Landmarks of World Literature: Virginia Woolf: The Waves.* Cambridge: Cambridge University Press, 1987.

Woolf, Virginia. *Between the Acts.* New York: Harcourt, 1941.

———. *Books and Portraits: Some Further Selections from the Literary and Biographical Writings of Virginia Woolf.* Ed. Mary Lyon. London: Hogarth, 1977.

———. *Collected Essays.* Ed. Leonard Woolf. 4 vols. London: Hogarth, 1966.

———. *Contemporary Writers.* New York: Harcourt, 1965.

————. *Jacob's Room and The Waves.* New York: Harcourt, 1959.

————. *Moments of Being: Unpublished Autobiographical Writings.* Ed. Jeanne Schulkind. New York: Harcourt, 1976.

————. *Mrs. Dalloway.* New York: Harcourt, 1953.

————. *Night and Day.* New York: Harcourt, 1973.

————. *To the Lighthouse.* New York: Harcourt, 1955.

————. *The Voyage Out.* New York: Harcourt, 1948.

Zwerdling, Alex. "Jacob's Room: Woolf's Satiric Elegy." *ELH* 48 (1981): 894–913.

Child as Ready-Made:
Baby-Talk and the Language of
Dos Passos's Children in *U.S.A.*

BRIAN McHALE

The Semiotic Child

Children, it appears, can get lost in translation. Breakfasting in Belgium a few years ago, one might have learned as much from examining the bilingual copy on the back of packages of Kellogg's Corn Flakes. There the breakfaster who could read both French and Dutch would have observed an odd discrepancy in the parallel texts describing a promotional "special offer." The product on offer was straightforward enough: a cereal bowl. But where the Dutch text specifies that this bowl had been designed for children's use, the parallel French text, which supposedly "translates" the Dutch, omits all mention of children. What had become of them?

Itamar Even-Zohar, whose example this is, answers that they were never there in the first place in French commercial discourse (1990a).[1] Unlike the parallel discourse in contemporary Dutch (or, in another of his examples, in British English), the French of advertising copy such as one finds on Kellogg's Corn Flakes boxes resists direct reference to children, preferring oblique reference or no reference at all. Now, while this particular referential blind spot with respect to children may be a peculiarity of French (and French in a particular, restricted range of uses, at that), the general principle is not. Indeed, Even-Zohar adduces the Kellogg's cereal bowl offer as evidence of a feature attributable to all discourses, in all cultures; namely, that they never represent reality in the "raw," so to speak, but always rely on a *preselection* from the universe of potentially representable items. Thus, the presence of children at the breakfast table must presumably belong to the real-world experience of French-speakers as much as it does to Dutch-speakers, but whereas Dutch commercial discourse admits children to its preselection of representable items, the equivalent French discourse excludes them. This preselection, which differs from culture to culture, from genre to genre, and from period to period, Even-Zohar proposes to call the *repertoire*, while for the items of reality constituting the repertoire he has coined the deliberately provocative neologism, *realemes.*

Even-Zohar's proposals recapitulate and systematize insights of very general currency in what might be thought of as the "semiotic" disciplines, including contrastive linguistics, cultural anthropology, translation studies, and of course semiotics itself. Indeed, among the semiotic disciplines there is only one to which the notion of a preselected repertoire seems alien, and that one, of course, is poetics. This is so for at least two reasons. First, traditional understandings of literature's mimetic function, still powerfully influential, rest on the assumption that literary works are free to represent whatever is "out there" in the real world, constrained by nothing but the limits of human insight and imagination. There would seem to be no room in traditional mimetic theory for prefabrication or codification; mimesis is understood to be direct reflection of reality, not reality routed through some mediating cultural code. Secondly, literary studies for at least the past two centuries have tended to value convention-flouting art over convention-bound art, and consequently to underestimate the role of literary repertoires. The result is a distorted picture of literary-historical processes, for artistic transgression of course implies the prior existence of norms capable of being transgressed. In the absence of constraints on what may or may not be represented, there could hardly be any lifting or loosening of constraints. Moreover, every such loosening tends to create a new system of constraints, a new repertoire, thus preparing the way for the next cycle of innovation.

Even-Zohar's approach to literary representation finds ample corroboration in studies of childhood in literature. Children, as is well known, figure relatively rarely as objects of literary representation before the Romantic period. A naively mimetic theory of representation would presumably require us to believe that the absence of children from literature reflects, in some sense, their absence from writers' real-world experience. This is a good deal less satisfactory than saying, along with Even-Zohar, that this zero degree of representation reflects, rather, the conventional organization of the literary repertoire whereby, as in French commercial discourse down to the present day, no realeme corresponding to the reality of children was readily available for writers' use.

Having identified the presence or absence of children as a matter, not of the imitation of reality, but of the structure of the repertoire, we are still far from exhausting the usefulness of this approach. For the changing constitution of the image of the child—which items of reality are and are not admissible in representations of childhood, at various periods and in various genres—is also susceptible to analysis in terms of the literary repertoire. We might, for instance, find these terms useful for capturing the rapid, indeed explosive expansion and reorganization of the literary sub-repertoire of childhood around the turn of the century and into the modernist period, as successive waves of naturalistic and modernist innovation opened up the representation of childhood to such "new" realities—that is, realities newly codified and sanctioned—as formerly taboo bodily functions, children's interior life and dream-life, "adult" emotions (especially negative ones: hatred, resentment, jealousy, etc.), childhood violence (both towards and on the part of children) and, of course, childhood sexuality. It is this sudden and (at the time) shocking expansion of the childhood sub-repertoire that makes the novelists of this phase—in British fiction, for instance, Joyce and Lawrence; in the U.S., John Dos Passos, James T. Farrell, Edward Dahlberg, Henry Roth, and others—so interesting to students of literary childhood.

Moreover, it is not just the literary image of the child and its constituents that are susceptible to analysis in these terms, but also the *language* of the child. For the literary representation of linguistic reality is as much conditioned by the structure of the repertoire as the representation of any other order of reality, if not more so. Just as the literary child's appearance, behavior, psychology, and so forth, are to a large extent ready-mades, pieced together from prefabricated units available in the literary repertoire, so too is the language literary children speak. Here is another reason why the novels of the modernist "explosion" are of special interest to students of literary childhood, for in these novels—notably in Dos Passos's *U.S.A.* trilogy (*The 42nd Parallel*, 1930; *1919*, 1932; *The Big Money*, 1936)—the sub-repertoire of children's language can be isolated and described more readily than it can in most other periods and genres. This is because the sub-repertoire used at this period actually has an independent existence outside of literary representation, not in "reality" as such—not, that is, in the language that real children really speak—but rather in the layperson's *image* or stereotype of children's language. Ask an adult who is not a trained lingust to imitate the language of children, and he or she will probably produce a sample of baby-talk, which is demonstrably *not* the same thing as children's language, though it purports to represent the latter. As we shall see, it is upon the baby-talk stereotype, and not upon the language children really speak, that Dos Passos and others of his literary generation drew when seeking to represent children's language.

The notion of a preselected realeme repertoire carries us a long way toward capturing the process of representing children's language, but it does not carry us quite the whole way. Even-Zohar's theory of the repertoire needs to be supplemented by a different, more text-oriented kind of account, one that describes how prefabricated children's-language realemes are integrated in the fabric of texts, how they come to be *inscribed* or *textualized*.[2] Here, once again, the novels of Dos Passos and some of his contemporaries prove to be invaluable as case studies, not because they illustrate this inscription process in its simplest or most readily graspable form but, on the contrary, because they illustrate it in all its complexity.

This complexity is due largely to their preferred technique for introducing represented speech. The simplest technique for textually inscribing a sample of "exotic" discourse, such as children's language, is direct quotation, which in effect treats the imported discourse as a miniature text in its own right, a foreign enclave or inset within the textual fabric. Framed between quotation-marks and attributed to some appropriate speaker, directly-quoted discourse presents relatively few problems of textual integration and motivation. But from the moment one eliminates the quotation-marks and other syntactical framing devices (the *incipit* "he/she said," or the embedding clause of indirect discourse, "He/she said that"), the source of the "imported" discourse tends to become elusive, and problems of textualization begin to arise.[3] At the extreme of this tendency toward ambiguity one finds the techniques of so-called free indirect dicourse preferred by Dos Passos and his contemporaries (including, e.g., Lawrence in *Sons and Lovers* [1913], Joyce in *A Portrait of the Artist as a Young Man* [1916], Henry Green in *Living* [1929], Edward Dahlberg in *Bottom Dogs* [1930], and James T. Farrell in the *Studs Lonigan* trilogy [1932, 1934, 1935]).[4] Here, in the absence of unequivocal markers of who speaks, and of where the "imported" discourse of the inset leaves off and the "native" discourse of text proper begins, the reader has no choice but to fall back on more equivocal and *ad hoc*, though still systematic, indicators, some of which are described below in "The Inscribed Child."

BABY-TALK, OR, THE READY-MADE CHILD

How, then, do we recognize children's language in Dos Passos' *U.S.A.*? Here are two samples, widely separated in the text:

(1) Fainy's eyes smarted; in his ears was the continuous roar, the clatter clatter over crossings, the sudden snarl under bridges. It was tunnel, all the way to Chicago it was a tunnel. Opposite him Pop's and Uncle Tim's faces looked red and snarling, he didn't like the way they looked, and the light was smoky and jiggly and outside it was all a tunnel and his eyes hurt and wheels and rails roared in his ears and he fell asleep (*42nd Parallel* 16)

(2) Poor Daddy never did get tucked away in bed right after supper the way he liked with his reading light over his left shoulder and his glasses on and the paper in his hand and a fresh cigar in his mouth that the phone didn't ring, or else it would be a knocking at the back door and Mother would send little Mary to open it and she'd find a miner standing there whitefaced with his eyelashes and eyebrows very black from the coaldust saying, "Doc French, pliz . . . heem coma queek," and poor Daddy would get up out of bed yawning in his pyjamas and bathrobe and push his untidy grey hair off his forehead and tell Mary to go get his instrument case out of the office for him, and be off tying his necktie as he went, and half the time he'd be gone all night. (*Big Money* 106–7)

Even stripped of their contexts in this way, these passages unmistakably evoke a childish tone. If called upon to isolate the features responsible for this tone, the reader might first pick out the kin names (*Pop, Daddy, Mother*) and epithets (*poor Daddy, little Mary*), and then perhaps mention the breathless, run-on quality of the sentences. Even without knowing that the protagonist's given name in the first example is Fenian, one could recognize *Fainy* as a child's nickname. The onomatopoeia (*clatter clatter*) and naive-sounding *jiggly* also contribute to the childish tone of this passage. Finally, in the absence of a better explanation, one might regard the curious use of *it* as another marker of children's language.

Between them, these passages illustrate many of the most common markers of children's language in *U.S.A.* The complete repertoire of children's language features, including those that occur no more than once or twice in the text, will now be informally summarized.

(i) Causal coordination, invariably using the conjunction *and*. See (1) and (2).

(ii) Other run-on constructions. Examples include prepositional phrases in series (*1919* 257) and recursive embedding of that-clauses, a sort of "House That Jack Built" construction:

(3) The Trents lived in a house on Pleasant avenue that was the finest street in Dallas that was the biggest and fastest growing town in Texas that was the biggest state in the Union and had the blackest soil and the whitest people and America was the greatest country in the world and Daughter was Dad's onlyest sweetest little girl. (*1919* 256)

(iii) Deviant uses of ambient-*it*. The use of *it* in (1) clearly deviates from the familiar dummy-*it* or ambient-*it* found in expressions of weather, time of day, and so forth ("It was raining," "It was three o'clock"). Other examples of deviant ambient-*it* constructions include:

(4) When he woke up it was a town and the train was running right through the main street (*42nd Parallel*, 16).

(5) Poor Daddy got grey and worried and never laughed round the house any more after that and then it was all about the investment (*Big Money* 108).

(iv) Deletion of preposition and article in temporal phrases. Compare the standard constructions "On Sunday afternoons," "During the winters," "In the mornings," "In the afternoons," "On summer evenings" with the following:

(6) Sunday afternoons Janey and Joe and Ellen and Francie had to sit in the front room and look at pictures or read books. . . . Winters the brick sidewalks were icy and there were colored women out spreading cinders outside their doors when the children went to school mornings. . . . Afternoons Janey and Pearl walked home together. . . . Summer evenings when the twilight was long after supper they played lions and tigers with other kids from the neighborhood. (*42nd Parallel* 133–36; my ellipses)

Note that these phrases are all iterative, that is, they all indicate recurrent events (see Genette 145–82).

(v) Anomalous second-person pronoun *you* in third-person contexts.

(7) The backyard was the only place you could really feel safe to play in. (*42nd Parallel* 8)

(8) What she liked at the beach was playing the game where you rolled a little ball over the clean narrow varnished boards into holes with numbers. (*Big Money* 169)

What initially foregrounds this feature is the possibility it appears to raise of apostrophe to the reader, in direct violation of the rhetorical norms of this text.[5] This hypothesis is quickly abandoned, however, and the correct one selected: *you* here functions as the equivalent of the impersonal pronoun *one*; compare "the only place *one* could really feel safe," "the game where *one* rolled a little ball."

(vi) Kin names functioning as proper names and/or pronouns. See (1), (2), (3), (5). Other examples from *U.S.A.* include: *Popper, Mommer, Mom, Mummy, Momma, Grandfather*, and *Brother*. Such kin names, when appearing in third-person contexts without the appropriate genitive pronoun (cf. "his pop" or "her daddy"), have long been recognized as indicators of free indirect discourse, since they identify a *speaker* (the one who can appropriately say "Pop") at the same time as they designate the person who stands in the specified relationship to him or her.[6]

(vii) "Tags" and other constructions using pronouns and general nouns (*thing, kind, sort*). This category includes a number of colloquial variants of *et cetera*, which often serve evasive or euphemistic functions: *and/or everything, and all this/that, things like this/that, all sorts/kinds of things*, and so forth.

(7) He had a new black suit on, too, like a grownup suit with pockets and everything. (*42nd Parallel* 10)

(8) Dick felt Mrs. Glen might have said something about his carrying out the ashes and shoveling snow and all that (*1919* 74).

(9) Minette Hardy . . . used to pass her . . . bits of paper with little messages scrawled on them: To Goldilocks with love from her darling Minette, and things like that. (*Big Money* 73).

(10) All kinds of things got him terribly agitated so that it was hard not to show it. (*1919* 81)

(viii) Intensifiers *so* and *such*.

(11) The children couldn't make out why the strong nice tall conductor was so nice to Miss Mathilda who was so hateful and trainsick. (*1919* 108)

(12) . . . he had such nice blue eyes but Miss Mathilda had horrid blue eyes. (*1919* 107)

(ix) Prenominal-epithet constructions. See (2) *Poor Daddy* and *little Mary*, and (5).

(x) A limited set of adjectives and adverbs expressing general approbation or disappropriation. These may appear prenominally, as in (ix), or as predicates. Aside from the items mentioned in (ix), this set includes *nice* (see [13] and [14]), *lovely, wonderful, horrid, dreadful*, and *awful*.

(xi) Specifically child-oriented lexis and idioms. These items fall into several general lexical fields relating to children's preoccupations, attitudes, and perceptions.[7]

(a) Age, relative seniority, size: *grownup* (see [11]), *to get big*, and others.
(b) Games, play: *to play dolls, lions and tigers* (see [6]), *three o'cat, follow my leader, toad in the hole; to roughhouse*, and *to do funny pictures*.
(c) Punishment: *to get spanked, to give him a licking*.
(d) Miscellaneous: *picturebook, funnypaper, softie*, and *sandman*.

(xii) Nicknames. Unlike kin names, nicknames or pet names do not identify a speaker; they do, however, evoke the familial and peer-group situations in which such names originate. Regular nickname forms, those produced by adding the diminutive suffix *-y* or *-ie* ([1] *Fainy*, [6] *Janey, Francie*; also *Johnny, Dicky, Benny, Margie*), are not invariably markers of children's language since, after all, they may also be used to designate adults. Irregular forms may suggest more strongly a nursery origin—*Arget* (= Margaret), *Lade* (= Adelaide), *Gogo* (= George) (*1919* 107).

(xiii) Deviant adjectival and adverbial forms. Many of these are nonce-forms produced by adding the regular *-y* or *-ly* suffix to the verb. Examples include *jiggly* (see [1]), *frizzly, trembly, choky, tickly*, and *glary*.

(xiv) Deviant superlative forms. Examples include *onlyest* (see [3]) and *grown-upest*.

(xv) Onomatopoeic items. Examples include *clatter clatter* (see [1]), *click click* (*1919* 73), *rumblebump chug chug* (*1919* 108).

(xvi) Miscellaneous childish nonce-forms. Examples include *sickyfeeling, companyvoices, tightscared, cozywarm*, and *slimysmelly*.

(xvii) Mispronunciations and other approximate phonetic transcriptions. Certain deviant spellings must be interpreted as children's misconstructions of adult utterances,[8] such as *monia* (= pneumonia), *Ideals* (= Idylls) *of the King, Queen Whenever* (= Guinevere) (*1919* 108–9). Other examples of approximate phonetic transcription occurring in the context of children's language in *U.S.A.* include *Popper, Mommer, yaller, kinda*, and *'ud* (= would).

One immediately remarks how few of the features in this list correspond to one's intuitions about children's speech. To explain the presence of the counterintuitive features, we will need to take context into account. But, setting aside the problem of contextualization for the moment, how closely does Dos Passos's children's language copy reality?

Our evidence for real children's linguistic behavior will have to come from the literature on language acquisition. This immediately confronts us with a disparity between what a linguist finds noteworthy in a child's behavior and what a novelist, or at least *this* novelist, finds noteworthy. Contemporary linguists, predictably enough, have concentrated on describing the grammar(s) of children's sentences. Dos Passos, on the other hand, has chosen not to imitate, even distantly, the telescoped syntax that has been the focus of most linguists' attention. Indeed, the features I have listed are predominantly lexical, not syntactical. The reason is not far to seek: only lexical features and superficial syntactical features (such as items [i–v]) could readily be accommodated to the free indirect discourse that is the basis of Dos Passos's style in *U.S.A.* But the fact remains that, for whatever reason, children's language in *U.S.A.* fails to reflect one of the central features of real children's linguistic behavior. From the outset, mimesis is compromised.

Equally compromising is Dos Passos's failure to vary his children's styles with age, except in two interesting cases.[9] We know that children's speech changes in fairly well-defined stages as they get older, and this fact figures predominantly in the literature on language acquisition. Not so in *U.S.A.*, however, where children's language is largely consistent throughout, whatever the age of the child. Indeed, we seldom are told the exact age of the children in question, unless by way of indicating the *limit* of children's language, the point beyond which it disappears ("When Fainy was seventeen," *42nd Parallel* 19; "When Eveline was twelve years old," *1919* 109).

These disparities between Dos Passos's supposed representation and objective linguistic descriptions would all but seem to invalidate the claim to faithful imitation in *U.S.A.* Are there any respects in which Dos Passos and the linguists coincide? There are, of course. The literature on language acquisition confirms, for example, that conjunction (see item [i]) is acquired early by children, that its earliest exponents are *and* and *then*, and that only gradually, with age, do causal conjunctions replace these simple, temporal conjunctions.[10] We can easily find actual transcripts of children's narratives that echo the breathless, run-on quality of (1) and (2):

(15) A little girl lived with her mommy. And then she got spanked. And a bear came in and he was a long one and he ate the girl up. And then the mommy and Daddy came home and the bear flied away and they said, "Where's our little girl?" and they were sad.

And then an eagle came, flied in their house. And Little Red Riding Hood came in and said, "That's a naughty eagle." And then the princess cut off the eagle's head. And the little girl thanked the princess for taking her home. And then the basket broke, and her mommy said, "Oh, naughty girl Little Red Riding Hood." And the mommy said, "Naughty Girl, Little Red Riding Hood." (Boy, aged 3 years, 9 months; Pitcher and Prelinger 44)

According to Piaget, a child in the "preoperational" period of development (from 1.5 or 2 years to 6 or 7 years of age), instead of connecting elements logically by implication or by using models of cause and effect, merely juxtaposes them. Even if logical-causal connectives such as *because/since, therefore*, and *although* do appear in children's speech in this period, they are typically mismanaged, used with the meaning of *and* and *then*.[11] Thus Piagetian psychology corroborates the "realism" of Dos Passos's use of run-on coordination as a marker of children's language.

Piaget can also be invoked to justify the use of anomalous ambient-*it* constructions (item [iii]). One characteristic of the preoperational child, Piaget tells us, is "egocentricity," which is reflected linguistically in the inability to adapt utterances to the needs of the listener, and in particular in the failure to identify unambiguously the referents of pronouns.[12] Faulty specification of pronoun-reference is illustrated by the following transcript of an exchange between Nigel Halliday (aged 2 years, 11 months) and his mother:

(16) MOTHER: How on earth did you get all that sand in your hair?
    NIGEL: I was just standing up and I threw the sand to it and it got in my hair. (Halliday 1975)

The referents of the pronoun *it* in (1), (4), and (5) have been left unspecified in much the same way. Dos Passos's use of ambient-*it* resembles even more closely the childish use of a different deictic, *that*, in the following transcript:

(17) But after a while then the horse went back and found a covered wagon, and it was the same one because it had the same people in it so they pull and heaved and that was the state of Oregon. (Boy, aged 4 years, 10 months); Pitcher and Prelinger 77)

The anomalous appearance of the second-person pronoun in third person contexts (item [v]) has been explained as functionally equivalent to the impersonal pronoun *one*. The literature on language acquisition suggests an alternative explanation in light of children's systematic confusion of pronouns. At an early stage, many children use the pronouns *I* and *you* not as discourse "shifters" (*I* = addressor, *you* = addressee, regardless of the identity or relationship of the participants), but as stable, unshifting labels rather like proper names: *I* = adult, *you* = child.[13] This, for example, was young Nigel Halliday's practice in sentences like, "Uncle gave you [= Nigel] some marbles" (Halliday, 70–71).[14] Even if (7) and (8) could not plausibly be read with *I* substituted for *you*, these passages might still echo, however faintly, the childish misconstruction of shifters. Be that as it may, there is at least one indubitable case of such misconstruction in *U.S.A.*: the quasi-proper name *Yourfather*, as in the sentence, "Yourfather was Dr. Hutchins but Our Father art in heaven" (*1919* 107).

The item *Yourfather* reflects another misconstruction typical of children's linguistic behavior: the erroneous segmentation of sequences (Ervin-Trip 213; Brown 391–95). Erroneous segmentation would also account for such items as *Dearmother*, *kinda* (cf. the unsegmented catenatives mentioned by Brown, such as *wanna*, *hafta*, *gonna*), and perhaps such nonce-forms (item [xvi]) as *companyvoices* and *cozywarm*. Incidentally, the item *Dearmother*, like *Yourfather*, is mimetically doubly determined, reflecting not only children's erroneous segmentation of sequences, but also the early acquisition of prenominal attribution. Prenominal epithets (item ix), in actual children's speech as in *U.S.A.*, are drawn from an extremely limited set of modifiers (item x). Ervin-Tripp lists as typical *big*, *little*, *pretty*, *poor*, *broken*, while in Pitcher and Prelinger's collection of stories by children, the only modifiers to occur at all frequently are *naughty*, *nice*, and *little*, and these invariably in prenominal rather than predicate position.

The deviant superlatives (item xiv) and other deviant adverbial and adjectival forms (item xiii) found in the context of children's language in *U.S.A.* also correspond to actual children's behavior, but in a strangely oblique way. Apparently, Dos Passos has taken a general principle of actual children's language and applied it to features other than those to which children in fact apply it. The principle is that of overgeneralization of inflections. Once a child has learned one of the basic English inflections—for tense, person, plurality—he or she is liable to use it too generally, adding it to word stems where it does not belong. Having acquired the use of the past tense marker *-ed*, the child may produce *comed*, *falled*, *goed;* having learned the plural markers, he or she may produce *feets* and *mens*.[15] The overgeneralization of comparative and superlative inflections seems actually to occur, often in verbal play (*gooder*, *deadier*, *middlesizeder*, *slimmiest*, *weaklingest*.)[16] Thus far, Dos Passos's application of the principle is directly mimetic. But I have failed to find any evidence for children's generation of nonce-adjectives from *verbs* by overgeneralization of the inflection (as in Dos Passos's *trembly*, *choky*), although there are examples of inappropriate inflection on noun stems (*beary*, *hatty*, on the model of *fishy*, *snakey*).[17]

Up to this point, the attempt to correlate Dos Passos's supposed representation and objective linguistic descriptions of children's language has yielded at best spotty and oblique results. It might well be protested that I have left out of account precisely those features that not only are most widely attested to in the literature on language acquisition, but also accord best with the lay-reader's intuitions about children's speech: child-oriented lexis and idioms (xi) and kin- and nicknames (vi, xii). The omission has been deliberate. It is my contention that these features, partly because they do correspond so well to our intuitions about "speaking as a child," belong not so much to children's language per se as to baby talk, a speech variety whose status is rather different.

Baby-talk is the conventionalized register of language used by adults in addressing infants or small children. Adults may also use it in various displaced and extended functions, such as to address pets or lovers.[18] Baby-talk may also be used by children themselves to address still smaller children, or to dramatize their own babyishness before adults. Obviously, it would be impossible to segregate baby-talk features and genuine children's language, since the two varieties interpenetrate so completely in real nursery situations. Still, the distinction is clear, in principle at least: the baby-talk features in children's speech are those nonstandard (non-adult) features that have been imitated directly from adults, while the genuine children's language features are those anomalies that have been generated by the children themselves on the basis of standard adult usage. No adult uses the pro-nominal system, for instance, in such a way that a child, in using *I* and *you* as equivalents of proper names, could be imitating him directly; rather, this is the child's misconstruction. Conversely, no child ever spontaneously invented the forms *doggie* or *kittycat;* these could only originate in the language adults use in addressing the child (Ferguson 1971, 114–16).

Baby-talk, although originally part of the adult's range of registers, and only derivatively part of the child's, is nevertheless generally believed by adults to reflect children's usage. Indeed, as C. A. Ferguson has observed, it is used by adults when mimicking children's language, even in prose fiction (1977, 231). In short, baby-talk is a classic linguistic stereotype, in David Crystal's sense of the term (107–8). Crystal distinguishes between two modes of knowing: linguistic stereotype and professional competence. The first is the layperson's *image* of a speech variety that he or she does not actually use; the second, the actual user's objective behavior. Professional competence manifests itself in the appropriate context of situation, such as legal language in the law office and courtroom; while the linguistic stereo-type manifests itself in jokes, parodies, and fiction. If children's language can be thought of as manifesting a sort of professional competence, then baby-talk is the corresponding linguistic stereotype.

The relevance of this distinction to Dos Passos's children's language is plain. Kin-names functioning as proper names and pronouns, nicknames, the child-lexi-con (including the modifiers listed under item [x] and the onomatopoeic forms in item [xv])—all of these are mentioned regularly in linguistic descriptions of the baby-talk register.[19] Thus an important part of the children's language repertoire in *U.S.A.*—statistically and contextually the most prominent features—has not been based directly on children's language per se, but on a conventionalized model of children's language, baby-talk. This means that Dos Passos's representation is actually a selection from a stereotypical repertoire of features, a selection from a preselection, an imitation of an imitation. It is this mediation by a stereotypical model, or repertoire in Even-Zohar's sense, that makes it possible for readers to decode Dos Passos's representation correctly. How could readers who were unfa-miliar with, or inattentive to, children's speech correctly identify this speech vari-ety in *U.S.A.* if identification depended upon direct comparison with real, objective behavior? But of course the reader has no need to compare passages of *U.S.A.* with real children's behavior; she or he only needs to be conversant with a widely known linguistic stereotype.

The Inscribed Child

The hypothesis of a mediated relationship between the raw material of (linguistic) reality and its literary representation, refracted, as it were, through a linguistic stereotype, solves many (but not all) of the problems raised by our list of children's language features. We are still left with a number of features unaccounted for, explicable neither in relation to children's language per se nor in relation to the baby-talk register. Embarrassingly enough, some of these as yet unexplained features, as well as some of the features we have already accounted for, seem to imitate speech varieties other than children's language. For example, the subset of run-on coordination, ambient-*it* constructions, restricted set of modifiers, and even tags using general nouns and pronouns (items [i], [iii], [vii], [x]), evoke the so-called Restricted Code of working-class speakers as readily as they do children's language.[20] Compare (3) or (4) with the following synthetic sample narrative in Restricted Code:

(18) They're playing football and he kicks it and it goes through there it breaks the window and they're looking at it and he comes out and shouts at them because they've broken it so they run away and then she looks out and she tells them off. (Hawkins 86)

Among the middle classes, according to Bernstein, the Restricted Code is supplemented by an Elaborated Code for use in educational and professional situations. Competence in the Restricted Code alone, without the Elaborated Code, identifies working-class speakers. Thus this subset of features from the list apparently reflects not children's language (or not only children's language), but the working-class social dialect.

Another subset, partly overlapping with this one, evokes yet another speech variety: women's language. In our culture "talking like a lady," as Robin Lakoff suggested some time ago (see also Edelsky), is a powerful linguistic stereotype, an image or expectation of how women should behave verbally (rather than a category of observable behavior, as Bernstein's Restricted Code is purported to be). Among its features Lakoff lists the intensifier *so* and a set of sex-linked modifiers, such as items (viii) and (x) on our list of children's language features. Thus in this case, as in the case of the Restricted Code features mentioned above, we have more than one (quasi-) mimetic motivation competing for the same features.

Dos Passos actually exploits the linguistic stereotype of "talking like a lady" in much the same way as he does baby-talk.[21] To evoke women's language in the "Eleanor Stoddard" and "Eveline Hutchins" narratives, Dos Passos uses intensifiers (*so, such, all too, just too*) and sex-linked modifiers (*nice, lovely, horrid*), together with some features not predicted by Lakoff, such as tags using general nouns and pronouns (vii) and multiple ("gushing") prenominal modification (*a bright definite little way of talking, a crisp little refined monied voice; 42nd Parallel* 244–45). The problem with this stereotypical representation of women's language is that it uses features already used to represent children's language.

This is the crowning embarrassment: not only are certain children's language features potentially imitative of other speech varieties (Restricted Code, "talking like a lady"), but they *actually* function in certain contexts as markers of those varieties. The anomalous second-person pronoun (item [v]) furnishes another example. It appears in children's language contexts, but also in the context of various working-class dialects and registers, such as the maritime register:

(19) When he came out of the galley they were further up the river, you could see towns on both sides, the sky was entirely overcast with brown smoke and fog. The Argyle was steaming under one bell. (*1919* 32)

Similarly, one might predict, on the basis of the comparison with Bernstein's Restricted Code, that run-on coordination would appear in working-class contexts as well as children's language contexts in *U.S.A.* And so it does:

(20) When they went to the girls' apartment they took a quart of whiskey with them and Mac almost dropped it on the steps and the girls said, "For crissake don't make so much noise or you'll have the cops on us," and the apartment smelt of musk and facepowder and there was women's underwear around on all the chairs and the girls got fifteen bucks out of each of them first thing. . . . Mac laughed, it was so very funny, but he was sitting on the floor and when he tried to get up he fell on his face and all of a sudden he was being sick in the bathtub and Gladys was cursing hell out of him. She got him dressed, only he couldn't find his necktie, and everybody said he was too drunk and pushed him out and he was walking down the street singing *Make a Noise Like a Hoop and Just Roll Away, Roll Away*, and he asked a cop where the Y.M.C.A. was and the cop pushed him into a cell at the stationhouse and locked him up. (*42nd Parallel* 75–76; my ellipsis)

Evidently, however, the functions of this rambling coordinate syntax are not exhausted by identifying it with working-class social dialect any more than with children's language, for it appears in genteel and low-life contexts alike. Further analysis shows that the common factor in most occurrences of run-on coordination is not dialect or register at all, but mental state. This feature regularly correlates with drunkenness (as in [20]; cf. also *42nd Parallel* 374), fatigue and confusion (1), exhilaration (*42nd Parallel* 141; *1919* 193), dream (*42nd Parallel* 209)—in short, with some extreme, abnormal, or altered state of consciousness.[22] Thus, in many contexts this feature of children's language belongs to a different repertoire, falling under a different set of literary conventions altogether, namely, those governing the mimesis of nonverbal states of mind rather than the mimesis of speech varieties.

These facts leave us with an extremely messy picture. In place of the well-defined, mutually exclusive sets of features we might have hoped for, we have found several subsets doing double, or even triple, duty as markers of different speech varieties in different contexts, or as markers of speech varieties in some contexts and markers of nonverbal states of mind in others. How are we to introduce some order into this apparent confusion? We could hypothesize some sort of complex or superimposed imitation. We could say, since Fainy in (1) is, at one and the same time, a child, a member of the working class, and in a state of fatigue and confusion, that the foregrounded features in this passage imitate children's language *and* Restricted Code *and* an altered state of consciousness; and so on for all our other problematical passages. This is ingenious enough, but implausible perceptually. Is it likely that a reader would be able to recognize superimposed layers of imitation in complex mimesis of speech? Isn't it more likely she or he would be satisfied to identify one object of imitation?

A better solution would be to allow for the play of context in the mimesis of speech. If the imitation of speech varieties is in some respects faithful to a linguistic sterotype, if not to objective linguistic reality, it is also in some respects arbitrary, determined not by the supposed object of imitation, but by strictly internal textual relations, that is, by *textual context* in the largest sense.

Contextualization, I would propose, operates at three levels or spheres: sentence context, discourse context, and virtual context.

Sentence Context. The continuing interest in "dual-voiced" structures of speech and thought representation—direct indirect, and free indirect discourse, and their variants and hybrids—has tended to obscure certain facts about the normal reception of sentences in fiction. First, dual-voiced structures normally confront a narrator's voice—or speech variety, which is what concerns us here—with the alien or intrusive voice of a character, and not one character's voice with another's. Second, readers will always try to naturalize a sentence as the utterance of a *single unitary voice*, unless there are very strong (contextual) reasons for reading it differently (that is, dually). There are, of course, sentences in which two characters' "voices" or varieties are heard, and which resist reduction to a unitary voice. In these cases, certain well-known strategies of reading are prescribed. One may, for example, read ironically:

(21) There followed a long wrangle between the firm of Truthseeker, Inc., and the management of Hummer's Livery Stable as to the rent of a springwagon and an elderly piebald horse with cruppers you could hang a hat on. (*42nd Parallel* 42)

No single register could assimilate both the formal businesslike items in this passage (*the firm of Truthseeker, Inc., the management of Hummer's Livery Stable, as to the rent of*) and the homely, colloquial, even rustic items (*wrangle, cruppers you could hang a hat on*). Rather, this clash of speech varieties is reconciled at a higher level, within a single ironic intention (see Booth 67).

Nevertheless, there are cases of less pronounced stylistic clash—and here, unhappily, we must resort to an ill-defined notion of *degrees* of disparity—in which it is possible to assimilate all the markers in the sentence in a unitary voice. For example, no reader of the final sentence of (1) would identify *Pop* and *jiggly* as markers of children's language, and at the same time identify the coordinate syntax and the ambient-*it* construction as markers of a *different* speech variety, say the Restricted Code. Instead, all these features will be assimilated to a *single* speech variety—children's language.

Discourse Context. But why children's language rather than the Restricted Code in this example? More generally: when features belonging to different speech varieties co-occur in a sentence, which register will be selected as the "dominant" to which the other will be assimilated? Apparently, the "given" register, as opposed to the "new" one, will be selected—the register already in play, if there is one, rather than the one newly introduced. Now, the "givenness" of a register may be determined either intertextually, or contextually: either strongly stereotypical features will dominate (such as the baby-talk items *Pop* and *jiggly* in [1]), or the dominant register of the preceding discourse will. "A text," as T. F. Mitchell put it some time ago in a classic article, "is a kind of snowball, and every lexical item and every collocation in it is part of its [the text's] own context" (186). This "snowballing" effect appears, for instance, in the contextualization of the sentence that immediately follows my example (2) in Dos Passos's original text:

(22) Mealtimes it was worse. (*Big Money* 107)

This elliptical prepositional phrase (cf. "*At/During* mealtimes . . ."), although it does correspond to an item (iv) on our list of children's language features, lacks mimetic motivation. Nowhere is such a construction mentioned in descriptions either of children's language per se or of baby-talk. Yet in this context it is readily perceived as a childish feature, under the lingering influence of the preceding discourse, whose tone is unmistakably childish. In this way, features that have no objective affiliation with either children's language or stereotypical baby-talk are pressed into service as ad hoc markers of children's language, and serve, in their turn, as part of the discourse context that determines the reader's perception of further items.

But this is somewhat disingenuous of me: it is not only the immediately preceding discourse that disposes us to read this feature as a marker of children's language, but also the fact that we have already encountered it a number of times in the context of other children's language markers (see [6] above; also *42nd Parallel* 371; *1919* 256). Thus the relevant discourse context may be much wider than merely the preceding sentence or sentences; it may, indeed, coincide with the physical limits of the text.

Virtual Context. It is also disingenuous to suggest that only the relation between one stretch of discourse and another, between one formal textual feature and another, counts as contextualization. On the contrary, the most important contextual relation subsists not between different stretches of discourse, but between different ontological levels: between the level of the text as linguistic entity, and the *fictive world* which the texts' sentences project or which, more accurately, the reader reconstructs at the text's instigation. We could follow Susanne Langer in calling this fictive world of the text its *virtual* level or virtual context, to distinguish it from the *actual* discourse of the text, upon which the fictive world depends for its existence.

The ideal case would be one in which these two types of contextual relation—that of discourse to *other* discourse, and that of discourse to fictive world—coincided. One stretch of discourse, say, would allow us to reconstruct a virtual (fictional) *context of situation*, while a *different* stretch would allow us to reconstruct the language uttered *in* that situation. Thus the relation between the two stretches of discourse would coincide with the relation between the two ontological levels, and we could proceed as we do in real-world sociolinguistics, finding correlations between the nonverbal context (in this case a virtual rather than actual one) and the language used in that context. Unfortunately, things are rarely so straightforward, even in the case of direct discourse, which most nearly approximates this ideal. When it comes to other modes of speech presentation, such as free indirect discourse, this ideal division of labor between different stretches of discourse is even less punctiliously observed.[23]

There are, however, rare cases even of free indirect discourse, of which we can say with some confidence that one segment gives rise to the (virtual) nonverbal context, while another constitutes the verbal component of the situation. For instance, in the opening sentence of Farrell's *Young Lonigan:*

(23a) Studs Lonigan, on the verge of fifteen, and wearing his first suit of long trousers, stood in the bathroom . . .

Thus far, we encounter no imitation of speech, no markers of register; the style is rather neutral, colorless. Decoded, these signs allow us to begin contructing a profile of the character in question: male, adolescent, and so forth. This profile-in-the-making, in turn, helps motivate the register-marker in the next segment:

(23b) . . . with a Sweet Caporal pasted in his mug. (Farrell 11)

We have no trouble correlating *pasted in his mug* with its (virtual) context of situation.

Much more typical of free indirect discourse, however, is the combination of

functions we find, for instance, in the opening passage of Dos Passos's "Daughter"
narrative (see [3] above), or the opening of "Eveline Hutchins":

(24) Little Eveline and Arget and Lade and Gogo lived on the top floor of a
yellowbrick house on the North Shore Drive. Arget and Lade were little Eveline's
sisters. Gogo was her little brother littler than Eveline; he had such nice blue eyes
but Miss Mathilda had horrid blue eyes. On the floor below was Dr. Hutchins'
study where Yourfather mustn't be disturbed, and Dearmother's room where she
stayed all morning painting dressed in a lavender smock. (*1919* 107)

Here, it would be futile to try to distinguish segments that give rise to the nonverbal component of the fictive world from those that imitate speech. The very same
items that allow us to reconstruct parts of a world—a genteel Chicago family,
four young children, a governess, something of the parents' approach to child-
rearing—also evoke the appropriate language for this virtual situation, namely,
children's language. Contextualization here proceeds not between different stretches of discourse, but between discourse (markers of children's language) and its
virtual context, the reconstructed fictional world.

THE "REAL" CHILD?

This has been an anti-traditionalist account of linguistic mimesis in the novel,
in the sense that it sharply contradicts the principles of what might be thought of
as "classical" literary dialectology. According to the "classical" account of, for
example, Krapp (225–73), Ives, Page, and others, the literary mimesis of speech
varieties (dialects, registers) can be adequately explained in terms of processes of
selection and *generalization*. The novelist represents a given dialect or register, first, by
choosing from the stock of features that actually constitutes the speech variety in
question a very few features to be treated as especially typical or distinctive; and,
second, by repeating these features in literary dialect passages relatively more frequently than would be the case in actual speech. The reader presumably decodes
the representation by locating the statistically emphasized features, and comparing
them with the various sets of features within the scope of his or her own sociolinguistic competence until one of them matches, thereby identifying the specific
set—the dialect or register—from which the features had been drawn in the first
place. Thus the mimetic contract is fulfilled, and literary art's power to hold the
mirror up to reality reaffirmed.

The present account of children's language in *U.S.A* counters this "classical"
version by proposing two alternative principles. In place of a principle of selection,
which implies that the entire range of real-world language behavior is freely and
directly accessible to novelist and reader alike, it proposes a principle of *preselection.*
The diversity of real language behavior, by this account, is available for representa-

tion only insofar as it has already been reduced to a much narrower code or repertoire of conventionally representable items, in our particular case a prefabricated "linguistic sterotype," that of baby-talk, which *stands in for* real children's language in novelistic representations. Similarly, in place of the straightforwardly statistical principle of generalization, the present account presupposes a much more complex set of textualizing and contextualizing operations, functioning at different textual levels, of which only a rough preliminary sketch could be offered here.

Nor are these alternative principles of representation restricted to literary dialectology alone; rather, they are themselves generalizable to literary representations of objects of all kinds. The literary representation of *anything* is, on the one hand, repertoire-based, and, on the other, textually produced through various processes of inscription and contextualization.

Having arrived at this conclusion, I find myself compelled to contest some of what I take to be the underlying premises of the present essay collection, in particular its assumption of a kind of "exceptionalism" with respect to the representation of children and childhood. The assumption would seem to be that children constitute a special case, presenting special difficulties of access and representation because, as objects of representation, they are always inevitably Other than the adult writers who undertake to represent them and their experience. This seems to me a fallacy. If representation is always culturally mediated, always repertoire-based, as I have argued here, then *no* object of representation is any more directly accessible than any other, and the representation of childhood presents no greater (or lesser) difficulties than does the representation of adulthood. Raw reality is always Other, and that Other is always inaccessible and unrepresentable except mediately, through the repertoires our cultures provide.

This is not to say that there is no world outside the text—a proposition that no one, except the straw men of anti-textualist polemics, could seriously maintain. The point is, rather, that there is no world *accessible to us through texts* that has not already been textualized. This is a tautology, of course, but no less the case for being tautological. More generally (but still tautologically), no semiotic system—language included; literature included—can give us direct access to extra-semiotic reality. No text can give us direct access to the experience or consciousness of a child; but neither can any text give us direct, unmediated access to *our own* (adult) experience, *our own* consciousness.[24]

NOTES

1. Cf. also an earlier version, "Constraints of Realeme Insertability." For the record, Even-Zohar himself credits Mia and Jose Lambert with having "contributed" the example of the Kellogg's cereal-bowl offer.

2. But see Even-Zohar, "Textemic Status," for indications of how Even-Zohar himself would handle the textualization aspect.

3. For details and an extensive critique of current treatments of quotation (my own included), see Meir Sternberg, "Proteus in Quotation-Land."

4. For a sampling of the extensive literature on free indirect discourse, see Genette, Pascal, McHale (1978), Cohn, Ron, and Banfield.

5. That is, the norms of the fictional narrative sections of *U.S.A.*; the norms of other sections, especially "The Camera Eye," are rather different (see note 14 below).

6. See, inter alia, Lips 68; Banfield 90. Note that kin-names may be used by *all* members of a family, including those who do not bear the specified relationship to the designated person: e.g., wives may refer to their husbands as *Dad*, to themselves as *Mother*, etc. Nevertheless, even if kin-names do not invariably identify *the* speaker, they always indicate the presence of *a* speaker, and consequently, in third-person contexts, of free indirect discourse.

7. The boundary between child-oriented items and adolescent slang is ill-defined. Some few items that impart an adolescent tone even when occurring in the same context as "childish" items can be identified, however: *tough* (adj.), *bully* (adj.), *gawky*, *stuck up*, *to kid [someone]* or *kid [someone] along*, *to get a crush on [someone]*, *to loosen up*, *to fall for*, *to pet*, etc. An interesting sub-category is ethnic epithets, which occasionally occur in the context of children's language in this text: e.g., *Polak, Bohunk, hunkies, greaser, Jap*, etc.

8. To this may be added certain "fixed routines" mimicked from adult speech: "On the groundfloor was the drawingroom and diningroom, where prisoners came and little children must be seen and not heard. . . . Your father was Dr. Hutchins but Our Father art in heaven" (*1919* 107; my ellipsis).

9. The opening pages of the "Richard Ellsworth Savage" narrative (*1919* 72–73) display two distinct styles of children's language: the first, less childish, corresponding to Dick's age at the point at which the narrative begins, and the second, more childish, corresponding to his age in an embedded flashback episode. In the opening pages of the "Eveline Hutchins" narrative (*1919* 107–15), the style varies literally from paragraph to paragraph, indicating Eveline's maturation from episode to episode.

10. See Ervin-Trip 212; Brown 30; Kernan 99–100. Weir (87, 91) reports that for children aged two to six *and* is the only frequently used connective.

The present section and the one that follows are reprinted, with minor changes, from McHale (1984). Consequently, the research on children's language and baby-talk reported and summarized here reflects the state of knowledge as of 1984, the publication date of the original article.

11. See Flavell 166, 275–76. However, if this account of the preoperational child tends to justify the appearance of item (i), it tends, by the same token, to invalidate the use of grammatically and semantically more sophisticated run-on constructions (item [ii]).

12. See Flavell 156, 272–73. This corresponds to the de Villiers's observations

(164, 152–65 and passim) that the general trend in the child's acquisition of language is toward ever-greater independence from immediate context. Thus children become increasingly better able to use pronouns and other deictics in ways that do not require the immediate context for their interpretation. For Bernstein's somewhat different perspective on context-dependent and -independent deixis, see note 20, below.

13. See especially Clark 100–2; also Weir 73–74; de Villiers and de Villiers 145, 262–63; and van der Geest 98–99.

14. One is irresistibly reminded of Michel Butor's second-person novel *La Modification* (1957) and his theoretical discussion in "L'Usage des pronoms personnels." As a matter of fact, Dos Passos substitutes the second-person pronoun for the expected quasi-autobiographical "I" in "The Camera Eye" (1, 3, 12, 19, 21, 36, 41, 46, 49).

15. See Ervin-Tripp 194–96; Brown 290–91, 296–97, 324–27 and passim.

16. The first two examples are from Pittcher and Prelinger 90, 109; the third from de Villiers and de Villiers 85; and the last two from Brenner and Lein 55.

17. See Garvey 38. Cf. the production of nonce-forms in children's game terminology by the addition of the suffixe *-ies/sy* to the word stem, e.g., *onesies, twosies, commonies, farsy-nearsy, plainsy, dumbsy* (Opie and Opie 155–56). Cf. also the baby-talk diminutive suffix *-ie.*

18. See Ervin-Tripp 270, 292; Ferguson, 1971 125–36.

19. For kin-names in baby-talk, see Jakobson 539; Ferguson 1971, 118–21; Ferguson 1977, 219–20; and Wells 277–78. For nicknames, see Ferguson 1977, 235 n 4; and Ervin-Tripp 328–29. For the baby-talk lexicon, see Ferguson 1971, 118–20; Ferguson 1977, 220–22; and de Villiers and de Villiers 124.

20. The term Restricted Code originates with the British sociologist Basil Bernstein. Building upon the findings of research carried out in London in the 1960s into class-based variation in language behavior, Bernstein distinguished between a Restricted Code of language practice, characteristic of working-class Londoners, and the Elaborated Code, i.e., standard educated English, which gives the speaker access to the institutions of social upward mobility. Bernstein's model, the findings on which it is based, and the ideology that seems to animate it have all been challenged, and there seems little doubt that the opposition Restricted versus Elaborated is far too crude to serve as a tool in sociolinguistic research. Nevertheless, the model does capture a viable *linguistic stereotype* of the class dialect of working-class speakers, and as such continues to be relevant in *poetics*, even if it has been discredited in sociolinguistics.

21. As in the case of children's language, where the opening passages of Joyce's *A Portrait of the Artist as a Young Man* (1916) is the crucial Modernist precedent, so too, in the case of literary representation of women's language, it is again Joyce who serves as the model; see "Eveline" in *Dubliners* (1914) and the "Nausicaa" section of *Ulysses* (1922).

22. Again, the model is Joyce: this time, Molly Bloom's syntactically disjointed soliloquy on the verge of sleep. I am indebted to John Spencer for this comparison.

23. A comparison between *U.S.A.* and Dos Passos's preceding novel, *Manhattan Transfer* (1925), illustrates the polar extremes of a spectrum of possibilities. In the

earlier novel, the syntactical boundary between reported discourse and reporting context is carefully maintained. So is the stylistic distinction between the two: where the reported discourse reflects the national, class, occupational, etc., diversity of the characters, the discourse of the reporting context excludes colloquial markers, instead exhibiting many self-consciously "literary" (quasi-poetic, lyrical, impressionistic) features. Here the distribution of functions between reported discourse and reported context approaches the ideal division of labor, the reporting context allowing us to reconstruct a (partial) picture of the noverbal context of situation within which the reported discourse is uttered. In *U.S.A.*, by contrast, the syntactical boundary is all but obliterated, and no stylistic distinction of the *Manhattan Transfer* type is observed; consequently, the division of labor is considerably complicated.

24. I take this position to be strictly parallel to the "irrealism" of Nelson Goodman and Richard Rorty, who contend that "the world," in the sense of some absolute, irreducible substratum of reality underlying all our versions of the real, and against which these versions must ultimately be measured, is (in Rorty's formulation) "well lost." Such an absolute substratum exists, no doubt, independently of all our worldversions, all our repertoires and representations; but since all we have access to are the versions, that substratum "world," whatever and wherever it is, is of no human use or interest whatsoever.

WORKS CITED

Banfield, Ann. *Unspeakable Sentences: Narration and Representation in the Language of Fiction.* Boston and London: Routledge and Kegan Paul, 1982.

Bernstein, Basil, ed. *Class, Codes and Control. Theoretical Studies towards a Sociology of Language,* Vol. I. London: Routledge and Kegan Paul, 1971.

Booth, Wayne. C. *A Rhetoric of Irony.* Chicago: University of Chicago Press, 1974.

Brenner, Donald, and Laura Lein. " 'Your Fruithead': A Sociolinguistic Approach to Children's Dispute Settlement." In *Child Discourse,* ed. Susan Ervin-Tripp and Claudia Mitchell-Kernan, 49–65. New York: Academic Press, 1977.

Brown, Roger. *A First Language: The Early Stages.* London: George Allen and Unwin, 1973.

Butor, Michel. "L'Usage des pronoms personnels dans le roman." In his *Repertoire 2,* 161–72. Paris: Minuit, 1964.

Clark, Eve V. "From Gesture to Word: On the Natural History of Deixis in Language Acquisition." In *Human Growth and Development: Wolfson College Lectures 1976,* ed. Jerome S. Bruner and Alison Garton, 85–120. New York and London: Oxford University Press, 1978.

Cohn, Dorrit. *Transparent Minds: Narrative Modes for Presenting Consciousness in Fiction.* Princeton, NJ: Princeton University Press, 1978.

Crystal, David. "Objective and Subjective in Stylistic Analysis." In *Current Trends in*

Stylistics, ed. Braj B. Kachru and H. F. W. Stahlke, 103–13. Edmonton: Linguistic Research, 1973.

De Villiers, Jill G., and Peter A. de Villiers. *Language Acquisition.* Cambridge and London: Harvard University Press, 1978.

Dos Passos, John. *U.S.A. [The 42nd Parallel; 1919; The Big Money.]* New York: Modern Library, 1939.

Edelsky, Carol. "Acquisition of an Aspect of Communicative Competence: Learning What It Means to Talk Like a Lady." In *Child Discourse,* ed. Susan Ervin-Tripp and Claudia Mitchell-Keenan, 225–43. New York: Academic Press, 1977.

Ervin-Tripp, Susan. *Language Acquisition and Communicative Choice.* Stanford: Stanford University Press, 1973.

Even-Zohar, Itamar. "Constraints of Realeme Insertability in Narrative." *Poetics Today* 1.3 (1980): 65–74.

———. "'Reality' and Realemes in Narrative." *Poetics Today* 11.1 (1990a): 207–18.

———. "The Textemic Status of Signs in Translation." *Poetics Today* 11.1 (1990b): 247–51.

Farrell, James T. *Studs Lonigan [Young Lonigan: The Young Manhood of Studs Lonigan; Judgment Day].* New York: Avon, 1977.

Ferguson, Charles A. "Baby Talk in a Simplified Register." In *Talking to Children: Language Input and Acquisition,* ed. Catherine E. Snow and Charles A. Ferguson, 219–35. London and New York: Cambridge University Press, 1977.

———. "Baby Talk in Six Languages." In his *Language Structure and Language Use,* 113–33. Stanford: Stanford University Press, 1971.

Flavell, John H. *The Developmental Psychology of Jean Piaget.* New York: Van Nostrand, 1963.

Garvey, Catherine. "Play with Language and Speech." In *Child Discourse,* ed. Susan Ervin-Tripp and Claudia Mitchell-Kernan, 27–47. New York: Academic Press, 1977.

Genette, Gerard. "Discours du recit." In his *Figures III,* 184–93. Paris: Seuil, 1972.

Goodman, Nelson. *Ways of Worldmaking.* Indianapolis and Cambridge: Hackett, 1978.

Halliday, M. A. K. *Learning How to Mean: Explorations in the Development of Language.* London: Edward Arnold, 1975.

Hawkins, P. R. "Social Class, the Nominal Group and Reference." In *Class, Codes and Control,* ed. Basil Bernstein, 81–92. *Applied Studies towards a Sociology of Language,* Vol. 2. London: Routledge and Kegan Paul, 1973.

Ives, Sumner. "A Theory of Literary Dialect." *Tulane Studies in English* 2 (1950): 137–82.

Jakobson, Roman. "Why 'Mama' and 'Papa'?" In his *Selected Writings,* vol. 1, 538–45. 'S-Gravenhage: Mouton, 1962.

Kernan, Keith T. "Semantic and Expressive Elaboration in Children's Narrative." In *Child Discourse,* ed. Susan Ervin-Tripp and Claudia Mitchell-Kernan, 91–102. New York: Academic Press, 1977.

Krapp, George Philip. *The English Language in America.* Vol. I. 1925. Rpt. New York: Ungar, 1960.

Lakoff, Robin. "Language and Woman's Place." *Language in Society* 2 (1973): 45–80.

Langer, Susanne K. *Feeling and Form: A Theory of Art Developed from "Philosophy in a New Key."* London: Routledge and Kegan Paul, 1967.

Lips, Marguerite. *Le style indirect libre.* Paris: Payot, 1926.

McHale, Brian. "Free Indirect Discourse: A Survey of Recent Accounts." *PTL* 3.2 (1978): 249–87.

———. "Speaking as a Child in *U.S.A.*: A Problem in the Mimesis of Speech." *Language and Style* 17.4 (1984): 352–70.

Mitchell, T. F. "The Language of Buying and Selling in Cyrenaica: A Situational Statement." 1957. In his *Principles of Firthian Linguistics,* 167–200. London: Longman, 1975.

Opie, Iona, and Peter Opie. *The Lore and Language of Schoolchildren.* Oxford: Oxford University Press, 1959.

Page, Norman. *Speech in the English Novel.* London: Longman, 1973.

Pascal, Roy. *The Dual Voice: Free Indirect Speech and Its Functioning in the Nineteenth Century European Novel.* Manchester: Manchester United Press, 1977.

Pitcher, Evelyn Goodenough, and Ernst Prelinger. *Children Tell Stories: An Analysis of Fantasy.* New York: International Universities Press, 1963.

Ron, Moshe. "Free Indirect Discourse, Mimetic Language Games, and the Subject of Fiction." *Poetics Today* 2.2 (1981): 17–39.

Rorty, Richard. "The World Well Lost." 1972. In his *Consequences of Pragmatism: Essays 1972–1980,* 3–18. Minneapolis: University of Minnesota Press, 1982.

Sternberg, Meir. "Proteus in Quotation-Land: Mimesis and the Forms of Reported Discourse." *Poetics Today* 3.2 (1982): 107–56.

van der Geest, Ton. "Some Interactional Aspects of Language Acquisition." In *Talking to Children: Language Input and Acquisition,* ed. Catherine E. Snow and Charles A. Ferguson, 89–107. London and New York: Cambridge University Press, 1977.

Weir, Ruth. *Language in the Crib.* The Hague: Mouton, 1962.

Wills, Dorothy Davis. "Participant Deixis in English and Baby Talk." In *Talking to Children: Language Input and Acquisition,* ed. Catherine E. Snow and Charles A. Ferguson, 271–95. London and New York: Cambridge University Press, 1977.

The Changing Language
of Black Child Characters
in American Children's Books

SUZANNE RAHN

To-day young Caesar, Roger Stafford's body servant, was helping Scipio, the butler, serve dinner since it was his master's thirteenth birthday and Roger was to dine with his father, Colonel Antony. The black boy was full of the importance of the occasion. He rearranged a flower in the big bouquet in the silver bowl and stood off to observe the effect. He, too, was thirteen.

"Dunno how young Massa gwine lak Missy comin' in fo' dinnah, too, lak she was nigh to growed-up. Missy only 'leben, an' seem lak somehow young Massa lak better to be by hisself." (3–4)

To-day young Caesar, Roger Stafford's body servant, was helping Scipio, the butler, serve dinner since it was his master's thirteenth birthday and Roger was to dine with his father, Colonel Antony. The boy was full of the importance of the occasion. He rearranged a flower in the big bouquet in the silver bowl and stood off to observe the effect. He, too, was thirteen.

"Don't know how young Master's going to like Missy coming in for dinner, too, like she was nigh to grown-up. Missy's only eleven, and seems like somehow young Master likes better to be by himself." (3–4)

The first passage comes from *The Golden Horseshoe*, a historical novel for children by Elizabeth Coatsworth, as published in 1935 and reprinted, unchanged, in 1947. The second comes from the edition "Reissued with revisions by the author" in 1968. These revisions are not extensive, focussing on the speech of a few minor black characters. Yet they make a difference—the young Caesar of 1968 is not quite the same "black boy" that he was in 1935. And his author's choices are part of a much bigger story. The changing language of black characters in American children's fiction has reflected changing attitudes toward blacks since the Civil War, and how both blacks and whites have fought for change. Indeed, book language has helped create the racial attitudes that American children absorb and grow up with and unconsciously maintain.

I will limit my investigation of this development mainly to children's books of the last hundred years, and especially their child characters, choosing some representative works from each period. My concern will be the literary phenomenon of book language, not actual speech. Black children from a particular geographical area may well have sounded about the same in 1890 as they do today—while black child *characters* from that same area would have "spoken" quite differently in 1890, in 1950, and in 1990. The first stage in this unnatural evolution is the so-called "Negro dialect" used by young Caesar in 1935, and by nearly all black characters between 1880 and 1940.[1] In the 1930s, some authors were experimenting with a more "natural" speech, but the major turning point came around the end of World War II. Suddenly, "Negro dialect" all but disappeared. Between 1950 and 1970, black child characters spoke the same "standard English" as their white counterparts. Around 1970 came the third shift—this time to a "Black English" distinct both from standard English and from the old "Negro dialect." The most radical forms of this book language appeared in the early seventies; since around 1974, various modified versions have appeared, leaving today's authors with an unprecedented range of options.

These successive transformations are closely related to large-scale cultural changes in the status and self-awareness of America's black community. Children's literature is by no means immune to contemporary pressures and problems, or to new currents of thought, though it tends to reveal its connections more slowly and in more subtle ways than books written for adults. We will find among children's books nothing so fiercely racist on one end of the spectrum as *The Klansman*, nor on the other so radical as *Soul on Ice*. Yet in their own proportion, gauged to the more impressionable minds of the young, children's books may be equally responsive to their times and significant in their effects.

"UNCLES AND LITTLES": THE LATE NINETEENTH CENTURY

Uncle Tom's Cabin (1852), though not a children's book, seems a logical place to begin. It was by far the best-known novel of its century to feature black characters—including a black child who became a special favorite with readers. According to *The Oxford Companion to Children's Literature*, retellings designed for children were soon available, and "in shortened form the book quickly became a nursery classic" (Carpenter and Prichard 550).

From Harriet Beecher Stowe, young readers would have learned that not all blacks speak alike. The genteel house slave Eliza naturally speaks the same standard English as Mrs. Shelby, the mistress who brought her up (10). So do her husband and her little boy. Uncle Tom and his wife Aunt Chloe speak a kind of "Negro dialect," though less exaggerated than many later examples. Topsy, the important black child character, speaks a heavy "Negro dialect," in strong contrast to the standard English of her white contemporary Little Eva. It is Topsy who doesn't know that she's supposed to say, "God made me," and says instead, famously, "I 'spect I grow'd. Don't think nobody never made me' " (221). The author does not, however, allow us to associate Topsy's ignorance of grammar and theology with lack of intelligence, but stresses the keen mind of this black girl from the outset (216).

Like the black characters, the whites do not all speak alike. Mr. and Mrs. Shelby, Eva and her father St. Clare, and others above a certain social level speak standard English, with no apparent distinction between Northerners and Southerners. The slave-trader Haley, the honest farmer John Van Trompe, and the villainous Simon Legree use a sort of uneducated "backwoods" speech. Whether a character speaks in dialect, then, depends neither or race nor on regional origin, but on social class and (presumably) education.

It is true that the "Negro dialect" used by Stowe deviates more conspicuously from standard English than the "backwoods" dialect. Both black and "backwoods" characters "drop their g's"; say "critter," "nigger," and "ye" (for "you"); and use certain ungrammatical or carelessly pronounced expressions such as "that ar," "this yer," and "kinder"—as in Haley's " 'kinder makes my blood run cold to think on't' " (5). In addition, uneducated black characters say "gwine" (for "going to"), use double negatives (like Topsy's "nobody never made me"), and in extreme cases (like Aunt Chloe's) turn their "th's" into "d's": " 'Now, I went over thar when Miss Mary was gwine to be married, and Jinny she jest showed me de weddin' pies. . . . Why, dey wan't no 'count 't all' " (20). Speakers of this dialect drop more letters and whole syllables, leading to a high visual occurrence of apostrophes. On the whole, though, the language of black characters in *Uncle Tom's Cabin* is not hard for a young reader to understand. Post-Civil War children's books took their black characters a long step deeper into unintelligibility.

Like Stowe, Joel Chandler Harris did not think of himself (originally) as a children's writer, but *Uncle Remus: His Songs and His Sayings* (1880) with its vivid retellings of black folk tales entered children's literature as quickly as the retellings of his fellow folklorists, the Brothers Grimm. Yet even adults find the dialect spoken by Uncle Remus extremely difficult; to the eye, at least, nearly every other word is non-standard, and a puzzlement: "One day atter Brer Rabbit foll 'im wid dat calamus root, Brer Fox went ter wuk en got 'im some tar, en mix it wid some turken time, en fix up a contrapshun wat he call a Tar-Baby, en he tuck dish yer Tar-Baby en he sot 'er in de big road, en den he lay off in de bushes fer to see wat de news wuz gwineter be" (7).

As a folklorist, Harris was concerned primarily with authenticity. Despising the "intolerable misrepresentations" of black speech "on the minstrel stage," he claimed that his own version was "at least phonetically genuine" (vii–viii). Such misspelled words as "wuk" for "work" are thus not intended as "mistakes" on the part of Uncle Remus, but attempts to reproduce his exact pronunciation. And for the listener, the difficulties disappear. A good reader-aloud of any race can, with a little practice, bring back to life a great black storyteller of a hundred years ago.

The white characters in the frame portions of *Uncle Remus*—including the little boy who listens to the stories—all speak in standard, normally spelled English. Although this may mean simply that Harris was interested only in black speech, his choice lent inadvertent support to the new convention beginning to dictate the language of black and white child characters in the 1880s and '90s. White children were to speak standard English, with a permissible degree of colloquialism. Black children were to speak "Negro dialect." Even plantation-raised white children, who had played with black children all their lives, must remain linguistically uncontaminated. In Thomas Nelson Page's *Two Little Confederates* (1888), for example, the white boy protagonists, Frank and Willy, speak perfect standard English. Yet their nursemaid Lucy Ann, their "boon comrade and adviser" Uncle Balla (7), and their playmates Peter and Cole—the family slaves they have grown up with—speak "Negro dialect."

Annie Fellows Johnston, in *The Little Colonel* (1896), goes so far as to give Lloyd, her heroine, a Southern accent. Lloyd says "mothah" and "fathah." But her speech is still quite distinct from the conventional "Negro dialect" of her nurse-maid Mom Beck and her playmate May Lilly. Indeed, just where Lloyd could have acquired her own accent is something of a mystery. Neither her Northern father nor her Southern mother shows a trace of it—yet, by some fortunate quirk of heredity, perhaps, it is precisely the accent of the long-estranged "gran'fathah" she has never seen before.[2]

The book language of black characters in this period must be judged in the whole context of nineteenth-century American literature, for the use of dialect was widespread. The 1880s and '90s, in particular, saw the rise of "local color" writing, with its special focus on regional cultures; authentically rendered local dialect was a key feature of the genre. Humorous writing might be couched entirely in dialect—Mark Twain's "Celebrated Jumping Frog," for example. Thus, not only black characters spoke in dialect, but Southerners, Westerners, New Englanders, German immigrants, Irish immigrants, and so on. In historical novels set in Tudor, medieval, and even ancient Roman times, the characters spoke a pseudo-Elizabethan dialect derived from Walter Scott. Even small children had a conventional dialect of their own—a "baby-talk" that revolts us today, but sounded adorable a hundred years ago. What the Little Colonel speaks is, in fact, baby-talk with a Southern accent. "'An' isn't you glad we've got a gran'fathah with such good 'trawberries?'" she asks her dog—to which the author adds dotingly, "it was hard for her to put the *s* before her consonants" (7).

The black characters of *Two Little Confederates* speak in dialect—but so do the "poor whites" of the area. As we have seen with the "backwoods" speech of *Uncle Tom's Cabin*, these "poor whites" talk very much like blacks. Both say "ef" for "if," "I's" ("I is") for "I am," "heah" for "here." Most tellingly, the "gwine" that becomes one of the most reliable indicators of conventional "Negro dialect" is here a regular feature of "poor white" speech as well. " 'I ain' rightly well enough to go back now, but I's anxious to git back,' " says the typical "poor white" Tim Miller; " 'I'm gwine to-morrow mornin' ef I don' go this evenin' " (56). This could be the black Uncle Balla speaking. The most noticeable differences in black speech are the "d's" instead of "th's" and such idioms as "Go 'long!"

In books of this period, there is no sense that only blacks have their own variant of English, and their dialect seems as much a factor of class and region as of race. Some writers, like Harris, took pains to reproduce the actual dialects of black speech. At the same time, a line was already being drawn between black and white child characters. And as dialect became less common in American fiction overall, the continuing use of an often spurious "Negro dialect" was to make black characters more and more conspicuous.

Politically, the late nineteenth century was a time of retreat from Reconstruction policies. In 1883, the Supreme Court declared the Civil Rights Act of 1875 unconstitutional; in 1896, it ruled that "separate but equal" public accommodations were legal. "Jim Crow" laws were enacted throughout the South. These events help explain what was happening in children's literature. The indifference of most Northerners to black problems coincides with an absence of black characters in books by Northern authors. Nearly all the black characters of this period live in Southern plantation settings that are or might as well be pre-Civil War, while their roles are increasingly subordinate and inferior. In *Uncle Tom's Cabin*, blacks play most of the leading parts; the white reader is encouraged to identify with Eliza, George, and Tom. In the early 1880s, Uncle Remus is still central and impressive. By 1888 and *Two Little Confederates*, the two white boys have all the big adventures without the black boys who are supposedly their playmates. On the one occasion that all four are together, watching a skirmish, the black boys are too afraid of being shot to help a dying soldier; they seem to be there to make Frank and Willy look good. Between them, Peter and Cole speak, perhaps, half a dozen lines. Mom Beck, Lloyd's nurse, has more dignity than the farcical Uncle Balla, but she too is essentially a Faithful Servant who never controls the action. Lloyd plays with "little darkies" on two occasions (24–25 and 84–86), but is always unmistakably in charge. Her black playmate May Lilly speaks once in the entire story (85).

A key image in *Uncle Tom's Cabin* is that of Little Eva in the garden, sitting on Uncle Tom's knee and placing a wreath of roses around his neck (162); the scene appears in black on the blue cover of my old copy, with Eva picked out in silver, an emblem of the spiritual marriage between these two saints-to-be (no wonder the prim Miss Ophelia exclaims, " 'How can you let her?' " to Eva's father!).[3] Eva's innocence recognizes and pays tribute to Tom's greater wisdom, long before the adults of the household know him for what he is. She reads the Bible to him, but he can explain what the Bible means and tell her the truth about slavery (168–69, 199). Uncle Remus, too, is a source of rare wisdom from whom a little white child can learn much about human nature and how the powerless survive.

The black boys in this original *St. Nicholas Magazine* illustration for Thomas Nelson Page's *Two Little Confederates* (1888) are depicted as comically fearstricken, in contrast to their white masters.

The numerous and disparate analyses of the Uncle Remus books are themselves a testament to the richness of meaning found not only within the stories but in the complex relationship between Uncle Remus as storyteller and his young listener.[4]

This powerful interaction between black "Uncle" and white "Little" diminishes in later children's books. Uncle Balla is said to have taught Frank and Willy to ride, trap, and cobble shoes (7), but we never see him do any of these things—only make a fool of himself by releasing a chicken thief that the boys have caught. Mom Beck has nursed both Lloyd and her mother, but we see no evidence that she has special knowledge to impart. Where Uncle Tom and Uncle Remus are central figures of wisdom that a white "Little" must respect, their later counterparts are merely good servants, and kept—like the black playmates—"in their place."

PRANKS OF THE PICKANINNIES: FROM 1900 TO THE 1930S

After the turn of the century, black characters show up more frequently in children's books, even, occasionally, as protagonists. But what might seem like progress does not survive a closer look. In some respects, the children's books of the early twentieth century are more racist than those of the nineteenth.

Compare the roles of blacks in *The Little Colonel* (1895) to those in a later volume of the series, *The Little Colonel's House Party* (1900). Lloyd, now eleven, no longer plays with "little darkies," but only with boys and girls of her own race. Mom Beck, a constant presence five years ago, now makes a token entrance or two; when introduced to Betty, she does not even speak (Johnston 77–78). Black

Uncle Tom with Little Eva in the garden, an emblematic scene from *Uncle Tom's Cabin* (1852) by Harriet Beecher Stowe.

child characters do appear, however—as entertainment at a picnic, where "the funniest, blackest little pickaninnies that ever sung a song or danced a double shuffle" (139) have been trained to act a series of literary charades for the white children. On their other appearance, the six pickaninnies are described as "so black that their faces scarcely showed against the black background of the night. Only their rolling white eyeballs and gleaming teeth could be seen distinctly" (260). Questioned, they are "as unresponsive as six little black kittens," until their white trainer, Miss Allison, appears. These subhuman creatures can hardly be called "characters"; they are "clever little mimics" (139) who have all but lost their own power of speech, and exist only to amuse white boys and girls.

Such black child characters of the early twentieth century were invariably "pickaninnies." Their grotesque gestures and appearance, their outlandish names, their singing and dancing, their superstition, their gullibility, their laziness, their incompetence, their cowardice—all were sources of amusement. For three decades this image pervaded children's literature, a junior version of the black stereotype found throughout popular culture in this period. Derived in part from the black-face minstrel shows of the late nineteenth century, it took on new life in all-black film comedies, the "Sambo Series" (1910–11)[5] and "Rastus Series" (c. 1910), and in the faddish "pickaninny dolls" (Yuill 10). Radio's *Amos and Andy*—its comic black characters played by white actors speaking "Negro dialect"—was first broadcast in 1928, achieving enormous popularity over a quarter century; at its peak, over forty million daily listeners tuned in.[6]

"Negro dialect" was integral to this black stereotype. Not surprisingly, books of this period contain the most clear-cut examples of differentiation by dialect between black and white child characters—black children using heavy dialect set side by side with white Southern children speaking standard English (in *The Golden Horseshoe*, for example). The dialect itself varied from book to book. According to Augusta Baker, much was "author-created" rather than authentic (1972, 51); few authors possessed Joel Chandler Harris's knowledge of black speech or his respect for black culture. Careless writers like Inez Hogan, a specialist in "pickaninny stories," were not even consistent within their own texts. In her *Nicodemus and the Little Black Pig* (1934), Nicodemus says "dat old sow" and "those white pigs"— "belong" and "b'long"—on the same page (quoted in Broderick 151). But the main indicators, the slurred or dropped letters (with the consequent thicket of apostrophes), the double negatives, the substitution of "d" for "th," and the special words like "mammy" and "gwine" are instantly recognizable.

What was the effect of "Negro dialect" on young readers? Black children seem to have accepted it as a literary convention. Marjorie Hill Allee does not mention dialect as a problem in "Books Negro Children Like" (1938), though she is aware that black children find certain words offensive: "Books about Negro children are an especial pleasure, when they are well chosen, but many a well-intentioned but ignorant publisher has damned a book for Negro use for want of informed editing. 'Nigger' is a fighting word and is likely to be scratched out of the book by an indignant child. 'Picaninny' and 'darky' are almost as objection-able" (85). The effect on white children, I suspect, was sheer alienation from the characters. For young readers, at a stage when reading itself may still be challeng-ing, dialect poses added difficulties. They may skip such passages entirely, or even reject a book with much dialect in it. Moreover, characters whose speech is laden with strangely-spelled words and non-standard grammar are likely to look "stu-pid" to young readers who, again, are themselves still learning to spell and speak "correctly." What child will identify with stupid characters, whose speech he or she can hardly understand? If the actions of these characters also mark them as inferior—and the illustrations make them look subhuman—the negative impact grows even stronger.

Some black child characters were used explicitly to express racist concepts. Inez Hogan has Nicodemus tell the one black piglet in a litter of white ones, " 'Come here, little fellow, you don't belong among all those white pigs. You is black like me, and I spec' you b'long to me' " (quoted in Broderick 151). But even the liberal-minded children's books of this period seem to keep white readers at arm's length from their black characters. Lucy Fitch Perkins, whose famous "Twins" books were designed to promote intercultural understanding, added *The Pickaninny Twins* to her series in 1931. My "School Edition" points out in its note "To the Teacher" that little had been written for third or fourth graders "to acquaint them with the life and play of the children of Negroes, living in our own country, who have a history and culture of their own" (155). This sounds promis-ing. But nothing in the book itself suggests that blacks have either history or culture—not so much as a Brer Rabbit tale. The story concerns a pair of five-year-old twins, left in the charge of their older brother for the day, who get themselves into one predicament after another. The children are not stupid—just incredibly feckless—and the author's illustrations make them cute to look at. In other respects, however, Perkins reinforces the comic black stereotype. The twins have the usual outlandish names—Sammy and Dilly, short for Samson and Deli-lah; their big brother's name is Job. Their mother, Mammy Jinny, works for "Miz Lizbeth" at "de big house" (10). Their absentee father "had gone away up North to seek his fortune and had not come back" (9). The plot is one long farce, alternating between the naughtiness of the twins and the comic ineptitude of Job.

Although Perkins has made black children her protagonists, she does not involve young readers with them emotionally through their thoughts and feelings. When Sammy and Dilly panic and run from the angry Job, it's not scary—only funny; we never go far enough into the twins to feel their fear. Nor do we find anything in them to admire. In contrast, Kit and Kat of *The Dutch Twins* (1911), also five years old, take some important steps toward adulthood; they accompany their father to market, spend some money of their own, help their mother with the milking and churning, learn to skate. They suffer a few humorous mishaps, but their achievements more than compensate. The book ends triumphantly, with St. Nicholas rewarding them for having been good children. Sammy and Dilly return home at the end of *The Pickaninny Twins* "dirty as pigs, ragged, wet, and scared" (144), expecting a well-deserved spanking. It is hard to imagine them ever growing up at all.

As a child, I discovered the "Twins" books and read nearly all of them—except *The Pickaninny Twins*. Even my desire to complete the series (which can be a strong motivation for a young reader) could not get me through dialogue like this:

> "Is yo' mammy gone away, too?" Dilly asked politely.
> "Sho' she is," said Caroline, "an' she's gwine to be gone all de whole day, too."
> "Ain't nobody home but jes' you?" asked Dilly. "Ain't nobody lookin' after you same as Job?" (43–44)

For me, "Negro dialect" was a barrier not merely to understanding what these black characters were saying, but to encountering them at all.

Lucy Fitch Perkins avoided the touchy area of black-white relationships by including only black characters in *The Pickaninny Twins*.[7] In a book like Christine Noble Govan's *Those Plummer Children* (1934) we see the inevitable result of placing dialect-speaking black children and standard English-speaking white ones in the same fictional environment.

At first introduction, Govan's black characters seem to recapitulate all the stereotypes. The Plummers's cook is a black woman named Narcissus, who is thrown into fits of superstitious terror by a "hant." Her twin sons are Sears—"an earnest, serious-minded little pickaninny" (5)—and Roebuck, the archetypal black comic entertainer, who is "a source of delight to the white children. He could imitate any animal he had ever heard, could dance the buck-and-wing, the shuffle and the cake-walk, and was ready to take the most uninteresting or dangerous parts in the many make-believe games these children played. . . . His good-humor could stand the most vicious treatment or the grossest neglect. In other words, Roebuck was an ideal friend" (6). "Friend" seems an odd word for this relationship! In episode after episode, however, Roebuck's imagination and initiative make him at least as interesting as the Plummer children:

> "We could get Cis to tell our fortunes if she was awake," said Chris. . . .
> "Wouldn't do no good ter wake 'er," commented Roebuck. . . . "She'd tell you a fo'tune you wouldn't fergit. Why don't us play gypsies an' tell our own fo'tunes?" (6–7)

It's not what Roebuck says, but the dialect he is forced to say it in that makes him sound ignorant and inferior.

In one episode, Roebuck becomes the protagonist—when his beloved dog is lost on a trip to town. Here, for a few moments, there is nothing comical about him: "He did not see the things displayed in the stores, he did not even smell the fish and hamburger or see the drink-stands, he did not see the other boys they passed on the street—but he saw their dogs, and at every pair of cocky ears, and

'Dat's it!' she cried shrilly. 'Dere she goes! But how is I goner git in?'

The little Negro was knee-deep in water now, and the side of the tub was up to her chin. It looked for a moment as though she were going to be left behind.

Alice Caddy portrays black and white children as though they belonged to different species in her illustrations for *Those Plummer Children* (1934) by Christine Noble Govan.

stumpy, saucy tail, his heart leaped, and sank" (178). The young reader gets closer to Roebuck in this passage than to Sammy or Dilly in the whole of *The Pickaninny Twins*—not only because the author allows him some real feelings, but because they are expressed in standard English, a neutral book language that sends no special message about a character. In standard English, Roebuck can be every child who has lost a pet. The moment he speaks, he is a pickaninny again.

The tension is strong in *Those Plummer Children* between stereotype and reality. Sears and Roebuck and the black girl Emily are more life-like and individual than any black child characters since Topsy. Yet their unquestioning acceptance of orders from the white children, their grotesque appearance in the illustrations (in contrast to the pretty Plummer girls), the frequent humor at their expense, and, not least, their dialect—all this still keeps them at a safe distance from the young reader.

Those Plummer Children was prominently featured in "Pickaninny Pranks," a

Horn Book article of 1935. Here Nellie Page Carter suggests that children's books may provide "a leaven of understanding" and "an entering wedge of affection that could mature into largeness of heart in our dealings with the races within our boundaries" (18). To supply this "understanding" and "affection" for small children, she approves Inez Hogan's Nicodemus books, which she calls "gay little stories" about "a wide-mouthed, bare-footed pickaninny" (18). For older readers, she recommends *Those Plummer Children*. Her descriptions of Sears, Roebuck, and Emily focus on their most stereotypical aspects, and ignore those episodes in which the reader shares their thoughts and feelings. The two "hants," however, receive special attention, for "no Negro story is complete without an actual 'hant,' or at least the whisper of one" (21). The understanding and affection Carter wants white children to acquire are for the "Negro race" created in the white imagination.

In 1935 an article like "Pickaninny Pranks" could still gain the approval of *The Horn Book*, an established guardian of quality in children's books. A few short years would see a major change.

"NATURAL RHYTHMS": EXPERIMENTS OF THE THIRTIES AND FORTIES

The period just after World War I was especially turbulent for black Americans. The rebirth of the Ku Klux Klan in 1915—the same year that D. W. Griffith released his pro-Klan *Birth of a Nation*—triggered a surge of racist violence. Blacks were lynched by the hundreds in the Red Summer of 1919. But blacks were also disavowing the old "lie low" strategy of Booker T. Washington, and fighting back with organizations like the Niagara Movement of W. E. B. DuBois, the NAACP, the National American Political League, and Marcus Garvey's Universal Improvement Association. In the arts, the twenties were the years when black music, art, and literature exploded out of the ghetto in the great flowering called the Harlem Renaissance. One key concept of this renaissance was the "New Negro." Instead of adopting and imitating white culture, New Negroes embraced and celebrated their own heritage, both African and Afro-American.

It took time, as usual, for these developments to filter down into children's literature. In 1920 W. E. B. DuBois founded *The Brownies' Book*, a daring though short-lived children's magazine designed to further interracial brotherhood.[8] And in 1932 Arna Bontemps collaborated with Harlem Renaissance poet Langston Hughes to write *Popo and Fifina*, a children's book set in Haiti. Bontemps went on to become the first black writer of national stature to make children's books a specialty, with *You Can't Pet a Possum* (1934) and *Sad-Faced Boy* (1937).

In a *Horn Book* article of 1939, Ione Morrison Rider stresses Bontemps's concern for language, "in particular the problem of freeing the natural rhythms of colloquial speech from the tyranny of traditional renderings, [sic] that prevent its enjoyment by children" (14). These "traditional renderings" were, of course, those of "Negro dialect." Recognizing the barrier they created for young readers, while possessing a poet's ear for the rhythms of black speech and a deep fondness for folk culture, Bontemps attempted to create a new book language, authentic yet comprehensible, for the black characters of children's fiction.

His first experiment, a simple boy and dog story called *You Can't Pet a Possum*, was only partially successful. Its dialogue is sometimes stilted and unnatural— " 'That big ole truck which I was riding musta outrun the train' " (55)—or spattered (in the old style) with apostrophes: " 'I 'spect I'll be gone free o' fo' days' " (38). The ignorance and comic incompetence of the young protagonist (whom Bontemps should surely not have named Shine Boy) cannot help reminding us of the familiar stereotype. Still, Rider called it "a great advance in the rendering of Negro life and speech for children" (15).

Three years later, Bontemps had advanced to *Sad-Faced Boy*, the story of three brothers from Alabama who make their way to Harlem. A glance shows that Bontemps has done away entirely with the traditional phonetic spellings and apostrophes, to create an invitingly "normal"-looking page. Yet the dialogue also reflects a distinctive way of speech, with its own grammar, rhythm, and idiom:

"Listen, big shorty. I know what."
"What you know, little half-pint?" his brother said, smiling.
"Let's us go play some music and forget about what we has and what we hasn't got." (90)

A young reader can admire these three boys too, despite their funny names (Rags, Slumber, and Willy) and country-boy naiveté. They get to the big city on their own, they learn their way around, they even earn money as the "Dozier Brothers Band." Bontemps's pervasive humor is never at the boys' expense; rather, it reflects their own wry, easy-tempered outlook on the world.

Ione Rider's article on Bontemps and Marjorie Hill Allee's "Books Negro Children Like" in 1938 were themselves symptoms of change. Only three years after "Pickaninny Pranks," Allee was explaining how much Negro children disliked the word "pickaninny." And while Allee says nothing overt against "Negro dialect," her book list recommends neither *The Pickaninny Twins* nor *Those Plummer Children*. Instead, listed among the few stories with black child characters are *Sad-Faced Boy* and *Araminta*.

The "Araminta" stories of Eva Knox Evans—*Araminta* (1935), *Jerome Anthony* (1936), and *Araminta's Goat* (1938)—were experiments along another line. These simple, amusing tales for young children use no dialect at all; in fact, Araminta and Jerome Anthony can be identified as black only by the illustrations. Even black children were disconcerted by this innovation. The author relates in "The Negro in Children's Fiction" how her own class of black kindergarteners protested that Araminta did not speak as she was supposed to. When Evans pointed out that the children themselves did not use "Negro dialect," they insisted that the colored people in books did (650).

Bontemps had evolved his own book language; Evans eliminated distinctive language entirely. Yet another experiment, this time for teenage readers, was that of Florence Crannell Means in *Shuttered Windows* (1938). Known for her pioneer, Hopi, and Navajo heroines, Means was visiting the Mather School, a black girls' school in South Carolina, when one of the students told her, " 'We-all wish you'd write a book about us, M'm. Like we were white girls' " (Means 1940, 40). Thus a white woman became the first author of any race to write a teenage girls' book with a black heroine. Well aware that "it's dangerous business to try to interpret other peoples" (1940, 40), Means did not attempt to project her own consciousness into that of an uneducated Southern country girl. Instead, she gave Harriet Freeman a Northern, middle-class background not unlike her own. The cultures Harriet encounters when she enters Landers School (a thinly-disguised Mather) or visits her great-grandmother on an island off the South Carolina coast are as new and strange to her as they were to the author. Means also read her book aloud, chapter by chapter as she wrote, to two English classes at Mather, and incorporated the girls' suggestions into her story (see Rahn 102). The result was an authenticity that can still startle us today.

Harriet Freeman challenges the literary Jim Crow laws in many ways. She is Northern, at a time when Northern blacks were nonexistent in children's books. She is a strong heroine as well—proud, intelligent, independent, and a natural leader. And she is beautiful—"a bronze maiden, eyes straight-gazing under brows that frowned with thought; hair cloudy black; full lips well-cut; smooth, brown skin stained with dusky red" (6). Like the New Negroes, she takes pride in her ancestors, the mighty slave leader Black Moses and her brave and loving great-grandmother. She is not repelled but fascinated to discover a relic of her African heritage in Granny's morning prayer ritual, a fragment of Islam inherited from Black Moses.

Harriet herself speaks standard English. But when she hears the Gullah dialect of the islands, she is instantly attracted: "Here was a strange language, not only softly slurred, but pieced together with extra syllables—'Nevah did Ah reckon ma chillen duh-gwan lib lak duh whi' folks'—and with strange words: 'entry,' 'yeddy.' It was as lovely as French patois. Harriet wanted to hear more" (9). Means was certainly the first young people's author to call a black dialect "lovely," or to suggest that such distinctive speech might be something valuable. And this same dialect (rendered less phonetically, to make it read easily) is the speech of Harriet's own great-grandmother and of her "young man" Richie; thus the reader cannot dismiss it as mere local color, but must accept it along with these central and attractive characters. At the same time, Means makes the point, through Harriet, that some blacks speak standard English, and ensures that dialect will not raise a barrier between her heroine and the white girl reader. For Means hoped that girls of both races would identify with Harriet. She does not even reveal that Harriet

Florence Crannell Means was fortunate in her illustrator for
Shuttered Windows (1938); Armstrong Sperry's Harriet, Richie, and Granny are the strong, attractive, unmistakably
black individuals her text describes. (Copyright © 1938
Houghton Mifflin Co. Used by permission)

is black until six pages into the first chapter—by which point even a bigoted
white reader might be safely "hooked" (Rahn 108).

In the long battle over stereotyping that we see waged in children's books of
the late 1930s and early 40s, dialect was often where the battle lines were drawn,
and opponents tended to take absolute positions. Eleanor Weakley Nolen describes a "wholesale condemnation of specific books solely on the basis of whether
they are or are not written in dialect" in "The Colored Child in Contemporary
Literature," a *Horn Book* article of 1942. She tells of her own "mental wrestling"
with the dialect question while writing her stories of Jeremiah and Susannah, two
young house slaves at George Washington's Mount Vernon estate. Because, she

says, she was writing for young children, for whom "the simplest and most direct English, correctly spelled, is none too easy," and because she wanted the speech of her black child characters to show that they were "individuals with minds, wills, and characters of their own," "It appeared to me that the best solution was to use, as much as possible, the characteristic twists of expression, the idioms, and rhythmic phraseology of the well-bred Virginia Negro as I knew him, and to avoid grotesqueries both of spelling and of word usage. I do not believe that Susannah spoke so very differently from Nellie Custis. How should she, when they were together almost constantly?" (350–51). Nolen received, she says, "full measure both of priase and of blame" for her solution. She was told that "the head of the children's department in the public library of a Northern city did not buy my books since 'they could not be authentic pictures of plantation life, inasmuch as their author *did not even know enough about Negroes to write in dialect.*' Italics mine" (351). "Colored children do vary," Nolen insisted; "they vary as widely as do white children and for the same reasons" (349). "All colored children do not speak as does Nicodemus, but neither do they all speak like Jerome Anthony" (354).

Reading *A Job for Jeremiah* (1940) today, one is struck chiefly, I'm afraid, by its sheer dullness—its thin characters and minimal storyline. The comically timid and incompetent Jeremiah does little to threaten the pickaninny stereotype. The language is not unlike that of *Sad-Faced Boy*, though without Bontemps's poetic flair. "'I can't waste no more time on you,'" Susannah tells Jeremiah. "'I'm a-going up to the Big House 'n' see is Mistress Nellie awake yet'" (Nolen 1940, 35). (Note the avoidance here of "gwine"!) It is hard to imagine the passions aroused by this bland little book fifty years ago.

But for generations, dialect had provided a protective barrier between black and white characters, "proving" that even white children who played habitually with black ones would retain their linguistic (and by implication, racial) purity. "Negro dialect," moreover, demonstrated not only the purity but the superiority of the white child. White children possessed an innate ability to speak correct English; black children were incapable of mastering its grammar and pronunciation. Language was used to signify a biologically fixed hierarchy of intelligence. To write, like Nolen, "I do not believe that Susannah spoke so very differently from Nellie Custis," was to imply that the slave girl was as intelligent as her mistress. To add, "How should she, when they were together almost constantly?" was to suggest the unthinkable—a kind of linguistic miscegenation between that black girl and the stepdaughter of George Washington.

The new cultural self-awareness of black Americans and their growing ability to organize themselves and demand their rights made some white Americans realize for the first time the injustice of the old stereotypes. But larger currents of history also influenced the portrayal of black child characters. As Nolen acutely points out, the "World Fellowship" movement in the aftermath of World War I had inspired a flock of children's books set in foreign countries, while in the

1930s, possibly as a result of the Depression, came a focus inward on "the fabric of life in America," including American minority groups (1942, 348). As World War II began—the war for democracy, as many saw it—the struggle against race prejudice gained urgency. Writing in 1942, Nolen maintained that "concern over the quality of American life . . . is going to increase during the difficult period which is ahead of us. . . . Race prejudice has no place in a democracy, and the place to combat race prejudice is with the child's first books" (349).

For both black and white writers at this time, changes in book language stood for changed attitudes toward blacks themselves. But no consensus, even among those most opposed to race prejudice, had determined just what language black child characters should speak. By 1942 a wide range of possibilities, from the traditional "Negro dialect" of Nicodemus to the standard English of Jerome Anthony, maintained a state of uneasy coexistence. Even as the war ended, however, a new convention was emerging, which was to determine the language of black child characters—and a good deal else about them—for the next twenty years.

COLOR BLIND AND COLOR DEAF: 1945 TO 1970

As black soldiers came home from the still segregated armed forces to face segregation in housing, in schooling, in employment, in parks, on buses, and in public restrooms, pressure mounted for substantial civil rights reform. Under the Truman Administration, the armed forces were integrated for the first time in history, literacy tests for voting were declared unconstitutional, and a Civil Rights Commission was appointed.

In the world of children's books, these hopeful years produced the first fictional attempts to look head-on at racial prejudice and injustice, Jesse Jackson's *Call Me Charley* (1945) and Marguerite De Angeli's *Bright April* (1946).[9] Charley, the only black child in a white neighborhood, attends an all-white school and faces bigotry both from other boys and from the teacher, who denies him a part in the school play. April's school and her Brownie troop in *Bright April* are integrated, but she too encounters prejudice when a strange child points at her, or another refuses to sit next to her. In both stories, the main conflict is resolved, at least on the child's level. After some realistic maneuvering by concerned adults, Charley acts in the play after all. And the little white girl who had refused to sit next to April gets to know her and becomes her friend.

During this same period, *Two Is a Team* (1945) by Lorraine and Jerrold Beim became the first picture book to show an interracial friendship—and without mentioning race in the text. Only Ernest Crichlow's illustrations revealed that one little boy was black and the other white. *Two Is a Team* was to prove as prophetic in the area of illustration as *Call Me Charley* and *Bright April* in that of language.

Both Charley and April speak and think in undiluted standard English. " 'My name is Charles. . . . Sometimes I'm called Charley. Nobody calls me Sambo and gets away with it' " (Jackson 8). " 'You see, Mamma . . . she didn't know at first that my skin is just like hers, only a different color' " (De Angeli 88). The voices are indistinguishable from those of white child characters. This makes sense, because both books clearly aim to educate white children about race prejudice and the pain it causes; as in *Shuttered Windows*, standard English prevents alienation between the black protagonist and the white reader. The common language, exterior (speech) and interior (thought), also "proves" that blacks are essentially "like us." Here *Bright April* is the more successful of the two. Charley is so two-dimensional and his story so poorly told, that we can't put ourselves inside him. April is more convincing, and De Angeli stays so close to her point of view that we wince with her when someone hurts her feelings.[10]

With amazing swiftness, the pickaninny disappeared from children's literature, and a new pattern for black child characters was established; suddenly, from being radically different from white children, they became virtually identical. Regional and distinctive cultural influences were wiped from their speech—and from their minds. April is just a nice, average little girl, entirely middle-class in her values, conventionally feminine in her tastes, and devoted to her Brownie troop. Even Arna Bontemps adapted to this trend in his later work; the black protagonists in his *Chariot in the Sky* (1951) and *Lonesome Boy* (1955) use a far less distinctive, less "black" language than his protagonists of the thirties.

Dialect had become so unacceptable that a process of rewriting it out of old children's books was soon under way.[11] Real integration—in children's books as elsewhere—was another matter. After the brief flurry of postwar idealism, one finds few black characters of any sort; their mere presence had become too unsettling in a decade whose surface conformity masked increasing discontent, dissent, and fear. The Newbery Medal awarded to Elizabeth Yates's *Amos Fortune, Free Man* (1950) was taken at the time for a sign of progress; after all, this story-biography of a slave was the first Newbery winner with a black protagonist. But some were not so sure. Dorothy Sterling writes that she was "a bit suspicious about the thinking behind the award. Almost until the end, Amos kept saying 'No, I'm not ready for freedom—don't give it to me yet.' I couldn't help wondering if his humility wasn't a part of the book's appeal" (1972, 176–77). Indeed, patient Amos Fortune, who "earns" his freedom by a lifetime of faithful service rather than by demanding it, now reads as white wish-fulfillment—the award as a retreat by the children's literature establishment to a timid accommodation with the segregationist status quo.

Nor did the opening salvos of the Civil Rights Movement—the Montgomery bus boycott of 1955, the crisis over school integration in 1957, the first sit-ins at lunch counters in 1960, the Freedom Rides and voter registration drives of 1961—inspire children's book publishers to join the fight. As the depth and violence of Southern resistance to integration became clear, publishers tended to avoid any book that might cost them Southern sales. The hysterical reaction to Garth Williams's *The Rabbits' Wedding* (1958) was sufficient warning. If Southerners could interpret the wedding of a black rabbit to a white one as miscegenist propaganda, who would risk a book about black and white boys and girls? In "The All-White World of Children's Books" (published in 1965), Nancy Larrick quotes several editors who faced Southern boycotts when they included black characters in their children's books (161–63). " 'Why jeopardize sales by putting one or two Negro faces in an illustration?' " one sales manager asked her (162).

One of the few exceptions that defied Southern censorship to describe the civil rights struggle taking place was Dorothy Sterling's *Mary Jane* (1959). Sterling had "traveled through the mid-South to talk with the Negro and white children who were entering integrated schools for the first time," and felt impelled to recast what she had learned into fiction—the story of "a Negro girl's first year in an integrated school" (1972, 178). " 'Couldn't you set it in the North?' " pleaded her editor. But, "after some backing and forthing," Doubleday let Sterling have her way. Luckily, *Mary Jane* sold well from the start, and by 1965 had been translated into five foreign languages (Larrick 164). It has outlived its enemies and is still read today.

In *Mary Jane*, Sterling was asking white readers to do more than identify with a black protagonist; she asked them to take sides with her in a black-white conflict. So it was essential to bring them close to her—to show them her thoughts, her feelings, her reactions, and to convince them that "ours" would be just the same. Like Means in *Shuttered Windows*, Sterling even avoids mentioning that Mary Jane is black until chapter 2 (though the dust jacket gives the game away). And when Mary Jane first sees the mob awaiting her on the school steps, she is as incredulous as a white child would be: "They couldn't be screaming at her—but they were" (52). Sterling is also careful not to make her heroine a saint. Mary Jane's reasons for attending the formerly all-white Wilson High are not idealistic, but ambitious: " 'Douglass has just plain science—stuff I mostly know already. Wilson has physics and chemistry and biology. How'm I going to be a biologist if I don't go to Wilson?' " (18).

Language, as usual, becomes part of the strategy. There can be nothing unusual—nothing even distinctively Southern—in Mary Jane's speech. Not only what she says aloud, but the words we hear running through her mind must be the normal colloquial standard English of any white American child character of the 1950s:

Eating alone, with everyone staring and no one to talk to. No one to joke with so that you could laugh and pretend you didn't care.

"But I don't care," Mary Jane told herself. "They hate me and I hate them." (86)

At one point, Sterling deliberately raises the issue of "Negro dialect." One white girl asks Mary Jane if she comes "from the North"; when Mary Jane tells her black friend Fred, he laughs. " 'Don't you get it?' " he asks. " 'You don't talk the way she thinks Negroes talk. You're supposed to say, "Dis-here chile sho' nuff bawn in de Souf," like Aunt Jemima or Old Black Joe or somebody' " (75). It seems unlikely that in real life the white girl would not have recognized a Southern accent identical to her own. But the incident makes an important point for readers still programmed to expect the traditional dialect from black characters.

The reality of Mary Jane as an individual and the reader's involvement in her experiences made her story an immediate success. But the book remained a maverick in its direct confrontation of racial problems. As the Civil Rights Movement grew in strength and popular support, yet violent resistance to it continued, children's literature found a different solution—a safer way to include yet not quite include black characters—to sidestep conflict by sidestepping difference itself. The 1960s became the decade when black child characters were "integrated" by nearly ceasing to be black at all.

Ezra Jack Keats's picture book *The Snowy Day* (1962) was one of the earliest examples. Its protagonist, Peter, is brown-skinned in the pictures, where his color creates an effective contrast with the white world of snow. The brief text says nothing of his race. Keats's Caldecott Award, though certainly deserved, suggests the delight with which this solution was received by teachers, librarians, and reviewers. Other picture books of this period adopted the same device—Millicent Selsam's *Tony's Birds* (1961), for example, and Joan M. Lexau's *Benjie* (1964). *We Build Together*, the book list first created in 1941 for the National Council of Teachers of English to highlight good children's books with non-stereotypical black characters, commented with wholehearted approbation on the solution in its 1967 edition, crediting *Two Is a Team* with having originated "this simple device, so much appreciated when it first appeared by all who were aware of the importance of such an advance, that has had a profound effect on children's illustrations and continues to do so. . . . Other books which ignore color, taking it for granted that it is of no importance in human relations, are just beginning to appear in significant numbers" (Rollins, xvii, xxv). The book list goes on to commend *What Mary Jo Shared* (1966) by Janice May Udry, emphasizing that Mary Jo's family, too, is identified as black "only through the illustrations" (xxv).

This painless trend of integration-through-illustration spread to stories for older children, in which the absence of racial identity seems far less plausible. *Roosevelt Grady* (1963) by Louisa Shotwell is one of the better-known examples. The Gradys are migrant workers, and much is made of the conditions they live and work in, yet the text never mentions how race prejudice would have added to their problems or defined their expectations. In fact, the reader knows they are black "only through the illustrations," which, being largely in tones of gray, are not wholly unambiguous. Needless to say, the Gradys's speech equally lacks any regional or ethnic flavor. The book was well received, and won the Nancy Bloch Award for the Best Intercultural Children's Book of its year, but Nancy Larrick, at least, remained unconvinced. Young Roosevelt, she pointed out, was really a kind of "counter stereotype"—"the Negro who is always good, generous, and smiling in the face of difficulties" (160). And it seemed odd to her that an "intercultural" award should be given to a book that "includes no whites except the teacher, the social worker, and the owner of the trailer camp. Only the pictures indicate that the Gradys and their friends are Negroes" (160). How, she implies, can a book be furthering intercultural relations, if its whites are barely present and its blacks barely black?

In *Jennifer, Hecate, Macbeth, William McKinley, and Me, Elizabeth* (1967) by E. L. Konigsburg, the case for integration-through-illustration becomes even more tenuous. Again, the text does not mention that Jennifer is black; only the author's illustrations suggest her race. The illustrations, moreover, are executed in a sketchy, impressionistic style that does not show features or skin color clearly. It would be interesting to know how many young readers of this highly commended Newbery Honor Book actually notice any difference between Jennifer and her white friend Elizabeth.

The idealism generated by the Civil Rights Movement in the early 1960s saw a fully integrated, color-blind society as its goal. Children's books of that time reflected this goal as though it had somehow already been achieved. In their fictional world, color became the one, entirely visual difference between races—a difference "of no importance in human relations." The disappearance of the old difference in language had heralded the disappearance of all ethnic difference. In the new world, black children not only sounded like white children, but thought, felt, behaved, and sometimes practically looked like them as well.

BLACK BECOMES BEAUTIFUL: 1965 TO NOW

As an ideal toward which both whites and non-whites were striving, color-blindness did not last long. By the mid-1960s, opposition had already arisen within the black community to Martin Luther King's integrationist and nonviolent policies; the Black Muslim Movement led by Malcolm X and Stokely Carmichael's Black Power Movement were pursuing their own paths to social justice. Yet a new sense of ethnic self-esteem permeated and united the entire black community. Indeed, it had become the *black* community. Just as leaders in the 1920s had campaigned successfully to be "Negroes" (with a capital N), those of the sixties renamed themselves. As Geneva Smitherman explains, "leaders of this era deliberately chose a racial label that required blacks to purify themselves of white ideas and values. . . . Black calls to mind power, black magic, even evil. . . . A black man, as opposed to a Negro man, is someone to be feared, reckoned with, and thus respected" (41).

Ethnicity encompassed far more in the sixties than it had in the twenties— from Afro hairstyles and dashikis and "soul food" and the new holiday of Kwanzaa, to the defense of black English as a dialect no less legitimate than standard. A slogan, "Black is beautiful," was coined to counteract the negative connotations of dark skin color. Picture books like Ann McGovern's *Black Is Beautiful* (1969), Rose Blue's *Black, Black, Beautiful Black* (1969), Jean Carey Bond's *Brown Is a Beautiful Color* (1969), and Lucille Clifton's *The Black BC's* (1970) sought to give young black children positive images of themselves. A subtler and more complex expression of this theme can be found in *Zeely* (1967), the first children's book by a new black author, Virginia Hamilton.

Eleven-year-old Elizabeth decides to call herself Geeder for the summer, while she and her younger brother (renamed Toeboy) are visiting Uncle Ross's farm. She becomes fascinated by a young neighbor woman, Zeely Tayber—watches her secretly, and invents stories about her. Geeder wants to be Zeely, or thinks she does. At this level, *Zeely* is not about being black at all; Geeder could be any imaginative girl with a preadolescent crush. The issues of race prejudice and civil rights are unmentioned. Yet we can also read this book as a thoughtful response to the Black Revolution of the 1960s, as we consider what Zeely looks like, how Geeder fantasizes her, and what the truth about her turns out to be:

> Zeely Tayber was more than six and a half feet tall, thin and deeply dark as a pole of Ceylon ebony. She wore a long smock that reached to her ankles. Her arms, hands and feet were bare, and her thin, oblong head didn't seem to fit quite right on her shoulders.
> She had very high cheekbones and her eyes seemed to turn inward on themselves. Geeder couldn't say what expression she saw on Zeely's face. She knew only that it was calm, that it had pride in it, and that the face was the most beautiful she had ever seen. (31–32).

Later, in an old magazine, Geeder finds a picture of a Watutsi woman of royal birth who looks exactly like Zeely. She is convinced that Zeely, too, must be a Watutsi queen.

Zeely embodies "Black is beautiful." Not only Hamilton's precise description of her appearance, but Symeon Shimin's evocative illustrations show us a type of beauty that is not European but African. Like Afro clothes and hairstyles, it connects an American black woman with a proud African heritage, even with a specific African tribe.

Zeely's love of the night and her habit of taking long walks after dark show that she is comfortable with her own darkness. At the same time, they connect her with another chapter of black history. Uncle Ross tells Geeder and Toeboy about the "night travellers" who were escaping slaves: " 'I believe . . . a night traveller must be somebody who wants to walk tall. And to walk tall, you most certainly must have to run free. Yes,' he said, 'it is the free spirit in any of us breaking loose' " (83). The common qualities of pride and desire for freedom link Zeely to ancestors who broke free of slavery. She herself literally "walks tall." And her daily life, as Geeder gradually discovers, is, like slavery, both hard and degrading; Zeely tends and drives hogs for her harsh father, and the townspeople laugh at her for being "animal, like those hogs" (74). Yet she protects the hogs as best she can from mistreatment and walks fearlessly through the night. She has kept her spirit free.

At the same time, Hamilton carefully deflates the mystique of "royal blood." When Zeely and Geeder finally meet and talk, near the end of the book, Zeely says, " 'We all come out of Africa—what of it?' " (97). And she tells Geeder about her own girlhood, when she too had imagined herself a royal Watutsi. But " 'I stopped making up tales a long time ago . . . and now I am myself' " (114). Gently but firmly, she frees Geeder from illusion. And Geeder realizes that she does not want to be Zeely but " 'Myself. . . . Yes, I guess so' " (114). Later, telling Uncle Ross and Toeboy about the meeting, Geeder realizes the source of Zeely's pride—by implication, all black pride: not the social status of some imaginary African past, but her own nobility of spirit. The courage and kindness of Zeely's hard life make her what Geeder calls the "best kind" of queen: "I don't mean queen like you read in books or hear on the radio, with kingdoms and servants and diamonds and gold. I mean queen when you think how Miss Zeely *is*" (120–21).

Zeely reclaims and redefines a rediscovered ethnic heritage—not only thematically, but by using the storytelling mode intrinsic to black culture. Geeder tells stories about Zeely to herself, Toeboy, and other children. Zeely tells Geeder her own story, in which is embedded the ancient tale that her mother once told her about their distant ancestor, "a young woman who waited for a message to come" that would "tell her who she was and what she was to do" (98). Finally, Geeder transmits Zeely's mother's story to Uncle Ross and Toeboy, joining the generations of black women storytellers, and adding her own layer of experience to the collective wisdom of her race. As Zeely and Geeder sit together in the clearing, and Zeely shares this inherited oral wisdom with the young girl, we may be reminded of other scenes, of Little Eva listening to Uncle Tom, and Uncle Remus telling his old tales to the little boy. But now the child is black—and the author, too.

In *Zeely*, both narrator and characters speak standard English. Like Dorothy Sterling in *Mary Jane*, Hamilton allows her readers to hear Geeder thinking—yet with strikingly different results. Mary Jane is a rather ordinary, though intelligent young girl; she talks to herself more out of social isolation than from natural introspection. Geeder, on the other hand, revels in the activity of her own mind, creating her story-world from what she observes around her :

> "I smell cigars, too," she whispered, "and soap and—my goodness—hay!" Geeder stood still in the room, then slowly backed out of it. A chill crept up her neck. "Oh," she said. "Old things. Waiting for something new to happen." (23)

This almost dreamlike effect of drifting in and out of Geeder's consciousness was to become more pronounced—sometimes to the point of surrealism—and more closely linked to ethnicity in Hamilton's later novels of the seventies and eighties.

In the late sixties, most of the children's writers dealing with black characters were still white, though more numerous than ever before. The prevailing mood of liberation and revolution was making publishers a little bolder and inspiring good writers who had never used black protagonists until now—writers like Elizabeth Borton de Trevino in *I, Juan de Pareja* (1965) and Mary Stolz in *A Wonderful, Terrible Time* (1967). The new convention governing black language may have helped. No longer need authors master the artificial "Negro dialect" or wrestle with controversial alternatives; their black characters could simply speak and think in the idiom normal for children's fiction. Ethnic themes, moreover, had acquired real prestige, appearing with remarkable frequency in the lists of Newbery and Caldecott Award winners and Honor Books. Between 1966 and 1974, three Newbery Awards went to books focussing on black characters and racial issues: *I, Juan de Pareja*, about the black slave of Velasquez; *Sounder* by William Armstrong, about Southern blacks of two generations past; and *The Slave Dancer* by Paula Fox, about slave trading in the 1840s. Five Newbery Honor Books also featured central black characters.[12] Yet we sense a lingering reluctance to embrace the problems of contemporary blacks; the actual award-winning books are all removed in time from the struggles of today.

Thus far the awards had gone to white authors and artists, though blacks were being represented among the Honor Books. The breakthrough year was 1975, when Virginia Hamilton won the Newbery Award for *M. C. Higgins, the Great*; in 1977 another black author, Mildred D. Taylor, won with *Roll of Thunder, Hear My Cry*. In 1976 and again in 1977 the interracial husband-and-wife team of Leo and Diane Dillon captured the Caldecott, first for an African folk tale, *Why Mosquitoes Buzz in People's Ears*, and then for *Ashanti to Zulu: African Traditions*.

What happened in the mid-seventies was not simply an increase of status and visibility for black authors and artists, but something like an abrupt change of policy. By 1975, children's books about blacks by non-black authors were suddenly no longer appreciated. Not only did such books fail to win awards, but books which had won awards only a few years ago were being harshly criticized for ignorance, insensitivity, even racism. In *The Black American in Books for Children* (1972), for example, Donnarae MacCann and Gloria Woodard exposed "racist" assumptions in *I, Juan de Pareja* and *Sounder*, as well as older Newbery winners like *Amos Fortune* and *The Voyages of Doctor Dolittle*. The pioneers of the thirties and forties, including *Bright April* and *Shuttered Windows*, were targeted by Dorothy Broderick in *Image of the Black in Children's Fiction* (1973). The same white authors who had been praised for featuring black characters were now punished for having done so.

Increasingly, the claim was that only black authors could write authentically of the black experience. Ray Anthony Shepard's comparison of *The Snowy Day* and the picture books of black author-artist John Steptoe in a 1971 issue of the new journal *Interracial Books for Children* is typical: "In Keats there is someone who looks like me, and in Steptoe there is someone who knows what is going on." In "Black and White: An Exchange" (1970), black author Julius Lester puts it even more strongly: "When I review a book about blacks (no matter the race of the author), I ask two questions: 'Does it accurately present the black perspective?' 'Will it be relevant to black children?' The possibility of a book by a white answering these questions affirmatively is almost nil" (29).

For Lester, and others, these questions of black "perspective" and "relevance" connect with their sense of racial identity and hard-won pride. George Woods, the white respondent of "Black and White," still thinks of color-blindness as the ideal, saying, "I try not to look at kids as black or white" (30). Lester replies that "Even in the best of all possible worlds, I want to be looked upon as a black. . . . I must . . . write books that hopefully will give black children the strength and pride that have been deliberately kept from them" (34).

Inevitably, the new generation of black children's writers turned to black English to express themselves. Black English had been recognized in the sixties as a genuine dialect of English, an "Africanized form of English" with its own grammar, idioms, and vocabulary (Smitherman 2). At the height of the Black Power Movement, there was much debate over whether it should be "allowed" into the classroom.[13] For black children's writers, however, its advantages were obvious. Using black English was one way to support racial unity and identity, while "purifying" oneself of white influence. Black English might also foster ethnic self-esteem by implying that a book was meant primarily for black, not white children; it was the first time that writers had been able to designate black children as their primary audience, or to signal their own blackness through book language. Finally, it made sense to write for black children in the idiom that many of them knew best, and would find easiest to understand.

It was crucial, of course, to distinguish between black English (and other authentic vernaculars) and the artificial, now taboo "Negro dialect." The 1971 edition of Augusta Baker's recommended booklist, *The Black Experience in Children's Books*, attempts to help readers see the difference:

> Another language consideration is the use of dialect particularly when it is pho-netically written, as "gwine" for "goin'." It is too difficult for the child to read and understand, and, since it is often not authentic, it is misleading. The use of regional vernacular is acceptable, but dialect should be used with great care. . . . Informal grammar and idiom are being used very successfully by some authors. John Steptoe, in his books *Stevie* and *Uptown*, has caught the language of the street perfectly. (i–ii)

John Steptoe, one of the first black author-artists to create picture books, was also one of the first to attempt an entire text—narration as well as dialogue—in black English. *Uptown* (1970) still seems a bit awkward and self-conscious, over-loaded with black pride catchwords:

> Dennis is my main man; we hang out together. . . .
> "Remember the time when we went to that bookstore up near 135th Street?"

"Yeah, they got a lot of nice Black Power things in the window," said Dennis.
"The man in there was a nice cat. He told us a lot of things about black people, and it's a lot different from what they tell you in school."
"Dig that," Dennis agreed.
"Plus like with black pride you can wear all these fine clothes and beads. I'm gonna get a dashiki and a kufti to wear. Then everybody will call me Brother John and I'll be as bad as I wanna be."
The man in the bookstore taught us how to say hello in Arabic.
"Al-salam, Alaykum, Brother." (unpaginated)

In Steptoe's later books, the idiom seems more natural. *My Special Best Words* (1974), narrated by three-year-old Bweela, tells how she toilet-trained her little brother Javaka; its language stresses not ethnicity but frankness in describing body functions—"And then Javaka make pee-pee in the toilet!"—and what "word" means to a three-year-old:

My best words is, WHATSHAPPENINMAN and IWANTSOMEWATERDAD and PRETTYFUL and IDONTWANTTOTAKEANAP and my special best word to Javaka is YOUADUMMY! (unpaginated)

Some of the earliest experiments with black English were the most revolutionary—the furthest, that is, from standard English. Steptoe's counterpart for an older age level was the black poet June Jordan, who published *His Own Where* in 1971. Again, both narrative and dialogue of this teenage love story are in black English, implying that characters, author, and audience are all black. Buddy's thoughts, often fragmentary or metaphorical, are interwoven with the present-tense narration, producing a stream of consciousness effect more like poetry than prose:

Buddy feel depression in the clutter-stricken room. Feel like a carpenter hands tied. Want to toss out everything and start the room from scratch. Keep it bare enough so Angela feel free.
"Your parents think you pretty wild." Buddy not quite leaning on the edge of the table. "Are you?". . .
Buddy like this girl, this Angela. He hate the room she have. Make even Angela seem clumsy. Make him feel himself like overgrown from Mars. He hate the whole apartment skimpy on the people-space. Rooms crush small by stuffed-up piece of furniture huge sofa and huge matching lamps huge things that squeeze the family mix into a quarrel just to move around a little. (21–22)

Buddy's struggle to liberate Angela from this apartment can be read large as the black struggle for liberation—for a space in America where blacks can "feel free" and become undistorted selves. The ironic ending, with Buddy and Angela making love in a cemetery, stops just short of hopelessness and seems a logical prelude to

Jordan's nonfictional *Dry Victories* (1972), a comparison of Reconstruction and the Civil Rights Movement and their "dry" or meaningless victories for blacks.

Dry Victories is even more radically experimental in form and language than *His Own Where*. We can easily accept dialect in fiction. But twenty years later, it is still disconcerting to see a "Note to the Readers" that begins, "This is a book we make because we think there was two times, Reconstruction and the Civil Rights' Era, that still be hanging us up, bad" (viii). The book itself consists of a dialogue between two young blacks, Kenny and Jerome:

> KENNY: Well, man, let's run it through. Like tell me why, in general, those old times seem dry.
> JEROME: Because they was. Dry. No real action. (9)

Solid pages of photographs and newspaper headlines reinforce the parallels between the two eras. Malcolm X and Booker T. Washington face each other on full pages; VISTA volunteers teaching black children share a spread with black schools founded under Reconstruction. To express radical political ideas, Jordan has created something equally radical in form. Expecting the usual neutral-toned, semi-academic prose, the reader is to be shocked awake by strong visual imagery and the voices of Kenny and Jerome—angry, cynical, and black.

Black writers of the middle 1970s tended to tone down their dialect, and to combine it with standard English.[14] Bette Greene, for example, in *Philip Hall Likes Me, I Reckon Maybe* (1974), and Mildred D. Taylor, in *Roll of Thunder, Hear My Cry* (1976), use mainly standard for the narrative and dialect for the dialogue—even though both stories are told in the first person by a young black girl. The distinction is less consistent in *Philip Hall*, whose narrator often slides into the vernacular, even in mid-sentence: "From time to time Philip would show the way by gesturing to the right or to the left, but otherwise he, like me, didn't have nothing to say" (107). In *Roll of Thunder*, the contrast between the formal, even stilted, English of the narrative and the loose-flowing rhythms of the dialogue is so marked as to produce some incongruous effects: " 'Shoot,' I mumbled finally, unable to restrain myself from further comment, 'it ain't my fault you gotta be in Mama's class this year' " (4–5). (The dialect here, incidentally, is not the urban black English of Steptoe, but a rural Southern speech used identically by the local white families; both black and white characters, for example, use the Southern second person plural "y'all.") Sharon Bell Mathis tries a different combination in *The Hundred Penny Box* (1975). The third person narrative is in standard English; Michael, the young black protagonist, and his mother speak standard too—but his great-great Aunt Dew and his father (whom Aunt Dew raised) speak black English.

Such compromise solutions ensure a wider audience; unlike Steptoe and Jordan, Greene, Taylor, and Mathis do not demand that a young reader (white or black) unfamiliar with Black English master a new dialect to understand their books. They also ensure a readier acceptance by the children's literature establishment. *Roll of Thunder* received a Newbery Award, while both *Philip Hall* and *The*

Hundred Penny Box were Honor Books; *His Own Where*, though much discussed, was not.

The Black Revolution brought a new generation of black children's authors to the fore, and stimulated experiments with black English and other dialects. The inconsistency and occasional awkwardness are signs of vitality and change. Since the middle seventies, however, there have been no significant new developments. The conservative mood of the eighties did not favor ethnic literature for children; few new black authors emerged, and the number of new titles featuring black characters diminished.[15] No single book language became dominant; the variations used today are essentially those established fifteen years ago. This has left authors with the wide range of options invented and explored for them by the pioneers of the seventies.

Perhaps the most commonly chosen—for example, in Walter Dean Myers's Newbery Honor Book *Scorpions* (1988)—is the combination of simple standard English for the narrative and simple black for the dialogue. Mildred D. Taylor still combines a highly formal standard English narrative with Southern black dialect dialogue in *The Road to Memphis* (1990). For a more stylistically adventurous author like Virginia Hamilton, black English rhythms can permeate the entire text. In her recent *A White Romance* (1987), narrative, internal monologue, and direct speech blend seamlessly into a poetic whole:

> They were running. The rain started again; it rained lightly on them. Didi's hair shone with the rain in the light of streetlamps. Talley looked at it. Didi looked at Talley's hair, grinned, nodded at her.
> "Mine do the same?" Talley murmured. "All glinty?"
> " 'Course!" Didi said. Their hair, glistening with rain droplets. It was like the rain held the night coming on.
> "Feels so good," Talley said. (52)

The picture books of Patricia C. McKissack use a black rural dialect in both narrative and dialogue, with more concern for clarity than consistency. Her *Flossie and the Fox* (1986) includes on the same page some sentences like "Slowly the animal circled round Flossie" and others like "He was sittin' 'side the road like he was expectin' somebody" (unpaginated).

All these contemporary authors find ways to make Black English accessible to a multiracial, multicultural audience—by simplifying it, by minimizing its grammatical differences from standard English, by avoiding too many black idioms or special vocabulary words, by mixing it with standard in various proportions. All have inherited Arna Bontemps's crucial innovation of making black dialect look "normal" on the page by avoiding the misspellings and overuse of apostrophes which give the effect of "mistakes" made by the speaker.

Though not all these authors use first person narrators, another common element of their book language is the closeness between reader and black protagonist. Not only the protagonists of Virginia Hamilton, but Bette Greene's Beth, Patricia McKissack's Flossie, and Walter Dean Myers's Jamal have the habit of internal monologue—of talking mind-to-mind with the reader. An intimacy and identification with black child characters that would have been inconceivable one hundred or even forty years ago is taken for granted in today's children's books.

Yet another common element goes back to "Uncle" times and beyond—the transmission of black racial wisdom through oral narrative. Again and again, the black authors of today pay tribute to the storytellers they heard as children. Mildred D. Taylor's novels are based on stories her father told her about his boyhood in the South. *Flossie and the Fox* came from Patricia McKissack's grandfather: "He was a master storyteller who charmed his audience with humorous stories told in the rich and colorful dialect of the rural South. I never wanted to forget them. So, it is through me that my family's storytelling legacy lives on" ("Author's Note," unpaginated). Virginia Hamilton's Newbery acceptance speech for *M. C. Higgins, the Great* describes her own legacy—the stories she has heard all her life from her extended "clan," the Perrys. And in Eloise Greenfield's *Childtimes* (1979), three generations of black women storytellers share their childhoods, in their own words—the author's grandmother, her mother, and herself.

As we, the readers, listen to these storytellers, we—black or white—join all these families. We become the new generation absorbing wisdom from the past. Whatever language they speak is now our heritage as well.

Notes

1. "Negro dialect" will be enclosed by quotation marks throughout this essay, to indicate its status as more of an imaginative and literary construct than an observed reality. Whereas standard English and black English are real dialects with real speakers, "Negro dialect" is the speech of fictional black characters as imagined by (mainly) white authors, and its characteristic visual appearance is as much a part of the dialect as its grammar and vocabulary. While "Negro dialect" has some features (for example, the double negative) in common with actual dialects spoken by blacks, and some variations of it may have been fairly accurate approximations of actual speech, it became more and more conventionalized; by the early twentieth century, virtually all fictional blacks spoke the same "Negro dialect" (as it was called by contemporary authors), regardless of regional setting or upbringing.

2. Sarah Elbert's analysis of Page and Johnston finds *Two Little Confederates* a defense of the Old South and *The Little Colonel* of the New. But Johnston seems only marginally Newer than Page in the roles she assigns her black characters.

3. One may be reminded by this scene of the legendary marriage of St. Cecilia to Valerian—an earthly marriage transformed into a spiritual one. After Valerian agreed to respect Cecilia's vow of perpetual chastity, an angel appeared to them and crowned them with wreaths of celestial roses. The red rose is traditionally a symbol

of martyrdom in Christian art, and both Cecilia and her husband became martyrs. Stowe also uses the emblem of the crowning angel in connection with Eva when she describes the decoration of Eva's bedroom at Lake Pontchartrain: "Over the head of the bed was an alabaster bracket, on which a beautiful sculptured angel stood, with drooping wings, holding out a crown of myrtle-leaves" (260). The evergreen myrtle is an ancient symbol of love; medieval brides wore myrtle crowns, and Eva's clearly signifies her coming union with the heavenly Bridegroom. Given this, and the widespread Victorian knowledge of flower symbolism, it does not seem farfetched to read the Tom and Eva scene as consciously symbolic.

4. Serious analysis of the Uncle Remus stories began in the late 1940s, with such essays as Louise Dauner's "Myth and Humor in the Uncle Remus Fables" in *American Literature* 20.2 (1948): 129–43; John Stafford's "Patterns of Meaning in *Nights with Uncle Remus*" in *American Literature* 18 (1946–47): 89–108; and Bernard Wolfe's "Uncle Remus and the Malevolent Rabbit" in *Commentary* 8.1 (July 1949): 31–41. Two important new versions of the Uncle Remus stories were published in the 1980s: *Jump! The Adventures of Brer Rabbit* (1986) by Van Dyke Parks and Malcolm Jones, and Julius Lester's *The Tales of Uncle Remus* (1987). Essays by Jones and Lester in *The Voice of the Narrator in Children's Literature* (1989), edited by Charlotte F. Otten and Gary D. Schmidt, reveal that the issues of black dialect raised by Harris's original can still cause problems. Jones, for example, defends the dialect used by Harris but admits that he and Parks had to "dismantle" it. Lester describes his confrontation with a white editor who disapproved his use of black English grammar.

5. The long-debated *Little Black Sambo*, which reached America in 1900, will not be included in this discussion. Despite the undoubted fact that Helen Bannerman's picture book has contributed to black stereotyping in America, neither the book, its author, nor Sambo himself is American—which explains why Sambo does not speak "Negro dialect" but impeccable standard English. The complex question of his racial identity (he is probably not African either), the history of various illustrated versions, and the influence of *Little Black Sambo* are authoritatively discussed by Phyllis J. Yuill in *Little Black Sambo: A Closer Look.*

6. Movie theaters would actually interrupt their films to pipe in the broadcast of *Amos and Andy*. See "Amos and Andy" in the booklet accompanying *America before TV: September 21, 1939—A Day from the Golden Age of Radio* (Greatapes 1987); the tape itself includes a typical *Amos and Andy* show, broadcast at 6:00 p.m.

7. In *Image of the Black in Children's Fiction* Dorothy Broderick lists a number of books published in the 1930s and '40s that similarly include only black characters—a literary equivalent of segregated schools and playgrounds.

8. The literary editor of *The Brownies' Book* was Harlem Renaissance writer Jessie Redmon Fauset. See "*The Brownies' Book:* A Pioneer Publication for Children" by Elinor Desverney Sinnette, in *Black Titan, W. E. B. DuBois: An Anthology by the Editors of "Freedomways,"* edited by John Henrik Clarke et al., 164–76 (Boston: Beacon Press, 1970).

9. Important advances in nonfiction also took place during this postwar period. Shirley Graham began publishing the first series of black biographies, beginning with

There Was Once a Slave (1947), the story of Frederick Douglass. Another work of black history, Arna Bontemps's *Story of the Negro* (1948), became the first book by a black author to be designated a Newbery Honor Book (formerly "Runner-up").

10. Only six years before, the one black character in Marguerite De Angeli's *Thee, Hannah!* (1940), a story of the Underground Railroad, had spoken in traditional "Negro dialect." De Angeli's decision to use standard English in *Bright April* shows how quickly the transition from one book language to another was taking place.

11. Popular series which had been among the most egregious users of exaggerated "Negro dialect" led the way in eliminating it. By 1953, for example, the speech of Dinah and Sam, faithful servants of the Bobbseys, had been transformed into immaculate standard English. As Paul C. Deane points out, their subservient roles had not changed at all. But book language had assumed such importance that removing dialect was now in itself a worthwhile public gesture.

12. These were *The Jazz Man* (1966) by Mary H. Weik, *Jennifer, Hecate, MacBeth, William McKinley, and Me, Elizabeth* (1967) by E. L. Konigsburg, *The Egypt Game* (1967) by Zilpha Keatley Snyder, *To Be a Slave* (1968) by Julius Lester, and *The Planet of Junior Brown* (1971) by Virginia Hamilton. American ethnic minorities other than blacks were also strongly represented among the Newbery Award and Honor Books of this period—particularly American Indians. Newbery Awards were won in 1961 and 1973 by Scott O'Dell's *Island of the Blue Dolphins* and Jean Craighead George's *Julie of the Wolves*, whose heroines are, respectively, Chumash Indian and Alaskan Eskimo. Between 1966 and 1972, we find nine Honor Books with main characters who are Puerto Rican *(The Noonday Friends)*, Latin American *(The King's Fifth, The Black Pearl)*, Jewish *(Zlateh the Goat, The Fearsome Inn, When Shlemiel Went to Warsaw, Our Eddie)*, or Navajo *(Sing Down the Moon, Annie and the Old One)*. When these are added to the books featuring black characters, the percentage of ethnic fiction and nonfiction is nearly half of the total Newbery list. As for the Caldecott Award, while the only award winner with a black theme since *The Snowy Day* had been Gail E. Haley's *A Story—A Story* (1970), the Caldecott Honor Books for this period included *Goggles!* (1969) by Ezra Jack Keats, *Moja Means One: Swahili Counting Book* (1971) by Muriel Feelings and Tom Feelings, and *Anansi the Spider* (1972) by Gerald McDermott.

13. For discussions of this controversy, see *Black Language Reader*, edited by Robert H. Bentley and Samuel D. Crawford (Glenview, IL: Scott, Foresman, 1973), especially the section titled "Where Do We Go from Here: Language and Education."

14. *Me and Neesie* (1975) by the black author Eloise Greenfield provides an example of less extreme black English than Steptoe's that is designed for the same age group. Much of its first-person narrative and dialogue is indistinguishable from standard English:

Mama pulled my head back around. "Keep your head still, Janell," she said. "And stop talking to yourself."

"I was talking to Neesie, Mama," I said.

"Nobody's in this bedroom but me and you," Mama said. "So if you not talking to me, you talking to yourself."

"Your mother don't know nothing," Neesie said. (unpaginated)

15. The 1984 edition of *The Black Experience in Children's Books* records a sharp decline in the numbers of new books published since the 1979 edition, with an average of only twenty-five new publications a year during this five-year period. "The volumes of material on the Black Experience for children which were available in the late 1960s and early 1970's have dwindled to a trickle of titles by the same familiar authors" (Rollock 4).

Works Cited

Allee, Marjorie Hill. "Books Negro Children Like." *Horn Book* 12.2 (1938): 81–87.

Baker, Augusta, ed. *The Black Experience in Children's Books.* New York: New York Public Library, 1971.

———. "Guidelines for Black Books: An Open Letter to Juvenile Editors." In Mac-Cann and Woodard, 1972, 50–56.

Beim, Lorraine, and Jerrold Beim. *Two Is a Team.* New York: Harcourt, 1945.

Bontemps, Arna. *Sad-Faced Boy.* Boston: Houghton Mifflin, 1937.

———. *You Can't Pet a Possum.* Boston: Houghton Mifflin, 1934.

Broderick, Dorothy M. *Image of the Black in Children's Fiction.* New York: R. R. Bowker, 1973.

Bryant, Sara Cone. *Epaminondas and His Auntie.* Boston: Houghton Mifflin, 1907.

Carpenter, Humphrey, and Mari Prichard. *The Oxford Companion to Children's Literature.* Oxford: Oxford University Press, 1984.

Carter, Neille Page. "Pickaninny Pranks." *Horn Book* 9.1 (1935): 17–22.

Coatsworth, Elizabeth. *The Golden Horseshoe.* New York: Macmillan, 1935. Rev. ed., 1968.

Deane, Paul C. "The Persistence of Uncle Tom: An Examination of the Image of the Negro in Children's Fiction Series." In MacCann and Woodard, 116–23.

De Angeli, Marguerite. *Bright April.* New York: Doubleday, 1946.

———. *Thee, Hannah!* New York: Doubleday, 1940.

Elbert, Sarah. Preface to *Two Little Confederates,* by Thomas Nelson Page and *The Little Colonel,* by Annie Fellows Johnston. Classics of Children's Literature, no. 56. New York: Garland, 1976.

Evans, Eva Knox. *Araminta.* New York: Putnam, 1935.

———. "The Negro in Children's Fiction." *Publisher's Weekly* 140 (18 October 1941): 650.

Govan, Christine Noble. *Those Plummer Children.* Boston: Houghton Mifflin, 1934.

Greene, Bette. *Philip Hall Likes Me, I Reckon Maybe.* New York: Dial, 1974.

Greenfield, Eloise, *Me and Neesie.* New York: Thomas Y. Crowell, 1975.

———— and Lessie Jones Little. *Childtimes: A Three-Generation Memoir.* New York: Thomas Y. Crowell, 1979.

Hamilton, Virginia. "Newbery Award Acceptance." In *Newbery and Caldecott Medal Books, 1966–1975,* ed. Lee Kingman, 124–36. Boston: Horn Book, 1975.

————. *A White Romance.* New York: Philomel, 1987.

————. *Zeely.* New York: Macmillan, 1967.

Harris, Joel Chandler. *Uncle Remus: His Songs and His Sayings.* New York: Appleton, 1880.

Jackson, Jesse. *Call Me Charley.* New York: Harper, 1945.

Johnston, Annie Fellows. *The Little Colonel.* Boston: L. C. Page, 1895.

————. *The Little Colonel's House Party.* Boston: L. C. Page, 1900.

Jones, Malcolm. "The Talespinner's Mind." In Otten and Schmidt, 74–77.

Jordan, June. *Dry Victories.* New York: Holt, Rinehart, and Winston, 1972.

————. *His Own Where.* New York: Thomas Y. Crowell, 1971.

Keats, Ezra Jack. *The Snowy Day.* New York: Viking, 1962.

Konigsburg, E. L. *Jennifer, Hecate, MacBeth, William McKinley, and Me, Elizabeth.* New York: Atheneum, 1967.

Larrick, Nancy. "The All-White World of Children's Books." In MacCann and Woodard, 156–68.

Lester, Julius. "The Storyteller's Voice: Reflections on the Rewriting of Uncle Remus." In Otten and Schmidt, 69–73.

Lester, Julius, and George Woods. "Black and White: An Exchange." In MacCann and Woodard, 28–35.

MacCann, Donnarae, and Gloria Woodard, eds. *The Black American in Books for Children.* Metuchen, NJ: Scarecrow, 1972.

Mathis, Sharon Bell. *The Hundred Penny Box.* New York: Viking, 1975.

McKissack, Patricia C. *Flossie and the Fox.* New York: Dial, 1986.

Means, Florence Crannell. "Mosaic." *Horn Book* 16.1 (1940): 35–40.

————. *Shuttered Windows.* Boston: Houghton Mifflin, 1938.

Myers, Walter Dean. *Scorpions.* New York: Harper and Row, 1988.

Nolen, Eleanor Weakley. "The Colored Child in Contemporary Literature." *Horn Book* 18.5 (1942): 348–55.

————. *A Job for Jeremiah.* London: Oxford University Press, 1940.

Otten, Charlotte F., and Gary D. Schmidt, eds. *The Voice of the Narrator in Children's Literature: Insights from Writers and Critics.* Contributions to the Study of World Literature, no. 28. New York: Greenwood Press, 1989.

Page, Thomas Nelson. *Two Little Confederates.* 1888. New York: Scribner's, 1953.

Perkins, Lucy Fitch. *The Colonial Twins of Virginia.* Boston: Houghton Mifflin, 1924.

————. *The Dutch Twins.* Boston: Houghton Mifflin, 1911.

————. *The Pickaninny Twins.* School Edition. Boston: Houghton Mifflin, 1931.

Rahn, Suzanne. "Early Images of American Minorities: Rediscovering Florence Crannell Means." *The Lion and the Unicorn* 11.1 (1987): 98–115.

Rider, Ione Morrison. "Arna Bontemps." *Horn Book* 13.1 (1939): 13–19.

Rollins, Charlamae, ed. *We Build Together: A Reader's Guide to Negro Life and Literature for Elementary and High School Use.* Chicago: National Council of Teachers of English, 1948.

Rollock, Barbara, ed. *The Black Experience in Children's Books.* New York: New York Public Library, 1984.

Shepard, Ray Anthony. "Adventures in Blackland with Keats and Steptoe." *Bulletin of the Council on Interracial Books for Children* 3.4 (autumn 1971):3.

Shotwell, Louisa R. *Roosevelt Grady.* Cleveland: World, 1963.

Smitherman, Geneva. *Talkin and Testifyin: The Language of Black America.* Detroit: Wayne State University Press, 1986.

Steptoe, John. *My Special Best Words.* New York: Viking, 1974.

————. *Uptown.* New York: Harper and Row, 1970.

Sterling, Dorothy. *Mary Jane.* New York: Doubleday, 1959.

————. "The Soul of Learning." In MacCann and Woodard, 1972, 175–87.

Stowe, Harriet Beecher. *Uncle Tom's Cabin.* London: Frederick Warne, n.d. [1852].

Taylor, Mildred D. *The Road to Memphis.* New York: Dial, 1990.

————. *Roll of Thunder, Hear My Cry.* New York: Dial, 1976.

Yates, Elizabeth. *Amos Fortune, Free Man.* New York: Aladdin, 1950.

Yuill, Phyllis J. *Little Black Sambo: A Closer Look.* New York: Racism and Sexism Resource Center for Educators, 1976.

Childhood Lost:
Children's Voices in Holocaust Literature

NAOMI SOKOLOFF

Over one million Jewish children died in the Holocaust. Many others suffered from Nazi persecution, whether in hiding or before they managed to flee. Even when it did not spell death, this experience often robbed them of childhood or distorted it by denying them the normal joys of play or forcing them into precocious maturity.[1]

Early on Nazi decrees forbade Jewish children to enter parks, playgrounds, and swimming pools. Various edicts banned clubs, scouting, sports, and schools. Later, in the ghettoes and camps, widespread privation exacerbated the pressures to grow up quickly. Young children frequently assumed leadership in ghetto families; because of youthful adaptability, coupled with the adults' shock and disorientation, children adjusted better than their parents did to the demands of their horrifying situation. They became smugglers, or volunteered for labor companies or factory work; as couriers for the resistance they made their way through the sewers into and out of the ghetto. In the camps, Nazi ideology made no concessions for youth. Children were not considered in any way as innocents, but rather, the seed of the subhuman. Not only were they treated with no special leniency, being a child meant certain extermination. Consequently, some feigned greater age, in order to be eligible for hard labor rather than immediate execution.

The destruction of childhood, the need to grow up prematurely, and the clouding of boundaries between childhood and maturity are themes that surface in Holocaust literature for adults and for juvenile audiences, as well as in the writing of children authors. All these kinds of literature entail, of necessity, an intersection of grown-up and children's perspectives. Whether the adult attempts to speak for or in the name of children, to edit texts by children, to impersonate young voices, or to represent their consciousness, the child's vision is always mediated by that of someone more mature. In the various genres, these perspectives combine in different ways to convey a childhood which—shaped by violence—was not a childhood. In order to survey some of those differences, this essay briefly examines three kinds of texts: 1) adult narratives that imagine the child, particularly Louis Begley's novel *Wartime Lies;* 2) children's compositions from the Terezín (Theresienstadt) concentration camp, collected by Hana Volavková in *I Never Saw Another Butterfly;* and 3) Uri Orlev's juvenile fiction, *The Island on Bird Street.* The final portion of the essay turns to an examination of fiction—David Grossman's "Momik," from *See Under: Love*—that dramatizes interactions among these categories of writing and suggests how discussion of each may open out onto the others.

Wartime Lies (1991) recounts the early life of Maciek, a boy born in 1933, who spends the war years in disguise. Passing as an Aryan in Nazi-occupied Poland, he comes under the care of his aunt Tania, and the two of them move restlessly from one location to another, from Lwow to Warsaw and then to the countryside, frequently changing addresses and aliases. For most of Maciek's childhood remnants of play and schooling are a part of his life: he reads *Treasure Island* in hiding, he plots battles with his lead soldiers, his aunt's lover gives him lessons in mathematics. Nonetheless, he no longer attends school, he is isolated from other children, and he experiences severe cruelties as well: he is uprooted, he suffers the deaths of loved ones, he lives through the bombing of Warsaw, and he narrowly escapes from a train bound for Auschwitz.

The greatest loss is that of his own voice. He must learn at an early age to lie and to conceal his identity. However, this responsibility—one that demands from him a mature appreciation of the dangers involved—also paradoxically infantilizes him. Growing up for Maciek means accepting forced helplessness and dependence on the aunt. He must obey her without question in order to survive, and he must often internalize, without examination, what grown-ups say. Consequently, the only voice left him is theirs, as they appropriate him into their world, leaving him little room to grow, to explore the world at his own pace, or to assert his own views. By way of example, consider the following passage which, like many others, conveys reports of adult speech with little evaluation or response from the child:

> Tania told me to lie down on our mattress. She lay down too, put her arm around me and talked to me in a whisper. She said it was lucky that we had not forgotten for a moment we were Catholic Poles and that nobody seemed to suspect us. Our only hope was to be like all the others. The Germans weren't going to kill every Pole in Warsaw; there were too many of them, but they would kill every Jew they could catch. We would make ourselves very small and inconspicuous, and we would be very careful not to get separated in the crowd. If smething very bad happened and she was taken away, I wasn't to try to follow: it wouldn't help her and I might even make things worse for both of us. If possible I should wait for her. Otherwise, I should take the hand of whatever

grown-up near me had the nicest face, say I was an orphan, and hope for the best. I shouldn't say I was a Jew, or let myself be seen undressed if I could avoid it. She had me repeat these instructions and told me to go to sleep. (131)

The scene takes place in a Warsaw cellar, as the pair seek cover from German bombardments. Tania's voice is presented through description of her speech ([she] talked to me in a whisper"), through indirect discourse ("She said it was lucky"), and through free indirect discourse ("Our only hope"). For most of the passage the little boy does not speak. Instead, Tania's words emphasize what the boy cannot say, with the exception of the ending. There the aunt insists on Maciek's need to repeat her instructions—indicating his *modus vivendi* of muting his own voice and denying his own responses.

Even after the war this experience haunts him, and the effect is devastating. He continues to pose as a Catholic, afraid of the consequences of revealing that he is Jewish. To lie and to conceal have become second nature. Consequently, even when he finds a genuine friend, he still feels he cannot confide in him such basic feelings as whether he hated or loved a pet dog. All is a sham, an extension of having had to cover up the basic truth of his identity for so long. The novel ends with the narrator explaining clearly that Maciek's childhood—that is, his own childhood—simply perished: "And where is Maciek now? He became an embarrassment and slowly died. A man who bears one of the names Maciek used has replaced him. Is there much of Maciek in that man? No: Maciek was a child, and our man has no childhood that he can bear to remember, he has had to invent one" (198). This relationship between the child and the man parallels the author's relation to his own childhood. Begley spent his early years in hiding in wartime Poland. Many years later, as an American citizen and a successful lawyer, he chose to re-examine the events of those formative years not by writing a memoir, but by creating a fictional character.[2]

Within the novel itself the disjunction between the boy Maciek and the man he becomes is put into relief through a major shift of narrative voice. Most of the text is oriented to the child's view, and, while narrated retrospectively in first person by an adult, offers a simple, unembellished presentation of information available to the boy himself, in a form that often approaches deadpan. In stark contrast, a few sections of prose are oriented to the views of the adult narrator, who reveals himself to be erudite, who lays authoritative claim to his interpretations of the past, and who brings literary intertexts, ironic insights, and vehemence to his retrospective judgments. This voice emerges especially as the narrator meditates upon Dante, offering a personal reading of the motifs of self-pity and disdain in the *Inferno* (73–75, 120–22). Just as Dante sought spiritual insight by journeying through hell, this man journeys back in memory to the hell of his childhood. Drawing on parallels from the *Inferno*, he reflects bitterly on bystanders who weren't victims of the Holocaust yet spared little pity for those who were. He is especially resentful of people who hold the Jews in disdain for not fighting back, who do not understand the circumstances of the time and who reserve their compassion only for victims capable of showing defiance.

Altogether, two radically different narrative voices govern *Wartime Lies*. The perceptions of the child who was largely mute finally find expression in the silent register of writing, through the adult who remembers that early time. The erudite adult voice, emphasizing the great distance between his current and his former selves, puts into relief the very artifice of representing the child's consciousness; the child's voice makes itself heard only as a literary phenomenon.

Begley's construction of childhood is not an isolated phenomenon in literary accounts of the Holocaust. Rather, Maciek is part of a spectrum of young figures typified by greater or lesser degrees of muteness and incomprehension. *Wartime Lies* bears important affinities to fiction of various periods written in a range of languages (including Dutch, German, and Hebrew). Clara Asscher-Pinkhof's *Sterrenkinder* (Star Children, 1946), Ilse Aichinger's *Die Grösserer Hoffnung* (Herod's Children, 1948), Jerzy Kosinski's *The Painted Bird* (1965), Uri Orlev's *Ḥayalei 'oferet* (The Lead Soldiers, 1967), and Aharon Appelfeld's *Tor hapela'ot* (The Age of Wonders, 1978) are all oriented to a child's outlook. While the attitude toward childhood varies from text to text, the centrality of the child's perspective in each creates a significant bond among these books.

At issue is the fact that the child's voice in adult fiction is always problematic; it is a frequently suppressed voice, and one that cannot freely assert itself but must be mediated. However, this reticent voice is well-suited to treatments of the Holocaust, for these contend with a fundamental tension between silence and words. The critical literature has often pointed out that treatments of the Holocaust in imaginative writing encounter fundamental difficulties of expression: how to assimilate the unimaginable into the imagination, how to find a language commensurate with the enormity of events that took place during that period. The focus on a child's partial understanding helps alleviate the adult narrator's struggle with language and artistic expression, for the young character's incomprehension serves to indicate the incomprehensibility of the catastrophe.[3] In some texts, attention to incomprehension has yielded a young figure "who stands for the possibility of fictional discourse that registers rather than construes."[4] That is, the child serves as a way to sidestep trying to formulate an interpretation of evil that defies understanding. In other texts, emphasis on incomprehension is accompanied by direct thematic emphasis on a child's muteness. In *The Painted Bird*, the protagonist simply becomes mute in the face of overwhelming horror he cannot accept or explain. A similar reaction occurs to a young character in Elie Wiesel's *The Gates of the Forest*.

Altogether, adults writing of the Holocaust have sounded the consciousness and perceptions of children which the children themselves could not voice for a variety of reasons: because they were killed too young to speak for themselves; because they were overwhelmed by trauma; because they were forced to live in disguise; or because they were too young to try to interpret their suffering. These perceptions, however, are voiced by adult writers only in a realm of the imagination, which mediates between the past and the time of writing but is never present. This is expression that clouds the child's "I," filtered as it inevitably is through an adult's words. If the mature artistic representation of a child's consciousness or voice is always a peculiarly literary ventriloquism, such is even more the case in these texts.

There were, however, children writing literary texts during the Holocaust, and they bring out with painful immediacy the voices so subdued and mediated in adult writing about this period. One of the best known examples is the collection *I Never Saw Another Butterfly: Children's Drawings and Poems from Terezín Concentration Camp, 1942–1944.* Unusual circumstances fostered the writing of these poems. At Terezín (in Czechoslovakia) Jews were allowed to maintain schools as part of a massive deception which the German command arranged for the benefit of the Red Cross and world opinion. The Nazis claimed that this was a model ghetto, one that offered Jews benign segregation in a town of their own, free from undue hardships. Behind the facade of decency the internees suffered starvation, disease, deportation, and untold cruelties. Many continued on to extermination camps, and of the fifteen thousand children who entered this place, only one hundred survived the war. In the midst of all this, the Jewish prisoners at Terezín encouraged their children to study, to paint, and to write.[5]

By comparison with the mutenesses and the appropriations of children's voices in adult fiction, these poems in their frequent use of "I" seem strikingly bold. Take, for example, a poem called "At Terezín," by a young prisoner of unknown age identified as "Teddy." Here we find not only the poet's outspoken first person pronoun, but also other children's words of protest as Teddy reports them.

> When a new child comes
> Everything seems strange to him.
> "What, on the ground I have to lie?
> Eat black potatoes? No! Not I!"
>
> ....
>
> Here in Terezín, life is hell
> And when I'll go home again, I can't yet tell. (10)

Another poem, called "Terezín," offers very direct comment about the need to grow up too young. The author, 13 or 14 years old, stands on the brink of adolescence, but already laments long lost childhood.

> I was once a little child,
> Three years ago.
> That child who longed for other worlds.

But now I am no more a child
For I have learned to hate.
I am a grown-up person now,
I have known fear.

Bloody words and a dead day then.
That's something different than bogie men! (by Hanuš Hochenburg, p. 22)

Certainly, such poems are less skillful than adult writing; they lack the artistic depth of adult texts as well as the multiple dimensions attained there through the layering and intersections of children's views with adult perspectives. Yet the young poets turn to many of the same topics as the adults, endowing them with special forcefulness and impact.[6]

Like many adult writers, youngsters wrote of untimely death, juxtaposing childhood with death, innocence with evil. "The Garden" by Franta Bass (12–14 years old) is informed by a sense that childhood should have been something else.

A little boy, a sweet boy,
Like that growing blossom.
When the blossom comes to bloom
The little boy will be no more. (50)

Both historians and literary artists have remarked that during the Holocaust children came to accept more than adults, as they had less trouble adjusting to the upheavals of their lives. Aharon Appelfeld, for instance, has noted in his essays that adults were more shattered by events; beyond physical abuse, their entire understanding of the world was destroyed by the conflagration, whereas children absorbed their suffering and it became simply a part of their being. Similarly, Orlev's novel *The Lead Soldiers* paints children who accept gruesome atrocity as a matter of fact, for this suffering is what the young figures have known most of their lives. Nonetheless, there remain poems by children which testify clearly to an awareness that their youth has been interrupted and that this interruption is both terribly wrong and unnatural.

While the children in adult texts are often uncomprehending, the children's own poetry frequently features attempts at explanation—by way of philosophical observations or generalizations that take on the quality of aphorism, and that demonstrate an unmistakable desire to comprehend. One poem, titled "It All Depends on How You Look at It," notes

Death, after all claims, everyone.
You find it everywhere.
It catches up with even those
Who wear their noses in the air.

The whole, wide world is ruled
With a certain justice, so
That helps perhaps to sweeten
The poor man's pain and woe. (by Miroslav Košek, age 10–12; 17)

Another poem, "Man proposes, God disposes" remarks:

Who was toughened up before
He'll survive these days
But who was used to servants
Will sink into his grave. (signed "Koleba: Košek, Löwy, Bachner"; 19)

These poems come across less as mature reflections than as youthful attempts to sound grown-up and to mimic adult wisdom. They differ markedly from the way adults have actually expressed themselves in literary treatments of the Holocaust. Adult fiction often turns to child characters to stress the incomprehensibility of the events. These young poets, in contrast, try to see some justice in the world that would help make sense of their own suffering. In the first example, the universality of death provides a perspective that makes their own deaths easier to accept; the second example seeks a kind of poetic justice, suggesting that previous suffering, which makes people tough, will help them learn to cope better with suffering in Terezín. Precisely for these reasons the poems tug at the heartstrings. The attempt to be grown-up testifies to a lack of cynicism on the part of the children, and so to their innocence in the sense of naivete. The texts thereby also contrast ironically with the efforts by the adult editor of this collection, to make the contributors seem younger than they were and so to emphasize the innocence (i.e., guiltlessness) of the victims. Though the subtitle of the collection announces that the volume contains "Children's Drawings and Poems," many of the poems, in fact, are by any measure the work of adolescents (ages 14–16), and they merit reading and analysis in the context of adolescent compositions such as Anne Frank's diary.[7] Telling, too, is the title of the collection *I Never Saw Another Butterfly*, which comes from a poem by a 21-year-old named Pavel Friedmann. The editor offers the following explanation: "Although in years he belongs among the adult poets, his work does not differ much in style or subject matter from the work of younger poets" (78). The editor strives for pathos. And, while adult readers may well sympathize with this inclination to emphasize youth, it is well to remember that often the young poets themselves were struggling in the other direction, to be more than their years.[8]

Turning now to *The Island on Bird Street*, we find an author who, like Begley and the children of Terezín, knew the Holocaust first hand. Uri Orlev survived a childhood of disguises, ghettoes, and camps in wartime Poland. Later he made his way to Israel, where he was one of the first to write fiction about the Holocaust in Hebrew. His novel *The Lead Soldiers* anticipates Begley's in several ways, particularly in the disjunction between its adult narrator and child protagonist. Their perspectives remain clearly separate, even as the narrator steps in and out of narrated events. Observing his younger self, he notes that that boy inhabited a different world, holding assumptions and values quite other than those of the adult story-teller and his readers. But *The Island on Bird Street* (in Hebrew, Ha'i birḥov hatsiporim, published in 1981) presents an artificial yet seamless combination of adult and child perspectives, peculiar to juvenile fiction. This is writing designed to speak to children and in the name of a child, conveying a child's impressions. At the same time, it is clearly written, conceived, and ordered by an adult. The synthesis—the melding—of child and adult perspectives in this text helps ensure that the themes of growing up, acting grown-up, and precocious maturity carry a very different valence here than in adult fiction.

The novel recounts the experiences of an 11-year-old boy, Alex, who must fend for himself in the Warsaw ghetto. When his family members are killed or deported, he manages to hide in an abandoned building, and waits there for his father to return. He lives on his own for many months, taking as his role model Robinson Crusoe's solitary fight for survival on a deserted island.

The first-person narrator speaks retrospectively of his own past, but it is not clear if this narrator is an adult, a child, or an adolescent.[9] The story is told in language that a young audience could easily read and understand, and the prose includes only the information Alex would have had access to as a child, at the time of the war. In addition, the narrator is very close, emotionally, to the experiences recounted. There is minimal dissonance (shock, condescension, humor, pity, or irony) between the narrator's stance and the child's, and there are few traces of the cognitive privilege typical of an older and wiser adult judging the past. At the same time, the narration could not possibly be that of a youngster: it is much too writerly, too coherent, neat, and dramatically stylized.[10]

Most prominent here are the conventions of juvenile adventure fiction. There are many descriptions of heroic action, of the child's ingenuity (e.g., in building a hideaway, accessible only by rope ladders), his daring in moments of danger, and his participation in a grand and noble mission—in this case, the ghetto uprising. These all enhance the main theme: Alex's maturity and self-reliance, thrust upon him by circumstances which demand that he grow up quickly.

A key scene takes place when Alex kills a German soldier with a pistol in order to save the lives of two partisans who have infiltrated the ghetto on a rescue mission. They at first do not believe he's done something so mature and, as they look for a hiding place, they insist, "Go get a grown-up" (99). He then reveals his secret lair, and they are astonished that he has built it by himself. Driving home the point that he can manage by himself, he refuses all their offers of help and their invitation to join their band in the forests. He remains in the ghetto until his father does finally come back and discover him, many months later.

Added to this adventure fiction are touching reflections that function less as convincing psychological portraits of a child's inner life than as the kind of adult reassurances familiar from other juvenile fiction by Orlev.[11] These suggest that it is possible to make peace with one's fears. Consider the following passage, which describes Alex's trepidations on first moving into the abandoned ruin. Previously, before Alex's family was deported, he and a group of boys used to dare one another to play there:

> It was odd, but now that I had to, I explored it without thinking twice, while back in the days when we played here I didn't dare take two steps inside before all the boys went "hoooooo" like a ghost and I ran right back out again. And yet even if there really were ghosts and they hid in places like this, why would they want to harm me? Like as not, they wanted to help. They certainly had to hate the Germans too. (45)

If, in Holocaust fiction written for adults, children often serve as a way of talking about vulnerability, bitterness, and the incomprehensibility of evil, here the emphasis falls on hope. Orlev's novel highlights the value in acting grown up and the value of growing up itself—that is, in hanging on in order to survive and, especially, to be like an admired adult, the father. These are ideals the grown author wishes to inculcate in his young audience. The reassurance—that the child can survive an ordeal, like a great adventure—can be read as an attitude typical of the Israeli cultural milieu from within which Orlev writes and which has a tradition of emphasizing heroism and bravery.[12] In the decades immediately after World War II Hebrew literature repeatedly featured the heroism of Israelis and defined their role vis-à-vis Diaspora Jews as one of rescue and redemption. In recent years Israelis have come to identify more with Jews in the Diaspora, and this novel contributes to that cultural phenomenon as it sends children the message that young Diaspora Jews, as well as native Israelis, can be seen as brave and heroic.

More fundamentally, the message that the child can cope, and even triumph, is a staple of much writing for children and a quality celebrated by critics of juvenile literature (see, e.g., Butler and Rotert). This is an issue increasingly under discussion since the 1970s, as, throughout Western culture, there have appeared more and more juvenile titles that deal with trauma of various sorts and with life at its darkest. As part of this trend—away from attempts to shield children from exposure to unhappiness in literature—the Holocaust is but one of the difficult topics that has attracted new attention. Yet in this area there is an undeniable possibility of doing genuine damage to children by shocking them and exposing them to unbearable details at too young an age. This problem has, in fact, been an overriding concern of critics who evaluate juvenile literature that deals with the Holocaust. James Farnham (55), for instance, writes, "The middle ground is a presentation of life tragedies ending with an affirmation of the worth of living."[13]

Altogether, the combinations of adult and child perspectives which inform adult fiction and literature written by or for children on the subject of the Holocaust respond to distinctive needs and orientations. Adult fiction like *Wartime Lies* aspires to reconstruct childhood, or to make some kind of peace with the past. Though the thematic material is much the same, the emphases are quite other for the children writers of Terezín or for adult writers like Orlev, who struggle to provide lessons to help juveniles become adults.

A remarkable narrative that faces head on the difficulties of speaking to children about the Holocaust is David Grossman's "Momik" (1986), which deals with the second generation, and with what parents do and don't tell their children about the traumas of that time.[14] The author himself did not experience the Nazi era firsthand. A native Israeli, born in 1953, he is not a child of survivors, but he was one of the first in Jewish literature, and particularly in Hebrew, to address in his fiction the agonies of the second generation.

A variety of factors, then, distance Grossman from the events of the Holocaust, and yet his novel attempts to approach its epicenter, that is, to deal with some of its most ghastly events. The discussion in this essay has progressed through texts that (in the events referred to, if not in the manner of telling) highlight increasingly gruesome aspects of the catastrophe. The focus has moved from life in disguise *(Wartime Lies)*, to life in Terezín, where children are still able to draw and paint, to the deportations, murders, and doomed uprising of the Warsaw ghetto. Grossman writes about even worse violence and about more grotesque depravities. It is probably fair to say that this fiction succeeds in part because of the new perspective afforded the author by his distance. Multiple filters—especially distance in time and an orientation to a child protagonist's partial understandings—allow for understatement and irony in the narrative. The child's naivete and his difficulties in trying to fathom what happened to his parents put into relief and epitomize the horror he confronts. And Grossman succeeds in portraying this encounter between naivete and horror because this adult fiction demonstrates extraordinary respect for young intelligence, imagination, and sensitivity.[15] Furthermore, as it explores a child's inner life and imagines that child as an author, "Momik" strongly suggests the value in listening to children's voices. It is a tale, too, that acknowledges the importance of juvenile fiction as a formative influence in the thinking of children. For these reasons this narrative casts into new light the categories set up at the beginning of this essay—adult fiction, child-authored texts, and juvenile fiction—suggesting that they are not so much separate entities as interconnected components in a complex web of relations among literary texts, all of which may contribute to readers' understandings of the impact the Holocaust has had on children.

Grossman's protagonist is a nine-year-old, Momik Neuman, who is an only son of survivors and lives in Jerusalem. The year is 1959. The parents, very protective of their child, are secretive about the past. Momik, however, is determined to decode their secrets and to try to rescue them from their nightmares and fears. As he sets out to learn about their mysterious past, he prides himself on his high intelligence and exceptional memory. Calling himself, as his parents evidently also do, an *alter kopf* ("old head" in Yiddish, suggesting a wise old man; 8, 17), he is convinced that he can unravel the puzzle and conquer the obscure evil by means of reason and methodical strategy. He must work indirectly though. He besieges a neighbor, Bella—also a survivor—with questions, and she implores him to stop asking and "go play with children his own age please" (15).

But he cannot let the enigma rest, it is too basic a part of his life. The puzzle is complicated by a grand-uncle, an invalid, who comes to live with Momik's family, and whose needs often become the little boy's responsibility. Entirely helpless, broken by his suffering at the hands of the Nazis, Anshel is described as being like a baby. He needs to be fed, bathed, and taken to the toilet—all of them chores that Momik assumes as part of his daily routine. This situation enforces Momik's need to grow up quickly: basic roles have been reversed, since at an early age he must take care of an adult who has been rendered infantile.

Momik's attempts to break the secret code at first present an amusing if heartrending juxtaposition of naivete and horror. Here, too, as in other novels, a child's incomprehension serves to highlight the struggle of the imagination to grasp the magnitude of the catastrophe. This character undertakes his mission—of gathering information to save the survivors from their suffering—by patching together impressions of the war era he has received from overheard conversations, taciturn comments, and a variety of texts to which he assigns his own meaning. When, for instance, he hears about "the Nazi beast," he assumes that the phrase refers to some kind of animal. Subsequently, he begins to collect stray cats, birds, and other creatures to see if he can't identify the wicked one and exorcise the evil out of it. Compounding his confusion is mention in the papers and radio broadcasts about the noted Nazi hunter Simon Wiesenthal. Imagining Wiesenthal's home as a big game hunter's trophy room, Momik determines to write to this man and engage his help in tracking the beast. At least, he figures, he might ask for some tips: do the animals congregate in large herds? what kind of prey do they pursue? and so on. By trapping and overcoming the evil, he feels, he can restore his parents to wholeness and their former power. His ambition is to reconstruct the stories they never told him, and to become a writer by weaving these tales into a heroic narrative. Momik is convinced, for example, that his father was a kind of emperor and a war hero. He knows that his parents have been in camps "THERE," but he interprets this fact in a way commensurate with his own understanding, supposing that the adults he knows from THERE all lived together at a military base, training for glorious exploits. Momik is puzzled by the knowledge that there were trains at the camps, but he surmises that the scene must have resembled Westerns in which Indians attack the mail train and settlers defend their railroad.

He gradually finds out more and more, though, largely through books he reads at the library. Bella, too, finally agrees to answer his questions, as he presses her more and more insistently to explain to him about death camps, torture, and atrocity. At this point the boy's faith in reason begins to break down and he becomes more and more disturbed by what he learns. Pushed to too-early an awareness, he reverts to what looks like immature behavior. Instead of acting smart, capable, and reliable, he indulges in temper tantrums and disquieting make-believe, and then moves on to desperately irrational acts. Unable to eat, to sleep, or concentrate at school, he reaches a final crisis when he lures a group of elderly survivors down to his cellar to try to coax the Beast out. The bewildered old people find the walls covered with pictures Momik has drawn of death trains, hangings, mass graves, and crematoria.

As was clear from his view of trains at the camps, based on Westerns, Momik relies on a variety of literary models to understand his world. The Bible, Jules Verne, adventure stories written by his grand-uncle, and other texts all come into play in his thinking. Down in the cellar he makes one last appeal to those models to help him. Calling on fantasy, he adjures the old people to tempt the Beast: "Now, now, go on, be wizards and prophets and witches and let's give it one more battle, be so Jewish it won't know what to do with itself" (83). Then, furious at the survivors for not having fought back against their persecutors, he wishes for a time machine, à la Jules Verne, that would allow him to turn back the clock and defeat Hitler himself. While Orlev's Alex draws inspiration and strength from a juvenile classic, *Robinson Crusoe,* and while Begley's adult draws on Dante to help interpret his own hell, here the literary intertexts fail. What Momik confronts is too terrible to be interpreted in those old frames of reference. As Hanuš Hochenberg wrote in Terezín, rejecting another kind of intertext—the folklore of childhood—"Bloody words and a dead day then / That's something different than bogie men."

Momik breaks down entirely, as, amidst the animals crying out, flapping and beating at their cages, he falls to the floor and in a strange, wordless, inhuman scream urges the Beast to come out. This action brings about a new reversal of adult and child roles. The boy collapses, and the old people he has herded about become protective of him. Murmuring with inarticulate pity, they gather about him, and he welcomes their concern, hoping vaguely that the Beast will not be able to get at him once he is surrounded by the ring of old Jews. The outcome allows no room for simplistic resolution, though. The text notes: "but when he opened his eyes and saw them all around him, tall and ancient, gazing at him with pity, he knew with all his nine-and-a-half year old *alter kopf* intelligence that it was too late now" (86). Momik's precocious intelligence, maturity, and responsibility do not protect him; once again he is the child and they the adults, and even all of them together are no match for the Nazi Beast. With this realization Momik has also moved far beyond his early and naive perception of the "Nazi Beast" as some kind of creature. His interpretation of that phrase gave it new vitality and impact, inadvertently endowing past evils with palpable longevity. It is thanks to his creative misreading, which is more than a metaphor or a conceit, that the child character finally realizes just how great a terror his parents had faced. And it is through exploration of the child's inner life and Momik's dramatic attempts to grapple with the Beast that the author creates riveting images of the parents' suffering as a crushing, enduring, emotional force that cannot but affect the second generation as well.

This ending refuses to prettify or simplify the matter of how to protect the innocence of the child. The horror is too great for the imagination, and neither the child nor the artist can transform it, domesticate it, or render it less potent. The text, with its steady focus on the destructive effect these experiences exert on the child, serves, too, as a painful and sobering reminder that the Holocaust fostered not just heroism, bravery, and early maturity. The horror took its toll as an undeniably devastating and hideous force. Only at times did it lead to ennobling actions or responses. Historian George Eisen writes that many children who experienced the Holocaust grew up prematurely, at least mentally, but "psychological regression to almost infantile behavior became a common phenomenon" as well (23). Grossman's novel suggests that, nonetheless, not to deal with these issues, to maintain silence and secrecy, is no protection against them. And imaginative writing may offer some insight into how to remember the past or speak about it to the next generations.

NOTES

1. For historical accounts of childhood and children's lives during the Holocaust, see Eisen, and Dwork.

2. For comments by the author on the uneasy relationship of his fiction to autobiography, and on the need to fictionalize his past, see Begley's "Who the Novelist Really Is."

Judith Grossman has commented astutely on *Wartime Lies.* She notes that the age of the child is of great significance with regard to the theme of deception. In Yehuda Nir's autobiographical *Lost Childhood,* she finds evidence that older children managed better with multiple identities and deceptions.

3. For extended discussion of Appelfeld's, Kosinski's and Orlev's novels, see Sokoloff. For comments on the child as myth and symbol in literary treatments of the Holocaust, see Ezrahi (157–58).

4. This is Mintz's apt description of one of Appelfeld's young characters (219).

5. To put the children's creations into perspective with the other artistic efforts at Terezín, see Green.

6. Mendelsohn finds in these poems "austere majesty" and goes so far as to claim that the Holocaust stimulated that rare phenomenon, "literarily competent material actually penned by children" (80). There is no doubt that the poems are immensely moving, but I would argue that the circumstances of their composition make them so, more than any sustained artistic skills they demonstrate.

Uri Orlev's *The Lead Soldiers* is of interest in this regard, because it turns children's wartime poetry into an overt thematic element. The novel concentrates extensively on the child's perceptions of events, contrasts these with explicit commentary of the adult, who has the wisdom of hindsight, and includes poems that the young protagonist writes. As Shaked (1970, 1989) notes, the poems may seem ordinary expressions of *weltschmerz*, particularly when the young character has become an adolescent, but the words take on much greater resonance as expressions of the Holocaust.

7. For an excellent discussion of adolescent writing and the diary of Anne Frank, see Dalsimer.

8. These are but a few of the poems preserved at the Jewish Museum in Prague. The entire collection cries out for extended literary study and, though the situation of their writing was unique, these poems merit comparison with writing by children in other wartime circumstances.

My thanks to Dr. Alexander Putik of the Jewish Museum in Prague for sharing with me an inventory of unpublished materials. It should be noted that a handsome new edition of *I Never Saw Another Butterfly* was published after this essay was completed (New York: Schocken, 1993). This expanded edition was prepared by the U.S. Holocaust Memorial Museum.

9. Another juvenile novel by Orlev, *The Man from the Other Side*, makes for instructive contrast. In this text an older narrator clearly points out differences in his perceptions at the time of the writing and at the time of the narrated events. Such self-conscious commentary is singularly absent in *The Island on Bird Street.*

10. Orlev's *The Lead Soldiers*, an early novel, makes for instructive contrast. Aimed at adults, this text similarly recounts childhood experiences in the ghettoes. The narrative is often fragmentary, burdened by flitting changes of perspective and a proliferation of characters and setting that make the storyline hard for the reader to follow. The incoherence suggests the child's disorientation due to the trauma of war, and it also reflects a certain artistic immaturity on the part of the author. *The Island on Bird Street* is quite a different text. All is sequential and orderly, both in the narration and in the narrated events.

11. For example, in *Ḥayat haḥoshekh* (The Beast of Darkness) a little boy is convinced that a beast lives under his bed, but only comes out at night. By befriending the beast he learns to cope with the death of his father in Israel's 1973 war.

12. On Israeli literary responses to the Holocaust, see Mintz.

13. For opinions on this issue and for surveys of juvenile titles, in English, that deal with the Holocaust, see Kimmel, Farnham, Harrison, Sherman, and Bosmajian. My thanks to Margo MacVicar-Whelan for suggestions she made on additional bibliography while I was preparing this paper.

14. "Momik" is the first section of the novel *See Under: Love* (in Hebrew, *'Ayen 'erekh ahavah*). While it is part of a longer novel, it can be read comfortably as a self-contained novella.

15. Grossman's interest in children's voices comes through in his other literary work, especially *Gan Rikki* (Rikki's Kindergarten). In this play all the characters are four-year-olds, and the actors who play these parts use distinctively childish diction.

Works Cited

Appelfeld, Aharon. *Masot beguf rishon.* Jerusalem: Hasifriah Hatsionit, 1979.

Begley, Louis. *Wartime Lies.* New York: Alfred A. Knopf, 1991.

———. "Who the Novelist Really Is." *The New York Times Book Review,* 16 August 1992. I, 22–23.

Bosmajian, Hamida. "Narrative Voice in Young Readers' Fiction about Nazism, the Holocaust, and Nuclear War." In *The Voice of the Narrator in Children's Literature: Insights from Writers and Critics,* ed. Charlotte F. Otten and Gary D. Schmidt, 308–24. New York: Greenwood Press, 1989.

Butler, Francelia, and Richard Rotert, eds. *Triumphs of the Spirit in Children's Literature.* Hamden, CT: Library Professional Publications, 1986.

Dalsimer, Katherine. *Female Adolescence: Psychoanalytic Reflections on Literature.* New Haven: Yale University Press, 1986.

Dwork, Debórah. *Children with a Star: Jewish Youth in Nazi Europe.* New Haven: Yale University Press, 1991.

Eisen, George. *Children and Play in the Holocaust.* Amherst, MA: University of Massachusetts Press, 1988.

Ezrahi, Sidra Dekoven. *By Words Alone: The Holocaust in Literature.* Chicago: University of Chicago Press, 1980.

Farnham, James T. "Holocaust Literature for Children: The Presentation of Evil." *University of Hartford Studies in Literature: A Journal of Interdisciplinary Criticism* 18.2–3 (1986): 55–82.

Green, Gerald. *The Artists of Terezín.* New York: Hawthorn Books, 1969.

Grossman, David. *'Ayen 'erekh ahavah.* Jerusalem: Hakibbutz Hameuchad, 1986.

———. *See Under: Love.* Trans. Betsy Rosenberg. New York: Farrar, Strauss, Giroux, 1989.

Grossman, Judith. Review of *Wartime Lies. The New York Times Book Review* (5 May 1991): I, 27.

Harrison, Barbara. "Howl Like the Wolves." *Children's Literature* 15 (1987): 66–90.

Kimmel, Eric. "Confronting the Ovens: The Holocaust in Juvenile Fiction." *Horn Book Magazine* 53 (1977): 84–91.

Mendelsohn, Leonard M. "The Survival of the Spirit in Holocaust Literature for and about Children." In *Triumphs of the Spirit in Children's Literature,* ed. Francelia Butler and Richard Rotert, 76–87. Hamden CT: Library Professional Publications, 1986.

Mintz, Alan. *Hurban: Responses to Catastrophe in Hebrew Literature.* New York: Columbia University Press, 1984.

Orlev, Uri. *Ha'i birhov hatsiporim.* Jerusalem: Keter, 1981.

———. *Ha ish min hatsad ha'aher.* Jerusalem: Keter, 1988.

———. *Hayalei 'oferet.* Tel Aviv: Sifriat Poalim, 1956.

———. *Hayat hahoshekh* [The Beast of Darkness]. Tel Aviv: Am Oved, 1975.

————. *The Island on Bird Street.* Trans. Hillel Halkin. Boston: Houghton Mifflin, 1984.

————. *The Lead Soldiers.* Trans. Hillel Halkin. New York: Taplinger Publishing Company, 1979.

————. *The Man from the Other Side.* Trans. Hillel Halkin. Boston: Houghton Mifflin, 1991.

Shaked, Gershon. *Gal ḥadash basipporet ha'ivrit.* Merhavia: Hakibbutz Hameuchad, 1970.

————. Afterword. In *Facing the Holocaust,* ed. Gila Ramras-Rauch. Philadelphia: Jewish Publication Society, 1989.

Sherman, Ursula F. "Why Would a Child Want to Read about That? The Holocaust Period in Children's Literature." In *How Much Truth Do We Tell the Children? The Politics of Children's Literature,* ed. Betty Bacon, 173–84. Minneapolis: Marxist Educational Press, 1988.

Sokoloff, Naomi. *Imagining the Child in Modern Jewish Fiction.* Baltimore: Johns Hopkins University Press, 1992.

Volavková, Hana, ed. *I Never Saw Another Butterfly: Children's Drawings and Poems from Terezín Concentration Camp, 1942–1944.* Trans. Jeanne Němcová. New York: McGraw-Hill, 1976.

Is Anybody Out There Listening?
Fairy Tales and the Voice of the Child

MARIA TATAR

"They cannot represent themselves; they must be represented" (Marx 124). Karl Marx's famous pronouncement about French small-holding peasants has been cited to make the point that children depend on adults to advocate their needs in the social sphere and to depict their desires and anxieties in the aesthetic realm (Siemon and Wallace 13). That children lack voices, authority, and presence and that they are even more bereft of the power to represent themselves than Marx's peasants seems eminently clear if we imagine a child alone in a courtroom, trying to argue a legal case. In the judicial realm, children can assert their rights only through the authority of adult advocates—who make a case for the "best interests of the child."

Those who argue for "what is best for the child" are, to be sure, not necessarily representing the child's point of view. The legal profession is just beginning to ponder the critical distinction between "what is best for the child" and "what the child wants" by problematizing the relationship between attorney and child client and challenging the notion that a court-appointed attorney necessarily represents the child in the truest sense of the term. Children's voices can only be heard when they speak for themselves or are represented by attorneys prepared to serve as ventriloquists for the child. But we might pause here to ask whether it makes any sense at all to invest children with the authority to represent themselves, either as witnesses or through attorneys who argue their point of view. It depends, of course, on the age of the child. In the critical age range of seven to fourteen, children can often speak intelligently about their needs, yet they cannot necessarily sort out the complicated family issues that bring them to the courtroom in the first place and that become even more emotionally charged through the process of litigation.

275

While children have been and probably always will be excluded from participation in the actual production of laws, the judicial system has begun to create a space in which they can engage in a dialogue about the interpretation of those laws and participate in disentangling the problematic relations between adults and children. Once attorneys elect to represent the child's point of view, they can, however, become so enmeshed in legal conflicts with court-appointed experts that in the words of one legal analyst, "the kid is lost in the middle . . . just because a bunch of grownup attorneys are fighting with each other over her" (Hoffman). The move on the part of the American judicial system to authorize children's voices in the legal process may sometimes produce imperfect results or lead to self-defeating complications, but it can only be hailed as a salutary development in the struggle for children's rights.

In the literary sphere, as in the judicial realm, adults legislate the way in which children are represented. Children's literature is produced by adults—they write the books, edit them, publish them, market them, sell them, buy them, and (at least up to a certain age for children) read them out loud. As Jacqueline Rose has pointed out, children's fiction "sets up a world in which the adult comes first (author, maker, giver) and the child comes after (reader, product, receiver)" (1–2). In books for children, adults produce fictions of childhood, either recapturing their own experiences or creating stories about what it is like to see as a child does or to speak as a child does. In reconstructing this former self or constructing a fictional child, adult authors invariably use the child within the book to take in the child outside the book—to secure allegiance to the story and to the values represented in it (Rose 2).

Though children ceaselessly represent themselves in their private lives through pictures and in stories, few besides members of their immediate family pay much attention. Children can indeed raise their voices, but virtually no one bothers to listen; when their voices become too loud to ignore, there is usually irritation all around. Adults not only have almost exclusive control over the public production of words and images for children, they also have virtually exclusive rights when it comes to the task of interpretation. In this arena too, we have ignored the children outside the book, suppressed their voices, and failed to authorize the ways in which they negotiate the distance between their own childhood experiences and what is depicted in the stories written for them.

It is in the realm of interpretation—rather than in the actual material production of texts—that I see a missed opportunity for launching meaningful dialogues between children and adults about a subject that children's literature ceaselessly represents from one point of view alone: the relationship between children and adults. Readers, as we know from Wolfgang Iser and Stanley Fish, actively participate in the production of textual meaning, constructing new interpretations for texts as they engage in the process of reading. Iser observes that the literary text initiates " 'performances' of meaning rather than actually formulating meanings" (27). This is not to say that he endorses a form of uncontrolled subjectivism that licenses endless idiosyncratic recreations of a text. Iser emphasizes that literary texts are programmed with "intersubjectively verifiable instructions for meaning-production, but the meaning produced may then lead to a whole variety of different experiences and hence subjective judgments" (25).

Literary texts give us fixed words on a page—verbal signifiers that regulate interpretation and prevent it from slipping into the realm of the arbitrary. Fairy tales, on the other hand, are for the most part unstable "texts." They may have reached print in one or another of their variant forms, yet the words used to tell a particular version do not constitute a definitive text. In cultures predating the printing press and general adult literacy, these stories were created through performance—the tellers of tales collaborated with audiences to produce new stories based on old ones. The knowing laughter or approving nods of listeners authorized continued use and further elaboration of an episode; silent indifference or voiced derision turned listeners into agents of censorship for sensitive narrators. Tales like "Little Red Riding Hood" and "Snow White" were cast into canonical form by Perrault and by the Grimms, yet over time, even those versions of the stories have been reshaped and rewritten as they were received by new communities of readers. American books and films based on stories in collections by Perrault or the Grimms, for example, have never slavishly adhered to the letter of those texts. The performance of meaning for fairy tales thus becomes both an intratextual and an extratextual matter, one enacted by (re)writers of the tale, who rescript stories passed on to them, and by its readers, who collaborate with the (re)writers to negotiate yet another production of textual meaning.

Few books have done more in recent times to shape the performance of meaning for fairy tale texts than Bruno Bettelheim's *Uses of Enchantment.* Bettelheim, who endorses the notion of bibliotherapy, positions the child as the recipient of moral instruction and therapeutic intervention. By implication, adults exercise hegemonic power over the domain of textual production and interpretation, generating stories designed to regulate a child's desires. Fairy tales, Bettelheim asserts, can be mobilized to help children "master the psychological problems of growing up—overcoming narcissistic disappointments, oedipal dilemmas, sibling rivalries, becoming able to relinquish childhood dependencies; gaining a feeling of selfhood and self-worth, and a sense of moral obligation" (6–7).

Utterly absent from Bettelheim's account is an attempt to read the stories from the child's point of view—to validate the protagonists' feelings and actions or to empathize with their plights. The villains of the tales produced by Bettelheim's reading are never real threats to the child, nor are they endowed with perfidiously evil traits. Instead, they are nothing more than projections and externalizations of the child's own "badness." Take the case of the wolf in "The Three Little Pigs":

> The wolf . . . is obviously a bad animal because it wants to destroy. The wolf's badness is something the young child recognizes within himself: his wish to

devour, and its consequence—the anxiety about possibly suffering such a fate himself. So the wolf is an externalization, a projection of the child's badness—and the story tells how this can be dealt with constructively. (44)

Time and again we hear about this "badness," about "how violent, anxious, destructive, and even sadistic a child's imagination is" (120).

The adult figures in Bettelheim's interpretations, by contrast, can do no wrong. The father and stepmother of Hansel and Gretel, for example, never really plot to desert their children; rather, the two children, feeling "threatened by complete rejection and desertion," project their "inner anxiety onto those they fear might cut them off." In just a few pages, Bettelheim manages to accuse Hansel and Gretel of "denial and regression," "destructive desires," "uncontrolled craving," "oral greediness," "unrestrained giving in to gluttony," "cannibalistic inclinations," "untamed id impulses," "uncontrolled voraciousness," "primitive orality," and "oral anxiety" (160–65). Children who have not yet made the passage through Bettelheim's therapeutic course of action are the real monsters of fairy tales, relentless in their desires, demands, and accusations.

Even more astonishing than Bettelheim's demonization of the oedipal child is his inflated notion of the therapeutic benefits of a story like "Hansel and Gretel." The conclusion to the story shows us a child who has "overcome his [*sic*] oedipal difficulties, mastered his oral anxieties, sublimated those of his cravings which cannot be satisfied realistically, and learned that wishful thinking has to be replaced by intelligent action" (165). "Independence in thought and action," along with "self-reliance," constitutes the ideals to which the child both inside and outside the book is to be guided. Bettelheim applauds a conclusion that shows Hansel and Gretel becoming parents to their parents: "As dependent children they had become a burden to their parents; on their return they have become the family's support, as they bring home the treasures they have gained" (164). This agenda seems all the more far-fetched when we consider that Bettelheim views the story as having its "greatest appeal and value for the child at the age when fairy tales begin to exercise their beneficial impact, that is, *around the age of four or five*" (15; my emphasis).

Bettelheim's interpretations are predicated on the notion that adults/parents have mastered their anxieties, gained control over their desires, and lead serene lives, free of conflict. Children, by contrast, are volatile, unruly creatures whose every action is dictated by the pleasure principle. This denial of adult wrongdoing and insistence that the evil traits of fairy tale villains represent projections onto adults rather than reflections or distortions of real adult behavior is the dominant interpretive move in *The Uses of Enchantment*, a book that silences the child with almost unparalleled determination. In subjecting children to a therapeutic course of action through fairy tales, Bettelheim also denies them their own subjectivity and thus defeats the very goals that he sets them.

Scholars who have heeded the voices of children telling their own stories reveal a great deal about what happens to fairy tales when the interpretive energies of children are released. In studying the child as speaking subject, John Pickering and Steve Attridge observe that tales told by children blend tradition and innovation: cultural stories (frequently fairy tales) are reproduced even as personal elements are introduced to engender a new order (425). Monsters in these narratives are overdetermined—rather than being mere personifications of the child's defects, they can function *simultaneously* as doubles of the self (a self that fears rejection), of the parents (with all the attendant distortion one would expect from a child familiar with "Jack and the Beanstalk" or "Snow White"), or they may simply stand for the host of both specific and diffuse dangers in real life.

Children generally rewrite the cultural stories told to them by emphasizing the dangers (usually in the form of one monster or another) that imperil the protagonists. The ways in which these threats are countered vary greatly depending on the teller, though there is a strong correlation between age and the four levels of narrative strategies defined in Brian Sutton-Smith's study of children's "folkstories." At the first level, the protagonist of the story is threatened or overcome by a monster; at the second, the protagonist escapes or is rescued; at the third, the threat is neutralized in some way; at the fourth, a complete transformation takes place so that the threat is removed in perpetuity. The progression in the narrative strategies may seem at first blush to correspond with a child's growing sense of control over the world, but it may also simply reflect an older child's need to create in fantasy a sense of security that does not exist in the real world. At the fourth level, we find endings like the following: "So the fox went to live with the tiger and he was *never lonely again*"; "And so the family was safe and sound *for ever and ever* and they ate cookies and juice and invited Grandma over to eat with them"; or "His father said that the boy had been transformed. His mother, brothers, and sisters thought so too. At school he was *always* laughing. And he laughed *every day from then on* [the end of a story about a boy who could not laugh]" (Sutton-Smith 255, 197; Obrig 59–60; my emphasis). The italicized words mark a need to insulate the subjects of the story from the initial lack or threat and to ensure an untroubled present and future.

Children's narratives take a turn very different from those found in the fairy tales written for them. Whatever inspires fear and creates danger in children's stories is "made safe, or at least, manageable" (Pickering and Attridge 425). The strength of the protagonist lies in an ability to tame what is threatening or to take a conciliatory stand that accommodates the initial threat and leads to a peaceful resolution of conflicts. Empirical studies of children's storytelling differentiate to some extent on the basis of gender: boys often construct happy endings that stage a confrontation leading to a conquest of the villain and a resolution of differences, while girls resolve conflicts with other characters by establishing alliances and affiliating themselves with mediating powers (Sutton-Smith 24; Wardetzky 169).

When children reinterpret canonical cultural stories by retelling them, they are at pains to produce happy endings for the entire cast of characters. Heads

279

rarely roll, witches are not sent down hills in barrels studded with nails, and no one dances to death in red-hot iron shoes. Usually it is only imaginary creatures, such as dragons, who are put to death. In her extensive study of children's fashionings of fairy tales, Kristin Wardetzky has observed that the children whose narratives she studied invented "comparatively harmless demises. . . . Not a trace of sadistic blood-curdling revenge, no perfidious cruelty, no aggressive retaliation" (164). These youthful tellers (all were in the range of eight to ten years) did not invest their stories with issues of separation and autonomy—what was at stake was the resolution of conflicts and the reconstitution of a stable and harmonious family. For them, it was less important to kill monsters than to befriend them and to persuade others to accept them, warts and all.

A look at virtually any classic fairy tale reveals that variants of the story all have different endings—in many cases dramatically different endings. It may be true that Cinderella always lives happily ever after with the prince, but her stepsisters suffer a variety of fates. After the Grimms' Aschenputtel marries the prince, birds peck out the eyes of her stepsisters to punish them for their "wickedness and malice" (92). But even this punishment seems relatively mild when compared to what befalls other stepsisters. An Indonesian Cinderella forces her stepsister into a cauldron of boiling water, then has the body cut up, pickled, and sent to the girl's mother as "salt meat" for her next meal (Philip 30–31). Or consider a Filipino "Cinderella," in which the stepmother and her daughters are "pulled to pieces by wild horses" (Philip 121). Other versions of the story reveal a lighter touch at work. A Tuscan "Cinderella" shows the stepsisters making fools of themselves by wearing so much make-up that they seem to be wearing masks (Philip 160). An Italian version, elegant in its simplicity, reveals the jealous girls to be "furious as dogs" when they hear that Cinderella has married a prince (Philip 78).

Despite the profusion of retaliatory punishments for the stepsisters, numerous Cinderella stories end on a conciliatory note. An Armenian Cinderella falls at the feet of her wicked sisters as they are leaving church, weeps copious tears with them, and ends up forgiving them (Philip 51). Perrault's version of the story is perhaps the fullest in its description of a reconciliation between the heroine and her sisters, who throw themselves at Cinderella's feet and beg her forgiveness "for all the ill-treatment she had suffered at their hands." Not only does this Cinderella, who is "as good as she was beautiful," forgive them, she also takes her sisters to live in the palace and loses no time in marrying them to "two gentlemen of high rank about the Court" (77).

Much as these placatory endings may offend those who believe that inflicting violent retaliatory punishments is a marker of the heroine's strength and an indicator of folkloric authenticity (Yolen 301–2), they are no less "true to the story" than any other ending and may in fact conform more closely to the ending desired by the child listening to the story. There is no reason to adhere to any fixed script for the fate of the stepsisters—especially when addressing children in the age range when fairy tales have their greatest appeal. This is one of the points in the story where an adult can take the measure of the story with the child and can collaborate in producing a satisfying ending—one that may be retaliatory, conciliatory, or anything in between. Cinderella has been reinvented by so many different cultures that it hardly makes sense to decree that she must be cruel and vindictive or kind and forgiving. Looking at different versions of "Cinderella," we find that some heroines are genteel and selfless, others are clever and enterprising, and still others are coy and helpless (Bottigheimer 1992, 102–14). To stabilize the traits of this folk heroine is to declare that we live in a world that knows no change and is unwilling to interrogate the values passed on to us by those living in other times and in other places.

Empirical studies of children's storytelling reveal not only a need for endings that bring everyone into a relation of happy dependence but also an insistence on a wholly uncritical attitude to the protagonist. In stories produced by children, Kristin Wardetzky observes, the protagonists are never cast in the role of transgressors. Commands are always observed—in stark contrast to the interdiction/transgression established by Vladimir Propp as one of the fundamental narrative moves of the folk tale. Curiosity is "*not* punished, but rewarded," Wardetzky notes (165; emphasis in original). In short, each and every action of the protagonist is validated and builds toward a peaceful resolution.

Since fairy-tale heroes and heroines often function as agents of transgression, it has been easy enough to turn their stories into lessons on the evils of curiosity and disobedience (Tatar 22–50). No heroine has suffered more trials and tribulations (to quote Jack Zipes) in this respect than "Little Red Riding Hood," which has been transformed from a bawdy folktale into a story about what Bettelheim calls the "pleasure-seeking oedipal child" (172), only because Red Riding Hood disobeys her mother's command not to stray from the path (Bettelheim 172).

Gender issues, as Ruth B. Bottigheimer has shown, further complicate the question of transgression (1987, 81–94). In the Grimms' collection, for example, female protagonists are invariably severely punished for their curiosity. Mary's child, in the tale of that title, opens a door forbidden to her and has each child to which she gives birth taken from her; Bluebeard's wife is nearly put to death for a similar deed—her act of uxorial disobedience is condemned, even though the interdiction she violates is issued by a serial murderer; the youthful protagonist of "Dame Trudy" ends up as a log that fuels the title character's fire. For male protagonists, by contrast, curiosity often opens the door to one adventure after another. "The Golden Bird," for example, shows us a hero who is so distracted by the wonders of the world that he is forever disobeying commands—yet each transgression takes him closer to his goal and thereby takes on a positive coloring.

As we tell fairy tales to our children, we need to bear in mind that the concept of transgressive behavior is highly elastic and that numerous cultural variables—gender being one among them—determine the way in which it is evaluated. Even those who disapprove of conformity and idealize resistance to social regulation are often perfectly willing to endorse children's stories that advocate compliant behavior and condemn disobedience and curiosity. As we select and read stories to children, we need to reflect in particular on how judgments about transgressive behavior are encoded in the story's words and in the virtual text we construct. "Bluebeard" does not necessarily have to be read as a cautionary tale warning girls of the perils of curiosity and disobedience; critical readers can see, even in Perrault's rendition, with its irrelevant historical *moralités*, a celebration of the heroine's resistance to blind obedience. To be sure, not all fairy-tale heroes and heroines can be turned into models representing the particular traits we wish to cultivate in children. As George Cruikshank railed more than a century ago, some fairy tales (he had "Puss in Boots" in mind) give us "a succession of success-ful falsehoods—a clever lesson in lying!—a system of imposture rewarded by the greatest worldly advantage!" (3). But listening to the voice of the child outside the book can often give us a judicious second opinion about the behavior of the child within the book.

Many of the words in the fairy-tale collections that have become part of our cultural heritage make them resistant to the challenge of reshaping and rewriting. The Grimms' "Jew in the Thornbush," a starkly anti-Semitic story that was in-cluded in special children's editions of the tales, is a strong reminder that what nineteenth-century adults read to children is not necessarily appropriate bedtime reading today. But many of the tales that have been recorded over time lend themselves to critical appropriation, especially if we consider the malleability of the stories—the way in which they are part of an oral tradition that was constantly subject to revision by tellers and listeners alike. These texts can serve as opportuni-ties for creating new stories—for cooperative and collaborative performances of meaning enacted by adult *and* child.

WORKS CITED

Bettelheim, Bruno. *The Uses of Enchantment: The Meaning and Importance of Fairy Tales.* New York: Random House, 1976.

Bottigheimer, Ruth B. "Fairy Tales and Children's Literature: A Feminist Perspective." In *Teaching Children's Literature: Issues, Pedagogy, Resources,* ed. Glenn Edward Sadler, 101–18. New York: Modern Language Association, 1992.

———. *Grimms' Bad Girls and Bold Boys: The Moral and Social Vision of the Tales.* New Haven: Yale University Press, 1987.

Cruikshank, George, ed. and illus. *Puss in Boots.* London: David Bogue, 1853.

Fish, Stanley. *Is There a Text in This Class? The Authority of Interpretive Communities.* Cam-bridge: Harvard University Press, 1980.

Grimm, Jacob, and Wilhelm Grimm. *The Complete Fairy Tales of the Brothers Grimm.* Trans. Jack Zipes. New York: Bantam, 1987.

Hoffman, Jan. "When a Child-Client Disagrees with the Lawyer." *New York Times* (28 August 1992): 136.

Iser, Wolfgang. *The Act of Reading: A Theory of Aesthetic Response.* Baltimore: The Johns Hopkins University Press, 1978.

Marx, Karl. *The Eighteenth Brumaire of Louis Bonaparte.* New York: International Publishers, 1963.

Obrig, Ilse. *Kinder erzählen Geschichten weiter* (München: Beck, 1934).

Perrault, Charles. *Perrault's Fairy Tales.* Trans. A. E. Johnson. New York: Dover, 1969.

Philip, Neil, ed. *The Cinderella Story: The Origins and Variations of the Story Known as "Cinderella".* London: Penguin, 1989.

Pickering, John, and Steve Attridge. "Viewpoints: Metaphor and Monsters— Children's Storytelling." *Research in the Teaching of English* 24 (1990): 415–40.

Propp, Vladimir. *Morphology of the Folktale.* Trans. Laurence Scott. 2d rev. ed. Austin: University of Texas Press, 1968.

Rose, Jacqueline. *The Case of Peter Pan or The Impossibility of Children's Fiction.* London: Macmillan, 1984.

Siemon, Stephen, and Jo-Ann Wallace. "Into the Heart of Darkness? Teaching Children's Literature as a Problem in Theory." *Canadian Children's Literature* 63 (1991): 6–23.

Sutton-Smith, Brian. *The Folkstories of Children.* Philadelphia: University of Pennsylvania Press, 1981.

Tatar, Maria. *Off with Their Heads! Fairy Tales and the Culture of Childhood.* Princeton: Princeton University Press, 1992.

Wardetzky, Kristin. "The Structure and Interpretation of Fairy Tales Composed by Children." *Journal of American Folklore* 103 (1990): 157–76.

Yolen, Jane. "America's Cinderella." In *Cinderella: A Casebook,* ed. Alan Dundes, 294– 306. Madison: University of Wisconsin Press, 1988.

Zipes, Jack, ed. *The Trials and Tribulations of Little Red Riding Hood: Versions of the Tale in Sociocultural Context.* South Hadley, MA: Bergin and Garvey, 1983.

Modulate Your Voice, Please

MARK JONATHAN HARRIS

It is a late Sunday morning in the fall of 1946. My father and I, wearing matching leather jackets, are visiting Nay Aug Park Zoo in Scranton, Pennsylvania. The air is thick with the smell of straw and animal droppings and roasted peanuts. There is another man with us, a neighbor whose face has vanished from my memory. I don't know why he's accompanied us—he has no children of his own to lure him here—yet he is walking with us, smoking a pipe as I remember—although I could be imagining that now to make up for his forgotten face.

The zoo is a dirty, dreary place with cramped cages and listless animals who evoke more pity than wonder. But that is an adult view, formed by visits over many years. I can no longer recall how I felt about the zoo as a child. Did I laugh at the chattering monkeys? Did I clutch my father's hand in fear at the snakes coiled behind the glass? Or did I feel some sympathy for the aging lion, staring blankly out at us, his face pressed against the bars?

As a writer, I want to fill in these lost details because I need to set the scene for what I do vividly remember about that Sunday. I want to convey how much I adore my father and how thrilled I am to be with him, even though he is probably paying more attention to his friend. So I imagine that he lifts me up to throw some peanuts to the monkeys and that he continues to hold my hand after we pass by the boa constrictor, and that he buys me cotton candy to eat as we walk back to the car.

The car is new—our family's first—a black Pontiac sedan purchased a few months earlier. I remember my father driving it triumphantly home from work as I waited for him, as I did each evening, at the front window of our apartment. But now, when we reach the place along the road where he has parked, the Pontiac is no longer there. Stunned, we look down the hillside. The car has plunged down the steep slope and come to rest in the brush and rocks forty yards below. For a moment everyone is speechless. Then the neighbor, who after this Sunday has no other role in my life, sucks on his pipe and says to my father, "You didn't put on the hand brake, Norman." The look on my father's face acknowledges that he is right. He stares at the car in confusion. Other people stop to gape or laugh. I am not sure exactly what is happening, but I know they're making fun of my father. The man I eagerly watch for every night at the front window, looks helpless, lost. I want to come to his rescue, but I don't know how. I begin to cry . . .

After forty-five years, why does this memory still haunt me? As a five-year-old, how much of this experience had I language to express? a conceptual framework with which to understand? And what of that Sunday morning did I really experience as a child, and what have I invented later? As a writer of children's books, these questions are ones I constantly confront as I shift back and forth between a child's and an adult's perspective in an attempt to understand the formative experiences of childhood.

Children—and adults as well—don't have to understand the significance of their experience to be profoundly affected by it. Although I could not have articulated it at the time, I saw something that Sunday I had never seen before—my father's fallibility. The accident revealed him in a new way, one that was painful for both of us. I understood that he was to blame for the car's slide down the ravine and that he was ashamed because of it.

Yet, thinking about it now, I wonder if I also recognized the contempt in our neighbor's voice, realized the extent of my father's humiliation. Even now, I'm not sure why our neighbor was so contemptuous of my father's mistake. Had my father driven him to the park to impress him with our new car? Also, why did my father suffer his contempt in silence? Why, in fact, did he feel so defeated by what, after all, was such a minor accident? A tow truck came a short while later and pulled the car up the slope and we drove home. In retrospect, my father's paralysis, his helplessness, seem out of proportion to what prompted them. Perhaps because I sensed but could not voice all this as a child, I've kept coming back to it as an adult to try to clarify its impact on me.

Recently I asked my parents about what they remembered of the incident. My mother, who was not there that Sunday, remembered it as the neighbor's car which had rolled down the ravine. My father acknowledged that it was his Pontiac, but he blamed the accident on the failure of the car's brakes.

Our differing recollections of that day are another reason, I believe, that the memory of our car at the bottom of the culvert has remained such a powerful image for me. In many ways, this event, and its aftermath, crystallize my childhood. And, like most writers, my childhood has strongly influenced the kind of books I write.

When I was growing up in Scranton, our family was considered a model in the community. My father was a successful lawyer, my mother an energetic housewife, my sister and I bright, well-behaved, honor students as well as Curved Bar and Eagle scouts. But, like many American families, our emotional lives were very constricted. My family's denial of the events that occurred that Sunday at the zoo was typical of the way we processed painful experiences.

Not too long ago I was in a toy store and witnessed a scene that epitomized my own childhood. A four-year-old boy was eyeing a baby doll. Maybe the mother was in a hurry, or the doll was too expensive, or perhaps she thought her son was too old to play with female dolls, but she peremptorily pulled him away from the display. The little boy began to cry. "I want that doll," he sobbed. The harried mother, trying to flee the store as quickly as possible, grabbed him by the arm and pulled him toward the door. "Stop that!" she admonished. "You don't really want that doll."

That was how my parents often responded to situations that upset them. Many of the feelings I had as a child were considered either unjustified or improper. Anger, for example, was not considered to be polite. Angry people had poor breeding. My parents rarely raised their voices. If they were angry at each other, or at us, they often expressed it by not talking. Their silence conveyed their displeasure and disappointment, but not much more information.

This repression of feeling—the avoidance of messy emotions like anger, resentment, or grief—is characteristic of many families in our society. My parents' repression was relatively benign. "Modulate your voice, please," my mother would say when we showed the first signs of anger, or "You don't smile enough," she'd tell my sister when she was sad. Other families shame or punish their children for displaying the same feelings. We can all cite familiar examples: "Stop that whimpering or I'll give you something real to cry about." Or when a child is shy or fearful: "Quit being such a sissy." Or what a mother told a friend of mine whenever she was angry: "Look at that face. Nobody will want to marry you with a face like that."

Instead of recognizing and accepting these emotions in our children, we try to pretend they aren't there. The denial of what happened at the zoo made my own confused emotions even more bewildering. In a world where adults shame you for your feelings, or tell you that *you* don't want a doll because *they* don't want you to have one, or that what you saw didn't really happen, it can be difficult to make sense of what you're experiencing.

As children we all want to please our parents, retain their love, as limited as it may sometimes be. We quickly learn to suppress feelings they can't tolerate, to ignore perceptions they don't want to hear. Parents often call this process maturation. "He's growing up into such a nice boy," meaning he's responsive to all their cues and has accepted both their spoken and unspoken rules of social behavior.

Some children rebel, of course, and challenge their family's value system. Although rebellion may cause turmoil, it can also guarantee attention. In children starved for love, negative attention is better than no attention at all. "I don't know what I'm going to do with that child. He's impossible." But he can't be ignored either.

Most children experiment with both approaches. As a child, I came up with my own solution. Since displaying grown-up traits was so important to my parents I tried hard to please them and began, at an early age, to act far older than my years. (In very young children this precocious maturity is often regarded as "cute.") The cost of adopting this pose was high, though, and to make room for all those other unacceptable emotions, I created three imaginary brothers— Morris, Neal, and Bruce, all of whom were much bolder and more daring than I. Morris was very outspoken and used "bad language." Neal had a violent temper that got him into so much trouble that he frequently had to be locked up in jail. And Bruce was a lady's man. He kept getting married and divorced.

Although I still retain a strong sense of each of my imaginary brother's personalities, I don't remember many specific details of their behavior in my childhood. There is one story that my mother tells so often about Morris, though, that I almost believe I can recall it myself. One winter day when I was three and she was impatiently dressing me in boots and snowsuit so I could accompany her to a place where I no doubt had no desire to go, I suddenly turned to Morris and politely, but firmly (in my most adult voice) told him to shut up. As intended, this caught my mother's attention, and she asked me why I found it necessary to silence Morris. "I'm sorry," I apologized, "but I had to do that. Morris was calling you bad names."

My imaginary brothers appeared in my life some time around the age of two and lasted until the birth of my sister when I was five. Then they disappeared. My parents thought they vanished because there was now another child in the family, another companion. That may have been part of it, but I think my brothers disappeared because the feelings and perceptions they had allowed me to express were becoming more dangerous and unmanageable. Not even Morris was brave enough to bring up my father's humiliation at the park.

Five was also the age I learned to read and began to take refuge in books. Books are still one of the most important ways children can test their beliefs and perceptions without having to defend them against disapproving peers or parents. They also allow children, and all of us, to extend the range of our experience, to indulge in, if only vicariously, emotions not possible in our ordinary lives.

Alison Lurie has written that, "Most of the great works of juvenile literature are subversive in one way or another: they express ideas and emotions not generally approved of or even recognized at the time; they make fun of honored figures and piously-held beliefs; and they view social pretenses with clear-eyed directness, remarking—as in Andersen's famous tale—that the emperor has no clothes" (4).

When I was growing up, there was not the richness of contemporary children's books there is today. There were rebels like Tom Sawyer and Huck Finn and Peter Pan, but not enough stubborn nay-sayers like Maurice Sendak's Pierre, and too few tenchant observers of adult foolishness and hypocrisy like Harriet in Louise Fitzhugh's *Harriet the Spy*, or children with the splendid and sustaining anger of Katherine Paterson's Gilly Hopkins. The strongest role model I could find for the anger I was discouraged from expressing was Edmund Dantes, Alexander Dumas's falsely imprisoned hero in the *The Count of Monte Cristo*. I thrilled to Dantes's escape from prison and the righteousness of his coldly calculated revenge.

Many scenes from the books I read in my youth remain more vivid than my own childhood. I remember the copious tears I shed at Dora's death in *David Copperfield* and at Sydney Carton's sacrifice at the end of *A Tale of Two Cities*. To cry over my own disappointments, my real or imagined deprivations, was childish self-indulgence; to weep over Dickens was a sign of maturity. Memories of my own life are often muddied, indistinct. Because of my desire to please my parents, I dismissed or disregarded so many of my immediate responses as a child that they are now lost or inaccessible. Writing children's books is one way I've attempted to recover them.

P. L. Travers has said that one writes not so much for the child one used to be as the child one always is. She writes: "You do not chop off a section of your imaginative substance and make a book specifically for children for—if you are honest—you have, in fact, no idea where childhood ends and maturity begins. It's all endless and all one" (quoted in Cott 204).

Speaking of men who write children's books, Zilpha Keatley Snyder told me once, "If you squint your eyes right, you can always see the little boy inside." Morris, Neal, and Bruce keep struggling to express themselves. The adult part of me continues to discipline and interpret them.

The books I write naturally reflect my own upbringing and experience. The children in them are usually struggling to be grown up. Often this means coping with adult problems, like divorce or homelessness, problems created by adults, but whose consequences children have to suffer. The children in my books often feel that if only they could just be good enough, do everything expected of them—or more—they could make things right again, restore their parents' marriage, get them jobs and homes, live happily ever after.

Yet, even though my protagonists may still cling to these magical childhood beliefs, they often see more clearly than the adults around them. As innocents, children can speak truths which adults—knowing the consequences of such candor—are reluctant to admit even to themselves. In my novel, *Confessions of a Prime Time Kid*, Meg wants to tell what it's really like to be a child actor. Her agent is firmly opposed to the idea. "Writing your memoirs at 13 is in *extremely* bad taste," the agent warns. "If an actress is going to be rude enough to write her autobiography, she should at least have the good grace to wait until she's in her sixties and all the people she's gossiping about are dead. When you're too old to get any more good parts, then you can tell all" (p. 14).

Following in the literary tradition of other child heroines, Meg goes ahead and speaks her mind anyway. Writing in the guise of a child provides authors a wonderful cover for impertinence. The punishment for juvenile offenders is much more lenient than for adults who commit the same crime.

The conflicts between honesty and hypocrisy, truth and fantasy, reality and magical beliefs, are at the heart of many coming-of-age novels about 12- or 13-year-olds, the literary age that seems to demarcate childhood and adulthood. My protagonists struggle with these issues as they try to reconcile their astute perceptions of the world with their desire for happily-ever-after endings. It's a sometimes painful, sometimes exhilarating process, but, in the end, my characters usually reach some resolution—however tentative—that offers them hope for the future.

On my desk is a picture of my father and me taken in the fall of 1946, sometime around our visit to the zoo. We are posed in front of our house in our matching leather jackets. My father stands behind me, his long, slender fingers resting lightly on my shoulders. He wears a tie underneath his jacket and his smile is stiff, composed for the camera. His eyes, behind his rimless glasses, are shadowed, hidden. There is a softness, a vulnerability in his face. (Can others see this? Or is this just my own projection?)

I, on the other hand, look up brightly from beneath my cap at the unremembered photographer (perhaps my mother). My eyes are wide, my eyebrows lifted, my mouth half-open, my whole face alive with a child's eagerness to please.

I go to the mirror and study the face I see there now. I squint a little, and yes, despite the graying beard, I can still glimpse a little of that boy's eagerness and wonder; but also more of the father's pain than I would like to acknowledge.

I look at the boy in the photograph, his freshness, his innocence, and I want to protect him, shield him from all that I know is coming. I want to speak to the father too, to tell him to be stronger, more assertive, that he doesn't have to let people treat him so contemptuously, that if he expresses his anger more it would be easier to stand up for himself, and that I love him even though he doesn't. I think if I could have told him that when I was younger, or even later, it wouldn't have been so hard to say the same things to myself and to believe them. But the boy and his father are frozen in time.

So I write children's books instead, continuing the dialogue that Morris and I began as three-year-olds, trying to reconcile a child's feelings with an adult's understanding, in an ongoing debate that I suspect I am not alone in waging.

WORKS CITED

Cott, Jonathan. *Pipers at the Gates of Dawn: The Wisdom of Children's Literature.* New York: Random House, 1983.

Harris, Mark Jonathan. *Confessions of a Prime Time Kid.* Lothrop, Lee, and Shepard, 1985.

Lurie, Alison. *Don't Tell the Grown-ups: Subversive Children's Literature.* Boston: Little, Brown and Company, 1990.

Loud Sound

DAVID SHIELDS

At the same time I was earning a Master of Fine Arts degree at the University of Iowa Writers' Workshop, I was a patient in the same university's equally renowned Speech and Hearing Clinic. How had my life come to this, I wondered, shuttling back and forth between two four-story brick buildings, two houses of language? I was overwhelmed by the paradox that as a writer I could manipulate words but that as a stutterer I was at the mercy of them.

There are numerous novels—such as *Billy Budd*, *The Horse's Mouth*, *One Flew over the Cuckoo's Nest*, and *The World According to Garp*—that feature characters who stutter, but my novel, *Dead Languages*, is, I believe, the only one that takes as its principal subject the experience of stuttering. I wanted to communicate completely the impossibility of complete communication, to convey what it felt like to stutter so badly that one worshipped words. To be locked inside one's own dead language and vainly strive to articulate one's full essence: this, to me, is not only a fair summary of my protagonist Jeremy Zorn's particular predicament but the very definition of being human and, especially, perhaps, a child, whose essential powerlessness, isolation, and solipsism—combined with a fierce need to *communicate* these states—are but the more manifest, transparent versions of what an adult feels.

Writing the book over several years, I knew I needed to get past the impersonal behaviorism of the speech clinic. And yet I also wanted to avoid the bathos of a disease-of-the-week TV movie. I sought to impose a neoclassical (and thus self-consciously "eloquent") voice upon the very colloquial (apparently mundane) material. I wanted the sound of an adult Jeremy writing at precisely the same time as the child Jeremy was stuttering. I wanted the sound of literature glossing life while life was exploding the sound of literature. Through insistent, at times obsessional, alliteration, I hoped to bring together simultaneously the lyricism of Jeremy the writer and the anguish of Jeremy the stutterer. And who is Jeremy to me, or I to Jeremy? He is the more manifest, transparent version: smarter, more confused, crueler, sweeter, more serious, funnier, more disfluent, more desperate, both my best and worst self: a hyperrealized self.

At the beginning of chapter 6, Jeremy, at twenty-one, looks back at himself as a six-year-old:

> I had gotten it into my head that, because my interlocutor never knew what I was going to say and once I said it he never understood exactly what I meant, it was incumbent upon me to underscore the impossibility of human communication by stuttering. I actually believed that. I thought it was my duty to insert into every conversation the image of its own absurdity. Worse than that, I came to think all fluent speech was "fascistic" (a word I had learned from Mother); was an assertion of authority in the one enterprise in which any assertion of authority struck me as ludicrous. Whatever I did, wherever I went, whatever I said, I assumed it had already been judged to be unwanted and unneeded. My apology was to tremble. (36)

The incessant alliteration, doing double duty, conveys Jeremy's attempt to master his childhood by transforming it into elegant language at the same time it demonstrates his inability to leave behind his childhood by no longer stuttering.

Similarly, when Jeremy analyzes the "Time Passes" section of *To the Lighthouse,* he says that Virginia Woolf

> presents a verbal surface that, in its alliterative and rhyming schemes, its punning, its inverted syntax, its broken-record repetitions, its ceaseless metamorphosis, parallels the chaos of time received by memory. Her metaphor for consciousness haunted by the past is language that stresses loud sound rather than literal sense and produces a superficial reality for the reader that is incomprehensible and absurd until he acknowledges there exists no meaning other than scattered sounds, and enters—as reader, as historian of the self—the rhythms of reprise. (216)

Not only is Jeremy talking here about his own narrative voice, of course, but the passage itself "swoons in sound," which, as Jeremy notes, in an earlier passage, that old stutterer Winston Churchill's sentences invariably did:

> Fame? Virgil stuttered. He wrote and rewrote the *Aeneid* the entirety of his adult life, averaging one hexameter a day. In his will he told Tibullus to burn the poem because the last eleven lines of Book XII didn't scan properly. One can't help but want to go back to the *Aeneid* with greater patience after hearing that. In his first speech as prime minister, Winston Churchill sometimes paused as long as five seconds before crucial phrases. The House of Commons thought he was employing silence as a rhetorical device. He was trying not to hyperventilate. Later he said, "I have nothing to offer but blood, toil, tears, and sweat." He adored alliteration. There's hardly a sentence he wrote that doesn't swoon in sound. Handsome

Loud Blazer, instructor of Psychoanalysis and Literature at London Prep, once said, "In every staccato rhythm, every pinched phrase, every aborted clause, the alert reader can hear echoes of Mr. Maugham's speech defect." Which strikes me less as literary interpretation than pedagogical sadism. Demosthenes, of course. Moses, of course, whose Ten Commandments tablet God rived in half to remind him he couldn't control language. Aristotle. Aesop. Charles I. George VI. Erasmus. Marilyn. All tellers of tales, really, in one medium or another, and all people known by only one name, as if they'd contrived a way to contract their tongues' Tower of Babel to a manageable logo.

The pressure that underlies stuttering also generates the ambition to succeed—to succeed hysterically and on the same field as the original failure: somewhere within the world of words. (65)

Jeremy resents his teacher's equation of Somerset Maugham's somewhat clumsy literary style with Maugham's stutter; Jeremy wants gorgeous written language to be a revenge upon the Babel of his spoken language. At age eleven, Jeremy tries to read *Rabbit, Run*, and says that only later did he "realize the author of that book built such ornate syntax to retaliate against his own stutter" (71). "Somewhere within the world of words"—on the page, as the narrator of *Dead Languages*—he needs to succeed hysterically. Whether or not the novel succeeds is, of course, up to the reader to decide. What's interesting to me now, though, is how absolutely *Dead Languages* mattered to me when writing it: not only was it an autobiographical novel about growing up but an autobiographical novel about growing up *via* language, and thus I felt this was my one and last chance to get it right: go from stutterer to singer, from child to adult.

"It's an ancient story, beginning before Demosthenes, and it has a simple moral: we try to but cannot construct reality out of words," Jeremy says toward the end of the book, feigning reconciliation—"feigning," because the reconciliation itself is written in such a way as to cancel itself out: it's full of lyric stuttering, exultant self-abnegation. "Catullus has nothing to say to the cab driver. A poem isn't a person. Latin's only a language. Stuttering's only wasted sound. It can't become communication." In the very next paragraph, Jeremy manifestly undermines this note of healthy affirmation by saying: "Only in broken speech is the form of disfluency consonant with the chaos of the world's content. Stutterers are truth-tellers; everyone else is lying. I know it's insane [,] but I believe that" (181–82). The message is the opposite, but the strategy is the same, as in the above passage: praising the chaos of stuttering, Jeremy is rigorously fluent.

What is to me the central passage in the book occurs after Jeremy tries to join his friends in making a crank call and the intended victim instead lectures Jeremy about how to stop stuttering. "This dialogue was rather discouraging," Jeremy thinks,

but human intercourse is often one person's obstinate attempt to dominate another person, and one of the unfortunate facts about disfluency is that you never get to dominate. It's all very well and good to assert that communication comes down to a mad dogfight; it's something else altogether to confess you're always the poor pup who loses. Another unfortunate fact about disfluency is that it prevents you from ever entirely losing self-consciousness when expressing such traditional and truly important emotions as love, hate, joy, and deep pain. Always first aware not of the naked feeling itself but of the best way to phrase the feeling so as to avoid verbal repetition, you come to think of emotions as belonging to other people, being the world's happy property and not yours—not really yours except by way of disingenuous circumlocution. (96).

The passage itself, of course, is disingenuously circumlocutious: writing is Jeremy's one chance to dominate—this is the one verbal arena in which he is not the poor pup who loses—but it is precisely this overvaluation of written language that prevents him from ever entirely losing self-consciousness, as a writer, when "expressing such traditional and truly important emotions as love, hate, joy, and deep pain." In *Dead Languages*, alliteration serves as a metaphor for both the transformation of the wounds of childhood into the bow of art and the incapacity of anyone to transform the wounds of childhood into anything except scar tissue.

I still occasionally see a speech therapist for a quick refresher, but I'm done with disfluency—bored with it as label and trope. I have no more to say about it that I haven't already said in the book. Or so I tell myself until I experience—when giving a reading, for instance, or teaching a class—a severe stuttering block and feel, from my tongue to my toes, five years old again.

WORK CITED

Shields, David. *Dead Languages*. New York: Knopf, 1989.

Giving Tanks

Darrell H. Y. Lum

The brown and orange crayons always run out at Tanksgiving time. You gotta use um up for color da turkeys and da Indian feathers la dat. Yellow run out fast too. My teacher, Mrs. Perry, used to tell us dat we supposed to use dose colors cause ass da autumn colors. Supposed to be when all the leaves on da trees turn color, like da orange and brown crayons or da funny kine brown one in da big crayon box: burnt someting. I couldn't see how if da leaves turn color was pretty. For us, dat jes means dat da tree going die, or maybe stay dead awreadty. Or maybe like our lychee tree in da back yard, when da leaves turn color, dey fall off and Daddy tell me I gotta go rake before I can go play.

Tanksgiving was when you gotta learn about da Pilgrims and all dat. Ass when da Indians and da Pilgrims went get together, eat turkey or someting. Kinda hard to believe though, yeah. Me, I like da Indians mo bettah den da Pilgrims. Da Indians had da kine leather pants with da fringes and da small kine beads and dey fight wit bow and arrow la dat. Da Pilgrims had to wear da black suits, even da small kids, and da funny kine hat. Dey even had funny kine gun was fat at da end. My brother told me dat was one blundahbuss, dat da olden days guys wanted da bullets to spread all over so da gun was funny kine. He said dat kine gun couldn't shoot straight though. Ass why da Indians mo bettah. I betchu arrows could shoot mo straight den dat.

Da teacha told me I had to do one report on da pilgrims and draw one cornucopia. I nevah know what dat was. Even aftah I saw da picture I still couldn't figure out what dat was.

"Ass one horn of plenty," Louise went tell me. She smart, so she oughta know. "Stay like one basket fo put fruits inside, fo show you rich, dat you get food."

"Well how come always stay falling down and all da fruits spilling out?" I went ask her. "Funny kine basket, eh?" I not so dumb. So when I went home I went try draw one horn of plenty but I couldn't figure out what was fo. Look more like my brother's trombone den one basket. And you no can play music wit one horn of plenty. Ho, sometimes da teacher make us do crazy stuffs.

In school we always do the same old ting. You know, make one turkey out of one paper plate: da plate is the body and you paste on the head and the tail and the legs. Sometimes we make one napkin holder turkey: you staple half a paper plate to your turkey so get one place fo put da napkins. Den you paste da neck and da head and da feet like you stay looking at um from da front. And you gotta color dat too . . . brown and orange and yellow. Den you fold up da paper napkins and put um inside da plate and if you use color-koa napkins, look like da turkey tail. Mama really went like that one. She went hang um up on da wall and fill um up with napkins and put away da regular napkin holder until came all had it and da head went fall off.

Everybody like go to Auntie Jennie's and Uncle Jim's house fo Tanksgiving dinner cause Mama said Auntie's turkey always come out moist. Me, I only like eat skin and gravy . . . Auntie Jennie make good gravy. And I like the cranberry sauce da best. I no like da stuffing cause I think they hide all da ugly stuff from inside da turkey in dere.

Auntie Jennie's house was nice. Her kitchen table had real cloth kine table-cloth not da plastic kine on top and she no put sheets on top her couch and had anykine knitted stuff, like those hat things that cover the extra toilet paper on top the toilet tank. And get anykine neat stuff all around her house . . . anykine souvenirs from all over da world, da places they went go visit. J'like everyplace they went, she went buy one salt and pepper shaker. Fo collect. Some look like animals and look like one house or one car or one famous building. Some you couldn't even figure out where da salt or da pepper come out!

Uncle Jim had this teeny tiny collection of knives dat was da best. Wasn't real, was imitation; each one was about one inch long or maybe two inches long. Was anykine knives, like bolo knife and swords from all over the world and put on one piece of wood, j'like one shield. Maybe he went collect knives from every-place he went.

Uncle Jim was da fire chief and always had firemen at his house. And he park his car right in front his house, one big red station wagon. Da license plate says "HFD I," Honolulu Fire Department One. Dat means he da chief. Uncle Jim was tall and skinny and bolohead. Errybody call him "chief" and I know he da *fire* chief but he remind me of one Indian chief, tall and old and plenny wrinkles on his face. I betchu he get one Indian knife with one leather holder someplace.

My grandma, Ah Po Lee, was always dere too, sitting down on the couch in her plain stay-at-home clothes talking Chinese to my Auntie. I think she get nice clothes. One time, I seen one silk *cheong sam* hanging up on her door with the plastic from the dry clean man but I nevah seen her wear um. And she wear one wide cloth headband dat make her look like one old Indian lady: all small and bent ovah, plain blue khaki jacket and black Chinese pants and fancy cloth slippahs wit small beads making one dragon and anykine wrinkles and spots on her face. Look j'like warpaint.

So ass what we did Tanksgiving time. Go Auntie Jennie's house and eat turkey and make paper plate turkeys and try fo figgah out what one cornucopia was. And in school, I kept tinking, when we going learn about one Indian holiday. Would be neat if could, yeah? We could dance around . . . whoa, whoa, whoa, whoa! Anyways, all dat was jes one fairy tale. Like wrestling at da Civic Auditorium, fake. Same like da uddah tings in da books and da National School Broadcast, all fairy tales. Ah Po told me, one time, dat real Tanksgiving stay everyday. Ass why everyday she pray fo my grandfahdah. No miss. She burn incense and pour tea and whiskey fo him outside on da porch where get da bowl wit sand fo stick da red candles and da skinny kine incense. Sometimes I watch da ashes curl up, hanging on, hanging on. Da ting can go long time before it fall off.

I no can remembah my Ah Goong, my grandfahdah, except fo da big picture on da wall in da living room. But even my bruddah Russo said dat he nevah look like dat. He said he look mo old. Da picture stay one young guy. I guess ass one fairy tale too. Ah Goong was old, Russo said. Tall and skinny and old. So Ah Po burn candles and incense and pour whiskey and tea fo dis tall, skinny, old guy and I watch da ashes curling and da smoke go up like smoke signals. Once, I went ask Ah Po how come she pray so much and she tell me she pray dat Ah Goong stay okay, she pray dat us guys, Russo and me, be good boys, she pray "tank you" she get rice to eat. She tell me she get lots to pray about.

Everytime get sale, she go buy one bag rice. Could tell she felt rich when she had one bag rice extra in da closet. And toilet paper. Lots of toilet paper. And Spam and vienna sausages and Campbell's soup and can corned beef. Nevah mind she kept fixing and fixing her stay-home dress ovah and ovah, cause was stay-home anyway. Nevah mind dat she had one old washing machine you had to crank da clothes through da roller stuffs. Nevah mind sometimes she went eat *hahm gnee*, salt fish, and rice fo dinner fo three days when me and Russo went sleep her house and we wanted to eat plain meat and not all mixed up wit vegetables kine.

And I seen her finish eating da little bit meat off da bone from my piece of meat and how hardly had any slop for da slop man and how she went look in her button bottle for two quarters fo wrap up in red paper fo give us *lee-see* fo buy ice cream from da ice cream man. Ass how I knew dat my cornucopia wasn't one basket wit fruits and vegetables spilling out. Wasn't Indians and Pilgrims sitting down fo eat turkey. Was Russo and me sitting down at da table while Ah Po put her oily black frying pan on da stove and turned da fire up high until da oil smoke and she put noodles and carrots and a little bit oyster sauce and three, maybe four, pieces of green onion cut big, so that we could see um and pick it out of our plates. She nevah used to have one big fat turkey fo Tanksgiving.

"Lucky," she used to say anyways. "Lucky da ice cream man come," even though he always pass by about three-thirty every Thursday. "Lucky you get *lee-see* to spend. Lucky. Lucky you come visit Ah Po," she would say and we would tink about what if we nevah come and miss out on noodles and quarters and ice cream.

I guess we was lucky, yeah?

On Pidgin and Children in Literature

DARRELL H. Y. LUM

It's difficult to say why I write in the child's voice. I don't know really except that it is the voice that wants to tell the stories.

It took a long time for me to realize that this was my voice. Pidgin (Hawaii Creole English actually) is my language, my first language. And despite the efforts of parents, teachers, and the board of education to eradicate it, it simply is part of who I am. Indeed, how do you eradicate your native tongue?

The question is not so much a matter of using the child's voice as it is discovering one's own voice. And common to all writers is the difficult job of telling a story in a consistent and authentic voice. It is even more difficult if you have grown up being told that your native language is just "bad English" and that pidgin speakers will never amount to anything. Yet pidgin and the child narrator get closer to the "heart" of some stories (or perhaps give the stories "heart") than standard English or an adult point of view does.

My parents didn't want me speaking pidgin. "Speak good English," they'd say. My father would always be sure to point out to me whenever he met a local kid who spoke standard English, "Too good, eh? Dat kid, he talk like one *haole!*" (Caucasian). And of course, my teachers never let us use pidgin in the classroom.

Pidgin has been blamed for the ills of the educational system since the beginning of American schooling in Hawaii. As early as the 1880s, educators pronounced, "It is the sober duty for every instructor of Hawaiian youth to check the use of pidgin English" (Attributed to Rev. William Oleson in Stueber, 148). In 1932 it was called "mongrel, it follows no recognized usage in pronunciation or structure. The schools must remedy this disgraceful condition" (Stueber, 255). And in 1940, the local newspaper editorialized on the occasion of one hundred years of American schooling in Hawaii that "exhibitions of pidgin English on and off school grounds by students . . . should make teachers of English weep and all other teachers ashamed" (Stueber, 307). There should be little wonder then that the 1987 Board of Education faulted pidgin for the poor language skills of island children. They mandated that all teachers use standard English and encourage the use of standard English by students on and off campus because pidgin speakers were "severely limited" in their competitiveness and would be unable to "move up the ladder of success" (Board of Education).

The fact that pidgin still exists in the face of global communications and mass media is in itself amazing. Despite the opposition, pidgin survives because people nurture it as a cultural remnant of an earlier (but not necessarily simpler) time. It is all we have left. Native Hawaiians have been displaced from their land, their numbers have been decimated, their language all but lost. For people from immigrant stock, pidgin is an acknowledgement of our plantation past and a reminder of a colonial and paternalistic system that in some ways still exists in the state today.

The public use of pidgin has been largely relegated to comedians who spoof local culture,[1] comic books,[2] and thugs or simpletons on television.[3] The popular media has perpetuated stereotypes about pidgin speakers (that they are of lower class, inarticulate and stupid) even if our own experience runs counter to this stereotype. Most locals know of a downtown doctor, lawyer, or engineer who speaks pidgin fluently and has been known to utter it in the boardroom, the courtroom, and across the counter. Most will tell you that they have an uncle or aunt in their family who, at every family party, tells stories about "small kid time" when they sit around and "talk story" next to the buffet table and the cooler of beer in the carport. Stories in which the players are admirable, heroic, complex, brave, and real. And while I don't specifically write work for children, it seems that children recognize that the child narrator in the stories is speaking to them and for them. A community college reading teacher recently told me that her fifth-grade nephew who hated both reading and writing in school discovered my book and then spent two hours reading aloud to her. She reported, "Afterwards he went to the computer and told me, 'I'm gonna write like that!'"

I think kids recognize that here is a language of this place and of their lives and experience. Here is a language that allows them to say something. Something important. A language that they can play with and have fun with. A language that feels easy and comfortable. One that they already have mastered because it is *their* language. A language that is both oral, with its particular cadence and rhythm, *and* written.[4]

The pidgin narrator is almost always a child because for most pidgin speakers, the development of the language stopped somewhere around sixth or seventh grade, when the educational system had beat us down enough to realize that pidgin was not going to get us the approval of parents or teachers. We had already learned how to switch it on and off as we entered the classroom, but around age twelve or thirteen we stopped explaining things to ourselves in pidgin and the development of our own fluency in pidgin stopped. The pidgin-speaking narrator in my stories is stuck with a language and vocabulary that has not developed much past the seventh grade. Many adults tend to use pidgin to recall a pastoral, simpler time, but for me, it was a time of turmoil and anxiety.

By age twelve or so I realized that there was indeed something wrong with the way I spoke. And while we all spoke pidgin outside the classroom, we became more conscious about not speaking it in the classroom and some of us ended up not speaking at all. It was better to remain silent than to risk correction by the teacher and embarrassment. But the supposed reticence of local kids which plagued teachers in the classroom was certainly not evident on the playground. There were certainly those who could tell stories. Stories of dances and fights and girls and cigarettes and taking showers in P.E. and combing your hair into a thick pomaded wave with a long, skinny comb that you pulled out of a special custom-made pocket in your "drapes" (bell-bottom trousers). Of YMCA social clubs and intramural sports and belonging and not belonging. Of fear of being chosen last for basketball or of being called on first in algebra. Fear that you looked funny or smelled funny or talked funny, like one *haole*. Of hoping no one would notice your haircut and hoping everyone would notice your Beatle boots. Those pidgin-speaking years were deeply felt and anxious times. We were anything but silent and reticent. It was a painful, horrible, and memorable time. So why shouldn't stories come out of this?

My earliest stories, written in a college creative writing course, were awful "all-American" stories with characters named Smith and Jones that took place in cities like Chicago or New York, places I had never been. After all, I had never read any literature that was about Hawaii or about the people I knew lived here. I was writing what I thought a short story ought to be.

My experience growing up Asian American in Hawaii was unlike all the stories I had read before. It was an experience rooted in a plantation past. A past of immigrant laborers who were not sojourners but settlers who had come to make America their home. A past where my grandmother, at the age of twelve, came to the Kingdom of Hawaii in 1891 to be a housegirl. She spoke a Hawaiian-Chinese-English pidgin and took the name of the family who "adopted" her, her real surname lost or forgotten. A past where my grandfather, a Chinese-language school principal, led a court battle all the way up to the U.S. Supreme Court to strike down a law passed by the Territorial Legislature banning foreign language schools on the assumption that they were un-American. A past where family stories and "talking story" were an important part of our lives.

My memory of childhood is filled with clear, strong images of seemingly random and unrelated people, places, and events. The stuff of stories. The writer assembles these into a story that unfolds into a unity for the reader. The child narrator may not always know the true "meaning" of the story he tells, but then again, I often don't know the true meaning of what I write until long after those initial images are recorded. For me, the writing process is much like the child's discovery of the story he tells. I usually stumble around for a while and quite accidentally latch onto something that "drives" the story toward its resolution. I often only have an intuitive sense of what is important. A large part of the process is simply learning to pay attention to one's own voice. The wonderful thing about the child narrator is that he or she serves as a constant reminder of my responsibility to simply tell the story.

My desk is full of little objects to help me focus on telling the story: a crocheted beer can hat, a bird woven out of a coconut leaf, a black rubber handball. Things that are meaningful just to me but which help me capture the details. These images, real and concrete, ultimately lead me to the story. Perhaps it's the discovery of something that was plainly there all along. Perhaps it's the unconscious veering toward an object that has taken on new meaning because of the story.

In the end, using the child's voice means paying attention to it. Paying attention to what children are saying, paying attention to how your narrative voice speaks. Trusting your voice and believing that despite its limitations, you are capable of saying whatever you want to say. Trusting that we pidgin speakers are capable and fluent in a language that is expressive and communicative. And that we can tell these stories as no one else can.

NOTES

1. Andy Bumatai, Booga-Booga, Frank Delima, Mel Cabang, and others often depend on ethnic stereotypes, e.g., the big, violent Samoan, the lazy Hawaiian, the oversexed Filipino with a heavy accent, the tightwad Chinese, the slant-eyed Japanese, etc.

2. An example is *Pidgin to the Max*, a cartoon joke book which sometimes is mistaken for a dictionary of pidgin terms. In addition to relying on ethnic stereotypes, the portrayal of pidgin-speakers and women tends to be demeaning and of low intelligence.

3. Television shows such as *Hawaii Five-O*, *Magnum P.I.*, *Jake and the Fatman*, and others have usually depicted pidgin speakers as criminals. Even as the occasional law enforcer, the pidgin speakers are not much more than flunkeys or "yes-men" to the white male leads.

4. For a discussion of Hawaii's literary history, see Stephen Sumida's *And the View from the Shore: Literary Traditions of Hawaii* (University of Washington Press, 1991).

WORKS CITED

Board of Education minutes of 17 September 1987, meeting and appendices. State office—Board of Education, Honolulu.
Stueber, Ralph Kant. *Hawaii: A Case Study in Development Education 1778–1960.* Diss. University of Wisconsin, 1964.

AFTERWORD

LAURIE RICOU

> The child is a continent I cannot cross to reach
> you.
> —Alice Hokanson, *Mapping the Distance*

My three-year-old nephew, whose mother is francophone and father anglophone, promises he will be ready to play immediately "après breakfast." The bilingual phrase that for Alexi (I suppose) is simply spontaneous pragmatics, is novel enough in my ear to conjure a whole culture: a mid-morning version of après-ski, with oranges, complacent peignoirs, and a chocolate-brown carpet scattered with Legos. When I come back to the subject of children and literature—as I have with great pleasure in reading and re-reading *Infant Tongues*—I continue to be fascinated by the challenge of writing into this intersection of child speech and adult interpretation, and delighted by surprising solutions as diverse as the infinite variety of children's neologisms. The child, following some marvellously elastic "laws" of language acquisition, speaks a combination of words (or non-words) which may never have been spoken before. Within them adult listeners may discover a way of looking at things in their own language as unusual as if they were just learning a second language. The sequence seems at once logical and unpredictable. The writer/artist, in turn, draws on such glimpses into the child's mind, to mediate a child character, or a child's point of view, or a child narrator, or, less directly, to shape a way to write children's literature. To Alexandra Johnson the unself-conscious potential which rests in children's "accidents of language" promises a "serendipity of meaning." Serendipitous meaning forms on infant tongues, crying "pay attention," whether in a new collection of essays, or at your breakfast table.

Three-and-a-half-year-old Anna might be urging her father to be more energetic when she orders him to "roll up your leg sleeves [cuffs]," and she knows she can get the crumbs out of her hair with the "hairbroom." I have these examples because Anna's parents write them on the calendar near the phone. Of course, a novel, poem or children's story is more than a recording of such anecdotes. But children in literature often provide the same fascination: through them we are

302

awakened to accidents of language and their serendipities of meaning. Canadian poet Al Purdy finds the colour of infant tongues in the box of crayons:

Pre-School

Black was first of all
the place I came from
frightened because I couldn't remember
where I'd been or was going to
But when did I find yellow
in buttercup and dandelion
in the meadowlands and hill country
discover them in my mind
as if they had always been there
yellow eyes yellow eyes?
Red was about then too
and the river discovered me
lying upsidedown by the water
waiting for myself to happen
all the unfolding summer
while red willow roots waved
thru the water like a drowned girl's hair
I said as slowly as I could "You're red"
and it was so and I knew
I knew for the first time
that I could invent the world
Dark colours came later
of course after the blue sky
brown takes study to like much
tho some of the brown kind of people
have silver lights in their eyes
from the time the moon left here
because of a solemn promise
it gave the sun earlier on
and the brown people wanted to stay
in that gleaming landscape
and waited too long to leave:
in their minds they are not quite clear
they haven't dreamed their sleeping
why it was there were no shadows
in that country without colour
but silver silver silver

Later on
the house went smaller and smaller
and green moss grew on the shingles
and all vegetable things in red and yellow
flowed orange and gold into women
and the grey child
went searching for one more colour
beyond blue eyes and brown hair
past the red tremble of leaves in October
and the silver women
beyond the death-black forest
to where all colours begin. (209–10)

The poem is written in the first person and, with three significant exceptions, in the past tense. The adult speaker tries to remember when, or in what order, he experienced, or learned to differentiate colours. But the poem is in a different register from the aw-shucks diffidence and frequent crudity of a "typical" Al Purdy poem. The adult speaker tries to remember by writing, in various ways, through a child's sensibility. He creates accidents of language in which to remember. He is, I would argue, alert to the serendipity of meaning.

"Pre-School" is not, at least directly, a poem about infant tongues. At one level it concerns the pre-linguistic stage of human development, during which time everything is (so adults speculate) a boom of sensory diffuseness. Pre-school is pre-education by any institution, where the tutors are love and the senses, the colours of the spectrum (and beyond). To convey this world Purdy evidently uses some of the markers which Brian McHale identifies as "standard" in representing a child's speech: run-on phrasal and clausal coordination, for example, or deviant uses of ambient-*it*. Obviously, the gratuitous repetition ("I knew/I knew," etc.) and the general absence of punctuation add to the sense of breathlessness. As McHale notes, these strategies for representing literary children depend on what "prefabricated units [are] available in the literary repertoire." To imply, as I have in my first paragraph, that representing childhood poses a unique problem is, to McHale, naive.

In pre-school (Jean Piaget's period of concrete operations) color is not a descriptor, a characteristic—but a presence, a material reality, a surround, a noun, a place name. Adults can not remember their own learning of language. They suspect that "learning" may not even be the best word to describe the process. Young children have not developed the language to talk (or write) about their own experience. It is just this site of the unspoken, unwriteable that has provided such a challenge to writers. And increasingly, if somewhat belatedly, to *critics*, as this book exuberantly discovers—"as if they had always been there." Mary Galbraith's scrupulous study of the languages of Pip is a marvellous illustration.

The key to this book, the most prominent recurring idea, is surely the notion of the muted child—that a child, an infant, has its only written and spoken representation in an "adult discourse not yet inhabited by the child." Particularly, we discover a political side to a familiar subject which has itself been muted in much work on children in literature. The silenced child emerges as the definition of power in Mark Heberle's Shakespeare. That "Children's Bibles . . . rarely let children speak" is a demonstration, Ruth Bottigheimer argues, of their normative agenda. The Jewish child in the Warsaw ghetto voices incomprehensibility by barely speaking. To David Shields, stuttering (like the staccato repetitions in "Pre-School") is the way to speak the truth. In Virginia Woolf, the muted child is also unfettered and invincible.

Purdy's direct quotation of child's speech amounts only to two-and-a-half words. But the infant tongue, as written by the poet, runs at least through the first section of the poem, in dialogue with the adult tongue. It is realized in substantive adjectives, in drifting (and alliterated) modifiers ("while red willow roots waved"), in stacked modifiers, or in deviant syntax—"brown takes study to like much" rather than "to like brown takes much study." The repertoire is diverse. For Virginia Woolf, the apt construction is monosyllables; for Shakespeare, perhaps, the apostrophe; in catechisms a taste for riddle; for John Steptoe the capitalized compounds "PRETTYFUL" and "WHATSHAPPENINGMAN". These are all signs of language accidents, strategies available from the literary repertoire, for the child's corrective, radically Other, view of the world. They are conventions for our knowing for the first time, as Sklenicka and Spilka quote from Lawrence, "the entirely new, underived, underivable, something which is causeless."

In each of these, conventional and "mistaken" in some way as far as the psycholinguist is concerned, lies the potential intelligence of "creative misreading." These essays broaden the topic not only by writing the unwritten child, but by recognizing the child as reader: "listening to the voice of the child outside the book," promises Maria Tatar, "can often give us a judicious second opinion." Paralleling this interest is the emphasis on what child language will do to an adult's reading. In Mitzi Myers's discussion, the equating of bee and cow in an alphabet book provides a pivot on which the adult reader discovers both intellectual and *emotional* knowledge inherent in the "gender bender."

I asked Anna whether she was going to school yet. "I'm not big enough to go to school," she explained. "How big do you have to be?" "A little bit big," she concluded, triumphantly. That's it, I thought. When we come back to this subject of infant tongues, and we do, as teenagers, as parents, as grandparents, even if we are not writing scholarly articles about it, we constantly recognize the imprecise and shifting boundary between adult and child. As our houses "[go] smaller and smaller," we want to read our way back "to where all colours begin." Wanting to read and write infant tongues, we are all just a little bit big.

WORK CITED

Purdy, Al. *The Collected Poems of Al Purdy*, Russell Brown, ed, Toronto: McClelland and Stewart, 1986.

SELECTED BIBLIOGRAPHY

Some secondary works for further reading on the history and culture of childhood, the representation of children's voices and consciousness in sociology, linguistics, philosophy and psychology, and the child as author and subject in literature for adults and children. Articles on children's literature and language appear annually in *Children's Literature* (New Haven: Yale University Press, 1975–), quarterly in *The Children's Literature Association Quarterly* (Battle Creek, MI: 1975–) and *Children's Literature in Education* (New York: APS Publications, 1970–), and semiannually in *The Lion and the Unicorn* (Baltimore: Johns Hopkins Press, 1977–).

Adrian, Arthur A. *Dickens and the Parent-Child Relationship.* Athens: Ohio University Press, 1984.

Agress, Lynn. "Mothers and Children: The Relegated Roles." In *The Feminine Irony.* London: Associated University Presses, 1978.

Alderson, Brian. "Literary Criticism and Children's Books; or, 'Could Be Worse.'" In *Responses to Children's Literature: Proceedings of the Fourth Symposium of the International Research Society for Children's Literature,* 59–75. New York: Saur, 1980.

Allan, John. *Inscapes of the Child's World.* Dallas: Spring, 1988.

Anderson, Michael. *Approaches to the History of the Western Family 1500–1914.* Prepared for the Economic History Society. London: MacMillan, 1980.

Applebee, Arthur. *The Child's Concept of Story.* Chicago: University of Chicago Press, 1978.

Appleyard, J. A. *Becoming a Reader: The Experience of Fiction from Childhood to Adulthood.* New York: Cambridge University Press, 1990.

Arbuthnot, Mary Hill. *Children and Books.* Chicago: Scott, 1947.

Ariès, Philippe. *Centuries of Childhood: A Social History of Family Life.* Trans. Robert Baldick. New York: Knopf, 1962.

Aspects of Alice: Lewis Carroll's Dreamchild as seen through the Critics' Looking-Glasses, 1865–1971. Ed. Robert Phillips. New York: Vintage-Random, 1977.

Auerbach, Nina. "Falling Alice, Fallen Women, and Victorian Dream Children." In *Roman-*

tic Imprisonment: Women and Other Glorified Outcasts, 149–68. New York: Columbia University Press, 1985.

Avery, Gillian. *Childhood's Pattern: A Study of the Heroes and Heroines of Children's Fiction, 1770–1950*. London: Hodder and Stoughton, 1975.

————. *Nineteenth Century Children: English Children's Stories, 1780–1900*. London: Hodder and Stoughton, 1965.

Babenroth, A. C. *English Childhood: Wordsworth's Treatment of Childhood in the Light of English Poetry from Prior to Crabbe*. New York: Columbia University Press, 1922.

Bachelard, Gaston. *The Poetics of Reverie: Childhood, Language, and the Cosmos*. Trans. Daniel Russell. Boston: Beacon, 1971.

————. *The Poetics of Space*. 1985. Trans. Maria Jolas. Boston: Beacon, 1969.

Benjamin, Jessica. *The Bonds of Love: Psychoanalysis, Feminism, and the Problem of Domination*. New York: Pantheon, 1988.

Bettelheim, Bruno and Karen Zelan. *On Learning to Read: The Child's Fascination with Meaning*. New York: Knopf, 1972.

————. *The Uses of Enchantment: The Meaning and Importance of Fairy Tales*. New York: Knopf, 1976.

Birkin, Andrew. *J. M. Barrie and the Lost Boys*. London: Constable, 1979.

Boas, George. *The Cult of Childhood*. London: Warburg Institute, 1966.

Boswell, John. *The Kindness of Strangers: The Abandonment of Children in Western Europe from Late Antiquity to the Renaissance*. New York: Pantheon, 1988.

Bottigheimer, Ruth, ed. *Fairy Tales and Society, Illusion, Allusion and Paradigm*. Philadelphia: University of Pennsylvania Press, 1986.

————. *Grimms' Bad Girls and Bold Boys: The Moral and Social Vision of the Tales*. New Haven and London: Yale University Press, 1987.

Bower, T. G. R. *The Perceptual World of the Child*. Cambridge: Harvard University Press, 1976.

Bratton, J. S. *The Impact of Victorian Children's Fiction*. London: Croom Helm, 1981.

Brown, Mikel, and Carol Gilligan. *Meeting at the Crossroads: Women's Psychology and Girls' Development*. Cambridge: Harvard University Press, 1992.

Bruner, Jerome. *Child's Talk: Learning to Use Language*. New York: Norton, 1983.

Buckley, Jerome Hamilton. *Season of Youth: The Bildungsroman from Dickens to Golding*. Cambridge: Harvard University Press, 1974.

Burrow, Trigant. *Preconscious Foundations of Human Experience*. Ed. William E. Galt. New York: Basic, 1964.

Carnochan, W. B. "The Child Is Father of the Man." In *A Distant Prospect: Eighteenth-Century Views of Childhood*. Los Angeles: The William Andrews Clark Memorial Library, 1982.

Carpenter, Humphrey. *Secret Gardens: A Study of the Golden Age of Children's Literature*. Boston: Houghton Mifflin, 1985.

The Child. Ed. William Kessen. New York: John Wiley, 1965.

Child Language: A Reader. Eds. Margery B. Franklin and Sybil S. Barten. New York: Oxford University Press, 1988.

Children and Their Books: A Celebration of the Work of Iona and Peter Opie. Eds. Gillian Avery and Julia Briggs. Oxford: Clarendon, 1989.

Children and Youth in America: A Documented History (3 vols.). Ed. Robert H. Bremner. Cambridge, Harvard University Press, 1974.

Children's Literature: A Guide to Criticism. Ed. Linnea Hendrickson. Boston: G. K. Hall, 1987.

The Child's Part. Ed. Peter Brooks. Yale French Studies 43 (1969).

Cobb, Edith. *The Ecology of Imagination in Childhood*. Intro. Margaret Mead. New York: Columbia University Press, 1977.

Coe, Richard. *When the Grass Was Taller*. New Haven: Yale University Press, 1984.

Cogan, Frances B. *All-American Girl: The Ideal of Real Womanhood in Mid-Nineteenth-Century America*. Athens: University of Georgia Press, 1989.

Coles, Robert. *Children of Crisis*. 5 vols. Boston: Atlantic-Little Brown, 1967, 1972, 1978.

———. *The Moral Life of Children*. Boston: Atlantic Monthly Press, 1986.

———. *The Political Life of Children*. Boston: Atlantic Monthly Press, 1986.

———. *The Spiritual Life of Children*. Boston: Houghton Mifflin, 1990.

The Cool Web: The Pattern of Children's Reading. Eds. Margaret Meek, Aidan Warlow, and Griselda Barton. London: Bodley Head, 1977.

Cott, Jonathan. *Pipers at the Gates of Dawn: The Wisdom of Children's Literature*. New York: Random, 1983.

Courtney, Richard. "The Language and Thought of Children." *Play, Drama and Thought: The Intellectual Background*. London: Cassell, 1968.

Coveney, Peter. *The Image of Childhood: The Individual and Society: A Study of the Theme in English Literature*. Rev. ed. intro. F. R. Leavis. Baltimore: Penguin, 1967.

A Critical History of Children's Literature. Ed. Cornelia Meigs et al. New York: MacMillan, 1953.

Dalsimer, Katherine. *Female Adolescence: Psychoanalytic Reflections on Literature*. New Haven: Yale University Press, 1987.

Dally, Ann. *Inventing Motherhood: The Consequences of an Ideal*. New York: Schocken Books, 1983.

Damon, William. *The Social World of the Child*. San Francisco: Jossey-Bass, 1977.

Darton, F. J. Harvey. *Children's Books in England: Five Centuries of Social Life*. 1932. 3rd ed. Rev. Brian Alderson. Cambridge: Cambridge UP, 1982.

Darnton, Robert. "Peasant Tell Tales: The Meaning of Mother Goose." In *The Great Cat Massacre*. New York: Basic, 1984.

Darwin, Charles. "Biographical Sketch of an Infant." *Mind* 2 (July 1877): 285–94.

DeMause, Lloyd, ed. *The History of Childhood*. New York: The Psychoanalytical Press, 1974.

Dusinberre, Juliet. *Alice to the Lighthouse*. New York: St. Martin's Press, 1987.

———. "The Child's Eye and the Adult's Voice: Flora Thompson's *Lark Rise to Candleford*." *Review of English Studies*, n.s. 35, no. 137 (Feb. 1984): 61–70.

Dwork, Deborah. *War Is Good for Babies and Other Young Children: A History of the Infant and Child Welfare Movement in England 1898–1918*. London: Tavistock, 1987.

Empson, William. *Some Versions of Pastoral*. Norfolk, CT: New Directions, 1950.

Erikson, Erik H. *Childhood and Society*. New York: Norton, 1963.

Ewing, Elizabeth. *History of Children's Costumes*. New York: Scribners, 1977.

Fairy Tales and Society: Illusion, Allusion and Paradigm. Ed. Ruth Bottigheimer. Philadelphia: University of Pennsylvania Press, 1986.

Ferenczi, Sandor. "Confusion of Tongues between the Adult and the Child." *International Journal of Psychoanalysis* 30 (1949): 225–30.

Fiedler, Leslie. "The Eye of Innocence: Some Notes on the Role of the Child in Literature." *Collected Essays*, vol. 1, 471–511. New York: Stein and Day, 1971.

———. "The Invention of the Child." *New Leader* 41 (1958): 22–24.

Flandrin, Jean-Louis. *Families in Former Times: Kinship, Household, and Sexuality.* Trans. Richard Southern. New York: Cambridge University Press, 1979.

Fleishman, Avrom. *Figures of Autobiography: The Language of Self-Writing.* Los Angeles: University of California Press, 1983.

Foucault, Michel. *The History of Sexuality.* Vol. 1. Trans. Robert Hurley. New York: Random House, 1978.

Frey, Charles, and John Griffith. *The Literary Heritage of Childhood: An Appraisal of Children's Classics in the Western Tradition.* Westport, CT: Greenwood, 1987.

Garlitz, Barbara. "The Immortality Ode: Its Cultural Progeny." *Studies in English Literature* 6 (1966): 639–49.

Gathorne-Hardy, Jonathan. *The Rise and Fall of the British Nanny.* London: Hodder and Stoughton, 1972.

Gilligan, Carol. *In a Different Voice: Psychological Theory and Women's Development.* Cambridge: Harvard University Press, 1982.

Greenleaf, Barbara Kaye. *Children through the Ages: A History of Childhood.* New York: Barnes and Noble, 1978.

Greven, Philip. *The Protestant Temperament.* New York: Knopf, 1977.

Griswold, Jerry. *Audacious Kids: Coming of Age in America's Classic Children's Books.* New York and Oxford: Oxford University Press, 1992.

Grylls, David. *Guardians and Angels: Parents and Children in Nineteenth-Century Literature.* Boston: Faber and Faber, 1978.

Halperin, John. *Novelists in Their Youth.* New York: St. Martin's, 1990.

Hunt, Peter. *Children's Literature: The Development of Criticism.* Oxford: Basil Blackwell, 1990.

———. *Criticism, Theory, and Children's Literature.* Oxford: Basil Blackwood, 1991.

Hurst, Mary Jane. *The Voice of the Child in American Literature: Linguistic Approaches to Fictional Child Language.* Lexington: University Press of Kentucky, 1990.

Inglis, Fred. *The Promise of Happiness: Value and Meaning in Children's Literature.* Cambridge: Cambridge Univesity Press, 1981.

Innocence and Experience: Essays on Children's Literature. Eds. Barbara Harrison and Gregory Maguire. New York: Lothrop, Lee and Shepard, 1987.

Jackson, Mary. *Engines of Instruction, Mischief and Magic: Children's Literature in England from Its Beginnings to 1839.* Lincoln: University of Nebraska Press, 1989.

Jacobson, I. "The Child as Guilty Witness." *Literature and Psychology* 24 (1974): 12–13.

Jung, C. G., "The Psychology of the Child Archetype." *Essays on a Science of Mythology.* Trans. R. F. C. Hull. Princeton: Princeton University Press, 1969.

Kagan, Jerome. *The Nature of the Child.* New York: Basic, 1989.

Kegan, Robert. *The Evolving Self: Problem and Process in Human Development.* Cambridge: Harvard University Press, 1982.

Kincaid, James R. *Child-Loving: The Erotic Child and Victorian Culture.* New York: Routledge, 1992.

Knoepflmacher, U. C. "Of Babylands and Babylons: E. Nesbit and the Reclamation of the Fairy Tale." *Tulsa Studies in Women's Literature* 6.2 (fall 1987): 299–325.

———. "The Balancing of Child and Adult: An Approach to Victorian Fantasies for Children." *NCF* 37 (1983): 497–530.

Kohlberg, Lawrence. *Philosophy of Moral Development.* New York: Harper and Row, 1981.

Kuhn, Reinhard. *Corruption in Paradise: The Child in Western Literature.* Hanover, NH: University Press of New England, 1982.

Langbaum, Robert. *The Mysteries of Identity: A Theme in Modern Literature.* New York: Oxford University Press, 1977.

Language, Gender and Childhood. Eds. Carolyn Steedman, Cathy Unwin, and Valerie Walkerdine. Boston: Routledge, 1985.

Lieberman, Marcia. " 'Some Day My Prince Will Come': Female Acculturation through the Fairy Tale." *College English* 34 (1972): 383–95.

Livingston, Myra Cohn. *The Child as Poet: Myth or Reality?* Boston: Horn Book, 1984.

Locke, John. *The Educational Writings of John Locke: A Critical Edition.* Ed. James L. Axtell. Cambridge: Cambridge University Press, 1968.

Long, Michael. *Marvell, Nabokov: Childhood and Arcadia.* Oxford: Clarendon, 1984.

Lurie, Alison. *Don't Tell the Grown-Ups: Subversive Children's Literature.* Boston: Little, Brown, 1990.

Marcus, Leah Sinanoglou. *Childhood and Cultural Despair: A Theme in Seventeenth-Century Literature.* Pittsburgh: University of Pittsburgh Press, 1978.

Matthews, Gareth. *Dialogues with Children.* Cambridge: Harvard University Press, 1984.

———. *Philosophy and the Young Child.* Cambridge: Harvard University Press, 1980.

Moore, Robin. *Children's Domain.* London: Croom Helm, 1986.

Muir, Percy. *English Children's Books, 1600–1900.* New York: Praeger, 1954.

Myers, Mitzi. "Impeccable Governesses, Rational Dames, and Moral Mothers: Mary Wollstonecraft and the Female Tradition in Georgian Children's Books." *Children's Literature* 14 (1986): 31–59.

Nodelman, Perry. *The Pleasures of Children's Literature.* London: Longman, 1992.

———. *Words About Pictures.* Athens, GA: University of Georgia Press, 1990.

The Open Door: When Writers First Learned to Read. Ed. Steven Gilbar. Boston: Godine, 1989.

Opening Texts: Psychoanalysis and the Culture of the Child. Eds. Joseph H. Smith and William Kerrigan. Baltimore: Johns Hopkins University Press, 1985.

Opie, Iona. *The People in the Playground.* Oxford: Oxford University Press, 1993.

Opie, Peter, and Iona Opie. *The Lore and Language of Schoolchildren.* Oxford: Oxford University Press, 1967.

Patterson, Sylvia W. *Rousseau's Emile and Early Children's Literature.* Methuen: Scarecrow, 1971.

Pattison, Robert. *The Child Figure in English Literature.* Athens, GA: University of Georgia Press, 1978.

Pearce, Philippa. "The Writer's View of Childhood." *Horn Book* 38.1 (Feb. 1962): 74–78.

Pheiffer, John. *The Child in 19th-Century Fiction and Thought: A Typology.* Louisville: University of Kentucky Press, 1969.

Piaget, Jean. *Causal Thinking and the Child: A Genetic and Experimental Approach.* New York: International University Press, 1989.

———. *The Child's Conception of Time.* Trans. A. J. Pomerans. 1947. Rpt. London: 1969.

———. *The Moral Judgment of the Child.* New York: Free Press, 1965.

———. *Play, Dreams and Imitation in Childhood.* London, 1951.

Pickering, Samuel F., Jr. *John Locke and Children's Books in Eighteenth-Century England.* Knoxville: University of Tennessee Press, 1981.

Plumb, J. H. "The New World of Children in Eighteenth-Century England," *The Birth of a Consumer Society: The Commercialization of Eighteenth Century England.* Ed. Neil McKendrick. Bloomington: Indiana University Press, 1982. 286–315.

Pollock, Linda A. *Forgotten Children: Parent-Child Relations from 1500 to 1900.* Cambridge: Cambridge University Press, 1983.

————. *A Lasting Relationship: Parents and Children Over Three Centuries.* Hanover, N.H.: University Press of New England, 1987.

Prickett, Stephen. *Victorian Fantasy.* Bloomington: Indiana University Press, 1979.

Reclaiming the Inner Child. Ed. Jeremiah Abrams. Los Angeles: Jeremy P. Tarcher, 1990.

Richardson, Alan. "The Politics of Childhood: Wordsworth, Blake, and Catechistic Method." *ELH* 56 (1989): 853–68.

Ricou, Laurie. *Everyday Magic: Child Languages in Canadian Literature.* Vancouver: University of British Columbia, 1987.

Robinson, Edward. *The Original Vision: A Study of the Religious Experience of Childhood.* New York: Seabury Press, 1983.

Romaine, Suzanne. *The Language of Children and Adolescents.* Oxford: Basil Blackwell, 1984.

Romanticism and Children's Literature in Nineteenth-Century Literature. Ed. James Holt McGavran. Athens, GA: University of Georgia Press, 1991.

Rose, Jacqueline. *The Case of Peter Pan; or, The Impossibility of Children's Fiction.* London: MacMillan, 1984.

Rousseau, Jean-Jacques. *Emile; or, On Education.* 1762. Trans. Allan Bloom. New York: Basic, 1979.

Rowbotham, Judith. *Good Girls Make Good Wives: Guidance for Girls in Victorian Fiction.* Oxford: Basel Blackwell, 1989.

Rustin, Margaret, and Michael Rustin. *Narratives of Love and Loss: Studies in Modern Children's Fiction.* London: Verso, 1987.

Sale, Roger. *Fairy Tales and After: From Snow White to E. B. White.* Cambridge: Harvard University Press, 1978.

Schorsch, Anita. *Images of Childhood: An Illustrated Social History.* Pittstown, NJ: Main Street, 1979.

Shavit, Zohar. *The Poetics of Children's Literature.* Athens: University of Georgia Press, 1986.

Shengold, Leonard. *Soul Murder: The Effects of Childhood Abuse and Deprivation.* New Haven: Yale University Press, 1989.

Sklenicka, Carol. *D. H. Lawrence and the Child.* Columbia, Missouri: University of Missouri Press, 1991.

Sokoloff, Naomi. *Imagining the Child in Modern Jewish Fiction.* Baltimore: Johns Hopkins University Press, 1992.

Sommerville, C. John. *The Discovery of Childhood in Puritan England.* Athens: University of Georgia Press, 1992.

————. "Towards a History of Childhood and Youth." *Journal of Interdisciplinary History* 3 (1972): 438–47. Rpt. in *The Family in History: Interdisciplinary Essays,* eds. Theodore K. Rabb and Robert I. Rothberg, 277–35. New York: Harper, 1973.

Spacks, Patricia Meyer. *The Adolescent Idea: Myths of Youth and the Adult Imagination.* New York: Basic, 1981.

Spilka, Mark. "On the Enrichment of Poor Monkeys by Myth and Dream; or How Dickens Rousseauisticized and Pre-Freudianized Victorian Views of Childhood." *Sexuality and Victorian Literature,* ed. Don Richard Cox. *Tennessee Studies in Literature* 27 (1984): 161–79.

Stannard, David E. "Death and the Puritan Child," *American Quarterly* 26 (1974): 456–76.

Steedman, Carolyn. *Children, Culture, and Class in Britain: Margaret McMillan, 1860–1931.* London: Virago, 1990.

Stephens, John. *Language and Ideology in Children's Fiction.* New York: Longman, 1992.

Stern, Daniel. *Diary of a Baby.* New York: Basic, 1990.

———. *The Interpersonal World of the Infant.* New York: Basic Books, 1985.

Stone, Lawrence. *The Family, Sex and Marriage in England, 1500–1800.* Abridged ed. New York: Harper, 1977.

———. "Literacy and Education in England 1640–1900." *Past and Present* 42 (1969): 69–139.

Summerfield, Geoffrey. *Fantasy and Reason: Children's Literature in the Eighteenth Century.* Athens: University of Georgia Press, 1985.

Sunderland, Zena, et al. *Children and Books.* 6th ed. Glenview, IL: Scott, 1981.

Suransky, Valerie Polakov. *The Erosion of Childhood.* Chicago: University of Chicago Press, 1965.

Tanner, Tony. *The Reign of Wonder: Naivete and Reality in American Literature.* Cambridge: Cambridge University Press, 1965.

Tatar, Maria. *The Hard Facts of the Grimms' Fairy Tales.* Princeton: Princeton University Press, 1987.

———. *Off With Their Heads! Fairy Tales and the Culture of Childhood.* Princeton: Princeton University Press, 1992.

Teaching Children's Literature: Issues, Pedagogy, Resources. Options for Teaching. Ed. Glenn Sadler. Series ed. Joseph Gibaldi. New York: Modern Language Association, 1992.

Thorne, Barrie. *Gender Play: Girls and Boys in School.* New Brunswick, NJ: Rutgers University Press, 1993.

Thwaite, Mary F. *From Primer to Pleasure in Reading: An Introduction to the History of Children's Books in England from the Invention of Printing to 1914 with an Outline of Some Developments in Other Countries.* 1963. Rev. ed. Boston: Horn Book, 1972.

Touchstones: Reflections on the Best in Children's Literature (3 vols.). Ed. Perry Nodelman. West Lafayette, IN: Purdue University Press, 1987.

Townsend, John Rowe. *Written for Children: An Outline of English-Language Children's Literature.* Philadelphia: Lippincott, 1974.

Triumphs of the Spirit in Children's Literature. Ed. Francelia Butler. Hamden, CT: Library Professional Publications, 1986.

Tucker, Nicholas. *What Is a Child?* London: Fontana/Open Books, 1977.

———. *The Child and the Book: A Psychological and Literary Exploration.* Cambridge: Cambridge University Press, 1981.

Wachtel, Andrew Baruch. *The Battle for Childhood: Creation of a Russian Myth.* Stanford: Stanford University Press, 1990.

White, Barbara. *Growing Up Female: Adolescence in American Fiction.* Westport, CT: Greenwood, 1985.

Winnicott, D. W. *The Child, the Family and the Outside World.* Harmondsworth: Penguin Books, 1964.

———. *Playing and Reality.* Harmondsworth: Penguin, 1971.

Wooden, Warren W. *Children's Literature of the English Renaissance.* Ed. with Intro. Jeanie Watson. Lexington: University Press of Kentucky, 1986.

Zelinzer, Viviana. *Pricing the Priceless Child.* New York: Basic Books, 1985.

Zipes, Jack. *Breaking the Magic Spell: Radical Theories of Folk and Fairy Tales.* Austin: University of Texas Press, 1979.

———. *Fairy Tales and the Art of Subversion: The Classical Genre For Children and the Process of Civilization.* New York: Methuen, 1983.

CONTRIBUTORS

GILLIAN AVERY is a writer for children and a historian of children's literature. She has just completed a history of American children and their books (to be published by Bodley Head late in 1994), and is contributing the first essay, on the beginnings of children's books, to the forthcoming *Oxford Illustrated History of Children's Literature.*

RUTH B. BOTTIGHEIMER teaches at the State University of New York at Stony Brook. Her areas of specialization are folk narrative, children's literature, and cultural history. She has published *Fairy Tales and Society* (1986) and *Grimms' Bad Girls and Bold Boys* (1987), numerous articles, reviews, and review essays, and is currently working on a study of American and European Bible story collections entitled *The Bible for Children from the Age of Gutenberg to the Present.*

ROBERT COLES, professor of psychiatry at Harvard University, is widely known for work that spans the fields of psychology, education, and literature. He is the author of numerous books, including *The Spiritual Life of Children, The Moral Life of Children,* and *The Political Life of Children.*

MARY GALBRAITH received a doctorate in English and a master's degree in social work from the State University of New York at Buffalo. Her primary literary focus is on how narratives capture and create the experience of their characters and the ways in which readers enter into this experience. She is currently immersed in mothering twins and working with other families on issues of parent-child attachment.

ELIZABETH GOODENOUGH is an assistant professor of literature at Claremont McKenna College. She has published articles on Jung, Woolf, Hawthorne, and Laura Ingalls Wilder and has taught in the English Department at Harvard, Claremont McKenna, and the University of Michigan.

MARK JONATHAN HARRIS is an Academy award-winning documentary filmmaker and the author of five novels for children. *The Last Run* (1981) won the Golden Spur Award for Best Juvenile Western and *Come the Morning* (1989) was awarded the FOCAL prize for best children's book by a California author. His latest novel is *Solay* (1993). He is currently chair of Film and TV Production at the University of Southern California's School of Cinema-TV.

Mark A. Heberle is an associate professor of English at the University of Hawaii at Manoa, where he is on the working editorial committee of *Biography*. He has published on Spenser, Shakespeare, Vietnam war literature, and literary biography.

Alexandra Johnson is a lecturer at Wellesley College and currently teaches a class in memoir and women's autobiography at the Radcliffe Seminars at Harvard. In 1990, she won a PEN Special Citation (the PEN/Jerard Fund Award) for *The Novel Self*, a work-in-progress on women writers and their diaries. Her writing has also appeared in the *New Yorker, Nation, New York Times Book Review, Ms., Christian Science Monitor*, and the *Boston Review*, among other national publications.

Michael Lastinger is an assistant professor in the Department of Foreign Languages at West Virginia University, where he teaches French literature. He has written extensively on Zola.

Darrell H. Y. Lum is a Chinese-American writer born and raised in Hawaii. He has published two collections of short stories, *Sun, Short Stories and Drama* (Bamboo Ridge Press, 1980), and *Pass On, No Pass Back* (Bamboo Ridge Press, 1990), which was named a National Book Award winner by the Association for Asian American Studies in 1992. He has had three plays produced by Kumu Kahua and the Honolulu Theater for Youth and received a National Endowment for the Arts fellowship in 1990.

Brian McHale is a senior lecturer in poetics and comparative literature at Tel Aviv University, and co-editor of the international journal, *Poetics Today*. He is author of *Postmodernist Fiction* (1987) and *Constructing Postmodernism* (1993).

Mitzi Myers teaches writing and children's and adolescent literature at the University of California, Los Angeles. She has published extensively on eighteenth- and nineteenth-century women writers and historical children's literature. She is currently completing *Romancing the Family: Maria Edgeworth and the Scene of Instruction*.

Suzanne Rahn is an associate professor in the English Department of Pacific Lutheran University, and director of its Children's Literature Program. As an associate editor of *The Lion and the Unicorn*, she has edited issues on Heroes in Children's Literature, Historical Fiction and Nonfiction for Children, and Nature and Ecology in Children's Literature. She is the author of *Children's Literature: An Annotated Bibliography of the History and Criticism* and the forthcoming *Rediscoveries in Children's Literature*.

Laurie Ricou, professor of English and associate dean of graduate studies at the University of British Columbia, is the author of *Everyday Magic: Child Languages in Canadian Literature* (1986).

David Shields is the author of the novels *Dead Languages* (1989) and *Heroes* (1984) and a collection of linked stories, *A Handbook for Drowning* (1992). He has published stories and essays in *Harper's, Village Voice, Story, Conjunctions, Between C & D, Utne Reader,* and elsewhere. His work-in-progress, *Remote,* received the 1992 PEN/Revson Foundation Fellowship.

CAROL SKLENICKA is the author of *D. H. Lawrence and the Child* (1991) and articles on the fiction of Samuel Johnson and Henry James. She earned her Ph.D. at Washington University in St. Louis and is currently visiting assistant professor of English at Marquette University, where she teaches literature and creative writing. She has won a Wisconsin Arts Board award for her short fiction and the R. M. Ryan Novel Fellowship.

NAOMI B. SOKOLOFF, associate professor of Hebrew at the University of Washington in Seattle, is the author of *Imagining the Child in Modern Jewish Fiction* (1992) and co-editor of *Gender and Text in Modern Hebrew and Yiddish Literature* (1992).

MARK SPILKA received the Harry T. Moore Distinguished Scholar Award in 1988 for his lifelong contribution to Lawrence studies. His books include *The Love Ethic of D. H. Lawrence* (1955), *D. H. Lawrence: A Critical Collection* (1963), and *Renewing the Normative D. H. Lawrence: A Personal Progress* (1992). He is the Israel J. Kapstein Professor of English at Brown University and the editor of *Novel: A Forum on Fiction.*

MARIA TATAR is professor of German at Harvard University. She is the author of *Spellbound: Studies on Mesmerism and Literature; The Hard Facts of the Grimms' Fairy Tales;* and *Off with their Heads! Fairy Tales and the Culture of Childhood;* and she has edited a collection of essays entitled *Neverending Stories: Toward a Critical Narratology.*

ANDREW WACHTEL is an associate professor of Slavic Languages and Literatures at Northwestern University. In 1987, while a Junior Fellow in the Harvard Society of Fellows, he received his Ph.D. from the University of California, Berkeley. His first book, *The Battle for Childhood: Creation of a Russian Myth,* was published in 1990, and his second, *An Obsession with History: Russian Writers Confront the Past,* is due out from Stanford University Press in 1994. Professor Wachtel is currently working on a book on twentieth-century Russian drama, and another on the social role of literature in Yugoslavia.

INDEX

INDEX